WOMEN ARTISTS IN MIDCENTURY AMERICA

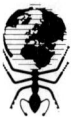

Women Artists
in Midcentury America
A History in Ten Exhibitions

Daniel Belasco

REAKTION BOOKS

In memory of Judith Cook Ferriter and Linda Nochlin

Published by
REAKTION BOOKS LTD
Unit 32, Waterside
44–48 Wharf Road
London N1 7UX, UK

www.reaktionbooks.co.uk

First published 2024
Copyright © Daniel Belasco 2024

Supported by Mildred Weissman / The Malka Fund

Printed and bound in India by Replika Press Pvt. Ltd

A catalogue record for this book is available from the British Library

ISBN 978 1 78914 843 5

CONTENTS

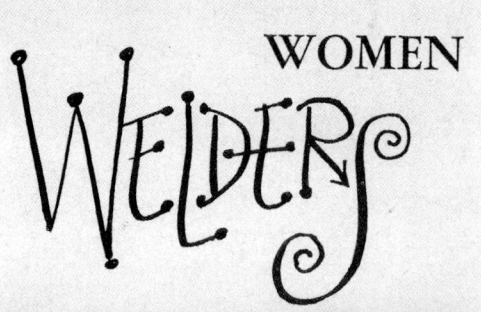

WOMEN

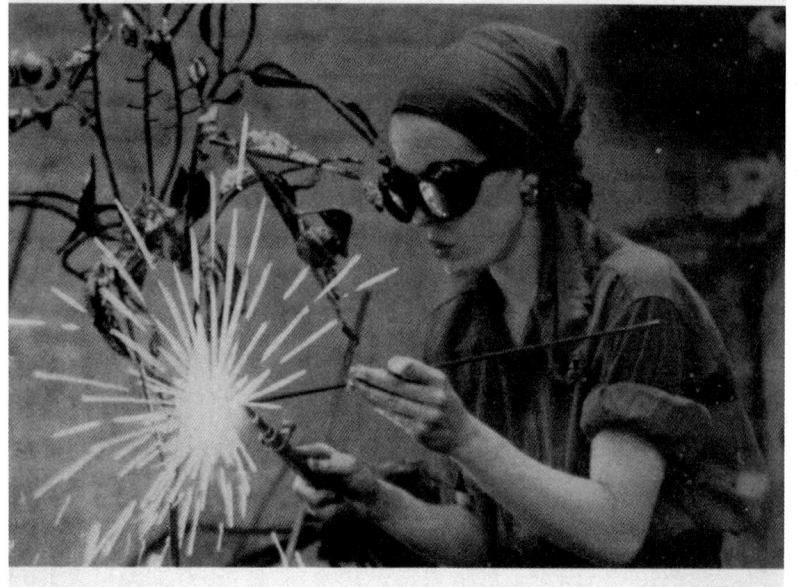

SCULPTURE
CENTER

1 Sculpture Center, New
York, *Women Welders*,
brochure, 1953.

Introduction

Barbara Lekberg wears dark-tinted goggles, a heavy button-up work shirt with rolled-up sleeves, and a head scarf (illus. 1). Sparks fly from the point of contact where she welds her abstract open-form sculpture. This image appears on the brochure cover of "Women Welders," a 1953 exhibition of works by eight female sculptors with two things in common: their gender and their work in the modernist technique of direct metal sculpture. American audiences became familiar with the image of the "woman welder" over a decade earlier, when thousands of women had gone to work in the war industries. The exhibition by the Sculpture Center, a membership organization then located in a carriage house on the Upper East Side of Manhattan, traded on the evergreen novelty of a woman doing a man's job while also recognizing the sociological reality of women's participation in the technical and stylistic development of modern art in America, a fact acknowledged in a review by critic Martica Sawin.[1] Yet to justify the all-women nature of the show, the center's director, Sahl Swarz, recapitulated old saws of sex difference. "Women are not categorized in this exhibition for the purpose of providing shelter for the female sex, but rather demonstrate that our proverbial weaker half is exceptionally strong in this new field of sculptural expression," he wrote in the opening lines of the brochure text.[2] His words, imbued with sexist stereotypes, exemplify the complex and contradictory situation for women artists in mid-twentieth-century America. On the one hand, supporters like Swarz framed women's personal psychology and techniques as natural outgrowths of essential feminine qualities inferior to the universal masculine. Yet on the other hand the exhibition was one of a growing trend providing important platforms for individual women artists to show their work and to be seen.

In the past decade, scholars and curators have significantly expanded our knowledge of American women artists in the mid-twentieth century, a period historicized as conservative and cautious overshadowed by the feminist art movement of the 1960s and '70s. There are a growing number of books and exhibitions about individual women working in this time period, some of which explore their relationships and interactions, yet all-women exhibitions remain a largely unexamined factor, presumed to have been either an invention of the feminist art movement or an irrelevant enterprise by staid organizations of women artists. Only a handful of these shows have received any scholarly or artistic interest, the most famous being "31 Women" at Peggy Guggenheim's Art of This Century gallery in 1943.

The all-women exhibition, in fact, was a widespread phenomenon at midcentury, and an investigation of its range and diversity can be a key to unlocking little-known narratives of either lionized artists like Georgia O'Keeffe or underrecognized artists like Norma Morgan. Most of these exhibitions were organized by long-standing women artists organizations or colleges as part of their mission to call attention to women's achievements. A few were organized for museums and galleries by sympathetic yet paternalistic men under the aegis of the period's emerging cultural liberalism. And a far fewer number were instigated by independent women artists and art professionals to further a specifically quasi-feminist agenda. Regardless of their curatorial underpinnings, once all-women shows entered the public realm, eager pronouncements of women's equality crashed against a capitalist reality of social restrictions and patriarchal cultural prejudices.

Women Artists in Midcentury America examines a significant cross-section of women artists of the period and the compelling and multifaceted historical contexts in which they lived and worked. It is a detailed chronological analysis of ten representative exhibitions from 1943 to 1962, couched in a critical engagement with issues around American culture, race, and aesthetics. Timely productions of individual passion and institutional negotiation, all-women exhibitions disclose the varied priorities and pervasive biases around women and gender in the midcentury art world. Both ongoing annual exhibitions and one-off projects affirm the limitations of discourse around women at midcentury, which generally proffered a more accommodationist than combative tone, celebrating the achievements of individual women artists rather than advocating for broader systemic change. This institutional history situates the biographies and artworks of individual artists within contemporary networks of other artists, critics, curators, and audiences. By shifting the focus from individual psychology to social history, I attempt to create an inclusive survey of women artists that both questions and reflects the period's biases. Ultimately, this analysis aims to present new information and open new perspectives to inform the complex history of gender in art prior to the reemergence of the feminist art movement of the 1960s and '70s.

Exhibitions are a constructive framework in the study of modern art. From the Salon des Refusés of 1863 in Paris to the artist-organized "9th St. Exhibition of Paintings and Sculpture" of 1951 in New York, group shows serve as landmarks of public discourse, critical response, and stylistic innovation. Archival documents, contemporary criticism, photographs, and oral histories record real-time points of contact among artists, critics, and audiences. Yet the canonical exhibitions of modern and contemporary art seldom acknowledged the significance of women artists' contributions to the field. Art historians have used such exhibitions to establish a male-dominated history of modernism as a series of social and stylistic revolutions in which women played supporting roles, such as Berthe Morisot as the sole woman in the first Impressionist Exhibition of 1874 and Hannah Höch as a late addition to the First International Dada Fair of 1920. The minority status of women in the canonical exhibitions of modernism confirmed preconceived notions of women as followers of men. Yet women have always been modern artists, and their limited numbers in milestone exhibitions underlined their constrained social, institutional, and familial parameters.

Women began organizing all-women exhibitions in the mid-nineteenth century as a tool to combat discrimination, advocate for acceptance of their work, and boost their professional prospects. Most shows were organized by the artists themselves, usually in the form of salons or annual exhibitions by members of women artists groups. Sometimes commercial galleries deemed it worthwhile to organize all-women exhibitions of contemporary artists. And on occasion museums and art societies devoted gallery space to exhibitions of women artists. Venues ranged from the famed Woman's Building at the World's Columbian Exposition, Chicago, in 1893, to the "Exhibition of Painting and Sculpture by Women Artists for the Benefit of the Woman Suffrage Campaign" at the prestigious Macbeth Gallery, New York, in 1915. Many thousands of women artists have shown their work at all-women exhibitions and otherwise benefited from public exposure through these shows. Yet critical responses, by men and women, often objected to the concept of segregation by gender and disdained the preponderance of amateurs and perceived dilettantes, giving these exhibitions an unfavorable reputation. Furthermore, all-women exhibitions rarely welcomed artists of color and participated in the larger systemic discrimination by the white-dominated art world.

Since the 1970s, feminist historians have reexamined women's groups, institutions, and social networks to decenter the history of art from male-dominated spaces. The revaluation of art and the dismantling of old hierarchies has opened new perspectives, and recently scholars have positioned all-women exhibitions, of which there have been thousands worldwide, as a discrete field of knowledge combining gender studies, aesthetics, sociology, and critical histories of art.[3] All-women exhibitions are essential documents of the lives and careers of women artists. They are rich nodes of public discourse around gender; they situate discussion of women artists and their careers within professional and social networks, and concretize artistic connections to a community of museums, galleries, collectors, art schools, and other women. And all-women exhibition catalogues, reviews, and other records provide the only evidence of the work of hundreds if not thousands of artists.

All-women shows intended for a general audience establish gender as an externalized context for art. They initiate a public discussion, criticism, and education about women artists that otherwise would not have existed. Through these shows, the artist and/or her representatives put forth specific works of art into a gendered space. In all-women exhibitions, gender is articulated in the historical moment, not as a retrospective interpretation. These shows and their critical responses established, published, and documented the identification of "women artists" as a category. As a male art historian committed to new research on the history of modern women artists, I have focused my scholarship on the public presentation and reception of art by women in explicitly gendered critical contexts in which the work is positively identified as by women artists. This book accepts the category as understood at the time, defined as people who self-identified as women artists. "Women artists" was not a static category and was continually negotiated and defined with each exhibition.

This book also interrogates the limitations of all-women exhibitions. Black, Indigenous, and other women artists of color rarely appeared in all-women exhibitions in the 1940s and '50s. The liberalizations of the postwar era and the emergence of the civil rights movement did not alter how exhibitions of "women artists" implicitly ascribed whiteness to the category. This made such exhibitions inherently exclusionary. There was little place for or acceptance of women of color in most art institutions, whether museums, art schools, or women's organizations. The exceptional instances when white collectors and curators included Black women in all-women shows occurred when their personal and professional networks overlapped and the artwork possessed styles or subject-matter explicitly engaged with the European tradition. For example, in 1948 the collector Duncan Phillips included Loïs Mailou Jones's *Place du Tertre* (1938) (illus. 2) in "A Group of Women Painters," an exhibition of 26 artists at the women's Centennial Club in then racially segregated Nashville, loaned from the collection of the Phillips Memorial Gallery in Washington, DC. Her impressionistic painting of a scene of Montmartre was likely created during her sabbatical in Paris. There she participated in the all-women exhibition "Femmes d'aujourd'hui à l'académie Julian" at the Galerie Jean Carpentier in 1938, showing a still-life titled *Nature morte aux pommes* along with work by 35 other painting students, including her French friend Céline Tabary. In 1940s

2 Loïs Mailou Jones, *Place du Tertre*, 1938, oil on canvas.

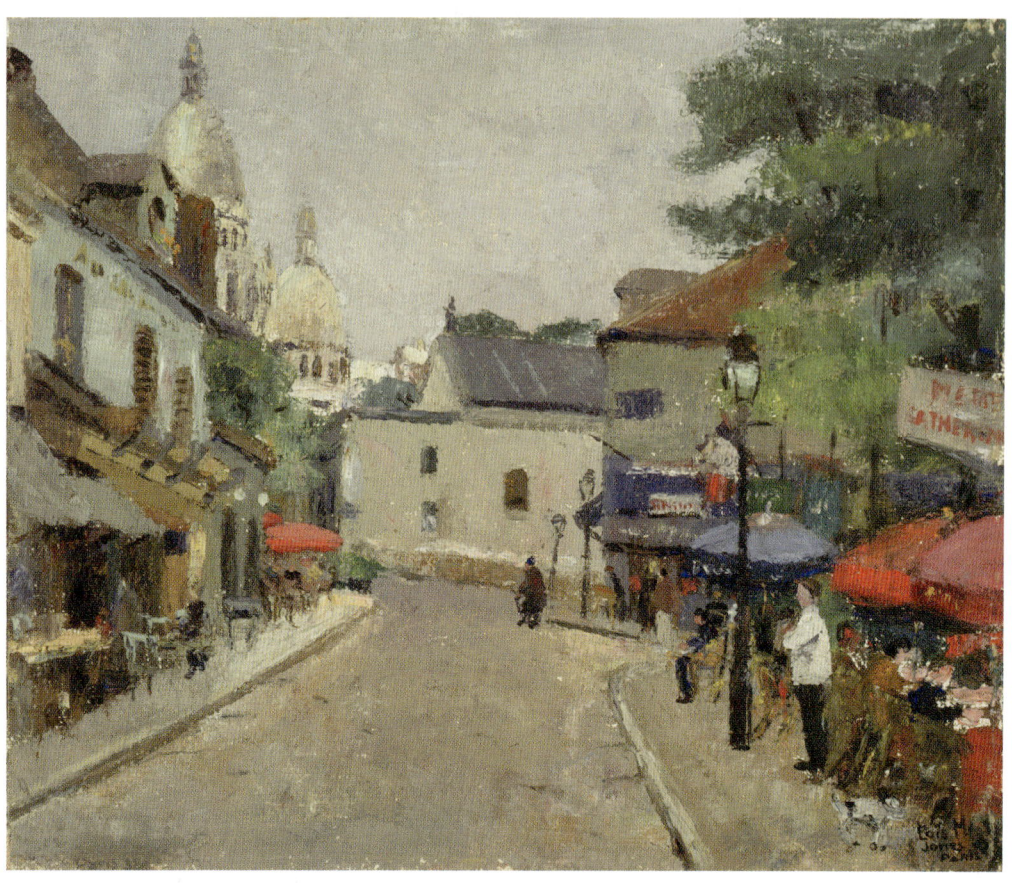

segregated America, Jones's painting of a Paris scene fit the context of the Phillips Gallery's collection, comfortably relating to such works as Janice Biala's painting *Spring, Rue de Seine* (1936), but she was likely prohibited from entering the gallery in Nashville together with her white peers.

Largely excluded from women artists organizations, Black women artists instead created independent spaces for the exhibition of their art. For example, Jones, with the help of Tabary, operated a European-style atelier known as the Little Paris Studio in Washington, DC, to train and exhibit artists of color in the 1940s. Black women's clubs, which originated in the 1890s, were crucial sites of resistance and community. These clubs maintained independent traditions with regular displays of members' watercolors, photography, and craft. These exhibitions and their constituent works were essentially ignored by the white art world, and documentation relating to them has yet to be surfaced. Much more work remains to fully recognize the self-directed exhibitions by women artists of color at midcentury.

* * *

Women Artists in Midcentury America is organized into ten chapters, each devoted to a milestone exhibition that highlights the advanced work of women artists at the time. This study begins with "Exhibition by 31 Women" (1943), an argument for women as leaders of the avant-garde, organized by one of its greatest patrons. It ends with "Women Artists in America Today" (1962), an impressive summation of the advanced art of the period on the cusp of a revived women's rights movement. Each of the selected exhibitions sparked dialogue, sometimes vigorous, in the media about the nature, history, and prospects of American women artists. Archival letters, journals, and publications allow the voices of artists, curators, and critics to speak across the decades. The narrative blends institutional histories and individual biographies, charting a social matrix of organizational priorities and artistic creativity. By attempting to reconstruct these exhibitions, the book investigates the complexity, challenges, and blind spots of the category of "women artists" in midcentury America.

To identify these shows I combed through volumes of art magazines, individual artist archives, newspaper indexes, and library catalogues. Most of these exhibitions did not appear in secondary literature outside of deeply researched institutional histories, artist monographs, and catalogues raisonnés, and many lacked basic documenation. I identified about fifty one-off exhibitions (not including annual exhibitions by women artists organizations) within the period of study and prioritized exhibitions that expanded representations of women artists according to medium, style, and geography as well as race, ethnicity, and national origin. The ten exhibitions in this volume were selected for their significance while avoiding repetition of themes. Several of the shows in this book focused on media other than painting and sculpture: photography, printmaking, and the decorative arts, specifically fiber and metalwork. Some shows reiterated established definitions of women artists and helped form a canon of nationally renowned painters like Georgia O'Keeffe, Isabel Bishop, and Irene Rice Pereira. Other exhibitions incrementally expanded the definitions of "woman artist" by welcoming a small number of experimental artists and the occasional artist of color. The geographic distribution of the selected shows captures the varied life experiences of women artists, many of whom built professional careers teaching art in cities across the country and worked to build their local art communities as well as their individual practices in New York, Washington, DC, Philadelphia, Houston, San Francisco, and Boston.

The book is organized chronologically to tell the story of the shifting discourses around gender through the mid-twentieth century, from the explosion of new opportunities in the war years, to the return to order in the postwar aftermath, to the malaise from phony proclamations of equality in the 1950s, to the reemergence of political feminism in the early 1960s. The book takes the reader on a journey over twenty years, from the Second World War to the Kennedy administration.

* * *

Psychological and sociological binaries of the masculine and the feminine framed much of the interpretation of women artists from the early 1940s. This climate was fueled by the rhetoric of psychoanalysis and Surrealism, which delved into the unconscious, guided by the theories of Sigmund Freud. Chapter One takes as its subject "Exhibition by 31 Women" at Peggy Guggenheim's gallery Art of This Century in New York: a critical touchstone to begin the exploration of the discourses of gender in midcentury American art. Juried by art world luminaries such as Marcel Duchamp and André Breton, the exhibition both confronted and affirmed the Surrealist movement's associations of women with sexuality and nature and men with politics and culture. The exhibition was mounted in 1943, when the Second World War reshuffled American society and women entered previously male-dominated spaces with new roles in industry, the armed forces, and government. This timing is significant, as critics found the exhibition to reveal a new assertive avant-garde of women artists distinct from the retiring professionalism of lady painters. Perhaps the most famous of all-women shows, "31 Women," is exceptional in its unabashed celebration of the European female avant-garde and its recognition of a new generation of American women painters and sculptors, flavored with publicity-grabbing oddities like Gypsy Rose Lee's collage self-portrait and Meret Oppenheim's already notorious fur-lined teacup *Object* (1936).

The Second World War was also a time of invigorated discourse on race in America. Black Americans were called on to serve a country whose entrenched cultural racism and legal segregation contradicted its unifying ideals of liberty and democracy. Across the political spectrum, a growing number of Americans supported the end of legal racial segregation, but women's voices were not initially given sufficient space in this conversation. Chapter Two explores one exhibition that attempted to engage the issue of race by promoting racial integration through the artwork of two women. "Portraits of Leading American Negro Citizens" opened on May 2, 1944, at the National Collection of Fine Arts, Smithsonian Institution, in Washington, DC, with 23 paintings by Black artist Laura Wheeler Waring and white artist Betsy Graves Reyneau. The portraits depicted Black scientists, educators, judges, and other prominent figures. Funded by the Harmon Foundation, the exhibition traveled for the next decade to over thirty additional museums, libraries, and community centers across the country, from towns to metropolises, stimulating educational opportunities and conversations on racial integration. The show was one of the few, if not the only, all-women exhibitions of the midcentury to address race and sheds light on the fraught intersection of race and gender in American art.

Women photographers were among those impacted by the societal upheaval of the Second World War and its aftermath, as new professional opportunities and public recognition became available to them. This shift minted new celebrities, like *Life* photojournalist Margaret Bourke-White. To take stock of women's increasing participation in the burgeoning diversity of photographic practices, Alouise Boker, the print director of the august Camera Club of New York, invited fifty women to submit four photographs that best represented their art. The resulting "First Women's Invitation Exhibition" presented 164 prints by 41 photographers, including Bourke-White, Ruth Bernhard, and Louise Dahl-Wolfe. It opened a new conversation on women in fine art, commercial, fashion, portrait, scientific, and medical photography, as discussed in Chapter Three. Unlike painting and sculpture, where long-standing prejudices limited women's roles, the comparatively new field of photography opened new opportunities for artistic and professional accomplishment.

The postwar "return to order," when men returning from the war reintegrated into society, displaced women (primarily white and middle class) from the workforce and university back to the home and unpaid domestic responsibilities. Women's colleges played a complex role in this history, training and supporting future artists and curators while teaching biased messages about gender differences and professional prospects. One such institution in rural western Massachusetts, Smith College—one of the "Seven Sisters" group of elite women's colleges—commemorated its 75th anniversary in 1949 with a celebration of distinguished women in science, art, politics, and the academy. The college's art museum contributed an exhibition, "Ten Women Who Paint," which gathered work by artists across three generations, from Elizabeth Sparhawk-Jones and Georgia O'Keeffe (born in the 1880s) to Isabel Bishop and Doris Lee (born in the 1900s) to Esther Geller (born in the 1920s). Chapter Four discusses the broader influence on modern art by women's colleges, like Smith, which employed women as art professors and historians and mounted early museum exhibitions of women artists.

Women artists organizations, some of which were founded in the late nineteenth century, played a pivotal role in midcentury American art by steadfastly advocating for gender equity. Chapter Five explores the discourses on gender within these organizations, focusing on the San Francisco Women Artists (SFWA) 27th annual exhibition in 1952 as a case study. The show typified the institutional structures and agendas of women artists organizations, while also demonstrating SFWA's unusual intergenerational support for experimental artists. The exhibition featured work by the pioneering Japanese American sculptor Ruth Asawa along with 91 other artists, including longtime members like photographer Imogen Cunningham and jeweler Margaret De Patta. This was not the only time Asian American artists and aesthetic innovators exhibited in SFWA annuals, but the 1952 edition especially demonstrated a forward-looking attitude toward new forms and materials, highlighting SFWA as an organization that differed in its outlook from the traditional women artists organizations of its day.

Postwar prosperity from the expansion of international corporations, real estate development, and domestic consumption led to burgeoning metropolitan areas across the country, with an accompanying surge in interest in contemporary art and design. Chapter Six takes us to Texas, where energy money and ambition transformed the state into a hub of arts patronage. Houston art teacher Norma Henderson observed the flourishing art scene and, concerned that women were being overlooked, organized an ambitious survey of art, craft, and design by nearly sixty women working in all media. Held at the Contemporary Arts Museum in 1953, "Women in Art" included a roundup of some of the established New York-based women of the time, including Loren MacIver and Mary Callery, but it was the show's catholic approach that defined it: it presented women from across the country in the emerging American craft movement, including textile and fiber artists Mariska Karasz, Dorothy Liebes, Florence Knoll, and others. The exhibition promoted women as forces in the new postwar fields of studio craft, interior design, and industrial ceramics, attributing their ancient excellence in the domestic arts.

"Why have there been no great women artists?" Linda Nochlin asked in her foundational feminist critique of art history published in 1971. The question was not a new one: it had been posed throughout the 1950s. However, at that time, critics and artists generally confronted institutional sexism in an oblique manner. The situation was addressed more directly in 1955 through the exhibition "Great Women Artists," organized by the Delius Gallery, a Manhattan commercial enterprise, as examined in Chapter Seven. The show surveyed four hundred years of painting and drawing, with works by Sofonisba Anguissola, Rachel Ruysch, Élisabeth Louise Vigée Le Brun, and Rosa Bonheur; Impressionists Berthe Morisot and Mary Cassatt; and modernists Paula Modersohn-Becker, Suzanne Valadon, and Sonia Delaunay. Room was made for contemporary works by Maria Helena Vieira da Silva, Georgia O'Keeffe, Irene Rice Pereira, and Janice Biala. The exhibition was one of a few during midcentury that gauged the history of women in Western art and provoked critics to ponder the contradictions of aesthetic quality and social exclusion.

Some individual women artists achieved renown in midcentury America, with retrospectives and monographic catalogues, yet the albatross of "greatness" inhibited most American museums from viewing women favorably. Large art museums with global collections rarely invested their staff time and collection resources in the history of women artists in Europe and the United States. Chapter Eight focuses on one notable exception, the print department of the Philadelphia Museum of Art, which organized "Women Printmakers" in 1956. The show featured 127 artists, with a substantial presentation of graphic work spanning nearly four hundred years. A review in the *Philadelphia Inquirer* noted the significance of this foray into "a still unexplored field," which demonstrated that initially women printmakers made careers as copyists of other artist's compositions and techniques, and starting in the late nineteenth century achieved individual reputations when they embarked on independent artistic experimentation. The exhibition included Cassatt and Morisot as modernist precursors and presented a wide array of contemporary printmakers, including Peggy Bacon and Wanda Gág, who created indelible black-and-white prints of women's new opportunities in the 1920s, and abstract experimentalists June Wayne and Sue Fuller. The exhibition represented a moment of institutional acknowledgment of women's achievements in printmaking and consideration of their larger place in Western art history.

By the late 1950s, Abstract Expressionism became the dominant art movement in the United States, practiced by hundreds of artists of diverse backgrounds across the country. Women seldom received public credit for their essential work in the formation and development of the style, especially in the New York scene headlined by Jackson Pollock and other male artists. It is against this backdrop that an unlikely gallery in Amarillo, Texas, organized an exhibition that for the first time presented women front and center as leaders in the movement, as examined in Chapter Nine. Contemporary artist and educator Dord Fitz partnered with New York artists Elaine de Kooning and Jeanne Reynal to organize "17 of the Women Tops in Art," the largest exhibition devoted to Abstract Expressionist painting by women mounted during the era, with three canvases each by Nell Blaine, Perle Fine, Helen Frankenthaler, Jane Freilicher, Miriam Schapiro, Hedda

Sterne, and Jane Wilson, among others. Six artists traveled to the Texas Panhandle to attend the opening, which included a ranch barbecue, a tea reception, and a symposium at a local college. The exhibition anticipated the subsequent celebration of women Abstract Expressionists in the realms of art-historical studies and museum exhibitions.

The Cold War rivalry between the United States and the Soviet Union shaped the politics of the era. To demonstrate the advantages of democracy, American politicians and museum professionals promoted the collective achievements of women artists as unparalleled in the history of art. The 1962 exhibition "Women Artists in America Today," part of the 125th anniversary celebration of the prestigious Mount Holyoke College in Massachusetts, presented a comprehensive exhibition of significant contemporary American women painters and sculptors. The timing of a campus speech by a federal official linked the exhibition with President John F. Kennedy's new agenda to promote artistic freedom and women's rights as democratic values. Chapter Ten explores how the show, which was curated by art history professor Jean C. Harris, celebrated contemporary sculpture, bringing together pioneering abstract sculptors (Lee Bontecou, Louise Bourgeois, Claire Falkenstein, and Louise Nevelson) and figural sculptors working in humanist content (Rhys Caparn, Minna Harkavy, Luise Kaish, and Marianna Pineda). "Women Artists in America Today" marked a highpoint in the recognition of women's excellence in modern American art—but at the same time serves as a reminder of the persistent structural and intellectual constraints on women artists' accomplishments prior to second-wave feminism.

These two decades of all-women exhibitions endeavored to bolster the legitimacy of the category of "women artists." Indeed, the term was pushed to its logical limit until the false promise of separate spheres collapsed in the 1960s. In 1963, Betty Friedan published *The Feminine Mystique*, reanimating the insights of Simone de Beauvoir, igniting the existential discontents among middle-class white women, and catalyzing a movement that grew to challenge political and institutional sex and gender discrimination. A new generation of feminist curators and artists recast the category of "women artists" as a basis for collective activism and rediscovered the all-woman exhibition as a rallying cry and source of solidarity and empowerment. The feminist artists involved in Womanhouse (1972), a collective art installation in Los Angeles, craved historical connections to their work. Recalled artist Judy Chicago,

> One day, while we were working in Womanhouse, one of the women in the Feminist Program returned from a thrift-shop expedition carrying an old book. It was an out-of-print edition about something called the Woman's Building, which none of us had ever heard about . . . As we examined the book, I was struck by the quality of consciousness evidenced by the women involved in the building and by the fact that they had apparently unearthed a good deal of historical material about women artists.[4]

This volume's focus on all-women exhibitions aims to provide more examples that can help to bridge the gap between a key feminist practice of the 1970s and the underappreciated work of women in the preceding decades.

EXHIBITION
by

31
WOMEN

30 W. 57   **Jan. 5-31**

201	Djuna Barnes	Portrait of Alice	1936
202	Zenia Cage	Mobile	1942
203	Leonora Carrington	The Horses of Lord Candlestick	1939
204	Leonora Carrington	Joie de Patinage	1942
205	Vera da Silva	Ballet	1939
206	Eyre de Lanux	Persiennes, Persiennes	1942
207	Leonor Fini	The Shepherdess of the Sphinxes	1941
208	Leonor Fini	Self Portrait	
209	Elsa Freytag von Loringhoven	Object	1926
210	Suzy Frelinghuysen	Composition	1942
212	Meraud Guevara	Still Life	1939
213	Annie Harvey	Still Life	1942
214	Valentine Hugo	Reve du 17/1/34	1934
215	Buffie Johnson	Dejeuner sur Mer	1942
216	Frida Kahlo	Self Portrait	1940
217	Jaqueline Lambal	No he is looking for them, I have told myself	1942
218	Gypsy Rose Lee	Self Portrait	1942
219	Aline Meyer Liebman	Story in Paint	1935
220	Hazel McKinley	Happy Land	1942
221	Milena	Insomnia	1942
222	Louise Nevelson	Column	1942
223	Meret Oppenheim	Fur Covered Cup and Spoon	1936
224	Barbara Reis	The Enchanted Bull	1942
225	I. Rice Pereira	View	1942
226	I. Rice Pereira	Defraction	1942
227	Kay Sage	At The Appointed Time	1942
228	Sonia Secula	Composition	1942
229	Gretchen Schoeninger	Abstraction	1942
230	Esphyr Slobodkina	Recollections	1942
231	Hedda Sterne	Catsonarock	1942
232	Dorothea Tanning	Birthday	1942
233	Dorothea Tanning	Jeu d'Enfant	1942
234	Sophie Taeuber Arp	Composition	1938
235	Julia Thecla	Magnifying Glass	1941
236	Pegeen Vail	Joie de Vivre	1942

3 Art of This Century, *Exhibition by 31 Women*, 1943, brochure.

1

Avant-Garde: "Exhibition by 31 Women," Art of This Century, 1943

"Here then is testimony to the fact that the creative ability of women is by no means restricted to the decorative vein, as could be deduced from the history of art by women throughout the ages."[1] So began the press release to "Exhibition by 31 Women," the landmark exhibition that opened at Peggy Guggenheim's Art of This Century on January 5, 1943. Guggenheim (1898–1979) sought to reclaim the category of "women's art" from negative associations with craft and dilettantism, transforming a debate that had been simmering for a century as women steadily became a larger force in the international art world as artists, collectors, educators, and dealers. This history seems to have informed the press release, which justified the exhibition's rationale as both aesthetic and sociological. The exhibition was conceived to make a sensation, and so it did: it became one of the most influential exhibitions of mid-twentieth-century America. The roundup of European and American artists initiated a new vision of women in the modernist avant-garde. The show created a space for women to *be* the avant-garde, leading the way into the future at a moment of global turmoil and conflict. Over eighty years later, the show remains the exemplar of the fashionable yet subversive all-woman exhibition, with the title "31 Women" appended to several twenty-first-century gallery shows in homage to Guggenheim's savvy positioning of women at the forefront of modern art.

Guggenheim's approach was radical in that it broke the rules of decorum that had largely guided the respectful all-women exhibitions of the prior century. In this regard, she built on the legacy of self-proclaimed modernist women artists who had presented their own group exhibitions to distinguish themselves from mainstream women artists organizations. In 1925, Marguerite Zorach, Anne Goldthwaite, and eleven other artists broke from the conservative National Association of Women Painters and Sculptors to form the New York Society of Women Artists (NYSWA). They wanted a jury-free system whereby members could select and install the work of their choosing, and desired a women's group dedicated to the progressive ideals of modern self-expression. The NYSWA was part of a small international wave of progressive women artists organizations, such as the Gemeinschaft Deutscher und Österreichischer Künstlerinnen (GEDOK), founded by feminist Ida Dehmel in 1926, and the Société des femmes artistes modernes, founded in 1930 by painter Marie-Anne Camax-Zoegger. The NYSWA's first exhibition, of thirty members in 1926, presented a variety of contemporary styles, with artists including Peggy Bacon (1895–1987) and Blanche Lazzell (1878–1956). The *New York Times* concluded that the focus on gender "heightens interest" in the show.[2] The artists sought new contexts for their work and founded new women artists groups to reconcile a woman-centered strategy with modernist aesthetics and analysis.

Guggenheim was probably familiar with at least some of these convergences of modern art and all-women exhibitions. The exhibition "31 Women" looms large in the history of mid-twentieth-century art because it probed the tensions between the binaries of Europe and America, abstraction and Surrealism, avant-garde and kitsch, and feminism and modernism. In its function as a conceptual intervention, the show presented a post-suffrage generation of women who came of age with new political rights, laying claim to a history of radical feminist aesthetics born from the suffrage and Dada movements of the 1910s. Not only did the artists identify as women, but their imagery was devoted almost entirely to women, from portraits and self-portraits to portrayals of women in evocative scenarios that invited audiences into symbolic realms of fantasy and imagination. Without any known installation photographs or plans, the legacy of "31 Women" rests on its terse title, eclectic checklist of artists, and passionate critical responses.

Why Guggenheim decided to mount this show remains a subject of debate. Perhaps she hoped that "31 Women" would attract a slew of publicity by stirring the gender pot of wartime's conflicting new symbols of femininity, from Rosie the Riveter to Hollywood's femme fatale. Perhaps she wished to riposte the rampant sexism in Surrealism, the dominant art movement of the moment, by singling out its many talented female practitioners. Perhaps she attempted to elevate a cohort of younger American artists in a New York art scene dominated by established male European modernists, many of them temporarily exiled in the United States. Perhaps she aimed to promote her friends and family to bolster a kinship network in the art world. Considering the selection of the artists and works in the exhibition, all these impulses seem to have been at play, which made for a raucous and contradictory show. In many ways Guggenheim thought and behaved like an artist, and she trusted her creative instincts, rightly or wrongly. As Lee Krasner (1908–1984) recalled of Guggenheim's impact, "What one should say about Peggy, is, simply, that she did it. That no matter what her motivations were, she did it."[3]

Born and raised in New York as the heir to two family fortunes, Peggy Guggenheim went on to live overseas for two decades before returning to the city in July 1941. About fifteen months later she opened a four-room gallery to display her personal art collection. Art of This Century was located on the seventh floor of a commercial building on 57th Street in the center of New York's gallery district. The theatrical interior was designed by Frederick Kiesler, a pioneer of interactive multimedia architecture, and possessed distinct spaces to accentuate the various art tendencies of the day. In the Surrealist room, the concave gumwood walls displayed unframed paintings, projected from the wall on baseball bat mounts. The abstract gallery walls were lined with blue-hued canvas screens, with paintings and sculptures mounted on industrial-looking metal-and-wire armatures that were strung from floor to ceiling. The kinetic gallery boasted a paternoster to display Paul Klee paintings, and in the same space Marcel Duchamp's *La Boîte-en-valise* (1935–41), a conceptual work of reproductions, was hidden behind a peephole—earning the area the moniker "Coney Island" in the media. Finally, the Daylight Gallery, with large street-facing windows, white walls, and two rooms totaling nearly 800 square feet (74 sq. m), was reserved for monthly special exhibitions of borrowed work.[4] Guggenheim kept her desk in this section, near several racks of framed works dubbed the Painting Library.

The gallery immediately became a center of modern art in New York and a crucial crossroads where aspiring American artists and the dislocated Parisian avant-garde could mingle and evaluate one another. Guggenheim had been away from the New York art scene since 1920, when she moved to Paris after receiving a substantial inheritance at the age of 21. She was a free spirit and adored the company of artists, in Paris becoming part of avant-garde literature and art circles associated with American expatriate bohemian writers Natalie Barney and Djuna Barnes. Guggenheim started collecting modern art under the tutelage of renowned art historians and opened her first gallery, Guggenheim Jeune, in London in 1938. She strove to build a collection representative of European modern art movements from 1910 to 1940, and in so doing she focused her attention on painting and sculpture by established European masters and longtime American expatriates, acquiring few works by women. She returned to Paris, where she planned to relocate the gallery, but following Germany's invasion of France she fled to New York in 1941 with her soon-to-be husband, painter Max Ernst. Once in New York, Guggenheim turned her attention to presenting her collection and exploring the new u.s. art scene, which fueled the program of Art of This Century. She aspired for her space to transcend the normal gallery experience and serve as an active "research studio for new ideas of creative effort."[5] The gallery's temporary exhibition program, which was established as part of this endeavor, exceeded the scope of Guggenheim's personal collection.

The catalogue of her original collection, also titled *Art of This Century*, was published in New York in conjunction with the gallery opening. An examination of its contents reveals women's minority status in her collection at the time. Surrealist painters Leonor Fini and Leonora Carrington were the only women to receive full-page treatments with biographies and illustrated works. The few other women in Guggenheim's collection were simply listed in the appendix: Berenice Abbott (two photographs), Elsa von Freytag-Loringhoven (Dadaist object), Jacqueline Lamba (one of many contributors to a collective Surrealist drawing), and Sophie Taeuber-Arp (drawing on paper). If any women or girls were among the artists included in the ethnocentric collections of "Children's Drawings," "Drawings of the Insane," and "Primitive Paintings," as titled in the catalogue, they were not afforded individual identities.

The political and economic landscape for women in the United States had shifted before Guggenheim returned to the country, with women achieving some legislative and social power and authority. No women sat in the u.s. Congress when Guggenheim moved overseas in 1920, but by the time of her return in 1941 ten did, including one in the Senate. First Lady Eleanor Roosevelt used her six-days-a-week newspaper column "My Day," read by millions, as a national platform to highlight vignettes in the halting progress in women's and civil rights. By 1942, women leveraged opportunities created by the war to move into trades and services previously restricted to men, from the factory floor to the Women's Army Auxiliary Corps, albeit in largely entry-level positions. Educators encouraged American women who had art training and drafting skills to contribute to the war effort.

Despite these gains, women continued to lack constitutional rights and equal protections in both public and private employment, which undermined their aspirations and blocked opportunities. Women's increased participation in the workforce also resulted in a conservative backlash. Philip Wylie's 1943 bestselling book *Generation of Vipers* decried what he perceived as the feminization of American culture and called for the restoration of women's place in the home. Something was in the air in early 1940s New York: a sense that power was shifting.

Over the course of five years, Guggenheim exhibited dozens of women artists in group and solo shows at Art of This Century, and she sanctioned the gallery to be a platform for socially conscious work. By one scholar's calculation, women comprised 40 percent of the artists in the gallery's exhibitions during its operations from 1942 to 1947.[6] Numerous women received solo shows at the gallery, although few of these led to museum acquisitions or exhibitions, which were the essential building blocks of a career.

Records indicate that Guggenheim developed the concept for an exhibition of experimental contemporary women simultaneously with her plans for her gallery. She corresponded with Museum of Modern Art (MOMA) director Alfred Barr about suggestions of women artists and loans of objects by Meret Oppenheim (1913–1985) and Barbara Hepworth (1903–1975) at least several weeks before Art of This Century's premiere in October 1942. With the gallery opened and the catalogue published, Guggenheim pursued the concept of an all-women exhibition—"31 Women"—for one of the first temporary shows in the Daylight Gallery. The show was sure to be an attention-grabber: an exhibition of women artists was uncommon in avant-garde circles, whose members, both male and female, opted to associate with each other and not conventional artist organizations.

Guggenheim recalled that Duchamp proposed the idea when they crossed paths in Paris, prior to their departures for the safe haven across the Atlantic.[7] The Dada provocateur had helped Guggenheim organize several shows in London. He had carved out a position as a male artist who took an interest in female subjectivity, through varied projects including his performative alter ego Rrose Sélavy and curatorial efforts. Indeed, Duchamp's collaboration with Guggenheim followed in the footsteps of his earlier work with Katherine S. Dreier (1877–1952), an American artist and patron of international avant-garde art. Dreier was a staunch feminist and publicly supported women artists; she was among the financial backers of NYSWA's first exhibition. In 1920, Duchamp and Dreier co-founded, with Man Ray, the Société Anonyme, an organization committed to promoting modern art in America. They opened a gallery in two rooms on East 47th Street in Manhattan with an exhibition of Duchamp, Constantin Brâncuşi, Francis Picabia, and Man Ray. The space remained open for about four years, during which time Société Anonyme also offered lectures and symposia on-site and in other venues as disparate as the Heterodoxy Club (a feminist debate society in Greenwich Village) and the Brooklyn Museum. It could be said that Dreier established the template for Guggenheim to build a collection of avant-garde art, install it in a publicly accessible gallery, and create spaces and opportunities for exhibitions and programs that surfaced new and marginalized voices.

In 1934, Dreier organized an exhibition of women artists in the collection of the Société Anonyme. "From Impressionism to Abstraction: 13 Women Painters from France, Germany, Belgium, Norway, Poland, and the United States" opened first in the gallery lounge of the American Woman's Association clubhouse in New York and then traveled to the Wadsworth Atheneum in Hartford, Connecticut, at the time a leading venue for experimental art and culture. The international flavor of the show, in addition to its feminist orientation, responded to the intensifying rise of nationalism and fascism. Yet the show provoked scant critical response. This could in part be attributed to it opening in a women's club, not a contemporary art gallery or museum, and to the pedestrian figural styles of ten of the artists. Abstract pictures were included by three artists: Suzanne Duchamp, Norwegian Cubist Ragnhild Keyser, and Dreier herself.

The following year, an unrelated exhibition concerning women and modernism—"15 Women in Modern Art"—opened at Beekman Tower gallery, New York. Centered on well-crafted modernism, "15 Women" presented a range of media—sculptures, photographs, litho- graphs, textiles, and furniture—by Bauhaus fiber artist Anni Albers, painter Mercedes Matter, and others, in a modern interior setting. Located in an out-of-the-way venue, like Dreier's "13 Women," the show stimulated little public response. Both served as tame precursors to the assertive attitude of "31 Women" at Art of This Century.

Guggenheim titled her show "31 Women," not "31 Women Artists" (illus. 3). The former can be categorized as artists who identified as women, whereas the latter would indicate "women artists," a histori- cally qualified and delimited category of artist. Regardless of the title, the show's premise allegedly displeased Georgia O'Keeffe (1887–1986), who declined Guggenheim's invitation to participate, apparently going so far as to visit the gallery with her entourage to declare, "I am not a woman painter."[8] On the one hand, this anecdote confirms O'Keeffe's reputation as a formidable artist who publicly insisted that she be presented as an individual without any qualifiers. She had been exhibiting in New York for over 25 years and was preparing a retro- spective at the Art Institute of Chicago that would open that same month. On the other hand, the story doesn't reflect O'Keeffe's actual participation in women-oriented exhibitions over the decades, either at women's organizations or in all-women group exhibitions. Her demurral might be read as her stating that she preferred not to partici- pate in *this* particular all-women exhibition.[9] Perhaps she didn't want to be identified as a certain sort of "woman artist"—a Surrealist with overtly sexualized art, a problem she already grappled with throughout her career. In 1926, a reviewer wrote that her exhibition of new paintings teased the viewer "like so many flappers on Broadway."[10]

Surrealism exerted an enormous gravitational pull in midcentury America and was largely the aesthetic context in which "31 Women" was conceived and interpreted. The landmark exhibition "Fantastic Art, Dada, Surrealism" (1936–7) at MOMA took New York by storm, followed a few years later by Salvador Dalí's sensationalist and sexualized "Dream of Venus" pavilion at the 1939 New York World's Fair. The Surrealist presence in New York increased with the start of the Second World War and the German invasion of France, which brought to the city many of its primary theorists and practitioners, such as Duchamp, André Breton, Max Ernst, André Masson, Yves Tanguy, and Wifredo Lam. Prior to this influx, the American art scene was dominated by figural School of Paris and Mexican-influenced Social Realist styles; with their arrival, the vogue shifted to new Surrealist mythic subject-matter and techniques of subconscious imagery, chance composition, and automatism. The male leaders and theorists of Surrealism sought to escape socially imposed structures of rationality and civility, instead valorizing the irrational and impudent—especially in what they considered to be their purest forms, such as the hysteric, the primitive, and the insane. The movement's theorists and artists associated women with natural forces beyond their control and obsessed over women as models, muses, and mannequins.

Despite, or perhaps because of, the intense foregrounding of male sexual desire in Surrealism, some women artists were attracted to the freedoms afforded by a movement that demanded the eradication of psychological inhibitions and thus participated in group exhibitions. Guggenheim attempted to proclaim her impartiality toward abstraction and Surrealism: at the opening of her gallery, she famously wore one earring designed by abstractionist Alexander Calder and the other designed by Surrealist Yves Tanguy. Yet her appointments to the jury to select the all-women exhibition suggest a clear bias toward Surrealism. The jurors were Duchamp, Ernst, and Breton, along with MOMA curators James Johnson Sweeney and James Thrall Soby, gallery assistants Howard Putzel and Jimmy Ernst (who later recused himself), and Guggenheim herself. Many of these men played essential roles in assembling and writing Guggenheim's collection catalogue. The panel of elite artists and curators convened on Christmas Eve a mere two weeks before the opening. Cementing the primacy of the male gaze in "31 Women," Guggenheim asked Max Ernst—by then her husband— to make studio visits and select works for the show.

Guggenheim charged the jury to select work by women primarily based on the criterion of the "fantastic."[11] An amorphous term that encapsulated Surrealism's tastes and styles, "fantastic art" included Surrealist paintings as well as all works of creation deemed in alignment with the Surrealist values of the irrational, unstudied, and sponta- neous: outsider, folk, ethnographic, and juvenile art. The category of the fantastic adroitly bridged the gap between U.S. artists and their European colleagues. Surrealism as a formal and philosophical move- ment may have been born of the French avant-garde and imported to the United States, but the fantastic is ubiquitous. The search for and apprehension of the fantastic came to be considered as much an artis- tic expression as was the creation of studio artworks. The ethics of this practice are complex, and there is a power imbalance in the European collection and elevation of non-Western culture, yet Surrealism did nourish postcolonialist activists like writers Aimé and Suzanne Césaire. Surrealists behaved as curators as much as artists and prided themselves on their collections of narrative-driven artifacts, which they sometimes arranged in cabinets of curiosities. American sculptor Louise Nevelson (1899–1988) earned Surrealist credentials when, around the time that "31 Women" was in development, she showed a shoeshine stand, gaud- ily decorated with baubles on wood by Italian immigrant Joe Milone, to Alfred Barr, who promptly installed it in the MOMA lobby as a Christmas folly.

In effect, as both a curatorial endeavor by Guggenheim and an eclectic group show, "31 Women" could be considered the first exhibi- tion of Surrealist women, though it was not declared as such. The checklist alone serves as an essential document of women Surrealists, many of whom became overlooked in the retrospective process of canon-formation in later decades, before all-women Surrealist survey books and exhibitions appeared in the 1980s. That is not to say that all of the artists in the show would self-identify as Surrealists; "31 Women" included both established Surrealists and newcomers brought in under the auspices of "the fantastic." Guggenheim and the jury clearly favored Surrealism's superabundance of imagery in tense juxtaposition and illusory landscapes, even if some of the artists themselves rejected the label. A solid contingent of abstract artists were included, as were a range of representational works that did not comfortably fit into either category, but these elements were overshadowed by Surrealism's dominance of "31 Women" in both its ethos and its reception.

The exhibition revisited several key works by women in previous Surrealist exhibitions. Swiss artist Meret Oppenheim's fur-lined teacup *Object* (1936) was already an icon of Surrealism in America. It

4 Leonora Carrington, *The Horses of Lord Candlestick*, 1938, oil on canvas.

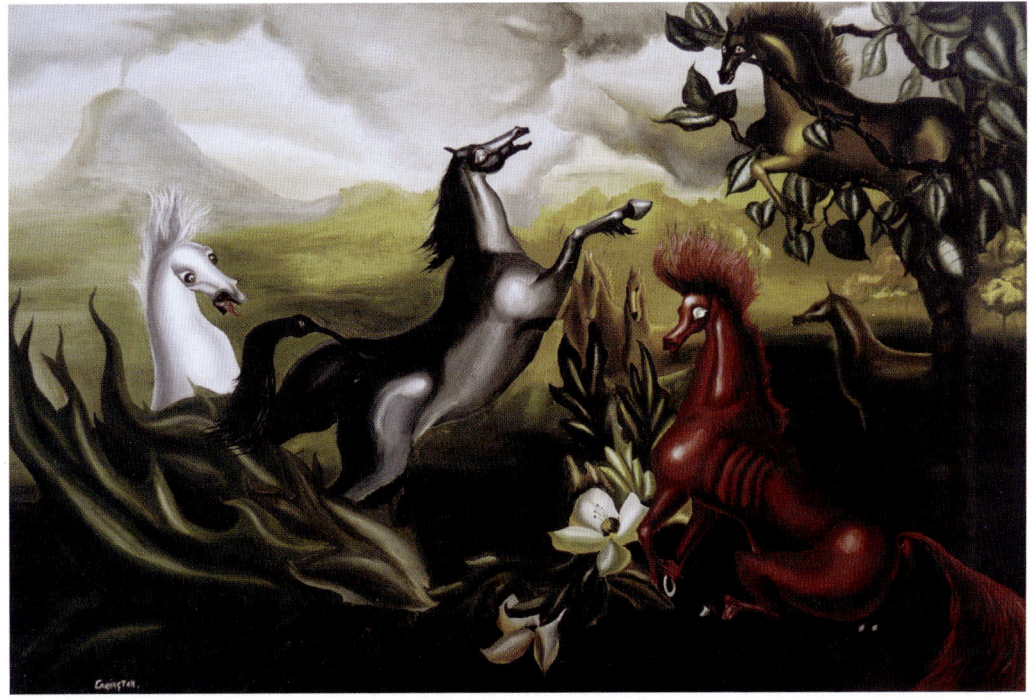

caused a sensation when it was exhibited at MoMA in 1936 and nine years later its violation of conventional notions of fine art continued to outrage the public. Guggenheim borrowed the disturbing work from the museum's study collection (it had not yet been formally accessioned to the permanent collection). Another work shown in "31 Women," the ethereal oil painting *Dream of January 17, 1934* (1934) by Valentine Hugo (1887–1968), had previously appeared in a Surrealist show in Belgium in 1934 and also was included in the MoMA survey. Two phantasmagorical paintings—*The Shepherdess of the Sphinxes* (1941) by Argentinian-born Italian artist and writer Leonor Fini (1907–1996) and *The Horses of Lord Candlestick* (1938) (illus. 4) by British-born Mexican artist Leonora Carrington (1917–2011)—were already in Guggenheim's collection and exhibited in the initial installation in Art of This Century's Surrealist gallery. By relocating these four works from a general Surrealist context to one centered around women's perspectives, Guggenheim surfaced interpretations of the works' psychological content and granted audiences the opportunity to connect women's self-expression to larger questions of social status.

At least nine other artists in "31 Women" previously exhibited in Surrealist exhibitions or employed Surrealist techniques and subject-matter. French painter Jacqueline Lamba (1910–1993) and American artist Kay Sage (1898–1963) were intimately involved in the movement, and each pioneered unique styles of biomorphic abstraction. Frida Kahlo (1907–1954), the sui generis Mexican artist whom Breton had famously proclaimed to be "a ribbon around a bomb" on the occasion of her first American solo show at the Julien Levy Gallery in New York, contributed a *Self-Portrait with Cropped Hair* (1940) depicting herself in a man's suit with hair clippings strewn across the ground.[12] Alluring paintings of scantily clad or topless women in dreamlike situations by younger Americans—such as *Birthday* (illus. 5) (1942), by Dorothea Tanning (1910–2012)—became signature images of the show, reproduced in reviews to illustrate critical interpretations of the exhibition as a frank examination of female sexuality. One such work, *La Déjeuner sur mer* (1942) by Buffie Johnson (1912–2006)—a painting depicting a scene of two mermaids picnicking on a raft adrift in a rolling ocean—appeared in the *New York Times*. The émigré artists Hedda Sterne (1910–2011) and Sonja Sekula (1918–1963), along with Nevelson and Portuguese painter Maria Helena Vieira da Silva (1908–1992), all created works aligned with Surrealist aesthetics.

The exhibition "31 Women" opened in the midst of the Second World War, before the horrors of the Holocaust became widely exposed. The show included several artists, including Nevelson and Sterne, who inscribed modernist displacement and reconfiguration in their work. Nevelson was born to a Yiddish-speaking Jewish family in Ukraine and raised in Maine. She went on to become an eminent abstract sculptor, but at the time of "31 Women" she was primarily known as a figural artist beginning to exhibit found wood sculpture. Her assemblage in the show, entitled *Column* (not extant, *c.* 1942), belonged to a body of work in which she created constructions from wood discarded on the streets of New York. A few months later she arranged a group of similar works in an immersive presentation at the upstart Norlyst Gallery, established by artist Elenore Lust with her boyfriend Jimmy Ernst after he left Art of This Century. Nevelson's audacious group of animal and caricature figures in a circus-themed exhibition presaged her later development of environmental art.

Sterne, born to a Jewish family in Romania in 1910, had fled Nazi aggression for the United States in 1941. She settled several blocks from Guggenheim's apartment on the east side of Manhattan. Her work initially aligned with the Surrealists and other European émigrés, and she showed at the landmark exhibition "First Papers of Surrealism" in 1942 at the Whitelaw Reid mansion, New York. Her contribution to "31 Women," entitled *Katsonarock (Portrait of V.X.)* (1941) (illus. 6), was a collage image created with the Surrealist technique of chance operations. She randomly tore brown paper, pasted the scraps on a large sheet of white paper, and completed the image by drawing whatever was suggested by the papers. This use of free association, a

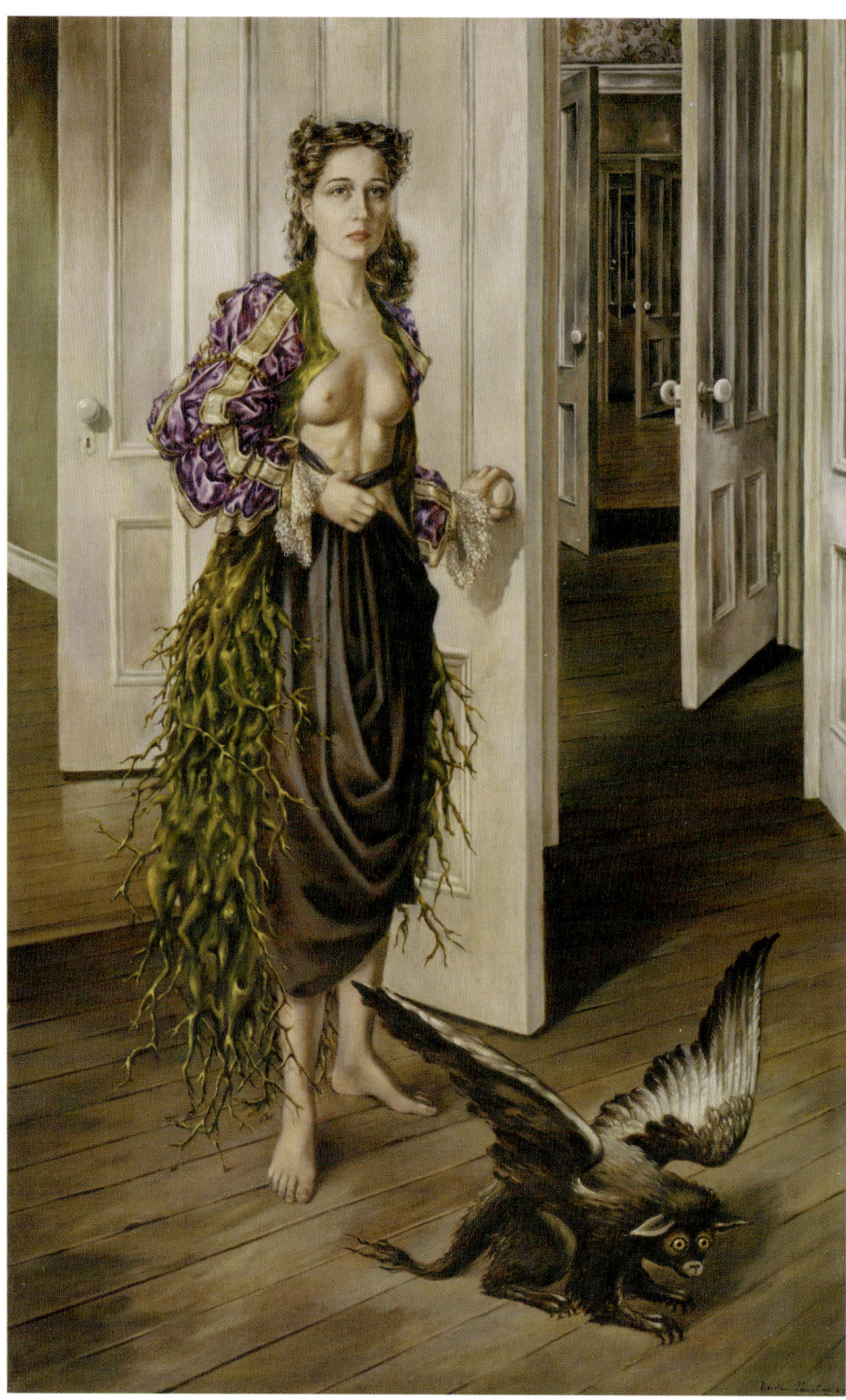

6 Hedda Sterne,
*Katsonarock
(Portrait of V.X.),*
1941, torn paper,
gouache, and
graphite on paper.

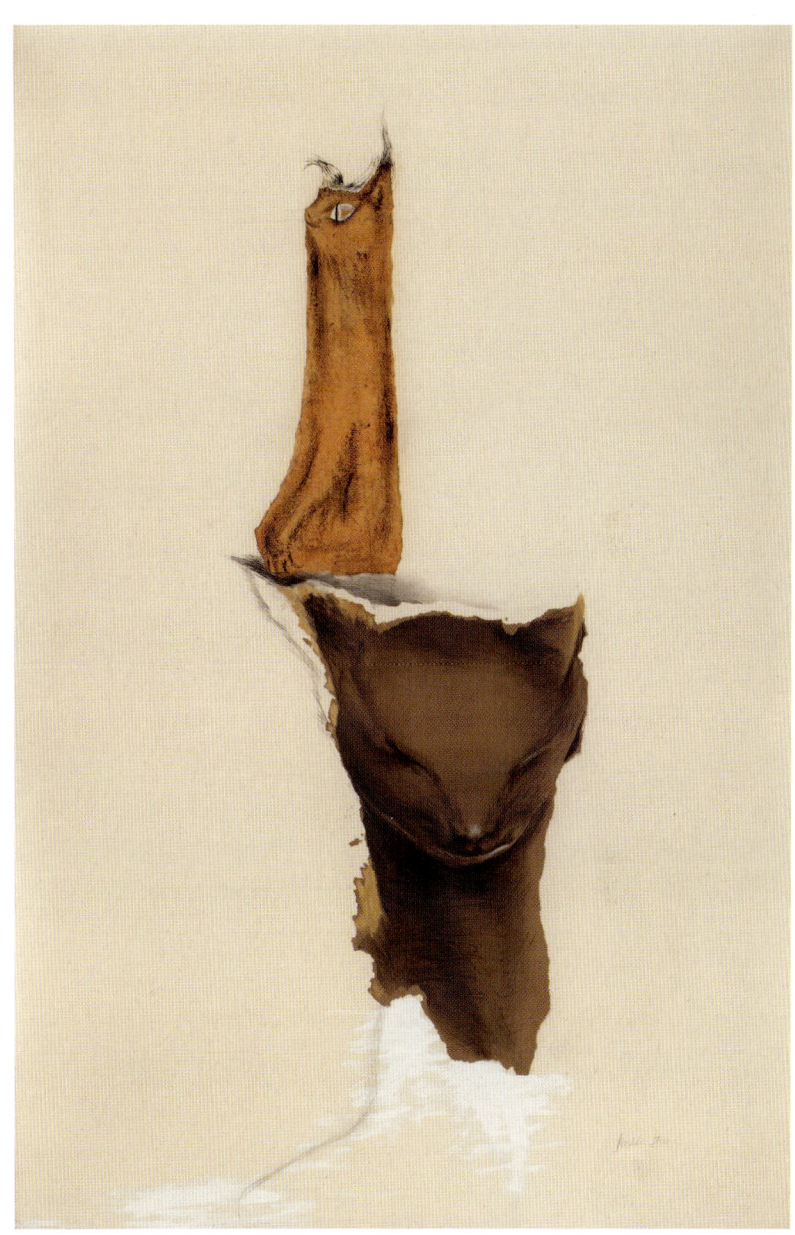

5 Dorothea Tanning,
Birthday, 1942,
oil on canvas.

psychoanalytic technique to unearth uninhibited imagery, later informed her painting process. So too may the tactile quality of Sekula's presently unlocated *Composition* (1942) be expressed in the active surface of *Untitled*, a contemporaneous work not known to have been in the show (illus. 7).

The expanding realm of Surrealism in the 1940s created spaces where women artists could work and gain recognition by exploring narratives specific to their lives. They resisted and undermined the negative stereotypes and myths of women in Freudian theory, as elevated by Dalí and Breton, by inhabiting and exploding them. This blurring of individual and mythic identities exposed the double consciousness that women faced as persons and symbols. To escape, transform, or transgress reality, modernist women painters have often portrayed women, frequently through self-portraiture, as goddesses or mythological beings. The clarity of the mythological images and fantasy settings in works by Tanning, Carrington, Fini, and Johnson invested self-portraiture with a dreamlike state. They addressed the particular problems of subjectivity and identity women faced during the traumas of fascism and the Second World War.

The Surrealist aura present in "31 Women" was heightened through an expansive selection of works embodying "the fantastic." This designation accommodated a colorful and eccentric group of works by nine artists with little in common other than appealing to the tastes of Guggenheim and her jury. This group included Americans Eyre de Lanux, Julia Thecla, Anne Harvey, and Aline Meyer Liebman and Europeans Elsa von Freytag-Loringhoven, Milena Pavlović-Barili, and Meraud Guevara. The portrait of *Alice Rohrer* (1936) by Djuna Barnes (1892–1982) rendered the titular art patron as an Expressionist icon embellished with bronze or gold powder (illus. 8). Another newsworthy inclusion was a collage by Gypsy Rose Lee (1911–1970), the well-known American burlesque performer who also ventured into visual art and creative writing. Nearly every review mentioned her *Self-Portrait* (1942) (illus. 9), a Joseph Cornell-like shadow box assemblage

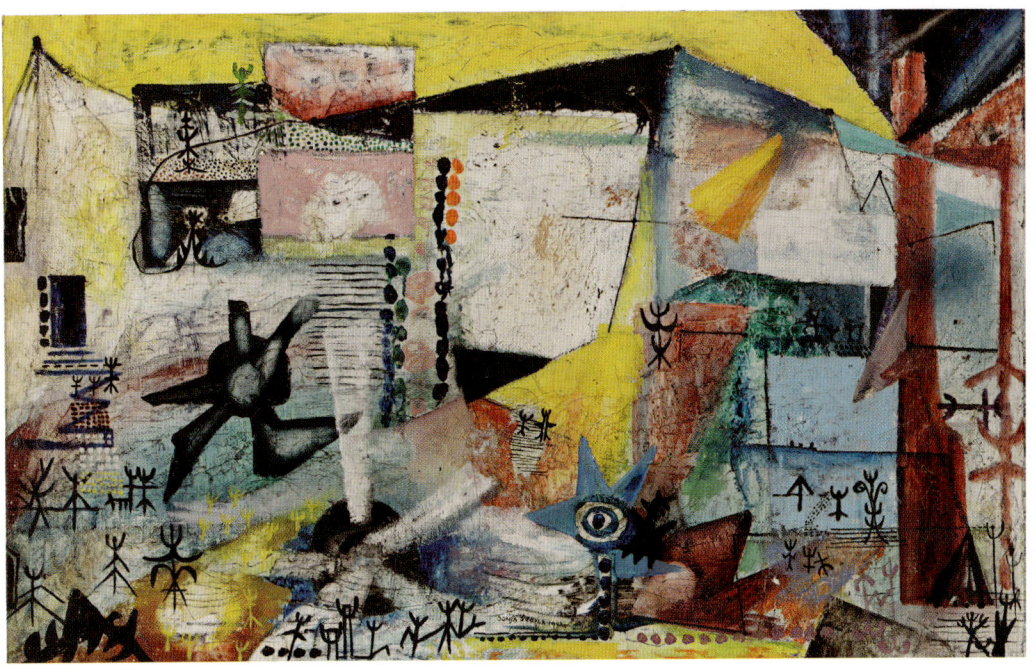

7 Sonja Sekula, *Untitled*, 1942, oil on canvas.

with magazine clippings and shells. The collaged image of a dog's head on her famous physique visualized the intertwined values of the Surrealist avant-garde and U.S. celebrity. As émigré artists like Sterne and Louise Bourgeois (1911–2010) have noted, America itself appeared inherently surreal: an unruly country lacking the formal class structure of European societies, a place where art is found as much as it is made.

The abstract contingent exhibited in "31 Women" was far smaller, with six artists who worked in Cubist, non-objective, or Constructivist veins. Abstract artists aspired to eliminate representation and reference to the (gendered) real world and invent pure images of shape, line, and color. Many women prized the freedom of abstraction to escape the strictures of gender and paint in a universal language that was frequently allied with science and philosophy, inspired by Albert Einstein and theories of the fourth dimension. Eight of the 39 founding members of American Abstract Artists, an arts organization formed in New York in 1936, were women. Though about one in five

39

was far from balanced, it still indicated a greater representation of women than other avant-garde groups. Relying as usual on male experts, Guggenheim turned to Barr for recommendations of female abstractionists for her show. He suggested five painters, praising them as "as good as the best of the men in the American Abstract Artists (AAA) group."[13] The jury selected three: Suzy Frelinghuysen (1911–1988), Esphyr Slobodkina (1908–2002), and Irene Rice Pereira (1902–1971). Their paintings of planar geometric forms in taut compositions embodied the non-objective approach to art as an impersonal means of public expression. The other abstract works in the show—a drawing by Swiss polymath Sophie Taeuber-Arp (1889–1943) and mixed-media constructions by Americans Xenia Cage (1913–1995) and Gretchen Schoeninger (1913–2016)—elicited little notice in contemporary reviews.

Pereira's meticulously layered paintings in particular demanded serious responses, and newspaper critic Emily Genauer (1911–2002), a perennial skeptic of avant-garde art, praised her paintings as tasteful and subtle in comparison to the libidinous quality of other pieces in "31 Women."[14] Pereira began her career as a secretary and stenographer before studying at the Art Students League of New York. She typically exhibited using the initial of her given name (I. Rice Pereira) as a means to degender her work, appropriate for an artist so engaged with the empirical discourses of science and technology distinct from individual identity. Her technique of layering planes of unconventional supports such as glass and parchment earned her a reputation as a pioneer of

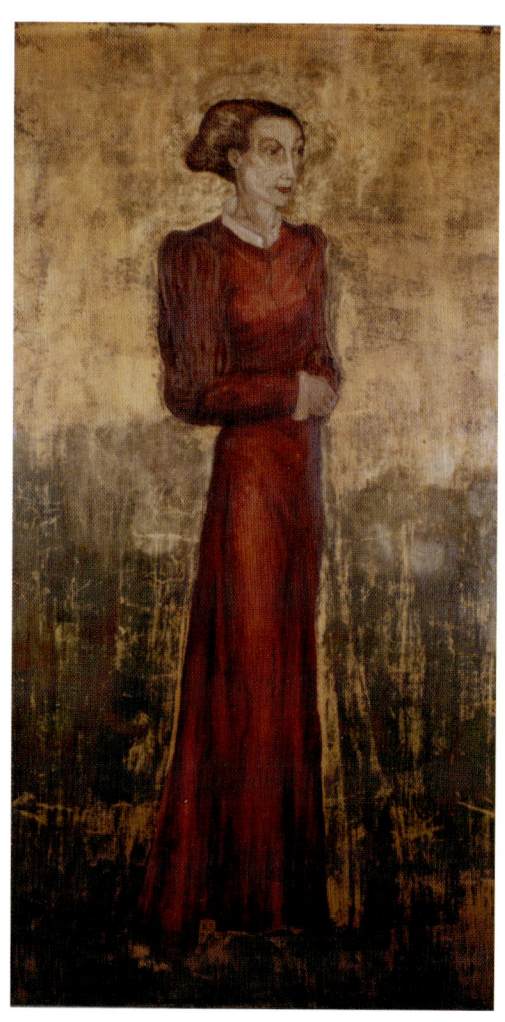

8 Djuna Barnes, *Alice Rohrer*, 1936, oil and bronze or gold powder on wood panel.

material experimentation and the extension of painting into three-dimensional space; in addition to her creative practice, Pereira taught and lectured widely. By the time her two abstractions appeared in "31 Women," Pereira had exhibited in New York with the Whitney Museum of American Art and the Museum of Non-Objective Painting (the future Solomon R. Guggenheim Museum). Of all the abstract painters in "31 Women," Pereira particularly captured Guggenheim's interest: she was the only abstract artist with two works in the show. Guggenheim gave her a solo show in 1944 and later purchased one of Pereira's pieces in "31 Women," *View* (1942)—an abstract work with interlocking

9 Gypsy Rose Lee, *Self-Portrait*, 1942, mixed-media collage.

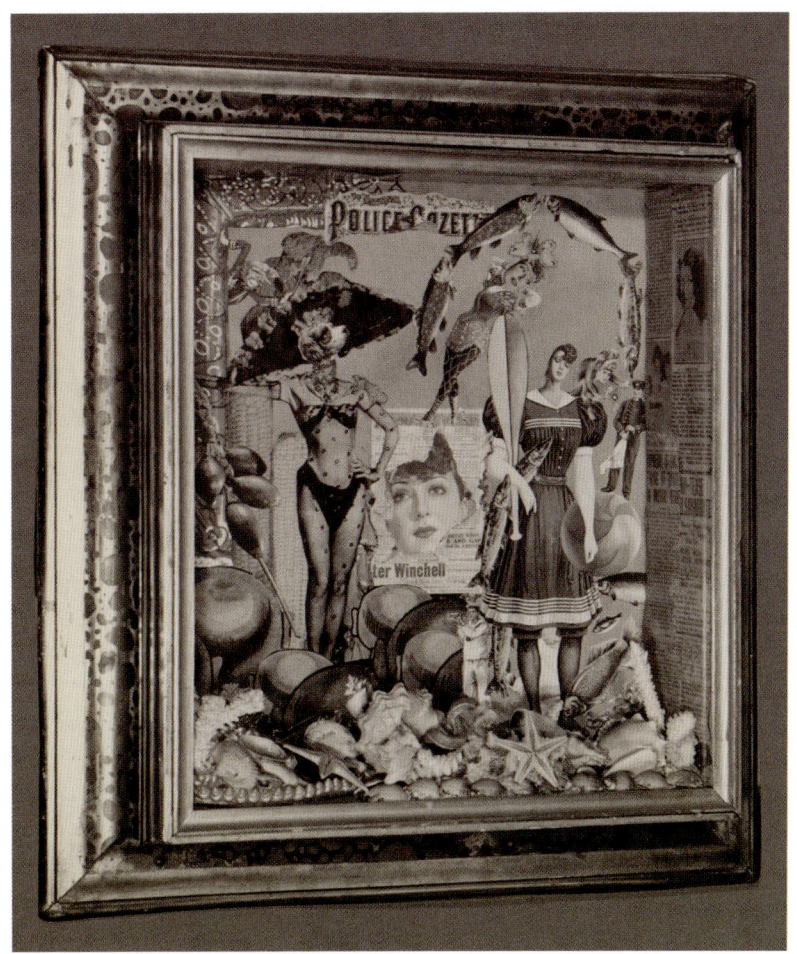

geometric forms superimposed on two planes—as a wedding present for her ex-husband Laurence Vail.[15]

In many ways, the media response confirmed O'Keeffe's concerns about "31 Women." Male critics resorted to stereotypes to portray the frivolity of the sororal milieu. "There is a slightly giggly air about the show," wrote *New Yorker* critic Robert Coates.[16] In the *Brooklyn Eagle*, Alexander Kruse wrote that the show "exudes a delightfully wacky air."[17] *New York Sun* critic Henry McBride unambiguously declared the show to be a Surrealist enterprise, deducing that "women ought to excel at Surrealism" because the movement is "70 percent hysterics, 20 percent literature, 5 percent good painting, and 5 percent just saying 'boo' to the innocent public."[18] Despite his dismissive tone, by linking Surrealism, hysteria, and women, he identified the show's power. Women expressed their inner demons and dreams through Surrealism. Male critics lavished attention on two of the physically smallest works—Lee's *Self-Portrait* and Oppenheim's *Object*—famous oddities that refashioned erotic and domestic symbols into mysterious forms with destabilizing power. Some of the exhibited works were interpreted as radical challenges to gender norms. One critic asserted that Kahlo's *Self-Portrait* "manifests women's determination to compete with men on the same artistic level."[19] *Time* magazine critic James Stern allegedly refused to review the exhibition because he believed that women artists should "stick to having babies."[20]

Rosamund Frost was one of the few women to review the show, and her perspective is notable in that she pinpointed what was really at stake in the exhibition:

Divisions of the sexes, or rather segregation of the female of the species, is ordinarily a dubious policy for an art show. This time, however, there is no outbreak of watercolor or flower painting. The women—they could never be laughingly referred to as ladies— present a chinkless armored front.[21]

Frost distinguished between Guggenheim's lively assembly of risk-takers and the predictable exhibitions of genteel "lady painters" typically proffered by midtown galleries and women artists associations. Like other reviewers, she spotlighted Surrealist art and praised works by Fini and Guevara, plus Kay Sage's ruminative *At the Appointed Time* (1942) (illus. 10), but Frost pushed her interpretation further: she deduced that the very appearance of these artists evidenced that the gallery was "living up to its promise of uncovering troublesome new talents."[22]

Frost's martial metaphor of a weaponized infantry was apposite. The term avant-garde originally referred to the advance force in an army, and the linkage between this and women artists evoked a new concept in the United States: the female avant-garde. Such forcefulness was appropriate at this moment of existential questioning. Critics worried that American contemporary art appeared weak compared to European modernism. Painter Robert Beverly Hale, when reviewing the annual exhibition of the National Association of Women Artists a few months later, lamented that the lack of vigor in the work stemmed from a general malaise and inhibition in American art. "Our full expression seems recurrently throttled, perhaps by some domestic puritan spirit," he wrote.[23] The critics, then, looked to enterprising gallerists like Guggenheim and "steely" artists like Sage to liberate American art from the thrall of European tradition.[24]

The exhibition documentation is thin, unfortunately, and there are no known installation photographs of the arrangement and juxtaposition of the works to confirm or challenge contemporary descriptions. Coates called the show "a mess of paintings, collages, constructions, and so on."[25] Viewers would find that "the exhibition yields one captivating surprise after another," Edward Alden Jewell noted.[26] Scholars, especially Siobhán Conaty, have attempted to reconstruct the checklist, but many images are missing and some works may be lost forever. As a concept and discursive intervention, the exhibition's greatest impact was to amplify the conversation around women Surrealists,

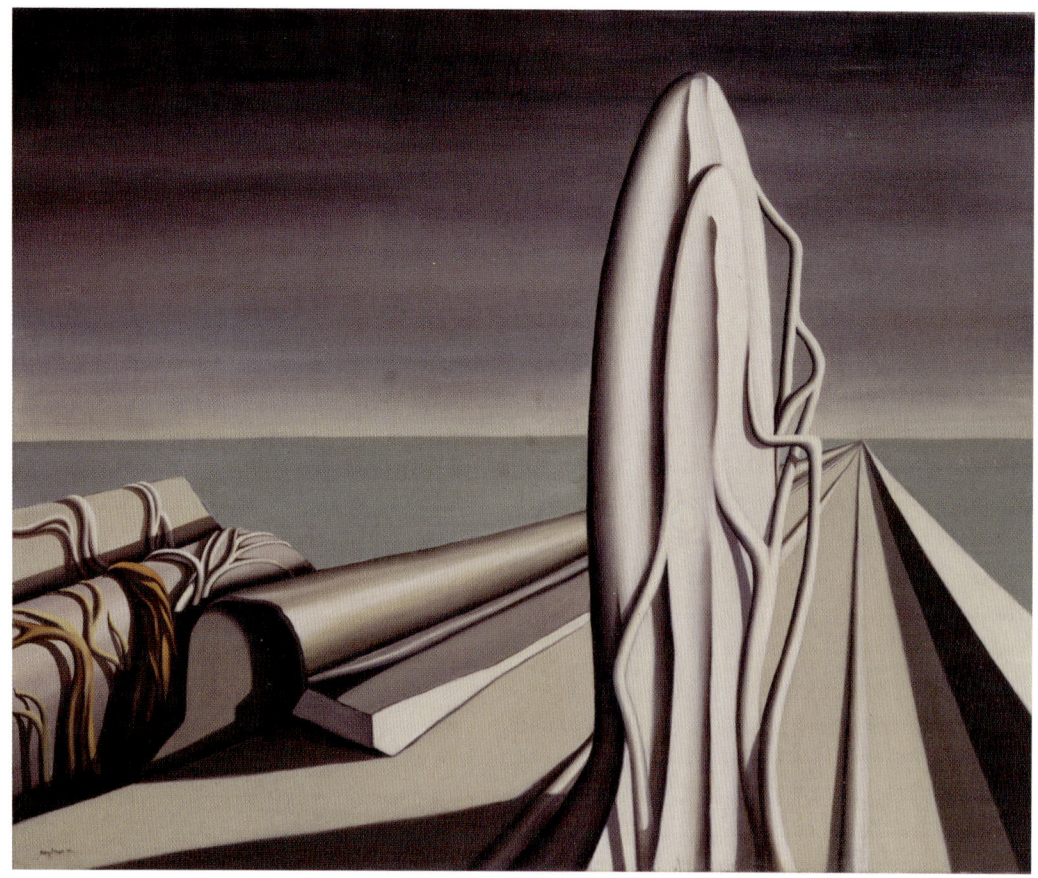

10 Kay Sage, *At the Appointed Time*, 1942, oil on canvas.

especially painters. One measure of this accomplishment came shortly after the exhibition closed. The March issue of the New York-based Surrealist journal *VVV*, edited by David Hare with advisors Breton, Ernst, and Duchamp, included work by eight women in Guggenheim's show: reproductions of exhibited artworks by Lee, Lamba, and Tanning; illustrations by Sage, Sekula, and Barbara Reis; short stories by Carrington ("The Seventh Horse") and Tanning ("Blind Date"); and an article on Nevelson's discovery of Joe Milone's shoeshine stand. Prior to "31 Women," the definitive American Surrealist journal generally overlooked women unless they were romantically attached to a man.

Half a year after "31 Women" closed, a solo show at Art of This Century achieved the critics' hopes for a homegrown American champion to rival European masters. Jackson Pollock's emergence in November 1943 altered the terms of modernist painting and broke the fever of Surrealism. "His abstractions are free of Paris and contain a disciplined American fury," is how one critic articulated the common sentiment.[27] Pollock came to be considered Guggenheim's greatest discovery, and her commitment to supporting his work is legendary. The masculinity of Pollock's public persona reshaped the reception of midcentury American art, especially as it began to cohere under the rubric of Abstract Expressionism circa 1945. As she ushered in the new movement with solo shows by Robert Motherwell and Mark Rothko, Guggenheim continued to provide an impressive number of solo exhibition opportunities to women, including Isabelle Waldberg, Alice Rahon, Janet Sobel, Sonja Sekula, Virginia Admiral, and Marjorie McKee. Yet Guggenheim's institutional support could not prevent them from being overlooked by critics and collectors and systematically excluded from the canon formation around the new American art.

Another immediate validation of the impact of "31 Women" came from the Washington, DC-based dealer David Porter, who ran the progressive G Street Gallery and presented both avant-garde and socially conscious art. Sometime in late 1944, he approached Guggenheim to help organize another all-women show. "I liked the idea I guess, and I knew so many women painters," Guggenheim recalled.[28] Together they assembled a list of artists and Porter arranged to circulate the show to several galleries and museums around the country. In the end, Guggenheim's and Porter's tastes differed too greatly, and instead of a single show traveling to both galleries, two parallel shows opened with the same title, "The Women," in homage to Clare Boothe Luce's well-known comedy of manners from 1936. Porter's well-meaning version appeared at two women's colleges, Western College in Oxford, Ohio, and Mary Baldwin College in Staunton, Virginia, before opening at his gallery in June 1945. Then it traveled to the San Francisco Museum of Art, opening in early 1946. Guggenheim's version opened at her gallery in New York on June 12, 1945, and did not travel. The competing exhibitions considerably overlapped, sharing fourteen artists by one count, but also contained telling differences stemming from the organizers' divergent sensibilities and networks.[29]

Guggenheim's "The Women" lacked the Surrealist esprit de corps and did not make nearly as big a splash as "31 Women," though eleven artists appeared in both shows. Jewell in the *New York Times* wistfully recalled the earlier show as a "piquant experiment" and deemed the second to be merely a repeat performance with thirty women "summoned into collaboration."[30] Indeed, the exhibition lacked the intersubjective frisson that animated "31 Women" and more placidly recorded the changing styles in New York. Surrealism waned after VE Day in May 1945, when many artists began returning to Europe. The pendulum had swung toward abstraction, and critics and historians noted the preponderance of such artists in the second iteration. "The Women" included Surrealist painting stalwarts Carrington and Sage, but they now formed a distinct minority. The shift in style was recorded in the work of other artists in "The Women," such as Jacqueline Lamba, whose painting evolved into pure abstraction with automatist techniques, and Hedda Sterne, who presented *The Neighbors* (1945), a semi-abstract painting with vaguely architectural imagery. Life in New York ingrained itself for Sterne and her imagery soon migrated toward the industrial environment. She said, "When I came to America, I lost interest [in Surrealism], because America was Surrealist. America had the kind of freedom the Surrealists wanted to show the European bourgeois."[31]

Some of the new exhibitors who had not appeared in "31 Women" were abstract painters and members of the AAA: Nell Blaine (1922–1996), Charmion von Wiegand (1896–1983), Alice Trumbull Mason (1904–1971), and Perle Fine (1905–1988). Lee Krasner, also an AAA member, was originally selected and her name appeared on the final printed checklist, but she never submitted a painting for the show. The overall content of "The Women," with its preponderance of abstraction, both non-objective and Expressionist, aspired to convey universal themes. "There is nothing save the catalogue to indicate that these artists are women. The work might just as well have been produced by 'The Men,'" Jewell wrote.[32] Meanwhile, the critic in *ARTnews* praised the artists' "almost masculine vigor of ideas" and concluded that "other all-female organizations should have a look-in at a show which is so refreshingly un-ladylike."[33] Guggenheim, at least according to these critics, created space for a group of women artists who positioned themselves as avant-garde and at the same time did not spurn being identified as women. If "31 Women" responded to the cultural trends of its moment, "The Women" looked forward. A cohort of painters, including Sterne, Blaine, Fine, and Krasner (in absentia), played key roles in the stylistic and social development of Abstract Expressionism. Other artists in "The Women," like painters Fannie Hillsmith and Alice Trumbull Mason, also emerged in the early 1950s associated with the new American abstraction. Louise Bourgeois, who showed an early wood construction in "The Women," evolved into one of the towering feminist artists of the twentieth century.

Taken together, "31 Women" and "The Women" encouraged a new generation of women artists to accept the thankless task of publicly working through the spectacle of being a woman and an artist. But there were significant gaps in who was welcomed and included. None of the artists in "31 Women" and "The Women" identified as Black. Painter and dancer Thelma Johnson Streat's name appeared on one of Porter's initial lists for "The Women," but she never participated in the exhibition. The one artist of color in either show was Mexican painter Frida Kahlo, who carefully controlled her public image and resisted all labels affixed to her work by critics. "They thought I was a surrealist, but I wasn't. I never painted dreams. I painted my own reality," she famously said in *Time* magazine.[34] By the Eurocentric standards of New York of the mid-1940s, Guggenheim's two all-women shows appeared vibrant and inclusive, with artists from various ethnic and national origins. Indeed, compared to the largely homogenous U.S.

mainstream art world of the late nineteenth and early twentieth centuries, artists from many economic, ethnic, and religious backgrounds participated in the Second World War-era New York scene. But still, galleries and museums upheld the Eurocentric classifications of modern art, which categorized artists by nation or style. In this system, Black artists were men and women artists were white.

A number of contemporary women artists of color experimenting with visual references to the fantastic would have been well-placed in a more inclusive version of "31 Women." Streat, in particular, shared a similar aesthetic sensibility and social circles with other artists in Guggenheim's all-women shows. Born in Washington state in 1912, she worked in the Works Progress Administration (WPA) and assisted Diego Rivera (1886–1957) on murals in San Francisco. In 1942 she became the first Black woman artist to have a work enter the collection of the Museum of Modern Art when the museum purchased her small gouache of a Northwest Native American-styled figure, *Rabbit Man* (1941). In Washington, DC, painter Loïs Mailou Jones also challenged the given hierarchies of European and "primitive" societies. Born in Boston in 1905, she began teaching at Howard University in 1930 and took a sabbatical in 1937–8 in Paris. Her *Les Fétiches* (1938) depicted masks from five different African cultural traditions, demonstrating the diversity of a continent that is typically homogenized in Western eyes. Both *Rabbit Man* and *Les Fétiches*, with culturally specific subject-matter painted by Black American women challenging European avant-garde traditions, would have enriched the global scope of Surrealism in Guggenheim's shows. But the default tendency for Guggenheim, as it was for her predecessor Katherine S. Dreier, was to favor white women artists and accept the boundaries of race in the art world.

Histories of modernism and the avant-garde privilege disruptive and paradigm-breaking artists. Traditional gender stereotypes restricted women from these realms, unless they affiliated with male originators through marriage or mentorship. Peggy Guggenheim challenged these perceptions around women and modern art, making convincing cases for the necessity of a new category: the avant-garde woman artist. Both "31 Women" and its successor "The Women" ushered in a new generation of American women, born in the first two decades of the twentieth century, who came of age with suffrage, the feminist era of the 1920s New Woman, and expanding opportunities through the New Deal of the 1930s. These artists became among the most prominent women artists in the 1940s and '50s, participating in all-women exhibitions at galleries and museums in the coming years.

PORTRAITS

OF

Outstanding Americans of Negro Origin

Painted by

Two Women Artists

Laura Wheeler Waring

Betsy Graves Reyneau

HARMON FOUNDATION
INCORPORATED

140 NASSAU STREET
NEW YORK 7, NEW YORK

2

Race: "Portraits of Leading American Negro Citizens," Smithsonian Institution, 1944

In the 1920s, artist Laura Wheeler Waring (1887–1948) set out to paint portraits of Black women as she saw them, not as they were typically portrayed in fine art and popular culture as laborers, maids, and nannies. A Black woman who had trained at the prestigious Pennsylvania Academy of the Fine Arts and in the Académie de la Grande Chaumière in Paris, Waring was likely aware of portrayals of Black female models by Thomas Eakins and Édouard Manet, and it is from this grounding that she confronted the critical importance of representation. She submitted a group of works, including at least three portraits of women, to the Harmon Foundation for consideration for its Award for Distinguished Achievement in 1927. Established in 1922 by white benefactor William E. Harmon, the New York-based Harmon Foundation provided grants and awards in various fields including medicine and education, and played a prominent role in supporting Black artists in the 1920s, '30s, and '40s through prizes, exhibitions, and publications. One of Waring's portraits, *Anna Washington Derry* (1927), won the Gold Award in Fine Art, which came with a $400 cash prize. She was the first woman to win the top award, and this accolade, together with the subsequent national acclaim that she received, encouraged her to devote more time to her studio practice alongside her other responsibilities as a recently married, full-time teacher at Cheyney College. "I have been planning to make a record of interesting characters of the American Negro in paint," she wrote to the foundation.[1] Over the next year and a half, Waring expanded this project, applying for a Guggenheim Fellowship and presenting her growing body of portraits in exhibitions in communal and educational settings at the Philadelphia YWCA and the Miner Normal School in Washington, DC. Both shows gained notices in local newspapers that attested to the public interest in Waring's refined portraits. These works circulated in solo and group exhibitions throughout the 1930s but generally remained below the radar of the white art world until the early 1940s, when a confluence of people and institutions joined up with her visionary project.

Building on the work of Waring, Harmon Foundation director Mary Beattie Brady assembled 23 portraits—consisting of both existing and newly commissioned paintings—in a groundbreaking exhibition at the Smithsonian Institution's National Collection of Fine Arts in Washington, DC. Initially titled "Portraits of Leading American Negro Citizens," the show opened on May 2, 1944, with eight paintings by Waring and fifteen by white artist Betsy Graves Reyneau portraying Black scientists, performers, educators, judges, and other prominent figures. The exhibition fulfilled the foundation's mission to advance progress toward equality for African Americans. The exhibition attracted more than 21,000 visitors in four weeks and received enthusiastic coverage in the press. Harnessing the power of these portraits to raise awareness about the accomplishments of African Americans and the need to expand civil rights, Brady, Waring, and Reyneau agreed to circulate the exhibition to communities across the country before it even opened in Washington.

"Portraits of Leading American Negro Citizens" initially did not conform to the standard definition of an all-women exhibition. Neither the original title nor the curatorial framework explicitly stated the gender of the artists. Nor was this fact mentioned in the press release circulated by the Office of War Information. Nevertheless, correspondence and other archival sources reveal that gender was a paramount concern, for Brady, who sought representation of women in the exhibition, and for the artists, who advocated for inclusion of their preferred female subjects. The pairing of two women artists and the initial commissions of portraits of several nationally known women, among them singer Marian Anderson (1897–1993) and educator Mary McLeod Bethune (1875–1955), affirmed the vital roles of Black women in the advancement of racial integration during wartime America. Over the course of the exhibition's ten-year run, gender became more integral to the exhibition, as evidenced by the new title given to a portfolio of 21 photogravures of exhibition works printed by the foundation to circulate to libraries and community centers in lieu of the original paintings: "Portraits of Outstanding Americans of Negro Origin, Painted by Two Women Artists" (illus. 11). As it traveled around the country, the show sparked conversations about the individual voices and achievements of Black women. And it created a rare opportunity for a Black woman artist—Waring—to gain visibility on a national stage. The subtitle situates the discussion of this show within the context of all-women exhibitions.

Waring and Reyneau had separate careers and presumably little interaction prior to their partnership on the exhibition. It is also unclear how much they even communicated directly, as Brady coordinated their efforts separately. Nevertheless, the two artists shared quite a bit in common. They were almost the same age, born in 1887 and 1888, respectively, and experienced youth and early adulthood prior to the achievement of women's right to vote with the Nineteenth Amendment in 1920. They both grew up in educated, middle-class homes with family histories of abolitionism. Both had grandfathers who were leaders within their communities—Waring's a minister, Reyneau's a state supreme court judge—and grandmothers reported to have aided escaped enslaved people seeking freedom. Both artists left home after graduating high school to pursue a career in the arts, with Waring moving from Hartford to Philadelphia and Reyneau from Michigan to Cincinnati and then Boston. Both studied with eminent American realist painters—Waring with Thomas Anschutz and William Merritt Chase, and Reyneau with Frank Duveneck—and gained exposure to the modernist avant-garde in Europe, but chose not to incorporate radical formal devices into their personal styles. In the 1910s, both began to entwine their artistic practices of naturalistic representationalism with social justice causes. Waring became a prolific contributor of illustrations to *The Crisis* after her friend W.E.B. Du Bois (1868–1963) became editor in 1918. Her illustration decrying lynching, "Lest We Forget," appeared on the magazine's cover in February 1924. Reyneau, meanwhile, became involved in feminist activism. She joined the National Woman's Party, which instigated provocative suffrage demonstrations, becoming one of a dozen women arrested for picketing outside the White House in 1917. Both Waring and Reyneau spent significant time in Europe furthering their artistic studies and making contacts with American and Continental artists, writers, and patrons.

There were significant differences between the two artists in terms of temperament and personal life. Waring appears to have been generally self-effacing and modest while Reyneau acted in an outspoken and assertive manner. Waring remained a committed educator, working full-time teaching art and music at Cheyney College (now Cheyney University) in Philadelphia—the nation's first institution of higher education for African Americans—for over forty years. She never had children, marrying when she was about forty years old, and balanced domestic responsibilities with her own career. Reyneau, on the other hand, married young and divorced by the time she was in her early thirties, and had one child, a daughter. If Waring was a pillar of her Philadelphia community, then Reyneau was less geographically grounded, pursuing new opportunities from New York to Washington, DC, and across the country. For the purposes of the exhibition, Waring and Reyneau both possessed facility as portrait painters in capturing the essence of their subjects, and used the format as an expression of their values and political beliefs, fostered by their conversations and interactions with women writers and political leaders.

Waring may have conceived her project to paint Black women when studying in Paris, a city famously welcoming to expatriate Black Americans, for fifteen months from 1924 to 1925. She traveled with a friend from Philadelphia, the opera sensation Lillian Evanti (1890–1967), and spent time there with the Black feminist writer and editor Jessie Fauset (1882–1961), who later became one of the leading figures in the Harlem Renaissance, achieving recognition for her bold female protagonists. Waring and Fauset collaborated on an article for *The Crisis* about their travels together to Algiers. Several years later, a contact in Paris, the salon host Madame Salmon, encouraged Waring to exhibit there. In a letter to Du Bois, Waring outlined her plans to present a dozen portraits of Black women of various ages and types.[2] The goal, she explained to William Harmon, was to "create more interest in interracial and international knowledge."[3] In 1929, Waring returned to Paris for her final visit and installed her portraits at the Galeries du Luxembourg on the Left Bank. The *New York Herald* announced the show as a group of "portrait studies," failing to mention that they depicted Black women.[4]

Scholar Lisa Farrington deems Waring's body of work "paradigmatic of the images of upscale blacks that marked the Harlem Renaissance."[5] Her double-portrait *Mother and Daughter* (1930) depicts in profile an older woman with darker skin and a younger woman with lighter skin, personifying the social facts of "racial mixing" and "generational differences" in American society, as interpreted by scholar Jacqueline Francis.[6] The painting was included in a traveling exhibition organized by the Harmon Foundation, and illustrated in Alain Locke's groundbreaking article on Black artists, but may have been too thematically complex for Brady's pragmatic objectives for the Smithsonian exhibition.[7] Throughout the 1920s and '30s, Waring employed portraiture as a medium to assert presence beyond stereotype, painting some images for her own interest and others as commissions by individuals and institutions.

Reyneau, for her part, allied portraiture with feminist activism. Not long after her arrest for picketing outside the White House in 1917, she painted portraits of several prominent leaders of the National Woman's Party. Her first New York exhibition, in 1922, was devoted to portraits. A painting of her grandfather, Benjamin F. Graves, gained attention in the *New York Times* for representing her defiance of gender restrictions. Reyneau allegedly won the commission because she was known only by her initials in the early 1910s after having first exhibited in Detroit without using her full name to evade a group's ban on women artists.[8] In 1927 she moved to Europe, living primarily in London, and, like Waring, published illustrations in magazines. Reyneau was interested in workers' politics, as evidenced by her portrayals of left-wing icons, such as her drawing of Italian anti-fascist writer Guglielmo Ferrero. She remained in Europe until war broke out, then returned to the United States. Race does not appear to have been a central focus or concern of her art until 1942, when she spent some months in Miami with her friend Marjory Stoneman Douglas (1890–1998), a writer, feminist, and conservationist. There Graves witnessed at first hand the harsh treatment and second-class status of African Americans in the Jim Crow South. Through this experience she became conscious of the contradiction that her allegedly democratic country, fighting Nazi Germany, also upheld a racial caste system. In an effort to make moral amends, Reyneau painted a portrait of a young man who worked on her friend's property, *Edward Lee* (1942), to portray in art the dignity that was not granted in daily life. After exhibiting this and other works at Douglas's home, which received some notice in the local press, Reyneau vowed to advance social change by painting portraits of Black Americans. "I was determined to fight fascism in any way I could," she recalled.[9] For her, fascism and racism were two sides of the same coin. She turned to portraiture as a tool to protest dehumanization.

The historical role of portraiture in European and American art has been to uphold individual status within a stable social order. Both Waring and Reyneau engaged in this genre throughout their careers to bring into history women and others whose humanity and accomplishments have been overlooked. Because Waring and Reyneau arrived at these parallel practices from different backgrounds, upbringings, and professional routes, their shared story became all the richer in affirming the goal of "Portraits of Leading American Negro Citizens" to promote recognition of the accomplishments of African Americans, as conceived by Harmon Foundation longtime director Mary Beattie Brady. A few years younger than the artists, Brady graduated from the elite women's Vassar College in 1916 and attended journalism school at Columbia University before being hired by William Harmon to run his foundation shortly before his death in 1928. She remained director until its closure in the 1960s and was known for her tireless activity as well as her well-intended meddling and oversharing with the people she relied on for advice and guidance. Neither an artist nor a curator, Brady viewed art not in aesthetic terms—art for art's sake—but as a didactic tool for education. The Harmon Foundation instrumentalized art to pursue its mission of racial integration through exhibitions and the dissemination of educational materials to libraries, schools, and universities in partnership with organizations like the Urban League and the Federal Council of Churches. Over time, the Harmon Foundation earned a reputation for conservative taste in its curation of Black art. In 1934 the artist Romare Bearden (1911–1988) published a critique of what he characterized as the foundation's condescending attitudes and its failure to support avant-garde Black artists.[10] Years later, art historian David Driskell, a beneficiary of Brady's patronage and advice (sometimes unsolicited), recalled her as a "staunch Republican" motivated by "noblesse oblige," the notion that with privilege comes responsibility.[11]

The stories of Reyneau and Brady converged in 1942, with portraiture and social justice serving as the connective tissues. After having painted Edward Lee, Reyneau determined to paint more portraits of African Americans, and sought institutional support for her project. The history at this juncture is a bit murky, and it is unclear as to whether it was Reyneau's or Brady's idea that Reyneau would travel to the historically Black Tuskegee Institute in Alabama to paint the young men training to become fighter pilots in the u.s. military's nationally renowned program. According to Brady, Reyneau visited the Harmon office in New York for assistance, and Brady connected Reyneau with administrators at Tuskegee.[12] Reyneau, however, recalled that she took the initiative and traveled to Alabama, not meeting Brady until afterwards.[13] Either way, her portrait of Lee became her calling card at Tuskegee, allowing her to earn the trust of potential sitters. Reyneau painted pilot Robert Deiz in an upward-facing posture typically reserved for white heroes. The u.s. Government Printing Office later used the image on a poster to sell u.s. war bonds, with the motivational words, "Keep us flying." Reyneau also approached the Tuskegee Institute's esteemed professor George Washington Carver (*c.* 1864 –1943) to sit for a portrait. A famed agricultural scientist, he dedicated his career to the study of crop diversification and soil preservation. Regardless of whether Brady smoothed the way or Reyneau enterprisingly seized the opportunity, Reyneau's portrait of Edward Lee was the clincher for Carver, demonstrating that she—despite being a white woman with no prior demonstrated allyship with the Black community—was a worthy artist capable of sensitively portraying Black people. Carver praised *Edward Lee* in a letter prized by Reyneau: "How true it is that you see within him the Pharaohs of Egypt. I can see it so plain in the way you have handled it. Even the tree and small vegetation takes on that character and shows such skillful work. This picture lifts the very soul up on a higher plane of living."[14] As an amateur painter, Carver knew something of the challenges of rendering the spark of life on canvas.

Reyneau portrayed the scientist and inventor in a relaxed state, pursuing one of his specialties, the crossbreeding of flowers. The empathetic portrait gained unanticipated significance when Carver died on January 5, 1943, a few months after Reyneau completed it, and became a readymade memorial. Assistant Secretary of the Interior Oscar L. Chapman, who was spearheading the effort to purchase Carver's birthplace and preserve it as a national monument, came across the portrait at the institute and recognized its potential as a promotional tool. Chapman illustrated it in black and white on the cover of a fundraising brochure and then assembled a group of patrons, who purchased the painting and donated it to the National Collection of Fine Arts.

Witnessing the enthusiastic response to the Carver portrait, Reyneau and Brady joined forces in early 1943 under their shared belief in portraiture as a vehicle to bring diverse peoples together for moments of racial progress. "I think there is some possible value in trying to help Mrs. Reyneau achieve her desires to do a series of study of the Negro in America," Brady wrote to Alain Locke on January 14, after hearing a report on the quality of the Carver portrait.[15] Brady recognized that a series of portraits of Black Americans solely by a white artist could potentially undermine the Harmon Foundation's mission.to promote Black artists. With Reyneau giving the project momentum, Brady circled back to Waring's ongoing portraiture practice as a potential stylistic and generational complement. Waring already had a relationship with the foundation, professional respect, and a considerable body of work in Black portraiture with prominent backers. Her portraits of Cheyney president Dr. Leslie P. Hill and Brigadier General Benjamin Oliver Davis hung in institutional settings (the college in Philadelphia and the 369th Regiment Armory in Harlem, respectively). In March, Brady called Waring and invited her to join in "getting together a collection of portraits by two women."[16] The selection of one Black artist and one white artist manifested the Harmon Foundation's mission to promote interracial cooperation. Because of the subject-matter and the artists' common gender, some reporters and critics jumped to the conclusion that they were also of the same race. "Negro Artists Give Exhibition," read the headline in a brief news item in Waring's hometown Philadelphia newspaper.[17]

To realize the Smithsonian exhibition, Brady obtained the encouragement and support of powerful men in art and government, including Secretary of the Interior Harold Ickes, Smithsonian director Charles Abbot, and federal art administrator Rene d'Harnoncourt, along with her longtime advisor, Howard University philosophy professor Alain Locke, the preeminent scholar of Black art in America. The formal presentation of Reyneau's *George Washington Carver* as a gift to the National Collection provided the impetus for the exhibition in the Smithsonian's National Museum. The opening featured laudatory presentations by government dignitaries. Vice President Henry Wallace proclaimed he could "think of no more deserving character" than Carver, whose success was "for all mankind."[18] To the government officials, the enshrinement of Carver's portrait confirmed the ongoing progress of American democracy to attain a more perfect union and ensure the civil rights and equality of all its citizens; they saw this notion as being exemplified by a portrait of a man who had been born into slavery, and who lived under Jim Crow, now being sanctified in the same halls as portraits of presidents who denied his humanity.

Waring wrote about the dedication ceremony and exhibition opening in *Pulse*, a monthly magazine published in Washington, DC, for a Black readership. She recounted Wallace's remarks about receiving a Christmas card from Carver painted with pigments made from Alabama clay, and Eleanor Roosevelt's dramatic late entrance. Amid her reportage, Waring offered a brief assessment of Carver, praising his humble values in pursuit of meaningful work: "The simplicity of Mr. Wallace's speech was completely in harmony with the man who[se] long and consecrated life had been marked by deep humility, absolute faith in God and selfless endeavor."[19] In discussing the contents of the exhibition, Waring listed Reyneau's portraits before her own, noting that "much credit" for the exhibition should go to her co-exhibitor. Theirs was an unexpected pairing of two artists facilitated by a foundation director with the express purpose of creating a model exhibition that walked the walk and talked the talk of integration in America.

Gender was always a secondary concern. Documentation of the twelve portraits of women that appeared in the initial Smithsonian exhibition and subsequent iterations as the show expanded and the checklist went through many vicissitudes reveal the varied priorities of Brady, Waring, and Reyneau, which did not always align. They continually negotiated their personal preferences, their mutual commitment to the representation of women, and the hindrance of the criterion of "outstanding." In the premiere show, four of the 23 paintings, or about 17 percent, depicted women: *Marian Anderson* and *Lillian Evanti* by Waring and *Mary McLeod Bethune* and *Jane Matilda Bolin* by Reyneau. Overshadowed by the pomp and circumstance around the Carver portrait, these paintings did not create much of an impression in news reports. Eleanor Roosevelt noted in her newspaper column that the quality of the portraits and the achievements of the "men" were equally interesting.[20] In an earlier column, she deemed the Carver "delightful" and the Bethune "extremely good" after encountering them in Chapman's office.[21] It is worth spending some time to analyze these four portraits as cogent prompts for conversations about professional Black women in the American public sphere.

Perhaps the best-known female subject was opera singer *Marian Anderson* (1944) (illus. 12). A classically trained contralto, Anderson sang on some of the world's prestigious stages. She is best remembered for her performance at the Lincoln Memorial in 1939, a powerful declaration for civil rights after she was barred from singing in the then-segregated Daughters of the American Revolution (DAR) concert hall. To right their wrong, the DAR invited her to perform in 1943 to raise funds for war relief, a tangible sign of the impact that artists can have on social progress. "A great artist, a great woman and a great citizen," author Cornelia Otis Skinner praised Anderson in a short biographical sketch circulated with the exhibition.[22] Waring's portrait depicts Anderson in her Victorian farmhouse in Connecticut, standing on a parquet floor with a vibrantly hued landscape visible through an open window behind her. She's wearing a floor-length gown: lushly painted, the red fabric gracefully drapes over the singer's torso and legs. The 76-inch-high (193 cm) painting was one of the exhibition's few full-length portraits, a format not uncommon for commanding female

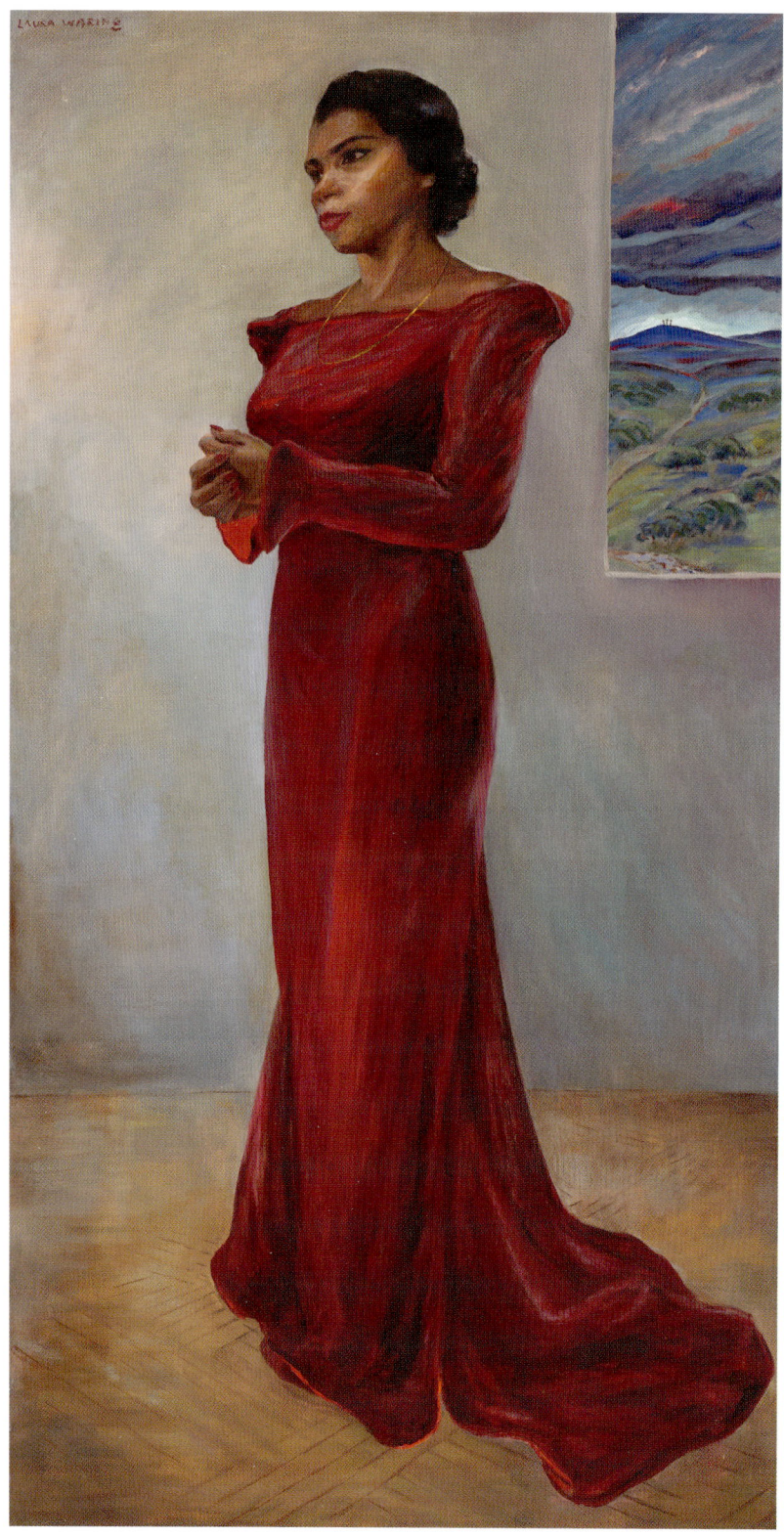

performers, suiting Anderson's national profile. At some point Waring reworked the original painting, which was disliked by both Brady and Locke, for unknown reasons. Waring's second portrait of a woman in the Smithsonian show was *Lillian Evanti* (undated). Evanti sang opera and, like Anderson, established her career in Europe to escape racism in the USA. Waring depicted Evanti sitting, hands gently resting before her, in an elegant dress: possibly her costume for *La Traviata*, as it was listed on the checklist. The present whereabouts of the painting are unknown, but in a contemporary snapshot (illus. 13) the work appears loosely painted, almost sketchy, and lacks the sophistication and vibrancy of Waring's other portraits in the exhibition, such as that of James Weldon Johnson.

The other two portraits of women in the Washington, DC, show were by Reyneau. *Mary McLeod Bethune* (1943) (illus. 14), 4 feet (122 cm) high, is especially well worked and detailed. Bethune achieved a national reputation as an educational leader, having founded a school in 1904 that evolved into Bethune-Cookman University, and served as a member of President Franklin D. Roosevelt's "Black Cabinet," a group of African American advisors. Reyneau carefully rendered Bethune wearing sumptuous clothes in a well-appointed interior in her Washington, DC, home, holding a cane and surrounded by symbols of her worldly accomplishments. An impressive globe is oriented so that her home state of Florida, rendered in pink, prominently appears in the center. The painting on the wall above her shoulder depicts the original Bethune College building. The biographical sketch by activist and civic leader Channing Tobias (also a subject in the exhibition) emphasized her renown as "not only the outstanding woman of her race, but, by general consent, one of the outstanding women of the world."[23]

Reyneau painted Bethune during a stint as a visiting artist at Howard University, the historically Black research university in Washington, DC. Locke arranged for her several-months-long residency there in the summer and fall of 1943. She was able to meet and paint from life some

12 Laura Wheeler Waring, *Marian Anderson*, 1944, oil on canvas.

of the university's eminent administrators and faculty members: Mordecai Johnson (the first Black president of Howard), Charles Houston (former vice dean of the law school), and Ralph Bunche (chair of the political science department). Reyneau's devotion to feminist activism and history was readily apparent to future civil rights lawyer Pauli Murray (1910–1985), already well known as a labor organizer, who met Reyneau during her third year as a student at Howard Law School. The two bonded over their mutual passion for women's rights and family roots in abolitionism. As Murray recalled,

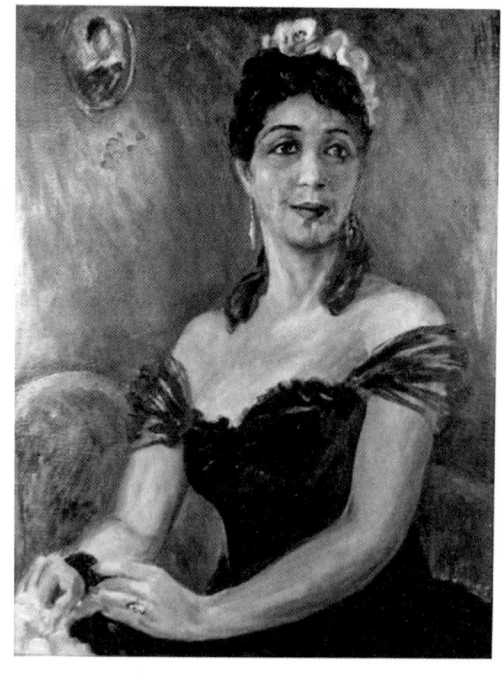

> Betsy Graves Reyneau was a fragile toothpick of a woman, in her fifties at the time, whose bodily frailness belied her fiery spirit and passion for social justice . . . Betsy was an engaging conversationalist with an encyclopedic knowledge of world affairs, and her reminiscences, sprinkled with caustic comments, were the stuff of oral history.[24]

13 Laura Wheeler Waring, *Lillian Evanti*, undated, oil on canvas.

Reyneau's encounter coincided with Murray's elaboration of her "Jane Crow" theory, a pioneering legal argument for civil rights based on an intersectional analysis of race and gender. Murray approved of Reyneau's work, writing retrospectively, "As an artist she also saw the rich variety of color among Negroes—from blond, blue-eyed Walter White of the NAACP to dark, mahogany-hued Mary McLeod Bethune."[25]

Reyneau's other female subject in the show was *Jane Matilda Bolin* (1944) (illus. 15), the first Black female judge appointed in the state of New York. New York City mayor Fiorello LaGuardia, in a brief tribute to Bolin (1908–2007) circulated in the exhibition materials,

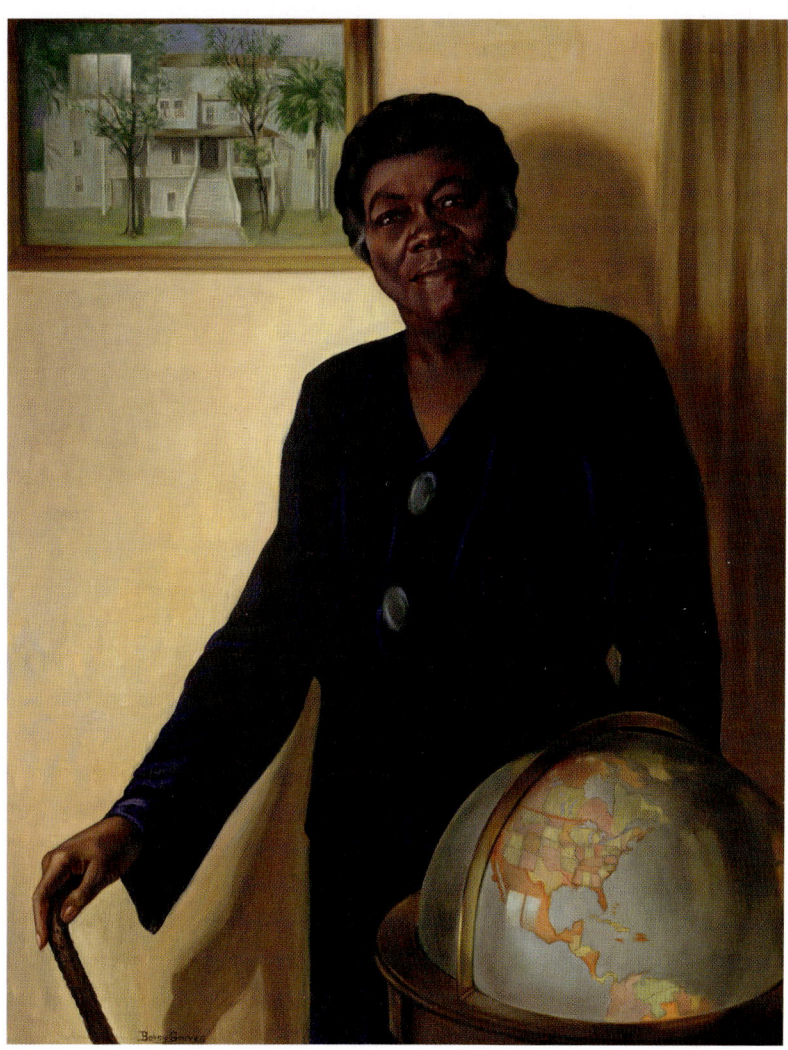

14 Betsy Graves Reyneau, *Mary McLeod Bethune*, 1943, oil on canvas.

concluded, "Her talents and heart are devoted entirely to the public good."[26] The painting is not as richly worked as the Carver or Bethune portraits. The flatter planes, vibrant color, and shallower depth appear illustrational, lending the image a graphic punch. Nevertheless, Bolin's large head and striking gaze impress the viewer with her presence and authority. The color contrast of her red coat set against the blue-gray background and her body's L-shaped arrangement provide structure. The placement of Bolin's left eye, gazing piercingly at the viewer, follows the compositional strategy of dividing an image into thirds for dynamic balance.

Enthusiastic about the success of the Washington exhibition, Brady, in consultation with Locke and others, decided to revise the checklist in preparation for the national tour. With about six months' lead time before the second stop at the Detroit Institute of Arts, sponsored by the city's Interracial Committee, they sought to commission new portraits of high-profile subjects and remove those who they felt failed to fit the essential criterion of "outstanding." Brady also hoped to increase the number of women among the portrait subjects but hesitated about whom to select. She relied on Locke's judgment, writing to him in June, "get your thinking cap on and suggest the people who are the very 'tops' that you think should be included with special emphasis on women."[27] Waring had already painted a considerable number of portraits of women over the previous two decades, but few of her subjects fulfilled Brady's criteria for national importance. Correspondence from Brady to Locke illustrates her ongoing concern with the underrepresentation of women. Early in the project, in October 1943, Brady wrote to Locke, "It seems to me that the exhibit is woefully shy on women. Who are the outstanding ones?"[28] Locke, for his part, recognized the importance of women's voices in articulating intersectional identities; in one such example he had included Elise Johnson McDougald's pioneering essay "The Double Task: The Struggle for Negro Women for Sex and Race Emancipation" in his 1925 anthology *The New Negro: An Interpretation*. Brady, Locke, and the two artists agreed in principle about the exhibition's need for a strong female presence. The selection of the sitters was a matter of negotiation.

Lillian Evanti was dropped from the 22 paintings in the Detroit exhibition, but two new portraits of women were added, bringing the show's female subjects from four to five. Waring successfully lobbied to include another old friend from her Paris sojourn.[29] Her new portrait *Jessie Redmon Fauset* (1944) (illus. 16) helped revive awareness of the writer and editor, a key agent in the Harlem Renaissance who had

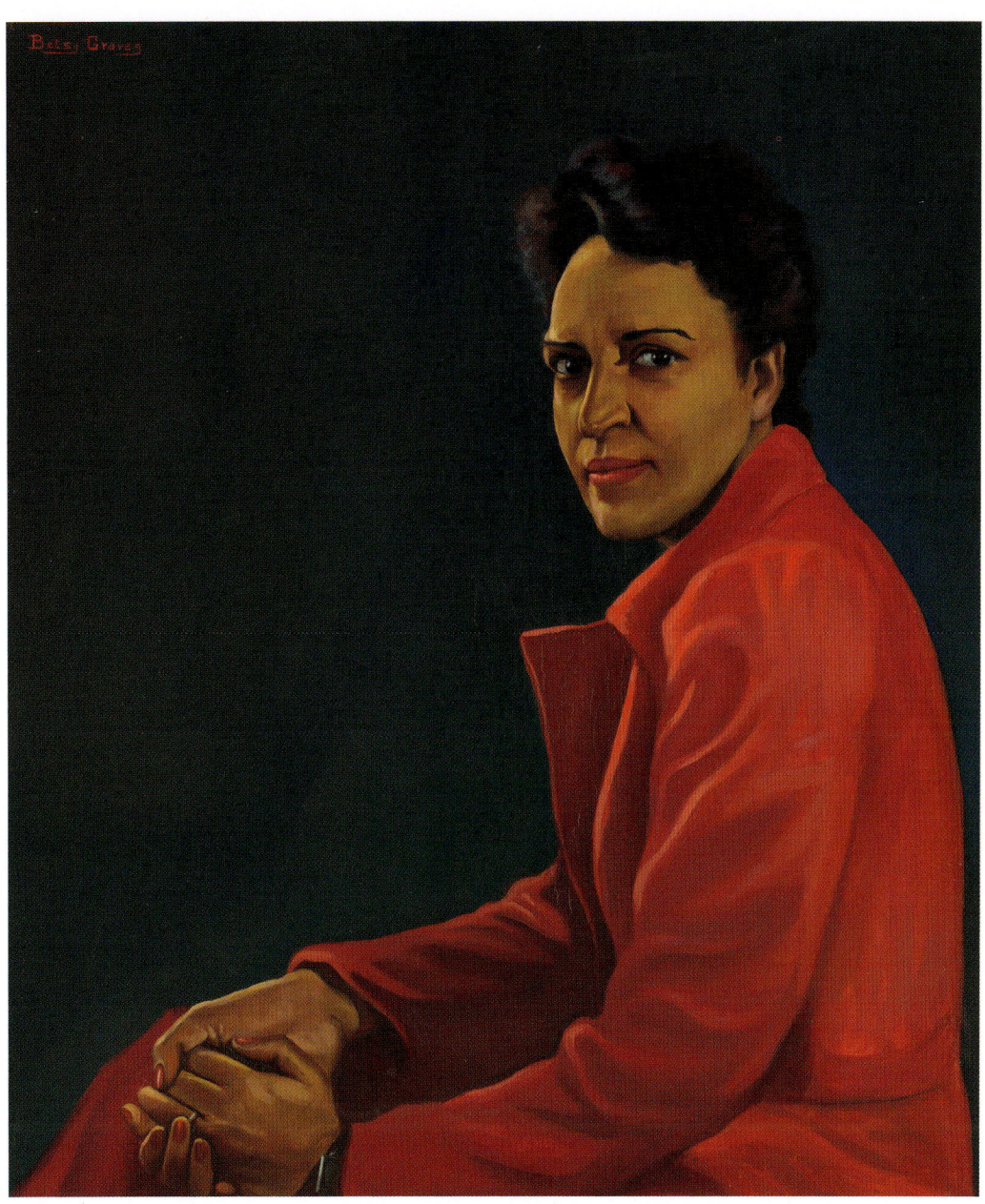

15 Betsy Graves Reyneau,
Jane Matilda Bolin, 1944,
oil on canvas.

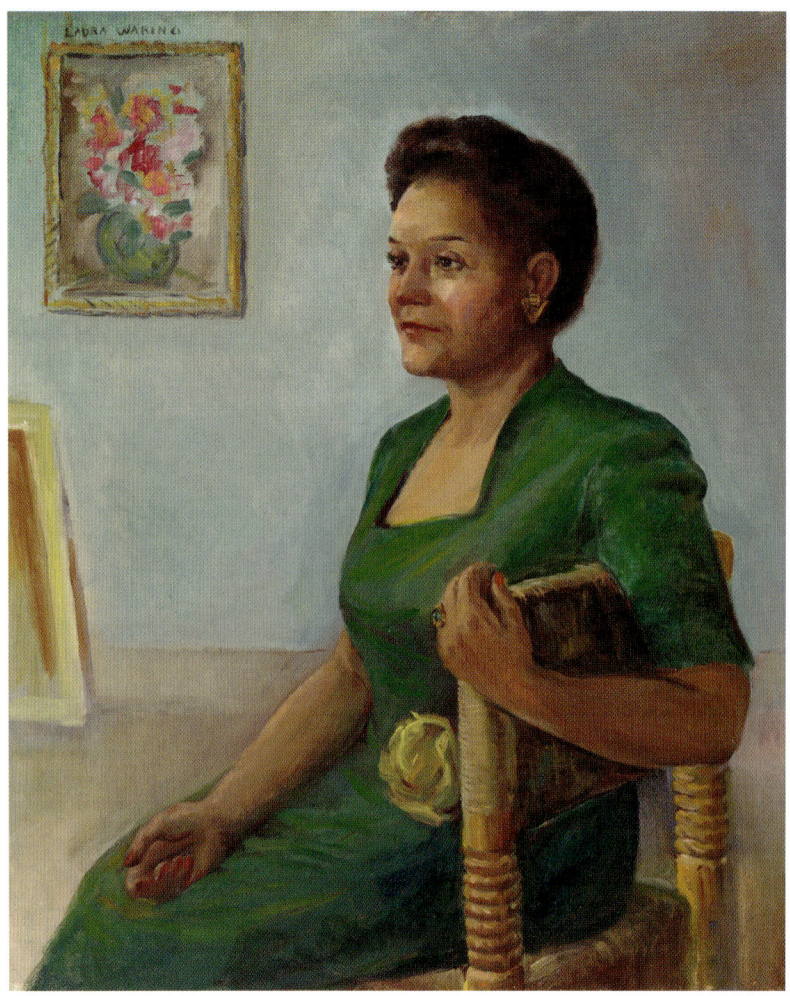

16 Laura Wheeler Waring, *Jessie Redmon Fauset,* 1944, oil on canvas.

faded from the public eye since her 1920s heyday and had been teaching French in a Bronx high school. Waring portrayed Fauset seated in three-quarter profile, eyes gazing beyond the frame. With looser brushstrokes, Waring alludes to a Renoiresque Impressionism, signified by the floral still-life painting depicted on the wall. The addition of Fauset to the roster achieved part of one goal of the exhibition: to bring attention to significant yet overlooked people, especially women.

The second new female portrait in Detroit was of educator Helen Adele Johnson Whiting (1885–1950), painted by Reyneau. Brady originally asked Reyneau to paint Whiting in her garden in Atlanta, when Reyneau was en route from Tuskegee (where she had returned to paint surgeon John A. Kenney and airman William Ayres Campbell) to her home in Washington. Whiting ended up sitting for Reyneau elsewhere, and the resulting portrait, *Helen A. Whiting* (1944), shows her in profile, with shadow on the side of her head, her face illuminated.

17 Laura Wheeler Waring, *Sadie Alexander, c. 1946*, oil on canvas.

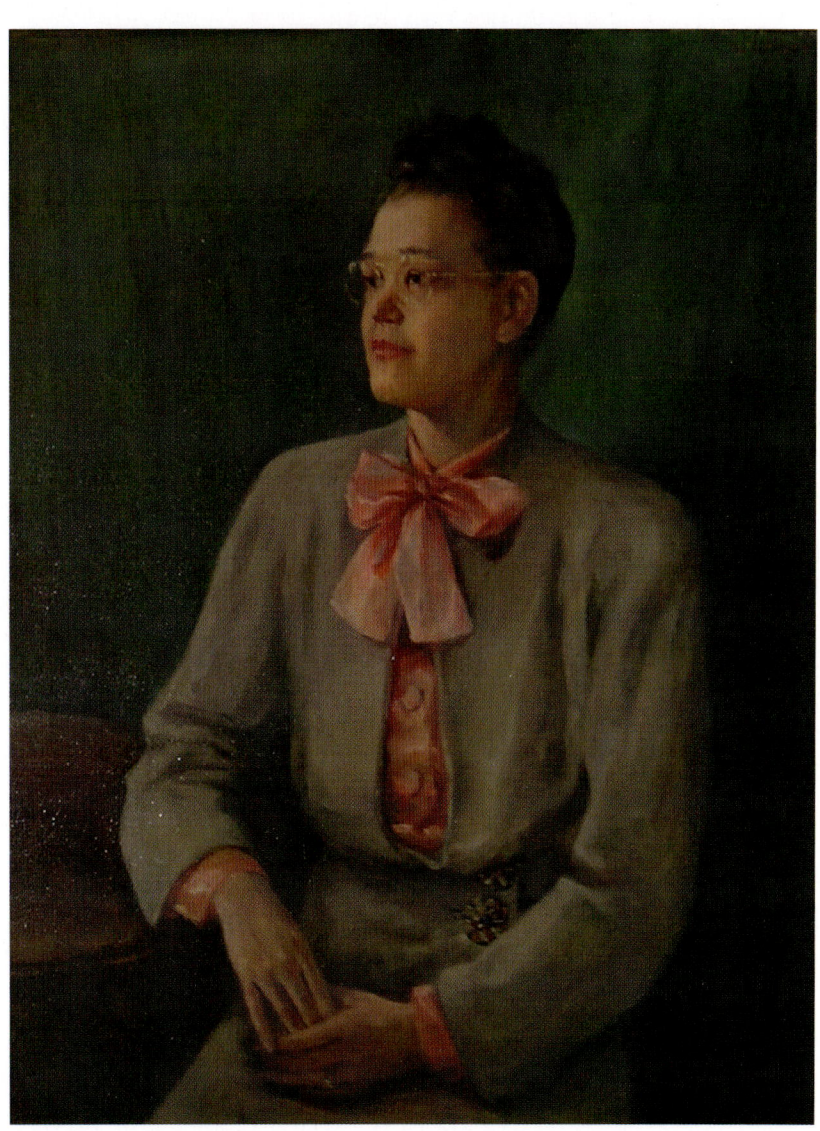

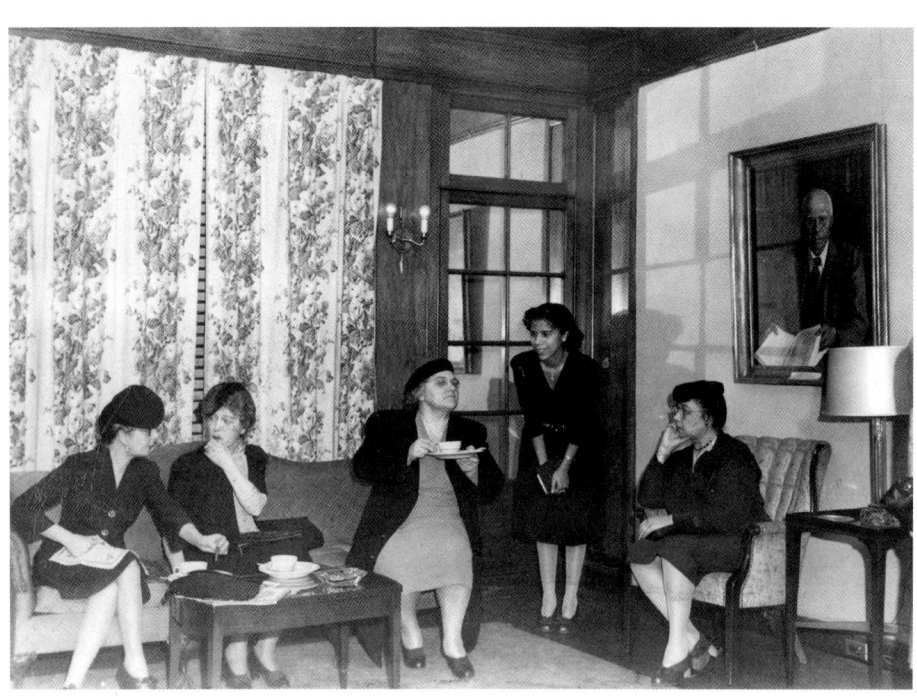

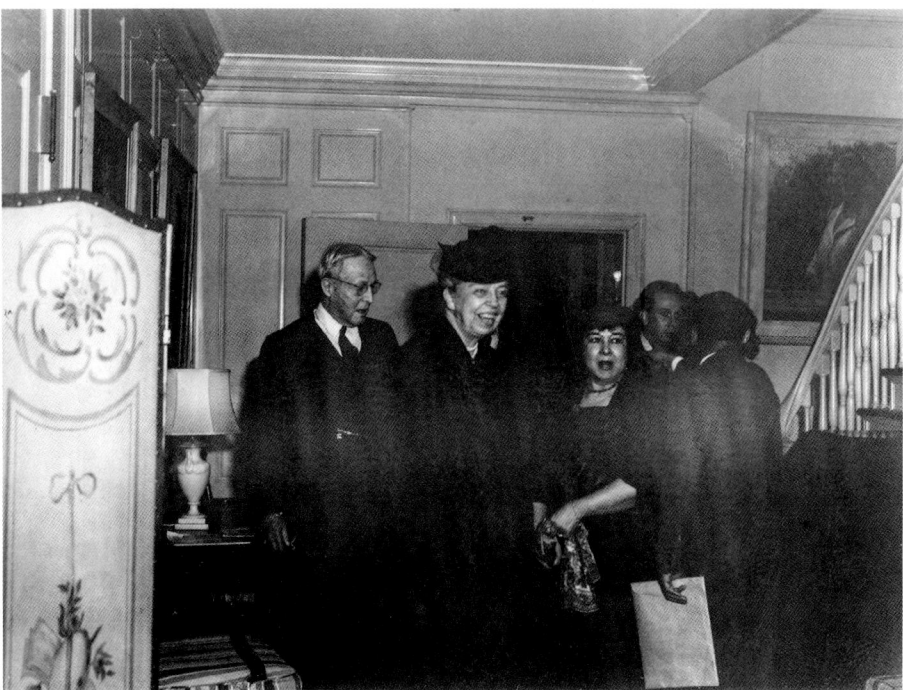

A dappled green background suggesting foliage creates a relaxed atmosphere and nods to the proposed garden setting.

After Detroit, the exhibition continued to travel, and Brady added new portraits. In the exhibition's fifth presentation, at the Brooklyn Museum in November 1945, the show consisted of 25 paintings. Six were of women, an increase to nearly one-quarter of the show. One of these additional paintings was *Anna Arnold Hedgeman* (1945) by Reyneau, who portrayed the civil rights leader Hedgeman (1899–1990) in a seated profile, her figure forming an L-shape on the lower half of the canvas, drawing the eye to the subject's vibrant green-and-white striped dress. A few days after the Brooklyn show closed, the key players in the exhibition gathered at the Roosevelt House, a multicultural center in Manhattan run by Hunter College, for the opening reception of its two-week presentation at the end of 1945. Installation photographs from the Harmon Foundation records show Waring, Reyneau, and Brady enjoying a cup of tea, hosted by Jean Campbell, student president of the Toussaint L'Ouverture Society of Hunter College (illus. 18). Other photographs document Campbell guiding a group of students to study Reyneau's portrait of Eugene Kinckle Jones (illus. 20), and the presence of the ubiquitous Eleanor Roosevelt, with the portrait of Whiting visible above the stairway (illus. 19).

At least five additional portraits of women joined the show in various locations as it traveled the country. Waring painted her friend the Philadelphia attorney Sadie Alexander (1898–1989) (illus. 17) in time for the portrait to be presented in the exhibition at the Cleveland Historical Society in 1946.[30] Waring also proposed to paint the dancer Katherine Dunham (1909–2006), pending approval from Brady, who as customary sought Locke's opinion. It appears that the commission was not granted, even though Brady lamented the imbalance between the numbers of paintings by the two artists.[31] Over the years, Reyneau painted several more portraits of women for the exhibition, including activist Mary Church Terrell in 1946, physician Ruth Temple in

18 (L–R) Unidentified, Betsy Graves Reyneau, Mary Beattie Brady, Jean Campbell, and Laura Wheeler Waring at Roosevelt House with Reyneau's portrait *Monroe Nathan Work*.

19 (L–R) Unidentified, Eleanor Roosevelt, and Laura Wheeler Waring at Roosevelt House with Reyneau's *Helen A. Whiting*.

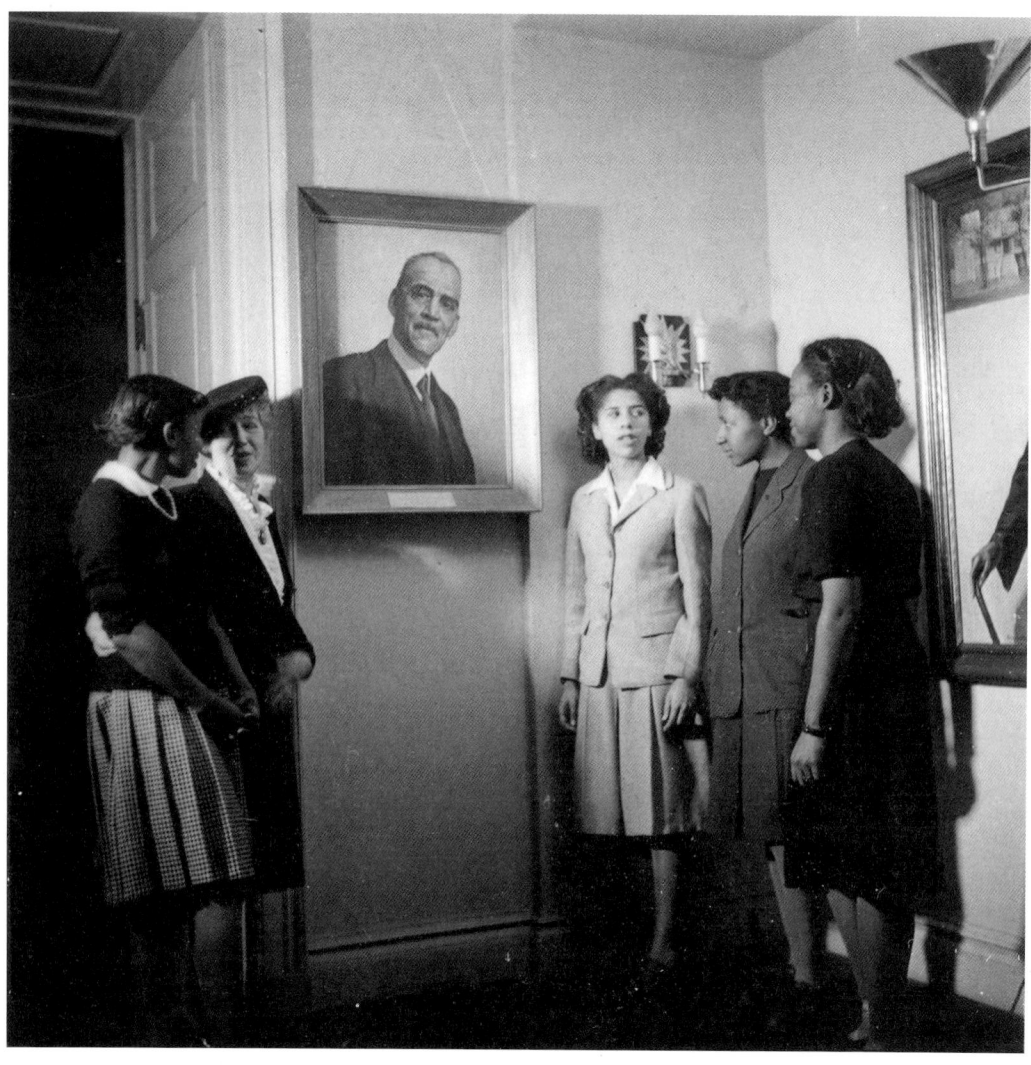

1948, nurse Mary Mills in 1952, and UN representative Edith Spurlock Sampson in 1953.

Shortly after the show opened, Brady identified the need to include a portrait of a visual artist to complement the performers and authors. She floated the names of several female painters as potential subjects, including Waring and Loïs Mailou Jones, in correspondence to Locke. But nothing came of it. Brady, ironically, did not consider Waring to be sufficiently prominent, and Locke did not disabuse her

20 Jean Campbell, president of the Toussaint L'Ouverture Society of Hunter College, center, and Betsy Graves Reyneau, second from left, at Roosevelt House with Reyneau's portrait *Eugene Kinckle Jones*, center, and *Mary McLeod Bethune*, right.

of her assumption. As for Jones, he demurred and deemed her "arty."[32] Another woman artist under discussion, sculptor Selma Burke (1900–1995), who had achieved national attention for her relief portrait of Franklin Roosevelt (later the source of his likeness on the dime), received some of Brady's unsolicited career advice. Around this time Waring completed an elegant portrait of artist Alma Thomas (1891–1978), who was at that time a junior high school art teacher, but it does not seem to have been considered for the exhibition. A number of male artists were proposed as well, including Hale Woodruff and Jacob Lawrence. In the end, for the artist slot Brady commissioned Reyneau to paint sculptor Richmond Barthé (1901–1989)—with whom the Harmon Foundation had been developing an exhibition and educational materials—in 1946, and later Aaron Douglas (1899–1979) in 1953.

Jones would have made for a fitting selection for the exhibition. She was an established painter and educator who created community and broke barriers of segregation. As seen in her *Self-Portrait* (1940), Jones included in her painting references to African art, here in the form of several figurines, as a crucial inspiration. In 1931 she received honorable mention in the Harmon Foundation prizes. Jones asked Céline Tabary to deliver her paintings to juried exhibitions to avoid racial discrimination, easing the way for her landscape *Indian Shops, Gay Head* (1940) to be awarded a prize at the Society of Washington Artists Fiftieth Annual Exhibition at the Corcoran Gallery in 1941. Several years later, collectors Marjorie and Duncan Phillips purchased another of her landscapes. This was in 1944, around the time that Locke and Brady deliberated Jones's merits for inclusion as a subject for the show. In the end, no portrait of a Black female visual artist appeared in the Harmon Foundation's traveling exhibition.

The discussion of "Portraits" as an example of a race-oriented all-women exhibition must also recognize the fact that Black women artists and crafters had organized group exhibitions of their work since at least the 1890s. References to such exhibitions, typically held at Black women's clubs, appeared in newspapers at the time. There is a need for more extensive archival research to surface and examine other public documentation that might exist of the artists and their work.

One of the rare documented Black all-women art and craft exhibitions took place at the World's Columbian Exposition in Chicago in 1893. The delegation from New York State presented the "Afro-American Women's Exhibit" in a corner gallery on the second floor of the Woman's Building. Boston-born New York City educator Joan Imogen Howard (1848–1937) organized the presentation of fine arts, including painting and drawing, and domestic handicrafts such as dressmaking and quilts. Howard was the only Black woman appointed to serve on any of the state boards, the governing bodies charged with organizing and financing exhibitions at the fair. A photograph of the exhibition's large display case was illustrated in the New York State report on its activities at the fair, serving as a key visual record of an exhibit that resembled a cabinet of curiosities.[33] Crusading journalist Ida B. Wells's scathing report on the fair's racist exclusions of African Americans found little to praise, an exception being Howard's initiative: "In the short period of her service she worked earnestly in behalf of her race, but met only with indifferent success."[34] Among the listed artists in the show were Ella Spencer, a watercolorist who graduated from Cooper Union in 1881, and Bertha Lattimore, who contributed a portrait drawing of abolitionist Robert Purvis, among other works. Howard also arranged to borrow a marble statuette by Edmonia Lewis (1844–1907), the most celebrated Black female artist of the nineteenth century, from the Boston YMCA, likely *The Wooing of Hiawatha* (1866), for the Woman's Building library.

It is notable that an educational, rather than primarily artistic, mission provided the framework for both the "Afro-American Women's Exhibit" in 1893 and "Portraits of Outstanding Americans of Negro Origin" in 1944. Both exhibitions have their origins in the creative vision and entrepreneurial efforts of Black female artist-educators (Howard and Waring), the didactic messaging of Black cultural advancement within mainstream white institutions (the world's fair and the Harmon Foundation), and the intersection of left-wing activism (Wells and Reyneau). As a project that allied art, history, and politics, with a robust educational component, "Portraits" successfully functioned in diverse venues from art museums to libraries to schools. The artists and Brady established at the outset that the primary focus of the show would be race, not gender.

The show circulated initially through the personal and professional networks of Reyneau and Brady, but it later began to take on a life of its own. In 1946 Brady hired the Black community organizer Bella Taylor McKnight (1900–1982) to arrange the tour and its local partnerships and community events. Over the next few years, she partnered with religious groups, school districts, sororities, local politicians, and civic organizations. Any integrated venue could host the show—which had grown to 32 paintings by 1946—for $200 for two weeks, or $250 for three, plus the cost of one-way transportation. As the exhibition traveled and the interpretation evolved, gender became part of the larger conversation. The addition of Knight to the team may have further amplified the visibility of women, as she made a point to discuss the women's portraits with visitors.[35] Women's groups and teams of hostesses often facilitated the presentation and public engagement.

To reinforce the educational value of the exhibition, many reviews included photographs of local dignitaries facing a painting in the show. In such photographs, the officials' gazes are firmly fixed on the image of an outstanding Black American, accompanied by captions describing the paintings as "admired" and "studied appreciatively"; as such, the images illustrate the power of art to work toward political ends through culture. Other photographs emphasize the importance of introducing school-age children to the portraits, such as an undated image of Reyneau and an interracial group of boys and girls looking at the portrait *Jane Matilda Bolin*, with her other works *Hugh Mulzac* (1946) and *Monroe Nathan Work* (1942) visible behind them. Waring did not travel with the show because of her commitments to teaching and disinterest in public speaking, so Reyneau became the face of the exhibition, traveling to venues and sometimes providing provocative quotes and hammy poses to the newspaper reporters and photographers. She confidently interfaced with officials, such as badgering Clyde Burroughs, secretary of the Detroit Institute of Arts, to provide a quote testifying that the paintings constituted a high-quality art exhibition in addition to a noble effort in community-building. As time progressed, Waring's voice diminished, and she was sometimes omitted from articles about the exhibition. Several of her works, like the portraits of Evanti and Alexander, were removed from the show. Her participation was further reduced by illness, and finally by her death in 1948. In the 1950s—in the presentation at the Dayton Art Institute, for example—only 6 of the 33 portraits were by Waring.

"Portraits of Leading American Negro Citizens" had originally been cloaked in the patriotic democracy of the war years, such as the Double V campaign by African Americans fighting for military victory abroad and political victory at home. (The title of the Surrealist journal *VVV* is thought to have been partly inspired by the campaign's vv logo). Yet the exhibition soldiered on through the rising tide of conservatism, nativism, and anti-communism of the late 1940s and early 1950s, bridging the short-lived optimism of true change for the status of Black people during the war to a calcification of the status quo in American life. The exhibition had remarkably long legs, traveling until 1954, when the foundation ended the tour after the Supreme Court's decision in *Brown v. Board of Education* to desegregate American public schools. Reyneau's commitment to the project did not end there, and even after the traveling show concluded, she continued to paint portraits, including of Marian Anderson in 1955 and Thurgood Marshall in 1956. The show still had a role to play, and libraries sometimes displayed reproductions from the portfolio during Negro History Week (changed to Black History Month in 1976). In 1967 the Harmon Foundation closed and dispersed its assets, donating 41 portraits to the National

Portrait Gallery (NPG) and over 1,000 other artworks to the National Collection of Fine Arts (now the Smithsonian American Art Museum). The following year, the Smithsonian's new Black history center in Maryland, the Anacostia Museum, displayed 28 of the portraits, attracting an estimated 5,000 visitors according to one report.[36] Two decades later, the Smithsonian showed 24 paintings from the Harmon donation in an exhibition titled "Portraits in Black," which circulated to university museums across the country. In 1997, the NPG reconstructed the original show in its own galleries with the exhibition "Breaking Racial Boundaries," accompanied by an essential catalogue by Tuliza K. Fleming. In 2020, ten of the portraits were on view in the NPG, with their subjects placed in thematic galleries by profession or historical period, not according to the original exhibition's racial framework. The exhibition never foregrounded specifically women's issues, but recent scholarship has brought new attention to the agency of its female exponents and the ways in which the exhibition facilitated the recognition and celebration of the individual merits and accomplishments of Black women.[37] In retrospect, Brady succinctly described the exhibition as "two races and two women banded together to fight injustice."[38]

. . . .

FIRST WOMEN'S INVITATION EXHIBITION

NOVEMBER 1st to 31st, 1947

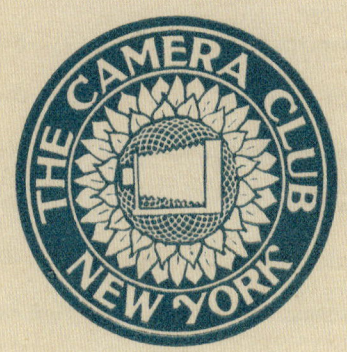

THE CAMERA CLUB
121 WEST 68th STREET
NEW YORK

. . . .

3

Photography: "First Women's Invitation Exhibition," The Camera Club, 1947

T he Second World War powerfully transformed the lives and careers of women in photography. With millions of men away at war, government, education, and industry tapped women's skills and labor as never before. "I doubt if there's ever been a war in history where women could play such a vital part," recalled photographer Margaret Bourke-White (1904–1971).[1] Already a famous photojournalist in the 1930s, Bourke-White was the first woman photographer to accompany a U.S. Air Force bomber on a combat mission. Other women photographers gained new opportunities to obtain technical skills, professional networks, and recognition through their work documenting the Women's Army Corps and the home front for the Woman's Land Army and the Office of War Information, or on assignment with news agencies. Women photographers experienced such a marked increase in professional standing that by 1946, *Popular Photography* claimed, "Virtually all fields of photography are open to women . . . In recent years, women have successfully invaded fields which were formerly regarded as being for men only."[2] Persistent sexism and racism limited or complicated women's ambitions, but there was a sense of postwar optimism that women were taking their place in all aspects of photography, the realization of over a half-century's concerted efforts to bring attention to women's accomplishments in one of the primary mass-media formats in the years before television.

21 The Camera Club, *First Women's Invitation Exhibition*, brochure, 1947.

When Alouise Boker (1897–1978) became the chair of the print committee of the Camera Club of New York in April 1947, she proposed to take stock of this trend. Over the next six months, she assembled a signal exhibition of u.s. women photographers. The "First Women's Invitation Exhibition" opened on October 31, 1947, at the Manhattan headquarters of the august photography society (illus. 21). The exhibition and its successor the following year played pivotal but heretofore unanalyzed roles in the recognition of women in twentieth-century American photography.

Since the turn of the century, the Camera Club had been associated with the legacy of celebrated photographer Alfred Stieglitz (1864–1946), who expanded and edited its journal *Camera Notes* to promote pictorialism, a movement of photography as an art form equivalent to painting. By the 1920s, pictorialism no longer stood on the avant-garde, yet camera clubs across the country upheld its principles of painterly composition and printing, which increasingly looked formulaic and sentimental in comparison to the new trends in Constructivist, Surrealist, and street photography. By the 1940s, the Camera Club struggled to demonstrate its relevance; it had an aging membership and shaky finances. The club's board recognized that a timely exhibition could capture the growing attention given to women in photography. Boker's concept was one facet of the club's efforts to energize its exhibition program to overcome its reputation for being a "stodgy outfit" and attract new membership.[3] In her two-year run as chair of the print committee, Boker also initiated shows by color photography pioneer Nickolas Muray and fashion photographer Philippe Halsman.[4] The "First Women's Invitation Exhibition" was Boker's attempt to compel the club to acknowledge the significant presence of women in the field of photography and among its own membership. "Photography, as a medium, is giving to the world expression[,] interpretation, research, record, and women are participating in this contribution," states the exhibition brochure.[5]

Boker achieved her goal of curating a diverse group of professionals and amateurs working in a variety of practices. The show included Bourke-White along with other photojournalists like Lisa

Larsen and Evelyn Straus, fine art photographers Lotte Jacobi and Imogen Cunningham, fashion photographers Louise Dahl-Wolfe and Toni Frissell, commercial photographers Eileen Darby, Constance Bannister, and Ruth Alexander Nichols, and specialists in medical and biological imaging. The largest contingent of the show, comprising over a third of the exhibited photographers, were pictorialists who regularly exhibited on the salon circuit, a portion of whom were club members. The "Women's Invitation" mixed the practical and the aspirational, serving the core amateur salon circuit exhibitors while showcasing an informed selection of prominent professional photographers. With women playing a larger role in public life, photography offered a literal vantage on women's perceptions of the world.

The Camera Club's newsletter, *Camera Club Notes*, did not update its pandering tone, however, and drew upon feminine foils to promote the exhibition's artists:

> This show is no sissy collection of shots of babies, babbling brooks, and pussy cats. Though pictorialists capture most salon space, other types of photographers are having their innings at the Gallery now. The forty-one exhibitors were selected because they are tops in the varied categories of abstract, animal, architectural, dance, documentary, fashion, medical, news, portrait, and theater photography as well as pictorial.[6]

Such unreconstructed language can be found in multiple unsigned items about the show in the newsletter's typewritten pages, which were edited by member Helen Milius. One cannot be sure of the precise authorship of the texts, but they evoke the era's "Girl Friday" image of the eager but overmatched female professional.

A complete inventory of the exhibition is unavailable. The brochure included a list of artists and their places of residence, but there is no extant checklist of the actual prints on view. A few published references provide illustrations and written descriptions, with one article in

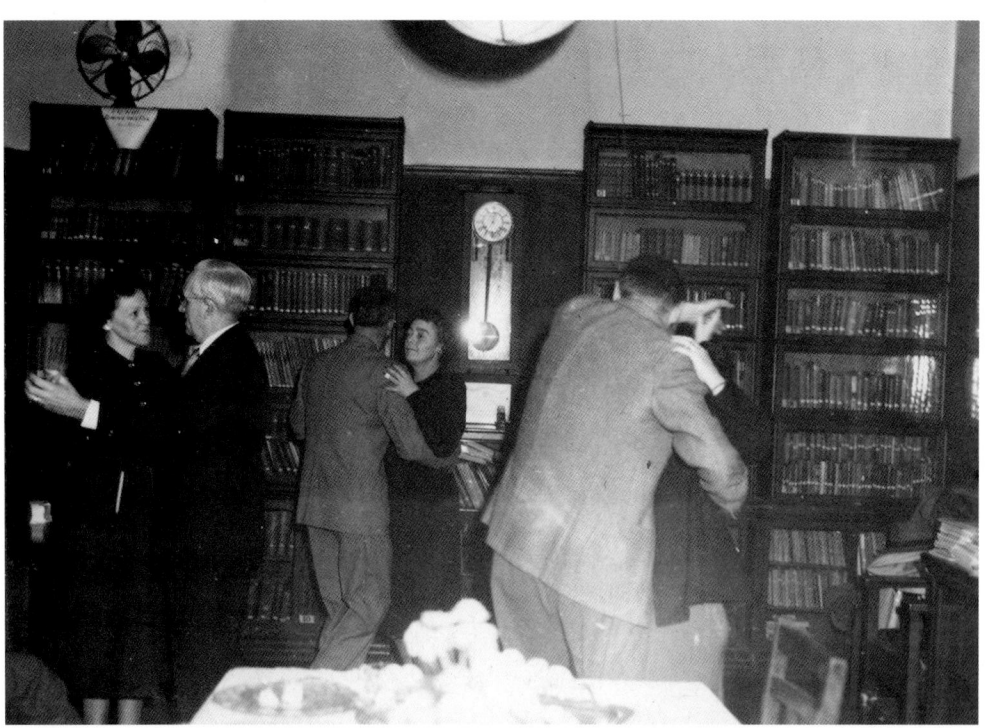

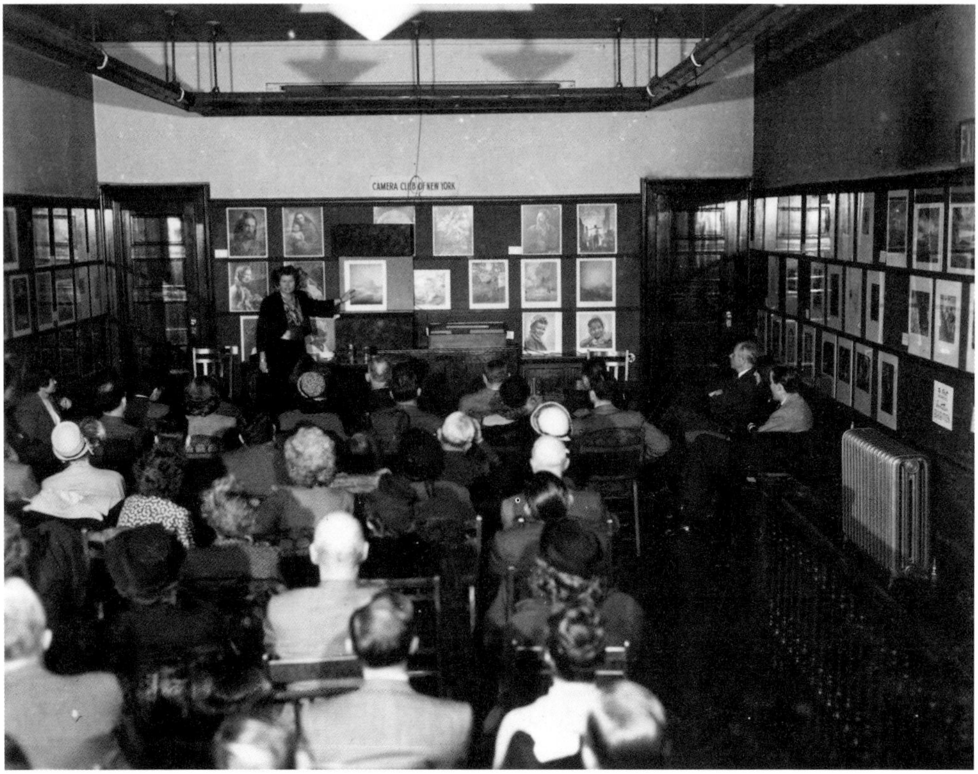

22 (L–R): Helen Wood, Francis Russell, T. Lopez, Alouise Boker, unidentified, dancing after the opening of the "First Women's Invitation Exhibition" at the Camera Club of New York, October 31, 1947.

23 Eleanor Parke Custis lecturing at the Camera Club, November 19, 1947.

24 Mildred Hatry (left) showing her work at the opening of the "First Women's Invitation Exhibition," October 31, 1947.

u.s. Camera fortunately printing images of a dozen exhibited works. The Camera Club institutional photo album includes two black-and-white snapshots of the opening with views of the gallery space; three rows of photographic prints are visible on the walls.[7] The snapshots do not document the exhibition per se but they do capture events that took place in the space simultaneous with the show, including Boker dancing at the opening (illus. 22) and a lecture by participating photographer Eleanor Parke Custis (1897–1983) (illus. 23). Because of the small size of the scrapbook photographs and the generalized subject-matter, few exhibited works can be clearly identified. An exception is the row of portraits by Lotte Jacobi (1896–1990), clearly depicting the famous faces of Eleanor Roosevelt, Margaret Truman (daughter of the president), and Albert Einstein above and to the right of photographer Mildred Hatry (1893–1973) (illus. 24). The lack of a checklist suggests

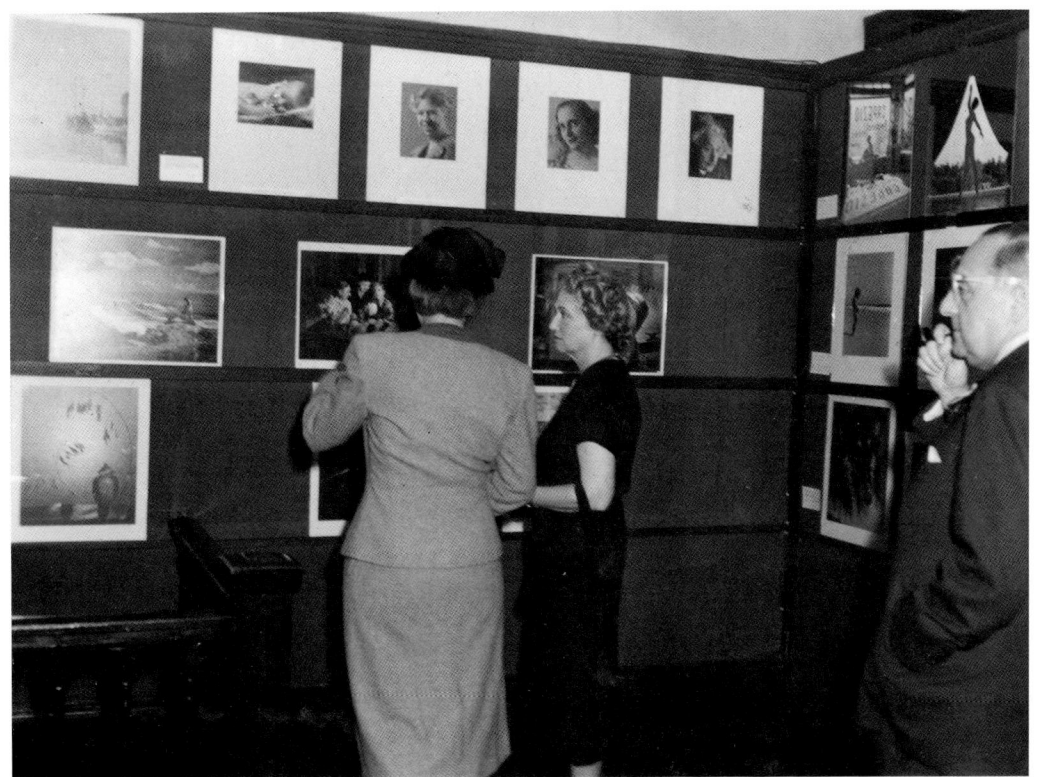

that the concept of the show, and the names and reputations of the participating artists, mattered more to Boker and the club than the aesthetic experience of the prints themselves. The show was not curated like a museum study of individual works assembled to explore a specific style or subject. Boker curated the artist, not the images. The artists, if they accepted the invitation to participate, offered their four preferred prints for the show, and Boker hung whatever they submitted.

The *New York Times* review by "Photo Notes" columnist Jacob Deschin, an amateur photographer with strict criteria for quality, composition, and taste, praised the exhibition's transcendence of the limits of gender-specificity: "Essentially, the exhibit is not markedly feminine, for the pictures displayed cover a wide range of photographic coverage, from medical photography to pictorialism. There are only a few pictures of babies, and these chiefly by photographers who specialize commercially in child photography."[8] Deschin saved his harshest criticism for the installation itself. He disliked in particular the large quantity of pictorialist works by the salon photographers, which he felt diminished the stature of other artists in the show, and argued that Boker should have imposed a stronger curatorial vision in the selection and presentation of the works. Boker, an amateur photographer herself, cast a wide net and did not create a hierarchy within the field of photography or adhere to any canon. She understood the field as flexible and diverse, with multiple avenues of success, following the typical approach for all-women exhibitions to facilitate their primary agenda of promoting women.

One identified work, Ruth Bernhard's *Hortons Point Lighthouse, Southold, Long Island* (1941) (illus. 25), exemplifies the cross-cutting themes and narratives that were explicit and implicit in the exhibition. The image is a still-life of two ruptured butterfly weed seedpods, with silky tendrils erupting from the confined casing. As suggested by the title, Bernhard (1905–2006) took this photograph at the lighthouse on the North Fork of Long Island, where she was staying at the time with her romantic partner, interior designer Evelyn Phimister.[9] On one

25 Ruth Bernhard, *Hortons Point Lighthouse, Southold, Long Island*, 1941, gelatin silver print.

84

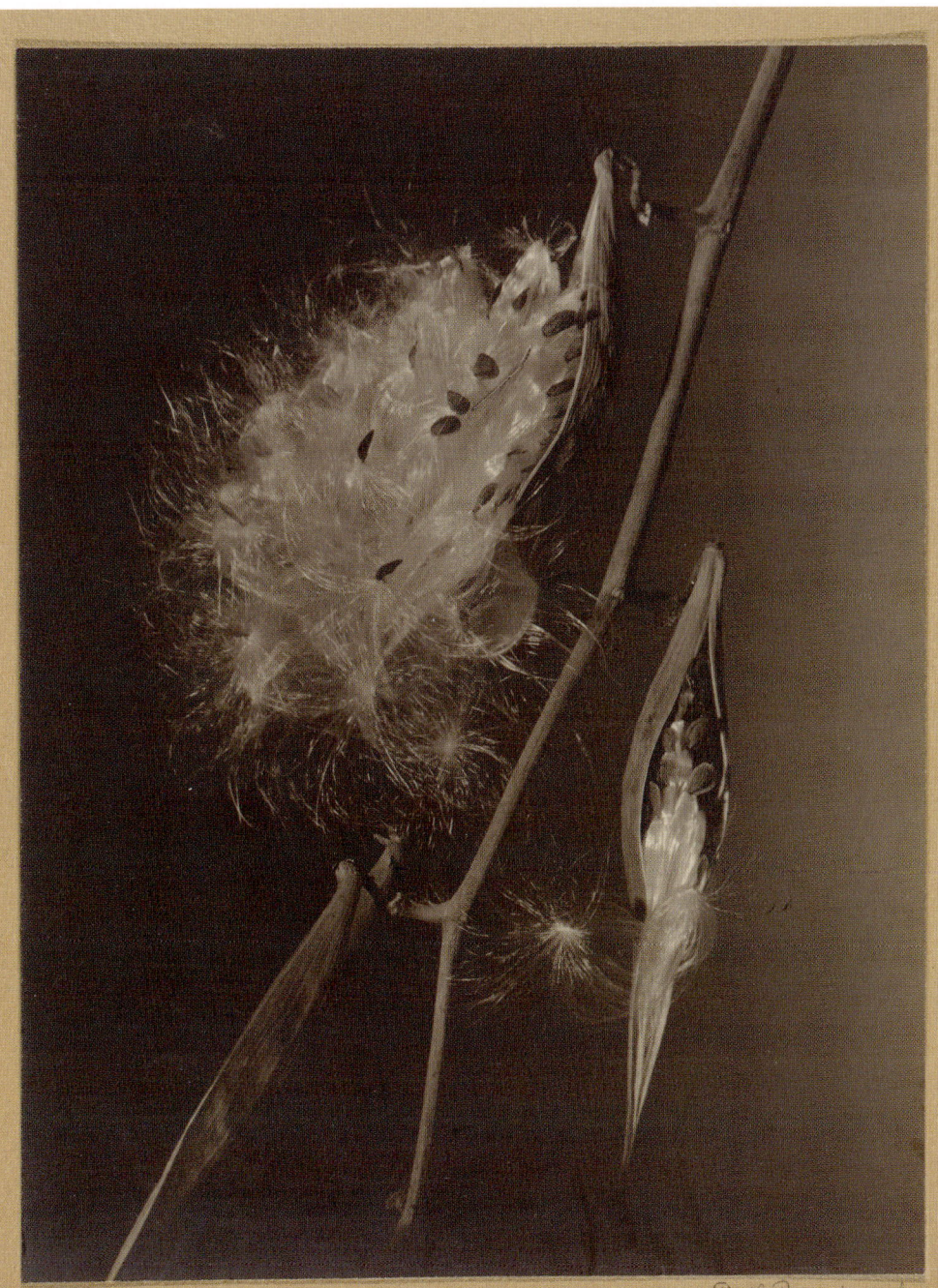

Ruth Bernhard

level, the photograph is a formalist study of natural plant structures in the tradition of early twentieth-century photographs by Imogen Cunningham and Edward Weston, whom Bernhard had met in California. On another level, the image also may encode the story of Bernhard's unconventional personal life. By the standards of the day, Bernhard was relatively open about her relationships with women, having disclosed her sexuality to her father, who was also an artist, years earlier. A second image by Bernhard in the exhibition, *Early Nude* (*c.* 1934), more explicitly delves into eroticism and the female gaze; it shows a dancer friend of the photographer posing nude in a fetal position in a metal tub. Bernhard's work relates to many of the photographers in the "Women's Invitation," as her willingness to express her personality through technical excellence in photography gained the support of leading curators and critics of the day.

The exhibition was installed in three rows of black-and-white prints, matted and unframed, resting on rails and leaning against the wall of the main gallery. Prints were grouped by artist and, according to the brochure, rearranged weekly so as not to disadvantage any artists with poor locations (the club used the gallery for lectures and meetings, and lines of sight of the photographs on the bottom row might have been obscured by furniture and activities). The dense hang, with prints sometimes several inches apart, suggested a fair-like environment aimed at the photography connoisseur for whom more is more. The photographic prints were not aestheticized to the point of fetishization as they would be in a traditional museum setting. Nor were subjects or styles grouped in any discernible way.

The selection process and presentation format mirrored the photography salons that were a staple of members-led camera societies across the country. Salons such as these provided spaces for photographers of all degrees of ability, from beginners to studio owners, to meet, share technical tips, enjoy lectures, and exhibit their prints. They were a home for serious amateur photographers who might not otherwise have had access to museums and galleries; these artists found the camera club network, and its open-call juried salons, to be a meritocratic opportunity to show their work. The Photographic Society of America (PSA) maintained and published annual rankings of the top photographers based on the number of prints accepted by salons. Women accounted for about 10 percent of the participants.[10] With the low proportion of women represented in these salons, some, like Custis, proudly proclaimed their achievement of a place in the PSA's annual list of the year's top ten.[11]

When Boker was appointed chair of the print committee (essentially the exhibition coordinator) at the Camera Club, she immediately set an agenda to bring more work by women to the club. She proposed to organize a solo presentation of Rosalind Maingot (1894–1947), a respected British photographer in the pictorialist tradition, and an exhibition of "outstanding women photographers" with a lecture by a prominent woman.[12] Boker's concept built on a fifty-year legacy of women photographers advocating to bring attention to their accomplishments to rectify the persistent marginalization of women in camera clubs and societies. Starting in the 1890s, photographer Catherine Weed Barnes (1851–1913) pushed for women to be admitted to all-male camera clubs and societies.[13] Periodic exhibitions of women photographers became an important measure of their institutional success, similar to all-women exhibitions in fine art and printmaking; one early example is the exhibition of between 150 and 200 prints by about 30 American women organized by photographer Frances Benjamin Johnston (1864–1952) at the 1900 Exposition Universelle in Paris. Six years later, the Camera Club of Hartford, Connecticut, presented about 200 prints by 32 of the foremost women photographers in the country, including Anne Brigman (1869–1950) and Jessie Tarbox Beals (1870–1942).[14] Even with women's increasing presence in the field, photography societies generally excluded them from leadership positions. In response, Mary Carnell (1861–1925) formed the Women's Federation of the Photographers' Association of America in 1909 to promote the work of female members, with workshops, demonstrations, lectures, and exhibitions in salons and private studios across the country. Three decades later, the women's committee of the Miniature Camera Club of Philadelphia responded to the same need and initiated the Annual National Photographic Salon for Women, which ran from 1937 to 1939, and exhibited scores of photographers from the United States and Canada.

Little is known about Alouise Boker's life and career. The documentation of her activities of the period records her economic and social privilege, community service, and artistic activities. During the Second World War, she volunteered through the Camera Club's War Service Photography program to teach photography to wounded servicemen rehabilitating in city hospitals. She was an amateur photographer, bringing her camera on her travels to the Alps and the Caribbean, as well as to Vermont, where she documented her encounter with the famed folk painter Anna "Grandma" Moses. Scrupulous and fair-minded, Boker consulted with curators, teachers, and photographers for suggestions in pursuit of the strongest possible list of participants for the "Women's Invitation." In June the roster was assembled, and by the end of the summer she had issued invitations to fifty women to submit up to four prints that best represented their recent work, following the salon model. By early September, 26 artists had accepted, and in the end 41 submitted 164 prints, all of which were hung. The list had considerable star power, yet Boker recognized its shortcomings and regretted that several illustrious women photographers, such as Dorothea Lange and Berenice Abbott, were not represented.

Among the photographers in the show, about fifteen could be classified as practicing the pictorialist photography predominant in salons and the Camera Club. Such photographers followed established rules of good technique and composition, choosing salon-friendly tried-and-true subjects like portraits, animals, and landscapes, without the provocative or alienating effects of Surrealist, Constructivist, or documentary photography. Even at the time the merits of pictorialism were hard to pin down. An *Oakland Tribune* article quotes one practitioner describing the style as "something pleasing . . . something you can 'live with' and hang on your living room wall."[15] The pictorialist photographers' primary affiliations were membership in the RPS (Royal Photographic Society) of Britain and the PSA (Photographic Society of America). These acronyms were attached to their names in the press like academic credentials to signify professional standing.

Boker's sympathy toward pictorialism also guided her choice of honorary exhibitor, the London-based Rosalind Maingot, who was known for her figures, costume studies, and flowers. At the time she was one of the few female members of the RPS. When she visited New York on a lecture tour in April 1947, the *New York Times* dubbed her "one of the greatest of contemporary portrait photographers."[16] Her work is little collected and studied today, however, which is typical for pictorialists excluded from modern art museum collections or exhibitions despite being celebrated in photography societies and magazines. The "Women's Invitation" included a few highly successful pictorialists, like Eleanor Parke Custis and Mildred Hatry. Both received solo exhibitions in the Brooklyn Museum's photographic gallery in 1946. One of Hatry's works in the Camera Club show, *The Women* (undated), now in the collection of the Brooklyn Museum, depicts a half-dozen mature women sitting at a table in what appears to be a knitting circle. The museum's press releases praised their international success in salons, claiming Custis to be "one of America's best known and most prolific photographers" and Hatry an "outstanding woman photographer."[17] An essential difference between the pictorialist culture and that of the modernist photographer is that success tends to be quantifiable. One reporter noted that Detroit-based Jean Elwell, who had a solo show of 60 prints at the Smithsonian in 1948, "has hung 758 photographs in 268 international salons, winning 102 awards, medals and honors for over 80 prints."[18]

In addition to the significant representation of pictorialists in the Camera Club exhibition, Boker invited women working in scientific capacities. Four photographers specializing in medical and scientific subjects appeared in the show: Avis Gregersen, Maria Ikenberg Lindberg, Stella Zimmer, and Grace MacMullen. Also included was Phyllis Dearborn Massar (1917–2011), who in the midcentury ran a studio in Seattle with her husband Robert, specializing in architectural photography; the studio created an important record of the rise of modernism in the Pacific Northwest. Boker's inclusion of these artists reinforced the importance of photography as a technical tool and the variety of career paths open to women in the field.

Despite the presence of women in medical, scientific, and architectural photography, the stereotype endured that professional women photographers exclusively specialized in putatively lightweight subjects such as infants and animals. Boker did not shy away from the negative associations and included baby portraits as a legitimate field of photography in which women were recognized as the leaders. Preeminent among them were Ruth Alexander Nichols (1893–1970) and Constance Bannister (1913–2005). Both ran successful commercial studios licensing baby images for advertising by nationally prominent brands. They also leveraged their success into other media by publishing photography books for children and adults, both frequently relying on humor and cuteness as narrative devices. Nichols, born in Nebraska, began taking pictures at age nine and graduated from Oberlin College, Ohio, in 1915. Her daughter starred in her first baby photos, and she went on to achieve commercial success, with clients including Johnson & Johnson, Prudential, and Steinway. Nichols was one of the four subjects—together with Toni Frissell, Berenice Abbott, and Margaret Bourke-White—of Irving Browning's documentary film short *Women in Photography*, released by Columbia Pictures in November 1941. It is possible that Nichols anticipated the increased demand for photography of adorable infants and toddlers during the postwar Baby Boom in the United States and the concurrent mass suburbanization. Bannister, a generation younger, was born in Tennessee. She battled gender discrimination from early in her career, when men sabotaged her work by scratching her negatives and spoiling her developing fluids; their targeting of her meant she had to print in the bathtub in her hotel room when she was a photographer for the *Chicago Tribune* and other news outlets.[19] She later branched into baby photography, such as the charming portrait of a ten-month-old (illus. 26) presented in the "Women's Invitation." She later repurposed the portrait and other images from the shoot in a "Baby Banters" strip, her nationally syndicated photographic comic.

While baby photography was not snubbed in the "Women's Invitation," it was kept to a minimum—a fact about which the *Times* reviewer noted his relief. The gravitas of Boker's production was, however, undermined by the newspaper's photo editors, who selected a

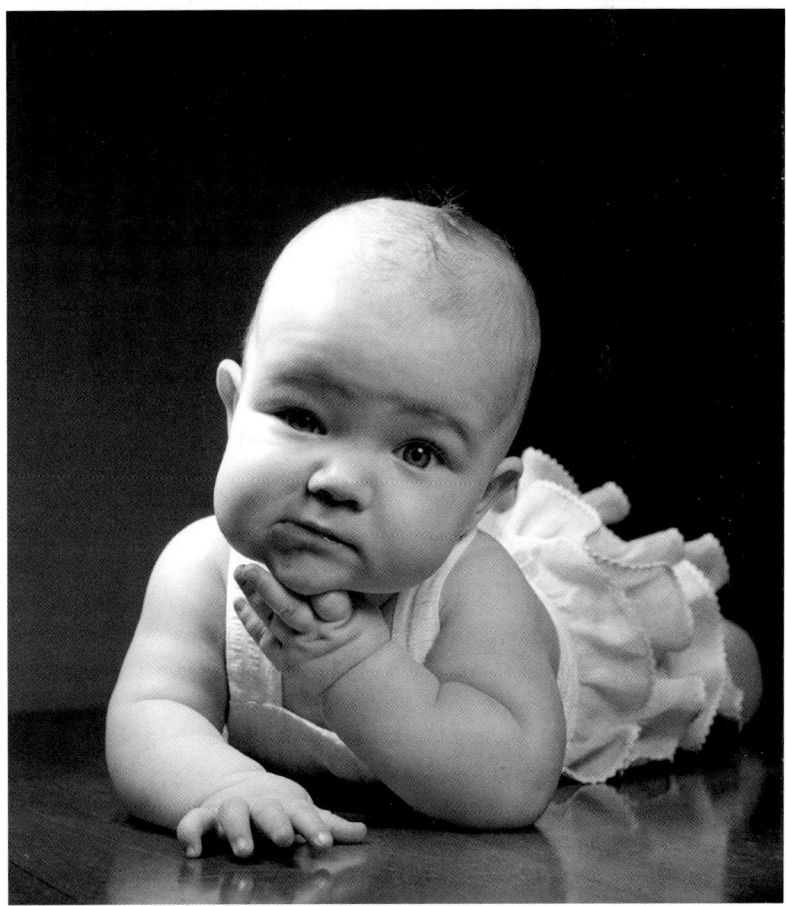

26 Constance Bannister, *Leslie Patricia Gordon, 10 Months Old,* 1946, gelatin silver print.

photograph of a juvenile orangutan, *Rusty* (1947) by Eileen Darby (1916–2004), as the sole illustration. The great ape was already famous, having been the subject of Darby's photographic report on the Saint Louis Zoo in *Life* in September.[20] Darby's career exemplified the resiliency required of professional women to overcome countless obstacles. Born in 1916, she built her own darkroom at the age of twelve and moved from Portland, Oregon, to New York to become a professional photographer in 1937. She gained employment in the darkroom of Pix, one of the many news agencies established by German refugees in the 1930s. Darby began to photograph Broadway theatrical productions and contributed freelance images to *Life*. The magazine offered her a staff position, which she turned down after learning that women's salaries were half those of men.[21] Instead Darby co-founded an independent photo agency, Graphic House, which became renowned for its superior darkroom processing, and soon *Life* photographers hired her to develop their prints. "Eileen Darby walked right into a man's world," proclaimed a 1945 newspaper profile on her national success as a theatrical photographer.[22] Darby revolutionized the genre by eschewing the stiff *tableaux vivants* of the previous era and shooting naturalistic images from the perspective of the audience. One celebrated example shows a tense confrontation between Marlon Brando and Jessica Tandy in *A Streetcar Named Desire*. Her photograph of the orangutan, *Rusty*, was an endearing work, but it did not represent the essence of her achievement.

Sportswomen's images of mountaineering, skiing, and other outdoor pursuits challenged stereotypes of women's photography. Boker represented this trend, which dated to the New Woman of the 1890s, in the exhibition through the inclusion of American Georgia Engelhard (1906–1986) and Swiss Helene Fischer (1900–1978), known at the time for their accomplishments in mountain climbing and skiing, respectively, and for their photographs taken during such excursions, which were reproduced in national magazines and books. Engelhard is probably best known in the art-historical literature as a niece of

Alfred Stieglitz and one-time travel companion of Georgia O'Keeffe, nicknamed "Georgia Minor." She established her own reputation as a sportswoman—setting climbing records in the Canadian Rockies—and as a "mountain photographer," joining news agencies like Black Star in the 1940s. A member of the Camera Club, she was chair of the publicity committee at the time of the "Women's Invitation." For her part, Fischer contributed four photographs of ski scenes, including one of well-known instructor Fred Iselin performing an acrobatic jump.

The show would have been incomplete without the presence of Margaret Bourke-White, an icon of female accomplishment, a glamorous globetrotting photojournalist who became synonymous with *Life* magazine. Born in New York in 1904, Bourke-White started her career at *Fortune* magazine in the early 1930s before joining *Life* in 1936. Her photograph of the Fort Peck Dam in Montana appeared on the cover of the inaugural issue. One of the preeminent mass-media outlets in midcentury America, *Life* elevated photography into an immersive storytelling device. "Women's Invitation" included Bourke-White's closely cropped portrait of a woman facing famine, part of her work on assignment with *Life* to document the social impact of the independence movement and partition in India in 1946–7.[23] Writer Lee Eitingon, who accompanied Bourke-White to India, recalled, "Being women, we had to be tougher. There were very few women doing things like that. One felt more pride in not knuckling under to any feminine weakness," using the gendered terminology of the time that idealized the so-called masculine virtues.[24] Bourke-White's work in the exhibition indicated both her worldliness and her political engagement.

With her sustained commercial and critical success, Bourke-White forged a different path than many contemporaneous photographers. At the time her career took off in the 1930s, the federal government responded to the crisis of the Great Depression and implemented a constellation of programs and agencies under the umbrella term of the New Deal. The Farm Security Administration (FSA), established in 1937 to provide aid to poor farmers, ran a photography division called the Historical Section. It sent photographers across the country to document the ongoing economic and environmental challenges and to gauge the efficacy of the agency's programs. Based in Washington, the FSA had its own darkroom and played a key role in supporting American photographers; it provided training, supplies, experience, and paychecks to women at the outset of their careers. After the United States entered the Second World War in late 1941, the government redeployed photographic and artistic resources to support the war effort. The FSA's photography department, led by Roy Stryker, was transferred to the Office of War Information (OWI) in 1942. Artists were sent out across the country to produce images of the impact of the war on the American people.

Boker included in the exhibition several women who worked for the OWI and documented the war's effect on the lives of women, including Marjory Collins (1912–1985) and Esther Bubley (1921–1998). Born in Wisconsin to Russian Jewish immigrants, Bubley worked as a darkroom technician at the OWI before going on assignment in the field. During long journeys on Greyhound coach buses crisscrossing the South and Midwest, she photographed the mobilization for the war and the innate restlessness of the modern age in the United States. She often used her work to record the injustices of racial segregation. After the war, Standard Oil commissioned her and several others to document working life in the oil industry in Texas. One photograph taken on assignment appeared in the "Women's Invitation," depicting seated cowboys in their bunkhouse adorned with pin-ups (illus. 27). Marjory Collins eschewed the affluent lifestyle of her childhood to become a photojournalist. After the Second World War, she worked as a freelance photographer in Europe and Africa for U.S. government agencies and the commercial press, producing images such as Ethiopian emperor Haile Selassie holding court (illus. 28), which appeared in the "Women's Invitation."

A few of the women photographers in the exhibition worked as staff photographers for news magazines. Others contributed

27 Esther Bubley, *Hayden Miles Ranch, evening in the bunkhouse at round-up time, Andrew County, Texas, Nov. '45,* 1945, gelatin silver print.

photographs on a freelance basis, or their work was licensed from an independent New York agency such as Graphic House, Black Star, or Monkmeyer, several of which were either founded or managed by women. Lisa Larsen (1925–1959), born in Germany, may have been the youngest participant in the "Women's Invitation." One of her photographs in the exhibition, *Shoe Fitting, Capezio Theatrical Shoes, New York City* (1947) (illus. 29), was published in *Liberty* magazine and nominated for a Picture of the Year award by the Missouri School of

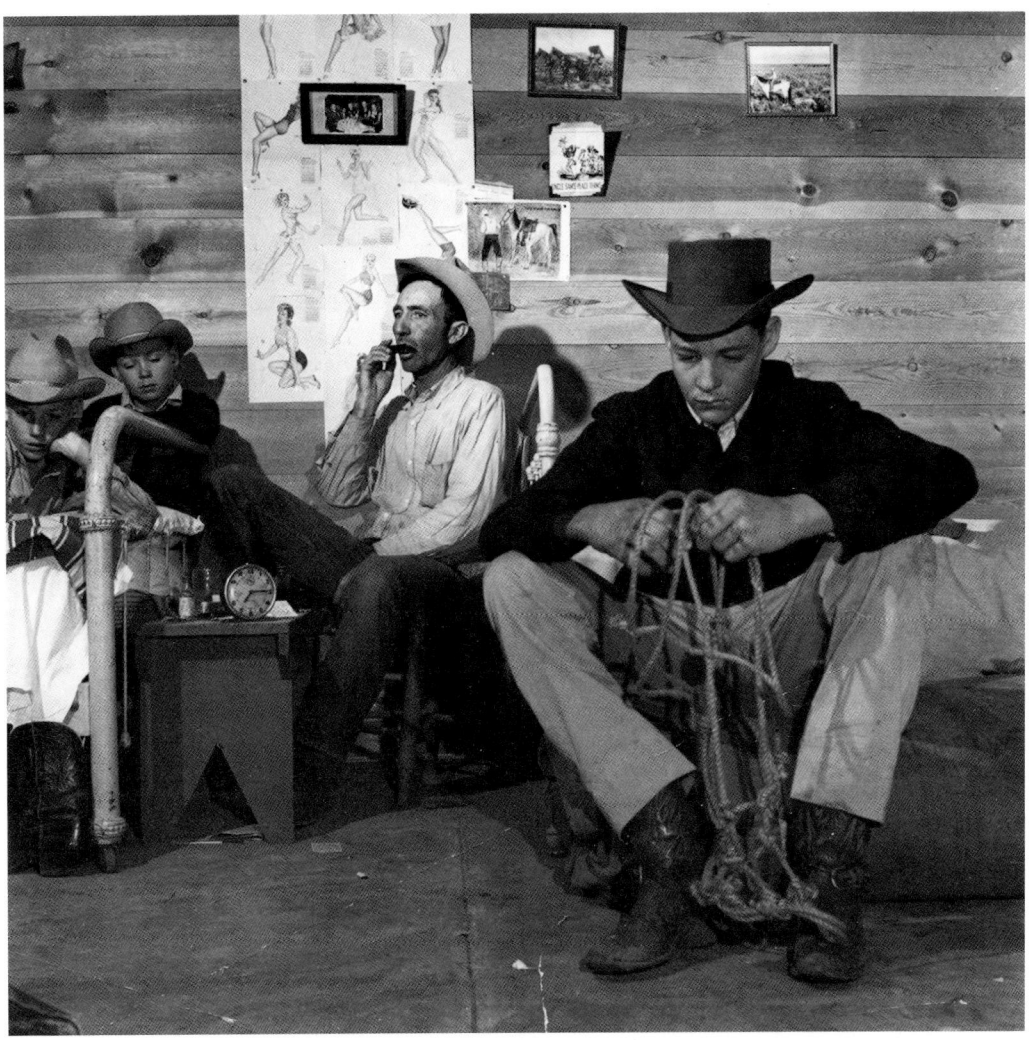

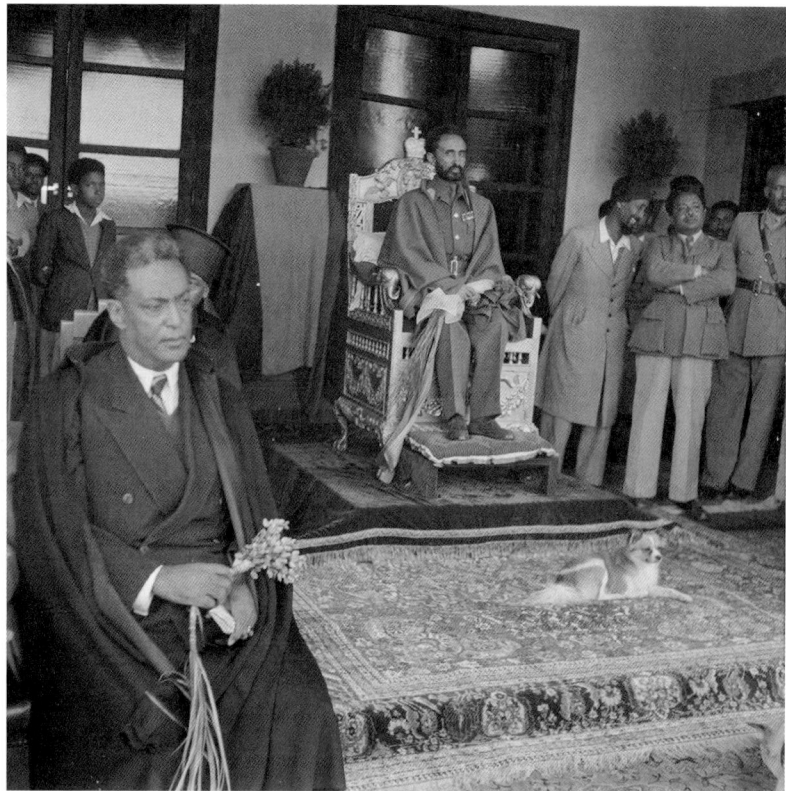

28 Marjory Collins, *Ethiopian Emperor Haile Selassie*, c. 1946.

Journalism. Shot from the interior, facing out through the storefront plate-glass window, the photograph exemplifies her striking compositions structured with graphic contrasts between dark and light. The shadow of the store name on the carpeted floor complements the classical pose of the female subject, with one bent knee, recalling a Degas painting. Larsen later joined the staff of *Life* in 1949, and after a decade of impressive photojournalism became the first woman to win the Magazine Photographer of the Year award in 1958 from the American National Press Photographers Association for her reporting on Nikita Khrushchev, the First Secretary of the Communist Party of the Soviet Union.

The "Women's Invitation" also included two eminent figures of the older generation: Imogen Cunningham (1883–1976) and Louise

29 Lisa Larsen, *Shoe Fitting, Capezio Theatrical Shoes, New York City,* 1947.

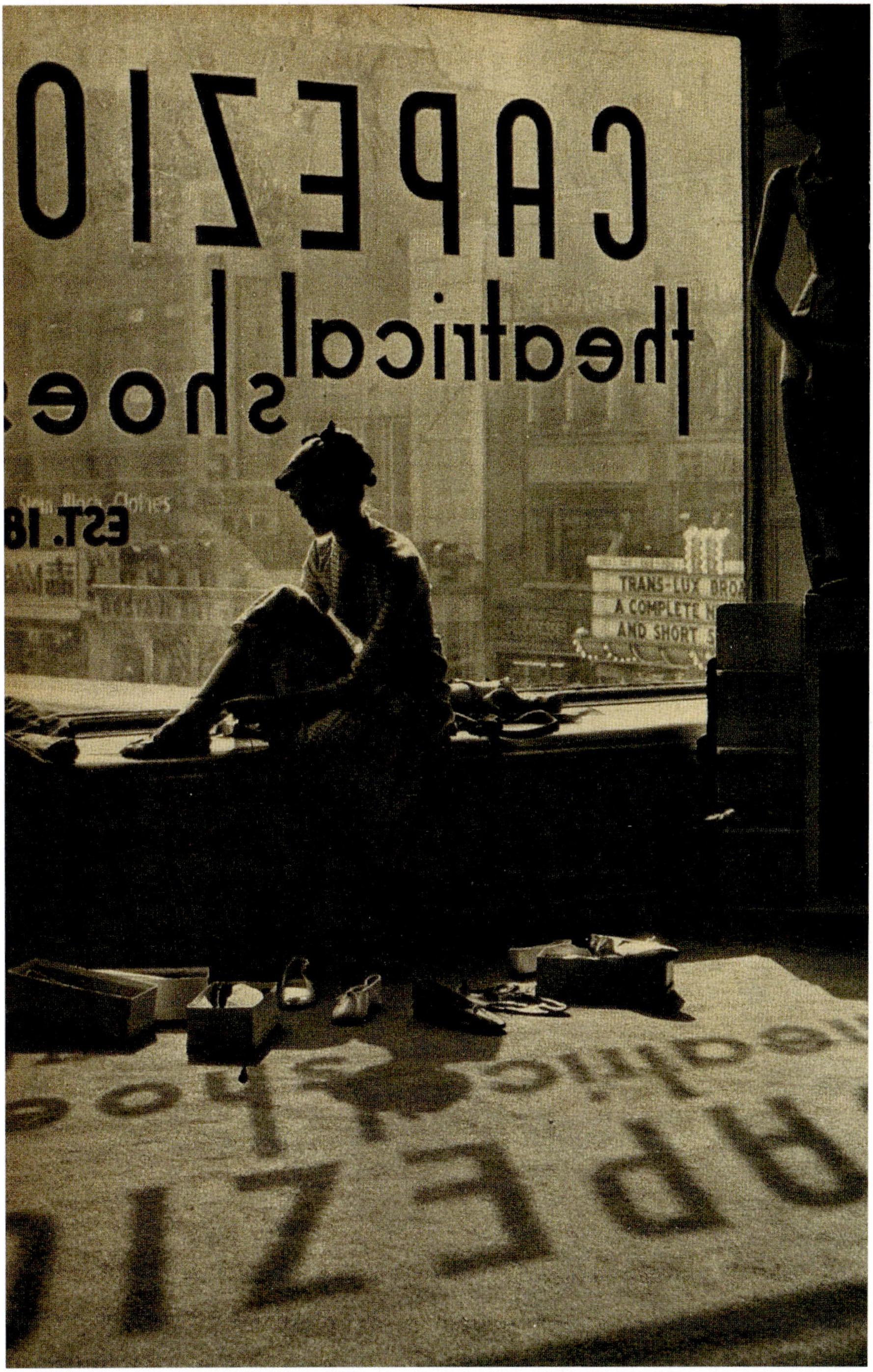
CAPEZIO
theatrical
shoes
TRANS-LUX
A COMPLETE
AND SHORT

Dahl-Wolfe (1895–1989). Both born and raised on the Pacific coast, the two photographers were each initially exposed to and stimulated by members of the Photo-Secession and pictorialist movements: Cunningham by Gertrude Käsebier in 1901, and Dahl-Wolfe by Anne Brigman in 1921. Their careers diverged from those stylistic paths as they traveled and expanded their intellectual and cultural horizons. Cunningham studied chemistry and technical photography in Germany in 1910, and Dahl-Wolfe traveled to Europe and North Africa with her friend the pioneering photojournalist Consuelo Kanaga in 1927. Dahl-Wolfe, who was trained in interior design and color theory, became a celebrated American fashion photographer in the 1930s and '40s, working for *Harper's Bazaar* and its formidable team of art director Carmel Snow and editor Diana Vreeland. When Kodachrome was released in 1935, Dahl-Wolfe quickly adopted it and became one of the first photographers to master color photography and printing. Her work is considered instrumental in the establishment of American fashion and the elevation of sportswear to haute couture and is known for innovating the staging of fashion shoots out of the studio, often in exotic locations.

Among the photographers in the "Women's Invitation," Cunningham was especially versatile and accomplished; her vast career encompassed several stylistic and social movements of the twentieth century. She was celebrated by Stieglitz in *Camera Work* and co-founded the influential collective f/64 in San Francisco, which established new aesthetic standards for sharp-focused modern photography. In 1913 she published an article in her college sorority magazine lamenting the lack of "conspicuously strong and individual work" by women in the fine arts. The cause, she wrote, was not women's innate weakness or inferiority but their lack of opportunity. She pondered, "Why women for so many years should have been supposed to be fitted only to the arts and industries of the home is hard to understand."[25] As will be seen in later chapters, Cunningham—like New York sculptor Louise Nevelson—allied herself with other women artists and expended her considerable credibility to support and elevate the work of younger women. Cunningham became wise elder of American art, equivalent to Georgia O'Keeffe in her redefinition of the feminine to establish her artistic identity and modernist credentials.

The contents of the "Women's Invitation" stemmed from Boker's affiliation with Camera Club pictorialists, her professional networks, and her awareness of the various typologies of professional photography. Yet these worlds of photography in which she operated largely excluded women of color, and these absences were mapped into the exhibition. In the United States, Black women had established careers in photography as studio practitioners, retouchers, and developers since the 1890s, as documented by photographer and historian Jeanne Moutoussamy-Ashe, but few attained recognition or visibility within historically white institutions and publications. The situation began to improve during the Second World War: for example, Elizabeth Williams and Emma Alice Downs served as photographers in the Women's Army Corps. In Los Angeles, Vera Jackson (1911–1999) achieved recognition as a student, winning a national high school photography competition, which led to a print displayed in the American Museum of Natural History in New York and coverage in Black newspapers. In 1946, *The Eagle* hired her as a staff photographer and she documented celebrities, such as Dorothea Dandridge, as well as society events and other news items.

A more inclusive exhibition could have involved international art photographers like Lola Álvarez Bravo (1903–1993) or some of the Black American women who were successfully working in various professional fields of photography, including photojournalism and studio work. Louise Martin (1911–1995) opened a studio in the segregated city of Houston in 1946, achieving her childhood dream to be a professional photographer. Segregated education prevented her from enrolling in local art schools so instead she earned money as a domestic worker to pay for tuition at the School of the Art Institute of Chicago. In 1952, Martin was invited to submit work to a salon at the Southwest

Photographers Association annual convention, held in a segregated hotel in Fort Worth, Texas. She accepted on the condition that the show relocate to a mezzanine level reached by stairs, since she was forbidden to use the elevator to reach the main exhibition hall.[26] Martin won several awards and later ironically noted how the commonplace practice of white photographers portraying Black children and elderly women solidified the misperception of Black people solely as subjects, not makers, in photography. This gap in representation cut across the field from the conservative precincts of salons to editorial photojournalism to socially concerned left-wing groups like the Photo League.

The exhibition achieved its goal of sparking a conversation within the club and in the broader world of photography, with uniformly favorable reviews in New York newspapers and national photography magazines. Encouraged by the positive response, Boker decided to mount a "Second Women's Invitation Exhibition," obtaining approval from the Camera Club board in April 1948. *Camera Club Notes*'s snarky announcement, "Powder-puff photography coming," again undercut the full acceptance of women as serious artists.[27] Boker did not wish to shoulder alone the administrative and fundraising responsibilities this time around, and formed an exhibition committee. She wisely enlisted the photographer and critic Nancy Newhall (1908–1974), who had joined the club a few months earlier. Newhall graduated from Smith College in 1933 and played a key role in the canon formation of modern photography. She had a professional and romantic partnership with Beaumont Newhall (1908–1993), founder of the MoMA photography department in 1940. When he served during the Second World War, she effectively ran the department and curated the first solo exhibition by a woman photographer at MoMA, "Children: Photographs by Helen Levitt" in 1943, which positioned her as an eagle-eyed street photographer in the vein of Henri Cartier-Bresson. Newhall's presence enhanced the curatorial rigor and presentation of the "Second Invitation." She activated her personal network to engage some heavyweight support, soliciting Ansel Adams to recommend names of women and inviting

Edward Steichen, director of the photography department at MOMA, to give remarks at the opening. (He declined, unwilling "to be used as a publicity agent."[28])

The collaboration between Boker and Newhall may have built on Newhall's work earlier that year to develop an exhibition of women photographers for the "Women's International Exposition" in Paris to promote international cooperation. In mid-March 1948 Newhall had been invited by Mary Jane Keeney, chair of the organizing committee of the Congress of American Women (CAW), the U.S. branch of the Women's International Democratic Federation, to serve as chair of the photographers committee. Newhall enlisted Berenice Abbott, Barbara Morgan, and Lisette Model to help quickly organize an exhibition of ten or twelve outstanding women photographers. "What a joy to realize that some of the world's most distinguished photographers happen to be both women and Americans!" Newhall exclaimed.[29] She hoped to persuade Bourke-White to participate, along with Bubley, Dahl-Wolfe, Kanaga, Laura Gilpin, Lange, Levitt, Morgan, and Model. They would each contribute about ten prints of their choosing to make a personal statement that need not address gender.[30] The photography exhibition never materialized at the June 1948 exposition, however: it was canceled by Keeney for lack of funding for fine art shipping and insurance. By contrast, the Camera Club, despite its lingering sexism, served as a reliable and malleable institution for Newhall and Boker to promote the advanced work of women photographers.

In planning the installation of the "Second Women's Invitation Exhibition," Newhall suggested that the gallery could use a bit of sprucing up. The drab walls of the Manhattan townhouse—head-quarters of the photography club since 1907—no longer suited their ambitions for a clean, bright installation appropriate for contemporary photography and the rejuvenation of the organization's program. For one week in August 1948, a team of twenty club members volunteered to paint matte white on the ceiling and gray on the burlap-covered walls of the picture channels, funded by a gift of $500 from an anonymous donor—Boker herself. The board praised the efforts to renovate the gallery, transforming it into an asset. Photography aficionados anticipated the exhibition before it opened on October 31. "Alouise Boker really started something last year when she lined up a 'Ladies Only' show for the Camera Club. The response was so great that she's going to do it again—this time it'll be even better," critic Mildred Stagg wrote in a popular photography magazine.[31] By the time the show opened, however, Nancy Newhall and her partner Beaumont Newhall had moved to Rochester and changed their club membership status from active to non-resident.

Boker took to heart the criticism that the first show overemphasized pictorialist work and devised a new curatorial procedure. Invited artists submitted up to four prints, one of which could be earmarked for exhibition. The rest would be selected by a professional jury that included Beaumont Newhall, photographers D. J. Ruzicka and Helene Saunders, and Mildred Stagg, the "Women in Photography" columnist for *u.s. Camera*. Newhall was quite familiar with the club, having spent hours cataloging its library, which included a number of unique volumes that informed his research for his 1949 book *The History of Photography from 1839 to the Present Day*. Photographer Ruzicka, a longtime club member, was a respected pictorialist. Saunders and Stagg were outspoken advocates for women in photography. Boker and Newhall's invitations, and the jury's selections, resulted in a balanced and thoughtful exhibition. In his *New York Times* review, Deschin approvingly noted the decreased proportion of pictorialists, limited to 10 of the 38 in total, but complained there were still too many baby pictures.[32] To confirm this impression, Tana Hoban's picture *The First Step* (undated), of a toddler, was the one work to illustrate the *Times* review.

There is no known extant list of participants, but contemporary documentation indicates that the show consisted of repeat presenters like Darby and Hatry and first-timers like Nina Leen and Lisette Model. Musya Sheeler presented a portrait of her husband, the painter and former club member Charles Sheeler. (They both attended the opening.[33]) Salon star Custis again traveled from Washington, DC, to the club to lecture on a comparison of her watercolors and photographs. The inclusion of Helen Levitt (1913–2009), whose poised composition *New York* (1938), of boys playing on a stoop in Harlem, as well as other documentarians like Marion Palfi (1907–1978), suggest that Newhall's contribution to the second exhibition added an interest in social documentation. She also introduced Laura Gilpin to Boker, who had seen the aesthetically refined print of *Rio Grande before a Storm* (1945) in Newhall's possession at the start of their research.[34]

The positive media coverage and willing participation of many important artists in the exhibition did not dissuade the club's print committee from terminating the "Women's Invitation" series. Instead of a third edition, they programmed a celebration of the club's 65th anniversary and an exhibition of Bourke-White's photographs from India in May 1949. As for Boker, she stepped down from her position as print director, after breaking another barrier within the club by serving as the first woman to oversee a print critique. "Where's that masculine stronghold that used to be at 121 W. 68th?" quipped the *Notes*.[35]

Six months after the second invitational closed, an all-women photography show appeared in an unexpected place. MOMA opened its first group exhibition dedicated to women photographers, organized by Edward Steichen, who had previously declined to lend publicity to the "Second Invitation" when asked to do so by Newhall. The untitled show—notably eschewing the word "women" in the title—included ten prints each by Bourke-White, Bubley, Hoban, Levitt, Lange, and Hazel-Frieda Larsen (later known as Hazel Larsen Archer). Four of the six had already participated in at least one of the Camera Club invitations. The women were among a larger group of artists invited by the museum to create new images for a poster campaign raising awareness about polio, and the exhibition had the didactic intention of providing the audience with an opportunity to compare commissioned design work and fine art photography. Grouped by artist, the exhibition with only sixty works received less attention in Deschin's *Times* column than did the two Camera Club shows.[36] His review was illustrated by Hoban's picture of a young blonde girl playing with a hoop, which, though appealing, didn't fully represent an exhibition that also included socially conscious imagery such as Lange's migrant workers or Levitt's documents of street life in Mexico.

These three exhibitions by Boker and Steichen—and Newhall's canceled endeavor—stood on a legacy of advocacy by women photographers and centered the work of women without making claims for a particular female sensibility in photography. The "First Women's Invitation Exhibition" boldly advanced the profile of women as a class of photographers in New York and helped to identify a canon of American women photographers later celebrated in feminist exhibitions and publications in the 1970s. At least 8 of the 48 women included in Margery Mann's groundbreaking "Women of Photography: An Historical Survey" at the San Francisco Museum of Modern Art in 1975 were in one of the two Camera Club shows. It was not until the 1980s, however, that scholarship documenting the activities of women of color in photography further expanded the field and began to acknowledge its true diversity.

4

Education: "Ten Women Who Paint," Smith College Museum of Art, 1949

In March 1949, artist Honoré Sharrer (1920–2009) received a "dreamboat chance."[1] Edgar C. Schenck (1909–1959), director of the Smith College Museum of Art in Northampton, Massachusetts, invited her to participate in a celebration of the elite women's college's 75th anniversary by proposing a painting of her choice to hang in a forthcoming exhibition, "Ten Women Who Paint." This contemporary art exhibition joined an anniversary celebration that honored "women distinguished in various fields," as Schenck explained in an invitation letter to Georgia O'Keeffe.[2] That framework inevitably involved artists with national reputations whose work addressed the contemporary life of women. The artists, like the dozen recipients of honorary degrees, were selected for their professional accomplishments. None had graduated from the college: Smith used its anniversary as a platform to celebrate women in general, not Smith women in particular.

Sharrer, who lived 8 miles (13 km) away from Smith in the college town of Amherst, was at the time working on one of her masterpieces, the five-panel polyptych *Tribute to the American Working People* (1951), painted in a precisionist style informed by both Renaissance and Social Realist painting. For the exhibition, Sharrer proposed one of her earlier celebrated works of the same ilk, *Workers and Paintings* (1943), which was in the collection of the Museum of Modern Art. Sharrer instructed Schenck to write to Dorothy C. Miller (1904–2003), curator of contemporary art at the museum: "I am sure they will be pleased to send it to Smith."[3] Her confidence was well placed, as Miller graduated from Smith College in the class of 1925, and had included Sharrer in her second of a series of influential surveys of American contemporary art, "Fourteen Americans," in 1946. The work was unavailable, however, and instead Sharrer asked the college to borrow another picture, *Woman with Pearls* (1946) (see illus. 37). By the time the show opened on October 14, it hung in the company of nine other pieces selected by the other participating artists, a cross-section of three generations of famous American women painters. The exhibition made a statement about both the position of women artists in the late 1940s and the college's history in educating modern and contemporary artists, curators, and critics.

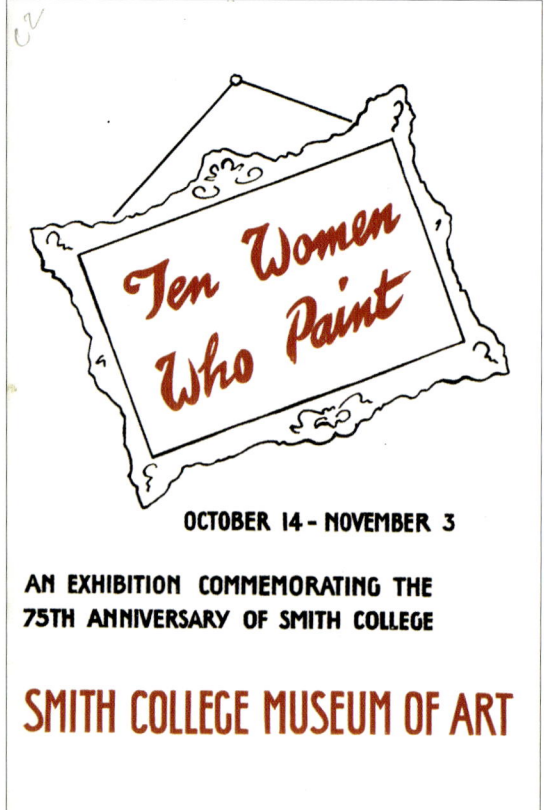

30 Smith College Museum of Art, "Ten Women Who Paint," exhibition catalogue, 1949.

Three years prior to "Ten Women," the architecture department of MOMA organized an exhibition of architectural plans submitted to a design competition for a new dormitory at Smith: a public imagining of the life of a contemporary college woman. The press release spoke in positive tones of building a communal home for young women embracing the modern moment, yet the situation was not so sanguine in the field of women's higher education. In absolute numbers the population of women on college campuses grew steadily after 1945, but the percentage of women among all enrolled students plummeted from a high of 49.8 percent in 1944 to a low of 28.8 percent four years later.[4] The wave of returning male veterans pushed women out of jobs and academic positions—even at women's colleges, where administrators made room for male professors. During this period there was a return to the traditional division of the sexes; women with advanced degrees confronted greater obstacles to obtain or retain a job, and younger female undergraduates became demoralized by their curtailed prospects. Black women faced persistent discrimination in national education bodies, particularly those with Southern chapters that abided by Jim Crow laws to maintain a white membership. Leaders of women's colleges responded to and perpetuated the problem, becoming vocal advocates for colleges to prepare women for work both inside and outside the home. With a rising tide of anti-feminism, women's colleges and other institutions muffled the progressive tone that some had adopted in the 1930s and focused on solving individual problems, not confronting systemic barriers.

Smith conceptualized its anniversary as both a celebration of its accomplishments as a college and as a moment to reflect on the current status of women in Western Europe and North America. The two-day convocation celebrated the installation of a new president and the awarding of honorary degrees to twelve international women of renown. The mood of the ceremony leavened triumph with caution. Benjamin Fletcher Wright, the newly installed Smith College president, lamented, "The place of woman in the present scheme of things is confused and unstable."[5] The following day, female Nobel Prize winners, high-ranking government officials, and women's rights activists from the USA, France, Denmark, the Netherlands, and Mexico received honorary degrees. One of them, former First Lady Eleanor Roosevelt, began her remarks by recounting that she would have loved to attend college but her grandmother, who raised her, forbade it. She ended on a hopeful note, citing the recent adoption by the United Nations of the Universal Declaration of Human Rights (UDHR), for which she served as committee chair, as a promise for women as individuals under the human rights umbrella that "all men are born free and equal in the dignity of human rights."[6]

The exhibition took place in the museum's Tryon Gallery, a neo-Georgian-style brick edifice at the center of campus. Through the vestibule one arrived on the long side of a skylit hall, flanked by a trio of galleries. The intimate proportions, unadorned walls, and natural light promoted thoughtful contemplation of artistic masterworks. A print study room in the basement supplemented the art teaching curriculum. One could call the gallery an archetypical university museum with the dual purpose of serving the student body and edifying a larger public audience. Opened in 1926, the gallery continued the college's vision since the 1870s to incorporate fine arts in the liberal arts curriculum: "the ideal of the cultured woman [that President Seelye] wished the College to produce meant the inclusion of the fine arts in her education."[7] Smith, like Wellesley, Vassar, and other elite women's colleges in the northeastern United States, was among the first institutions of higher education to establish on-campus art museums and art departments, a prioritizing of the liberal arts and humanities that distinguished them from seminaries and normal schools. Women's colleges played an essential role in educating women artists, curators, and art historians as undergraduates on campus and providing networks to support their professional development and contacts. But an exhibition of women artists was a departure for Smith. Since its founding in 1920, the museum had organized few notable solo shows of women, such as a memorial for Mary Cassatt in 1928.

An all-male museum leadership team and jury selected the ten artists. Outgoing director Schenck, who departed Smith before the opening to become the director of the Albright Art Gallery in Buffalo, New York, worked together with incoming director Henry-Russell Hitchcock, a historian of modern architecture (he coined the term "International Style"). The two men were advised by three Smith faculty members—art department painting instructors Mervin Jules and George Cohen, and art historian Oliver Larkin, a specialist in American art who later won a Pulitzer Prize. In their catalogue foreword, Schenck and Hitchcock outlined the conceptual limitations of the institutional context:

An exhibition in which the sex of the artist is a limiting factor would have little meaning were it not for the framework of the Seventy-fifth Anniversary of Smith College of which this is a part. Smith, who has taught young women the history and practice of art almost from its beginning, has chosen this time to honor distinguished achievements of women in many different fields.[8]

The illustration on the catalogue cover articulated the uncertain place of women in U.S. society at this time (illus. 30). The handwritten title of the show is presented within an ornate picture frame, suspended by a wire. The illustrator, Myrtle Affhauser Willard (1918–2006), drew the frame askew, as if it had been haphazardly hung from a nail and abandoned, waiting to be leveled. The off-balance image of women's art may have emerged from Willard's personal experience as a Smith College graduate (class of 1939). According to her obituary, she considered moving to New York and pursuing a career as an artist but decided to remain in Northampton. She worked at the museum as assistant to the director for much of the 1940s before leaving to raise her children, then returned to the museum as a photographer. Willard's efforts to integrate a career as a freelance illustrator with marriage and motherhood visualized the challenges of the era, when many women artists opted to minimize domestic duties. The artists in "Ten Women" with consistent success—Georgia O'Keeffe, Isabel Bishop, Irene Rice Pereira, Loren MacIver, and Perle Fine—enjoyed productive and mutually beneficial marriages with men, but never had children. Their career paths contradicted the college's postwar messaging to its students about harmonizing professional ambition and women's traditional childrearing responsibilities.

The tilted curatorial frame resulted in a rather narrowly drawn demographic of women artists. Nine were born in the United States, and one, Ruth Gikow, immigrated at age five. As Smith College is located in western Massachusetts, there was a distinctly New England flavor to the show, with three artists (Pereira, Esther Geller, and Fine) born in Boston and one (Sharrer) residing in nearby Amherst. The artists were raised in various regions across the country, and most moved to New York City and obtained art instruction at the Art Students League. Curiously for an exhibition meant to celebrate women's accomplishments within the context of higher education, only one artist, Doris Lee, graduated from a liberal arts college (Rockford College, Illinois), and two others, O'Keeffe and Sharrer, completed coursework at universities (Teachers College of Columbia University and Yale University, respectively). None studied for any considerable time in Europe. A similar numerical and geographic formula appeared in a related exhibition at the museum, "75 Books by 75 American Women"; the display was restricted to one book by one American per year, "somewhat arbitrary limitations," as college librarian Margaret L. Johnson admitted in the catalogue.[9] The national restriction of both museum projects offset the college's global perspective in celebrating women's efforts to promote democracy and freedom.

No artists of color were invited to participate in the show; they remained outside the prestige system of white institutions and were largely underrepresented in the realm of elite women's higher education. The National Association for the Advancement of Colored People (NAACP) national secretary Walter White—the subject of a Reyneau portrait in the Harmon Foundation exhibition (see Chapter Two)—had to negotiate with the Smith College president to permit his daughter, Jane White, to matriculate in the class of 1944. The American Association of University Women (AAUW) rarely admitted Black women as members, so educator Mary Church Terrell (another subject of a Reyneau portrait) co-founded a new group, the National Association of College Women, in 1923 and later successfully pushed to integrate AAUW's chapter in Washington, DC, in 1949. Black women found opportunities at historically Black universities like Howard in Washington, DC, which educated or employed Alma Thomas, Loïs Mailou Jones, and Elizabeth Catlett, among other artists. Scholar Linda Eisenmann noted that in the postwar years, white women received mixed messages about their innate abilities and professional prospects, but Black women had no illusions that there were places waiting for them in mainstream American education and society.[10] A 1964 sociological study of women in academia found it inconceivable that Black women would be college faculty. One chart referenced only the white birth rate to illustrate the reduced proportion of female faculty due to the impact of the rising pressure on women to have children.[11]

The exhibition's offer that the artists select their own work was a common feature of all-women and other invited exhibitions, but not one typically offered to artists by curators with their own cultivated standards of quality and importance. In the same spirit as Alouise Boker's Camera Club exhibition (see Chapter Three), Schenck invited the artists to "choose the work by which you feel yourself best represented—that is, the one that 'came off' best in your painting career."[12] The artists, many of whom averred in acceptance letters that they were honored to be invited to participate, proposed mostly recent works from their studios or on consignment with their galleries. The opportunity for artists to select their own work reinforced their individuality, indicating that their work would not be wedged into any curatorial agenda or aesthetic argument. The size of the allotted gallery prevented the museum from organizing a more comprehensive survey and limited artists to proposing small works. The largest canvas was only 55 inches (140 cm) wide.

Abstract painting had become a vital movement in contemporary American art by the mid-1940s, with group exhibitions coalescing what would soon become the dominant new Abstract Expressionist style. The Smith College Museum team played it safe, however, and selected living artists primarily working in varied figural modes. All-women shows of the 1940s, other than Peggy Guggenheim's experimental exhibitions, favored the familiar tropes of the American Scene and School of Paris. In the Detroit Institute of Arts's annual exhibition of 1943, which featured exclusively women artists, all fourteen painters worked in representational styles. Similarly, landscapes, still-lifes, and portraits dominated an exhibition of works by 26 women artists in the Phillips collection mounted at a women's club in Nashville in 1948. Both shows included works by Isabel Bishop (1902–1988) and Doris Lee (1905–1983), two of the most popular and accomplished contemporary figural artists of the 1940s, with distinctive styles, engaging subject-matter, and extensive professional credits. Both were selected for "Ten Women," and each chose works already in museum collections, purchased the year after their completion. Lee's faux naive landscape *Country Wedding* (1942) (illus. 31), borrowed from the Albright Art Gallery, is replete with narrative incident and visual interest, centered on a wooden church with Gothic windows. Bishop's depiction of urban working women, *Ice Cream Cones* (1942) (illus. 32), was borrowed from the Museum of Fine Arts, Boston, which had purchased it for $900. A 1943 article in *ARTnews* marveled at the success of Bishop, whose work had entered thirteen national

31 Doris Lee, *Country Wedding*, 1942, oil on canvas.

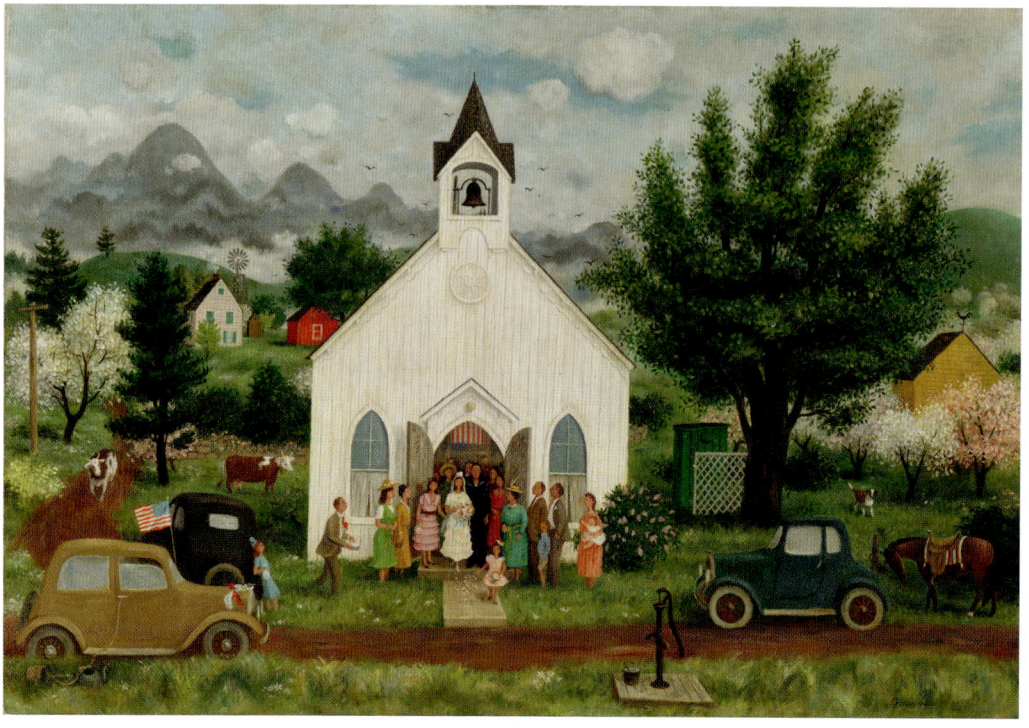

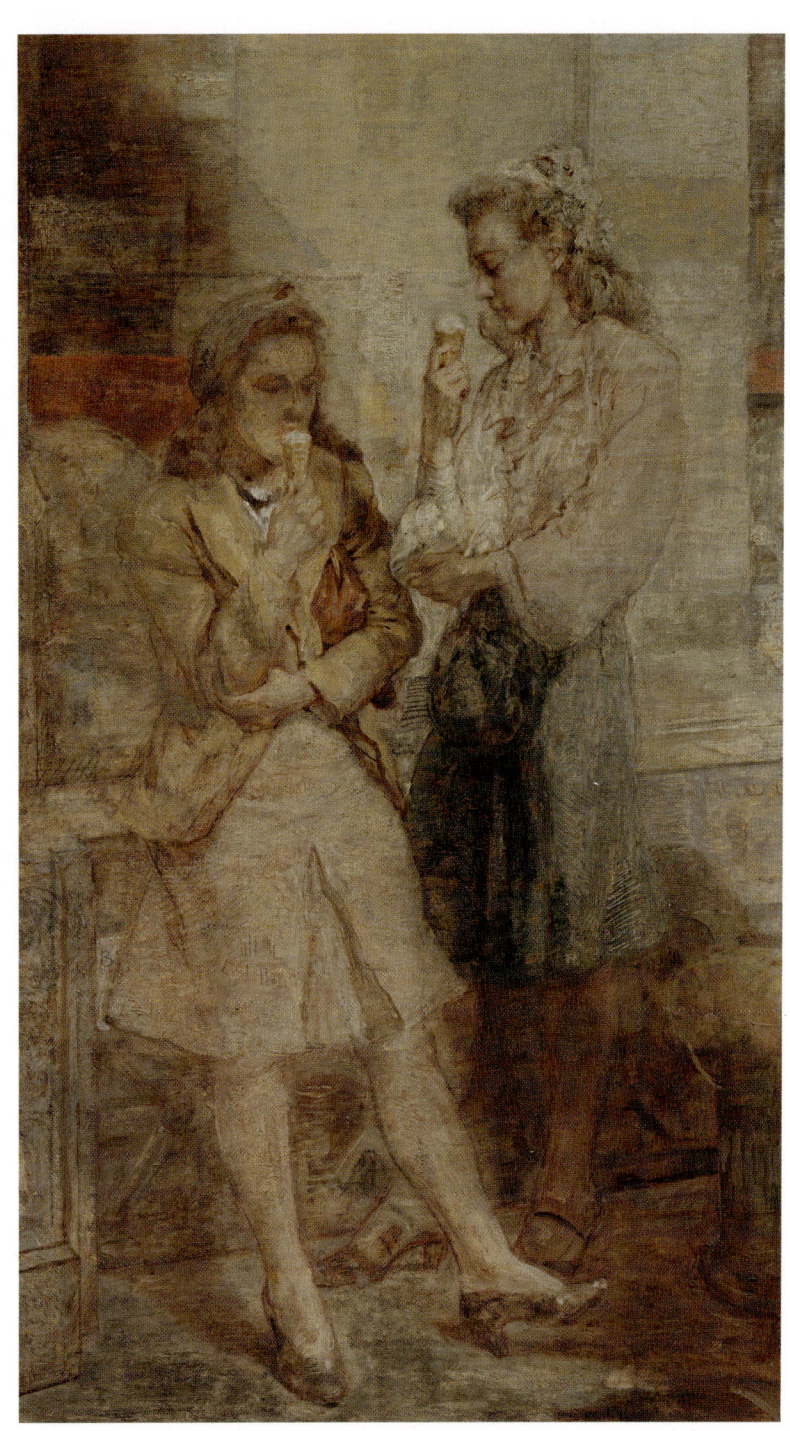

32 Isabel Bishop, *Ice Cream Cones*, 1942, oil and egg tempera on fiberboard.

museum collections and won a prize from the American Academy of Arts and Letters.[13] The Smith exhibition built on these established trends, highlighting leading women aligned with the styles that had remained popular in the United States since the 1930s, and avoiding the unsettling Surrealism of artists like Kay Sage and Dorothea Tanning.

The most unexpected selection might have been Elizabeth Sparhawk-Jones (1885–1968), a once-lauded artist who had dropped out of the art world for several decades before reviving her career as a painter of dreamlike imagery. Trained at the Pennsylvania Academy of the Fine Arts, she initially painted in a brushy Impressionism in the manner of

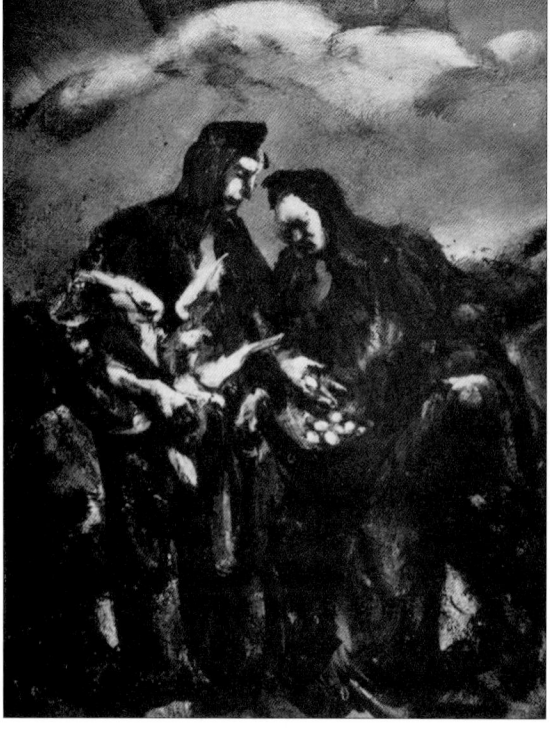

33 Elizabeth Sparhawk-Jones, *The Old Maids*, 1947, watercolor on canvas.

Cecilia Beaux and William Merritt Chase and rose to prominence in the early twentieth century. Her *Shop Girls* (*c.* 1912), depicting the modern subject of urban, independent women in bright colors with sanguine gestures, was the first painting by a woman to be purchased for the Art Institute of Chicago by the Friends of American Art. Soon, however, challenges with mental health arrested Sparhawk-Jones's ascent. When she resumed painting and exhibiting several decades later, her style had shifted markedly to obscure narrative compositions. The venerable Frank K. M. Rehn Galleries of New York City began showing her new work in the late 1930s, reinserting her mysterious paintings and watercolors into an American art world newly intrigued by images of the fantastic. "Strange that she is not recognized far and wide as among the ablest, most distinguished women painters in the United States," pondered a critic in *American Artist* magazine in 1944.[14]

The painting Sparhawk-Jones selected for "Ten Women" was titled *The Old Maids* (1947) (illus. 33), which she deemed "one of my best."[15] The watercolor on canvas, 28 inches (71 cm) high, depicts two cloaked figures, heads leaning toward each other in conversation or commiseration, one of them gesturing at the basket of fruit or eggs displayed by the other. The elliptical imagery and murky passages recall Goya's "Black Paintings," with their perplexing depictions of mysticism and arcane symbolism. *The Old Maids* appeared in the artist's 1947 Rehn solo show, where it was praised in ARTnews.[16] After Smith, the work traveled to Louisiana for a contemporary art exhibition organized by the Central Louisiana Art Association. One local critic lauded its "rugged strength that seemed to grow with one's familiarity with the picture."[17] Sparhawk-Jones's work possessed a seductive, visionary quality reminiscent of Albert Pinkham Ryder and a noirish viscosity shared by her friend Marsden Hartley. As she had been working at the margins of American art for over three decades, the title and subject-matter might be a commentary on a stereotype of the sexless single woman, traditionally an abject figure existing outside the dominant narratives encoded by male sexual desire.

If Sparhawk-Jones was the exhibition's forgotten great woman artist, then Georgia O'Keeffe was the show's most celebrated one. O'Keeffe initially worked as an itinerant art teacher until garnering attention as a modernist for chromatic near-abstractions championed by photographer and art dealer Alfred Stieglitz—her future husband—after they met in 1915. The painting she selected for the Smith show, *Ram's Head, White Hollyhock, New Mexico* (1935) (illus. 34), depicted a skull, flower, and desert landscape: icons from her precisionist vocabulary. The centralized composition forestalls intimacy and invests the imagery with a totemic power. The fact that O'Keeffe agreed to participate in the Smith show complicates her position vis-à-vis all-women exhibitions. She had famously rejected Guggenheim's offer to become one of the "31 Women" yet became personally involved in "Ten Women"; correspondence from her business agent Doris Bry shows the artist's concern for the disposition of the painting after the closing.[18] O'Keeffe had recently relocated to the New Mexico high desert, where she achieved a new phase of independence and authority. In 1946 her solo exhibition at the Museum of Modern Art—the museum's first retrospective of a woman (there had been several previous solo presentations of discrete bodies of work by women)—sealed her position as the preeminent living woman artist in the United States.

The retrospective prompted numerous reviews that assessed O'Keeffe's career in the larger context of the history of women in modern art. An article in *Independent Woman*, the official publication of the National Federation of Business and Professional Women's

34 Georgia O'Keeffe, *Ram's Head, White Hollyhock, New Mexico*, 1935, oil on canvas.

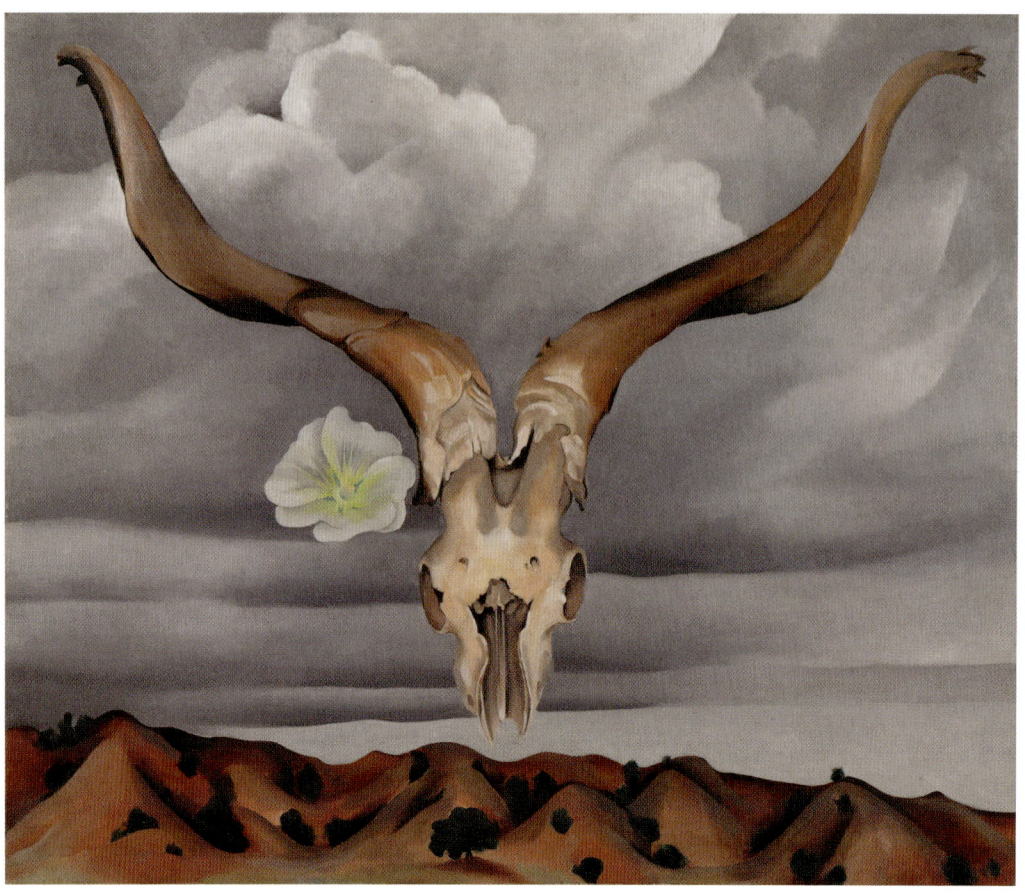

Clubs, evaluated O'Keeffe among eleven other artists, including three others in the Smith show—Lee, Bishop, and Pereira—using metrics like prizes, exhibitions, and museum purchases to compare the achievements of women artists in midcentury America.[19] O'Keeffe scored highest on the list, as determined by her MOMA show, honorary degree from the College of William & Mary, and the high prices of her work, such as $10,000 reportedly paid by Elizabeth Arden for a flower painting. James Thrall Soby (1906–1979), a MOMA curator, also published an appraisal of women in contemporary American art on the occasion of O'Keeffe's retrospective, titled "To the Ladies," a reference to Abigail Adams's directive to her husband, the future second U.S. president John Adams, in 1776. Soby's aesthetic assessment of women's progress began with the celebrated nineteenth-century painter and printmaker Mary Cassatt (1844–1926) as the definitive case study of the importance of individualization for American women to command respect in modern art: "women artists have usually taken their point of departure from men, yet many of them have achieved a fairly quick and complete independence."[20] In Soby's estimation, Cassatt's heirs to this legacy of female innovation were three contemporary American artists: O'Keeffe, Pereira, and MacIver.

In the late 1940s, non-objective painter Pereira and poetic imagist MacIver (1909–1998) were recognized by critics and curators in New York modernist circles as the leading women artists of their generation, following the trail blazed by Cassatt and O'Keeffe. "I know of no better younger American artists in their separate directions," Soby wrote in *Harper's Bazaar*.[21] From about 1945 to 1955, critics and curators fused the two women into a dyadic exemplar of the contemporary woman artist. Indeed, Pereira and MacIver shared lyrical, almost romantic tendencies in their imagery and thinking. Stylistically, however, they completely diverged, with Pereira working in a geometric non-objective idiom and MacIver developing a distinguished figural symbolism. Dorothy C. Miller selected them as two of the three women (the other was Sharrer) in "Fourteen Americans." And in 1948 both artists joined an eclectic group of 79 U.S. artists, from regionalist Grant Wood to budding Abstract Expressionist Mark Rothko, representing the United States in the Venice Biennale (for which Miller served on the four-person curatorial team).

For "Ten Women," Pereira lent an emblematic painting, *Vacillating Progression* (1949) (illus. 35), from her studio. The vibrant image, 28 inches (71 cm) high, represented her long-standing interest in using light and color to investigate scientific and spiritual realms. The work is constructed with three superimposed planes: a bottom layer of gesso painted with casein and two overlapping glass planes painted with oil and plastic paint. In this way, Pereira invented new ways to maximize the luminosity of paint by empirically experimenting with different supports and perspectives. "I have tried to achieve results by developing a working process using the medium itself rather than by creating an illusionistic interpretation," she said in an artist statement in *ARTnews* in 1947.[22] These concrete methods had interested her since 1935 when she co-founded the Federal Art Project's Design Laboratory, which emulated the Bauhaus's experimentation with non-traditional techniques and materials. She exhibited in a wide range of galleries in the late 1930s and early 1940s, including Howard University, the Surrealism-oriented Julien Levy Gallery, and Art of This Century, testifying to her central position as a leading abstract artist.

For the exhibition at Smith, MacIver opted for *The City* (1941) (illus. 36), a composition that had been previously shown in "Fourteen Americans" and illustrated in its catalogue. Composed of small vignettes of people, cars, packages, and signs, rendered in approximately equal sizes, the scene unfolds in a nearly gridlike pattern, suggestive of an all-over painting. The imagery, painted in muted shades of gray, is plainly legible in the canvas' abstract design, powerfully creating a non-narrative structure. In this, MacIver accomplished her stated goal of compressing the scene into mood: "In the catalyzing air of evening a city and its traffic merge; it is as if all the events of wheels and people, cobbling it, had left upon the avenue of their passing a stain of

35 Irene Rice Pereira, *Vacillating Progression*, 1949, three planes: two glass with oil and plastic paint, one casein paint on gesso.

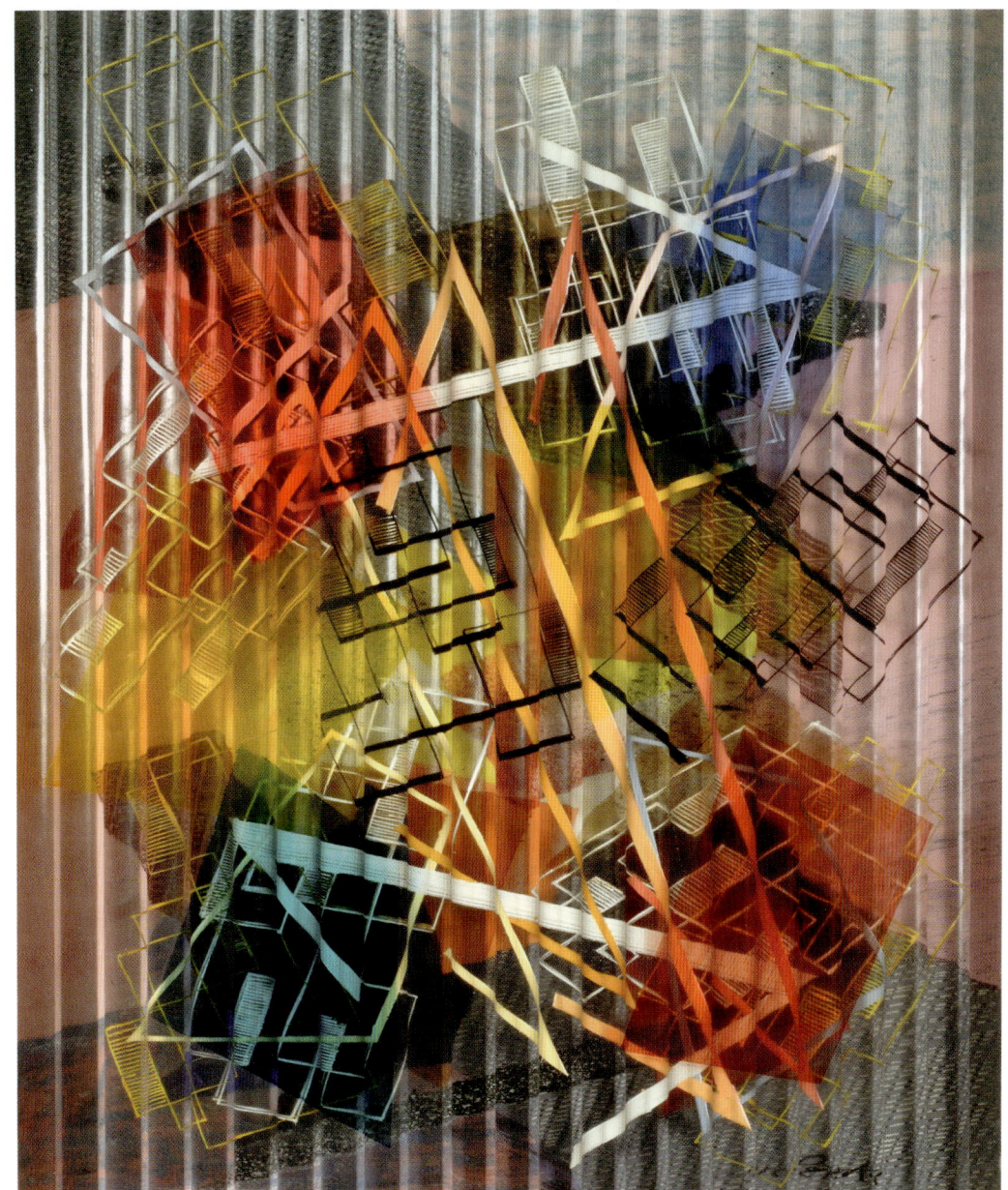

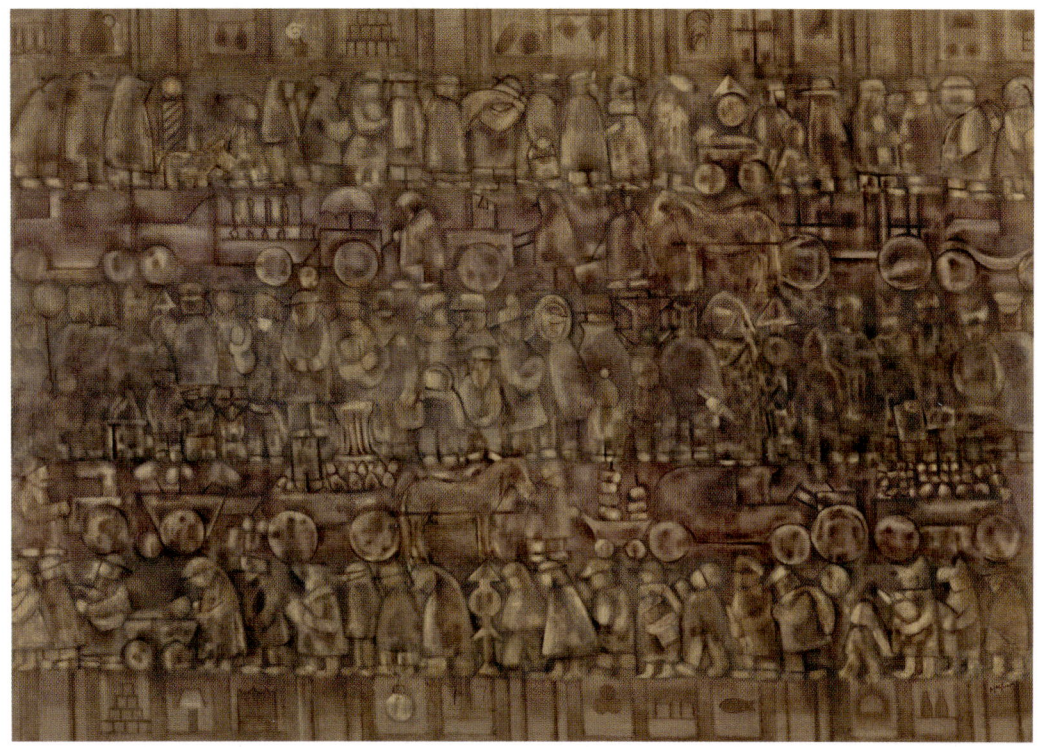

circumstance."[23] MacIver's poetics, according to many critics, embodied what art should be: an elegant and entrancing distillation of the visible world.

36 Loren MacIver, *The City*, 1941, oil on canvas.

Following the Smith exhibition, Pereira and MacIver attained conjoined status in two two-person museum exhibitions: the first, "Paintings: Loren MacIver and Irene Rice Pereira," originated at the Santa Barbara Museum of Art in 1950 with fifteen paintings, and the second, "Loren MacIver, I. Rice Pereira," an expanded version with sixty works, opened at the Whitney Museum of American Art in 1953. In total, these shows appeared in over half a dozen venues. The second iteration prompted Soby to revisit the topic of American women artists. With Pereira and MacIver at the fore, "women have made such conquests that they feel free to be wholly themselves in public expressions of thought and emotion, to be artists without shame or envy, adulation or fear," he proclaimed in "Again, to the Ladies!"[24] An art world unwilling to bestow solitary "genius" laurels upon women relied on their shared gender to celebrate their individual accomplishments.

Honoré Sharrer, frequently curated with Pereira and MacIver, imbued her representational paintings with political consciousness and satire. She published drawings of workers in the early 1940s, such as her illustrated article in the socialist magazine *People's World* about a Black woman welder facing sex and race discrimination in Oakland shipyards and housing. She also became known for intricately detailed multi-panel paintings of everyday life influenced by the Renaissance. For Smith, Sharrer arranged for a beguiling self-portrait to be borrowed from her parents in California. *Woman with Pearls* (1946) (illus. 37) was originally painted for the La Tausca Pearl Company's art competition, in which it won a prize, despite slyly playing on morbid tropes of the vanitas genre. An inscrutable woman, based on a photographic self-portrait, caresses a strand of cultured pearls arranged on a narrow shelf in the foreground near an empty bird's nest. Media attention to

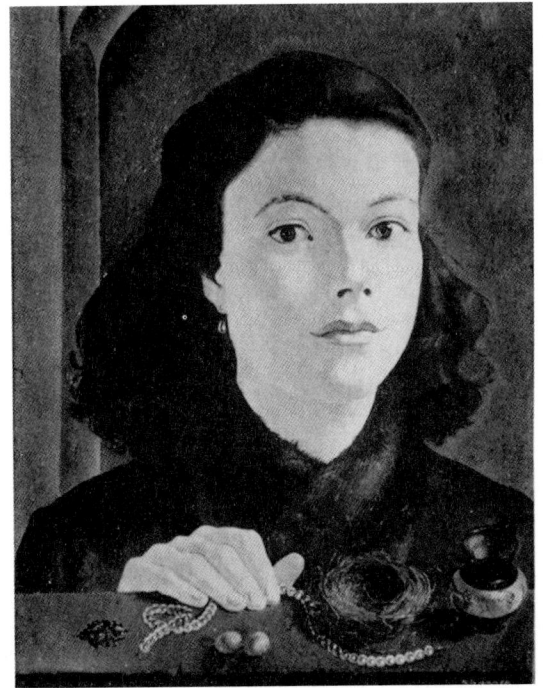

37 Honoré Sharrer, *Woman with Pearls*, 1946, oil on canvas.

Sharrer's career peaked in the early 1950s when she first exhibited *Tribute to the American Working People*, the subject of a photo essay in *Life* and an enviable "Paints a Picture" feature in *ARTnews*.[25] After this high point of recognition, however, Sharrer's style of magical realism fell out of favor. Though she continued to paint, she did not have another solo exhibition until 1969.

Consistent with this aesthetic, the Smith show leaned heavily toward representational artists who blended contemporary subject-matter with traditional techniques and materials. The youngest artist in "Ten Women," Esther Geller (1921–2015), was born in Boston, studied at the School of the Museum of Fine Arts, and became part of a group of artists, dubbed the Boston School, who blended French modernism and American social commentary. The work Geller selected for the Smith exhibition, *Rebec Player* (1947) (illus. 38), depicts a Cubist-derived expressionist figure painted in encaustic on board. Geller and other Boston peers opened up a new set of plastic possibilities for painting by reviving the anachronistic medium. Another work in "Ten Women," Ruth Gikow's *Pigalle Musicians* (1948), also evokes the continuing influence of the School of Paris on American artists.

In general, the works selected for "Ten Women" display a conspicuous degree of craft and finish. Traditional museum-goers respected abstract art so long as it politely demonstrated considerable workmanship, which partly accounts for the popularity of Pereira's well-constructed multi-plane paintings. The other artist with an abstract painting in "Ten Women," however, pushed against these conventions of refined taste. Perle Fine loaned an abstract canvas, *Pink Harlequin* (1948) (illus. 39), which she selected from her newest body of work presented at the Betty Parsons Gallery in New York that spring. A student of Hans Hofmann, Fine passed through a number of phases of abstraction, from Cubism to non-objectivity, before arriving at a personal version of gestural geometry. Also titled *Pink Troubadour*, the painting's central figure, splintered into numerous planes, provoked a critical debate over fragmenting an image past the point of "comprehension" when it was on view at Parsons.[26] The month before the Smith opening, Fine gave a talk at Forum 49, a modernist speaker series in a Provincetown gallery, on formal principles of abstraction.

The works in "Ten Women Who Paint" hung silently in the gallery without the presence of their makers, none of whom are known to have attended the opening festivities. The second exhibition, "75 Books by 75 American Women" at the Tryon Gallery, supplied additional sociological, historical, and creative contexts for the paintings. The Smith librarians selected only three books by visual artists (none painters, all highly accomplished in their respective fields): an illustrated memoir

38 Esther Geller, *Rebec Player*, 1947, encaustic on pressed wood board.

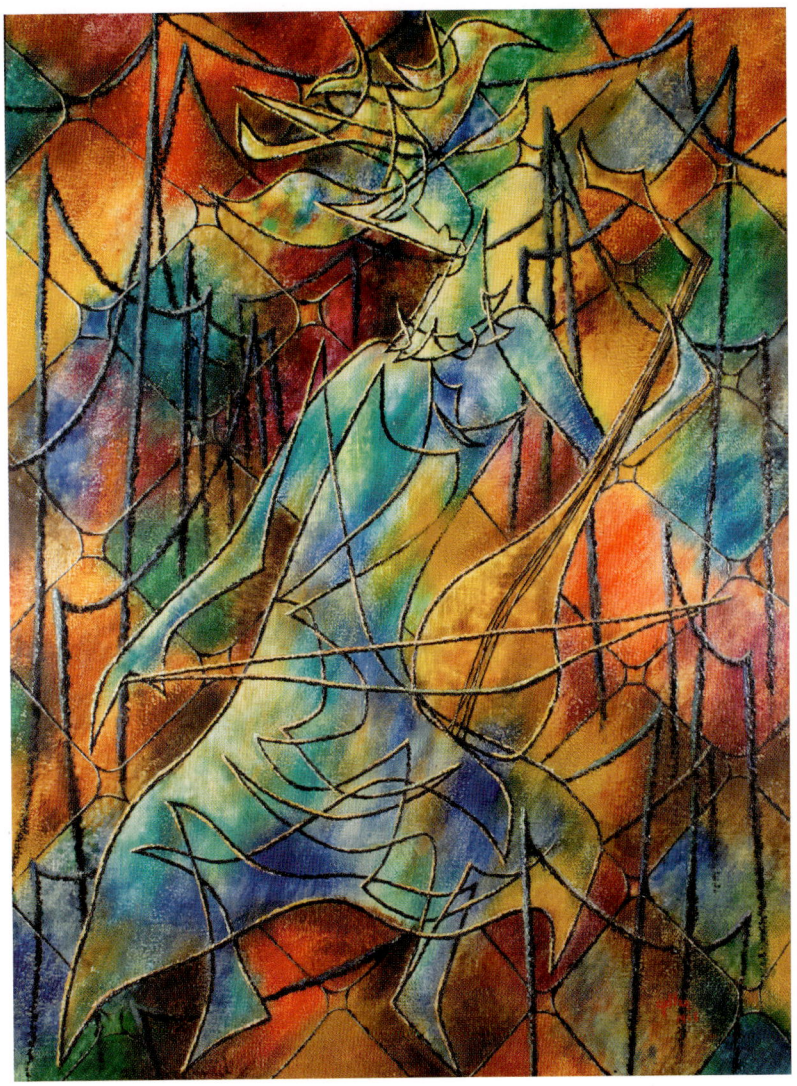

by sculptor Malvina Hoffman, a photo essay (*Say, Is This the USA*) by Margaret Bourke-White, and a compendium of illustrations by Mary Petty. Also included were groundbreaking studies of women's history such as Mary Ritter Beard's *Woman as Force in History* (1946), Kate Campbell Hurd-Mead's *Medical Women of America* (1933), and Sophie Drinker's *Music and Women* (1948).[27] None were by women of color. Nearly all of the books came from Smith's library, which had recently established the Sophia Smith Collection dedicated to women writers and women's history. Both "Ten Women" and "75 Books" are reminders that traditional women's colleges were making progress but still had much work to do in training scholars and building museum and library collections dedicated to the study of women's lives and creativity.

The museum's attention to distinguished individual achievement sidelined new documentation of the pervasive structural gender gap in U.S. art. Smith alumna Elizabeth McCausland had recently published a quantitative analysis of the income and professional standing of artists in the United States.[28] She found that about 15 percent

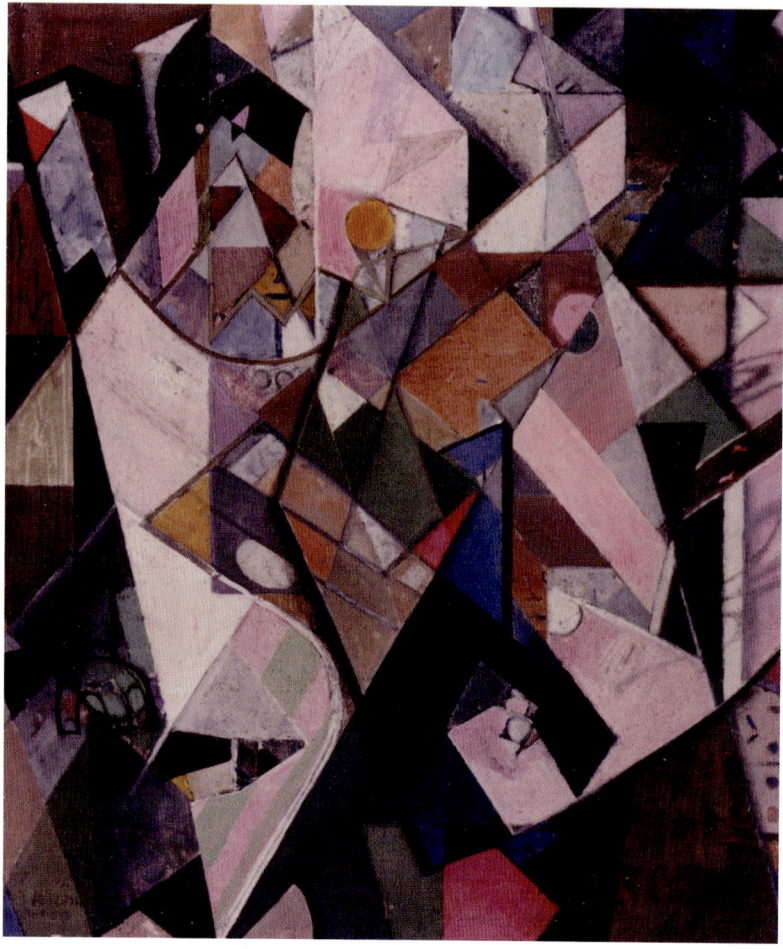

39 Perle Fine,
Pink Harlequin,
1948, oil on canvas.

of the five hundred leading artists in the United States, based on the empirical measurement of participation in national annual exhibitions, were women. Examining data from questionnaires received from about two hundred artists, McCausland documented the gross gender disparity, with women on average earning less than half of their male peers in both total income and art sales. Women acquired as many years of education, worked as hard, and exhibited as frequently, but they also bore the added burden of overcoming sex discrimination and keeping a household and family, she concluded. Isabel Bishop, likely one of the higher scorers in McCausland's rubric, elsewhere explained that even for women artists who gained some success, socioeconomic inequities persisted. "Once the girl has jumped from the amateur into the professional art field, a small private income is still a handy thing to have around, Miss Bishop maintains," wrote a reporter in the *Washington Post*.[29] Bishop's assumption of the necessity of privilege, and McCausland's critique of the unpaid labor of women artists, addressed the complex economic and social challenges faced by women artists.

"Ten Women Who Paint," an exhibition of ten paintings on view for two weeks, did not generate any critical reviews. The college's public relations strategy embedded the exhibition, along with "75 Books," within the larger campus-wide celebration of the present prospects of Smith as part of the larger ecosystem that can take some credit for women's impressive recent accomplishments in science, education, and politics. The *New York Times Magazine* ran a long article by Helen Markel Herrmann (class of 1940) surveying the college's history, and concluded that progress was measured by the fact that the class of 1950 believed that if "a home is no longer a full-time job, it is still a woman's most important one."[30] This statement effectively captured the paradoxical language around elite white women's education in midcentury America, which focused on empowering women to make informed choices to direct their own lives, without addressing the psychological and institutional discrimination that created obstacles to advancement or discouraged them from pursuing a professional path.

The museum's outreach to a high-caliber roster of contemporary artists and galleries, and notices about the exhibition in national art magazines, represented a tangible step in the college bolstering its contemporary art program and extending some much-needed resources to women artists. The museum, which remained under the directorship of Henry-Russell Hitchcock until 1955, expanded acquisitions of contemporary art. A high-powered advisory panel of experts and alumnae called the Visiting Committee—which included Soby and Miller along with Agnes Mongan (a Smith master's degree graduate and the first female curator at Harvard University's Fogg Art Museum)—helped plan the 25th anniversary celebrations of the museum's Tryon Gallery in 1951. Hitchcock wisely engaged Miller, who also facilitated long-term loans of Impressionist masterworks, and acquisitions by gift or purchase of several important modern paintings by American women, including Fine's *Silver Night* (1950), Pereira's *Inverted Light* (1949), and Florine Stettheimer's *Henry McBride, Art Critic* (1922). The museum organized a posthumous retrospective of Stettheimer's paintings in 1952.

Miller was one of several Smith graduates who impacted the mid-century American art world, others of whom included Elizabeth McCausland (class of 1920), leading New York art dealer Martha Jackson (class of 1928), and Nancy Newhall (class of 1930). Smith and other women's colleges played an outsized role in the training of women curators, collectors, and critics. In 1959 Vassar College economics professor Mabel Newcomer published a landmark study of the impact of women's colleges, relying on a broad range of statistics gleaned from public records. Scrutinizing the listings in *Who's Who in America*, an annual publication of notables, she found that graduates of eight elite women's colleges were significantly overrepresented among all female scholars, writers, and scientists.[31] Graduates of women's colleges had a leg up on other female aspirants to work in the art world, in part because of their economic privilege, their exposure to art on campus, and their social networks.

An education at an elite women's college potentially gave a pro-spective critic or curator a career boost, but the results were more mixed for studio art students. Alice Morgan Wright (1881–1975), Smith class of 1904, became a celebrated sculptor and suffragist. But decades later, Newcomer discovered that a college education played a negligible role in the real economy of the visual and performing arts.[32] Women seeking training and professional prospects in the arts gravitated to artist-led art schools or private study. Several talented young artists passed through Smith's studio classes before transferring out to obtain intensive train-ing elsewhere. Eleanor de Laittre (1911–1998) studied painting at Smith in 1929 but left before graduating to study at the School of the Museum of Fine Arts in Boston. Joan Mitchell (1925–1992) attended Smith for two years before returning to her hometown in 1944 to complete her BFA at the School of the Art Institute of Chicago. The same year, Japanese American artist Miyoko Ito (1918–1983) transferred to the School of the Art Institute of Chicago after two years as a graduate stu-dent at Smith; she found the program at Smith to be lacking, although it offered a safe harbor from internment with her family during the Second World War. Sylvia Plath (1932–1963) entered Smith in 1950 as a prospective studio art student and took painting and drawing classes with Mervin Jules and others, before switching her major to English and devoting herself to poetry.

Considering all the uncertainty around educating young women to be experimental artists, "Ten Women" reflected the cautious approach that women's colleges used to organize all-women exhibitions at midcentury. These few exhibitions favored professional accomplish-ment and were typically organized by male directors or curators. The Weatherspoon Gallery (now Art Museum) of the Woman's College of the University of North Carolina (UNC) Greensboro mounted an exhibition of works by contemporary women painters and sculptors in December 1950. Selected by Gregory Ivy, the chair of the art depart-ment, the show included New York artists with growing reputations, like Perle Fine and Louise Nevelson, as well as Southern artists Gwyn

Ferris, Maxine Gatewood, and Hazel McKinley. In 1954, the University of Michigan Museum of Art organized two women-themed exhibitions as components of an interdisciplinary summer program investigating "Woman in the World of Man." The elementary intellectual framework—which asked, "Does prejudice against women exist today?"—revealed the significant learning curve of a public research university that had established quotas limiting women's enrollment to make room for male Second World War veterans. Museum director Jean Paul Slusser and art professor Thomas J. Larkin curated an exhibition from the museum's collection with art depicting women and paintings by women. They also organized a contemporary art show, "Three Women Painters: Irene Rice Pereira, Kay Sage, Dorothea Tanning." Pereira played the starring role, participating in the interdisciplinary panel "The Artist's Values and Perspectives" and lecturing on "Women and Dimensions in Art." The typescript is preserved in her papers, and it is worth quoting one passage at length:

> One is constantly shocked into the realization that this inner world can only be preserved by understanding some of the problems that relate to the social conditions of the present. Once a woman ventures outside the traditional preoccupations with a family, she is confronted with this masculine world of objective statements, facts, aggression, competition, thinking, and logic. The role of this kind of a woman is very difficult and presents a dilemma; because, while participating in the objective, masculine world, she still must preserve her femininity or her personality suffers from the conflict.[33]

In delineating psychological and behavioral differences between men and women, Pereira accepts the category of "woman artist" as distinct from "artist." Interestingly, ten years earlier, a different Pereira lecture at Smith College avoided the topic of sex entirely, hewing to a closely argued philosophical and formal comparison between Renaissance and modern art. The Michigan program provided a platform for women to present and discuss art that directly addressed women at a time when contemporary society was largely unconcerned with the roles that education could play in the training and support of women artists.

Some women's colleges took proactive approaches to empowering women to oversee its art program. Vassar College, located in Poughkeepsie, New York, named its first female president, Sarah Gibson Blanding, in 1946. Unlike the male-dominated art department and museum of Smith, Vassar's art department and gallery were directed by Agnes Rindge Claflin (1900–1977), well known as a champion of women in the arts, through the 1940s and '50s. She hired Concetta Scaravaglione (1900–1975)—a noted figural sculptor who became the first female resident of the American Academy in Rome—as an art professor. The gallery organized solo exhibitions of Loren MacIver in 1950, Grace Hartigan in 1954, and Hedda Sterne in 1956. Nevertheless, by the 1950s the culture of Vassar had lost some of its feminist edge. Then-undergraduate (and later feminist art historian) Linda Nochlin (1931–2017), class of 1951, recalled that she was in the minority of students who did not aspire toward marriage and housewifery, and who admired Scaravaglione as a role model as an independent creative woman.[34]

At the experimental all-women Bennington College in Vermont, E. C. Goossen (1920–1997), a follower of critic Clement Greenberg's brand of formalist interpretation, curated "Nine Women Painters" in 1953. The show included work by recent alumna Helen Frankenthaler (1928–2011) (class of 1949) and offered an early appraisal of women painting in the Abstract Expressionist style. Unlike Smith's "Ten Women," with its two abstract painters, all the artists in Bennington's "Nine Women" painted in various modes of gestural abstraction. Three of the artists showed with the Betty Parsons Gallery, then still in its avant-garde prime: Fine, Sonja Sekula, and Sterne. Many were regulars in the Stable Gallery annual exhibitions in New York, which evolved out of the now legendary "9th St. Show" of 1951. Goossen's exhibition text for "Nine Women Painters" focused on the purely visual qualities of the work, argued that modern artists should function outside of politics, and refrained from speculation on the significance of gender in art, ignoring the framework imposed by the title and roster.[35] The focus on emerging artists working in advanced abstract styles contrasted with the Smith museum's preference for established artists primarily working in figural styles.

Smith, Vassar, UNC Greensboro, and Bennington all served female students and alumnae, but none of their all-women shows took a sociological stance and specifically addressed the situation of women in midcentury America. Only a handful of the artists in these all-women shows at women's colleges modeled the importance of undergraduate training and bachelor's degrees in their artistic maturation. Most of the featured artists' careers reified the conventional wisdom that all artists, and especially women, had to forge their own paths to success in postwar America. If women's colleges in general did not play a decisive role in the formative studio education of visual artists, they periodically gave professional artists a much-needed public platform, advancing individual careers and creating opportunities for conversations about women in the arts. By analyzing their work and tracing the artists' routes to and through the Smith exhibition, one can see how eager critics and audiences were to anoint a few women to the top rank of American art at the expense of collective activism.

"Ten Women Who Paint," notwithstanding its small scope and brief duration, consolidated women's accomplishments in the figural styles of modernism favored in American art in the 1920s, '30s, and '40s. It was one of the last surveys of women artists before Abstract Expressionism, undergirded by existentialism, transformed the fundamental expectations of art to be descriptive of individual subjectivity and physical presence. It took a quarter-century before the Smith College Museum of Art organized its next all-women exhibition in 1974. Yet the strict limit imposed on that show to four distinguished women representing different media—photographer Berenice Abbott, painter Helen Frankenthaler, printmaker Tatyana Grosman, and sculptor Louise Nevelson—continued the framework of "Ten Women" and did not advance a more inclusive or activist engagement. At the same time, the museum did host "c. 7,500," alumna Lucy Lippard's (class of 1958) decisive exhibition of female conceptual artists, which originated at the California Institute of the Arts the previous year.

If "Ten Women" culminated one era, a new one was beginning in a different department at Smith. In the summer of 1949, zoology professor Howard Parshley (1884–1953) was on Cape Cod, reading the French second volume of Simone de Beauvoir's *Le Deuxième Sexe* at the request of publisher Blanche Knopf, an old friend of Peggy Guggenheim's from Paris. She wanted him to evaluate the suitability of translating the monumental book into English for American readers. He agreed to take on the responsibility of translating the text himself, despite his lack of expertise in philosophy, Beauvoir's refusal to provide her references, and Knopf's ardor for abridgement. His translation of *The Second Sex*, published in March 1953, famously mischaracterized some of Beauvoir's philosophical terms and egregiously eliminated entire sections of Beauvoir's history of women. Despite its consequential errors and omissions, the Parshley translation nevertheless effectively channeled Beauvoir's voice and sparked the resurgence of feminist activism in the 1960s, including the writing of Betty Friedan (Smith class of 1942), whose book *The Feminine Mystique* (1963) delivered a lacerating diagnosis of the profound discontent of white educated women in America. Such a level of psychological realism was delimited by the intellectual boosterism of a circumscribed exhibition like "Ten Women Who Paint"; without a feminist perspective, educational leaders and female students struggled to resolve the tension between social pressures and the American standards of individual accomplishment.

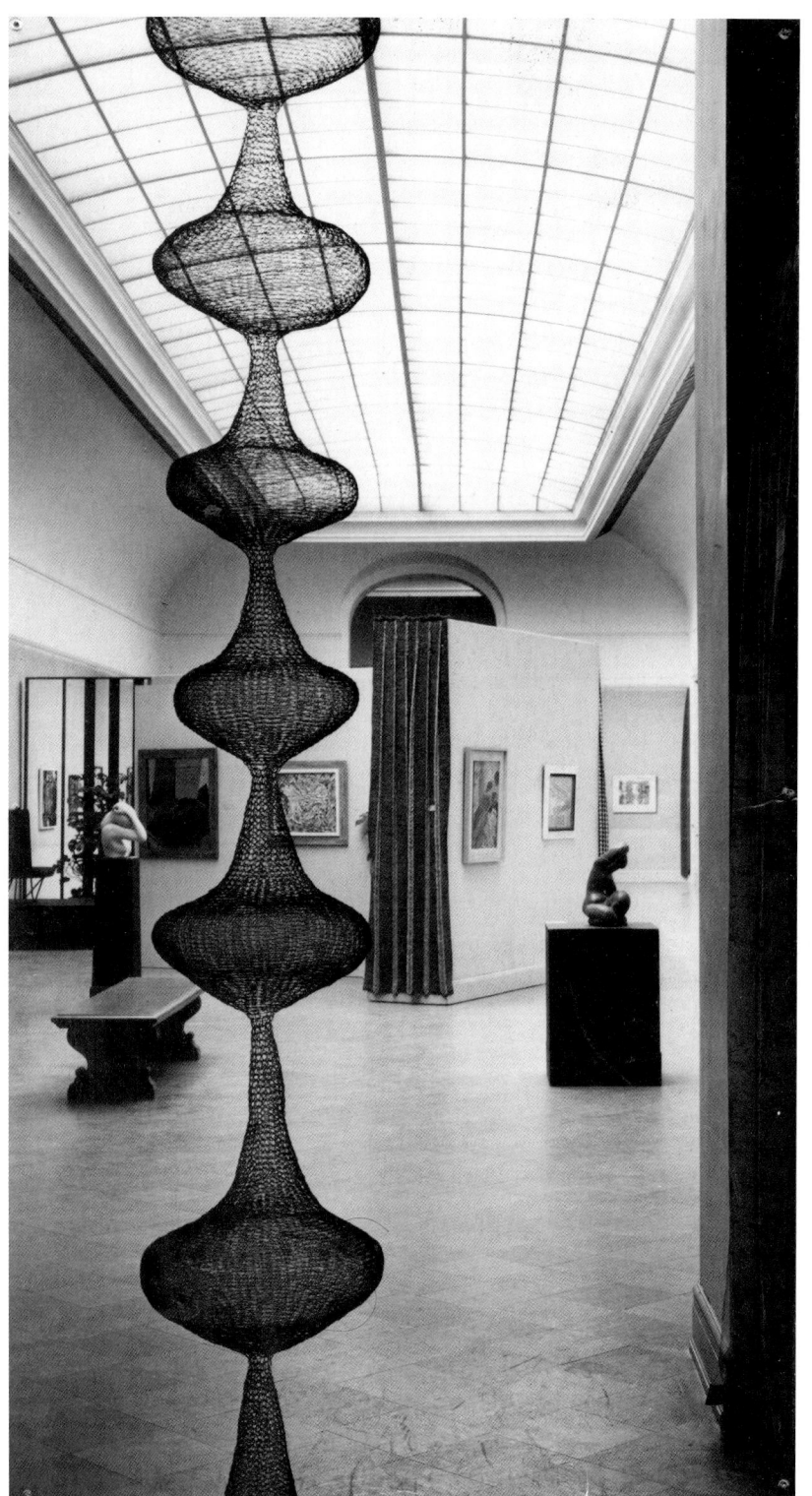

5

Women Artists Groups: "San Francisco Women Artists 27th Annual Exhibition," San Francisco Museum of Art, 1952

The sculpture suspended from the ceiling was unlike anything most people had ever seen. Virtually unclassifiable—was it sculpture, craft, or something else?—the untitled work by Ruth Asawa (1926–2013) was made from looped wire nearly 10 feet (3 m) tall, and comprised a stack of inverted mushroom-like forms of irregular size (illus. 40). "As people brushed by it moved back and forth like the pendulum of a clock," news reporter Wanda Ramey reported in her KCBS radio program *Jane Todd*. She concluded, "you could tell by the expression on their faces that people were fascinated—if somewhat mystified—by *Untitled Wire*."[1] In the 27th annual exhibition of San Francisco Women Artists (SFWA) (illus. 41), the work's organic shapes, open-weave looped wire, and kinetic responsiveness to its environment asserted a unique presence in American art. The iron wire piece, now identified as *Untitled* (s.435, Hanging Eight-Lobed, Single-Layered Continuous Teardrop Form) (1952), hung in an elegant skylight gallery of the San Francisco Museum of Art (SFMA), where it shared space with modeled figural sculptures on pedestals and framed landscapes and interiors rendered in oil paint and watercolor.

On the one hand, most reviewers in Bay Area daily newspapers noticed that Asawa's forms and process blurred the boundaries between art and design. "Ruth Asawa's fantastic crocheted wire sculptures are always fascinating," wrote painter Walter Snelgrove in the *Oakland Tribune*.[2] "Except for some wire-mesh creations by Ruth

40 Ruth Asawa, *Untitled* (S.435, Hanging Eight-Lobed, Single-Layered Continuous Teardrop Form), 1952, iron wire, on view in "San Francisco Women Artists 27th Annual Exhibition," 1952.

Asawa that look like nothing so much as long chains of interlocked jellyfish, the sculpture is fairly conventional," wrote R. H. Hagan in the *San Francisco Chronicle*.[3] On the other hand, Alexander Fried, writing in the *San Francisco Examiner*, made no mention of Asawa and instead devoted much of his review to pondering why there have been no great women artists, a familiar refrain of the day.[4] Asawa was emerging in the Bay Area and national scenes, and while her art and reputation were noticed, they were yet to be incorporated into the conventional understanding of American sculpture.

Moments such as Asawa's presentation in SFWA's 27th annual exhibition complicate the prevailing image of women artists organizations as bastions of conservatism and exclusivity. Little studied or appreciated, women artists organizations, some of which were founded in the late nineteenth century, staunchly advocated for gender equality in midcentury American art. The SFWA's 27th annual, and Asawa's participation in it, demonstrated a fostering of social and professional networks among women artists pursuing advanced aesthetic practices: an important instance of the alignment of women and experimental art in the context of an all-women show, at a moment in time poised between "31 Women" and the later feminist art movement.

Asawa was born in Southern California to Japanese immigrant parents and grew up as one of seven children tasked with chores to assist the family in operating a vegetable farm. In 1942, the U.S. government's executive order forced imprisonment of the Asawa family along with thousands of other Americans of Japanese descent. Asawa, her mother, and five of her siblings were detained for six months at the Santa Anita racetrack. They were then sent for a prolonged

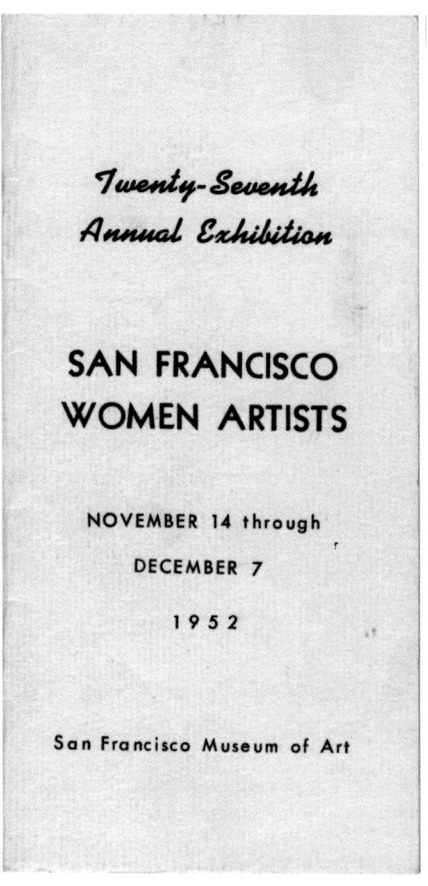

Twenty-Seventh Annual Exhibition

SAN FRANCISCO WOMEN ARTISTS

NOVEMBER 14 through
DECEMBER 7

1952

San Francisco Museum of Art

41 San Francisco Women Artists, *27th Annual Exhibition*, brochure, 1952.

internment at the Relocation Center in Rohwer, Arkansas, where Asawa took art classes and completed her senior year of high school. In 1943, she obtained indefinite leave to attend Milwaukee State Teachers College, where she continued to face discrimination and was denied opportunities to complete her student teaching. To further her education in a more inclusive environment, she continued her studies in 1946 at the experimental liberal arts Black Mountain College (BMC) in North Carolina, which had recently integrated with the enrollment of its first Black student, Alma Stone Williams, in 1944. In her three years there, Asawa thrived in a place that valued excellence and commitment over individual identity, studying art with Josef Albers and Ilya Bolotowsky, philosophy with Max Dehn, dance with Merce Cunningham, and architecture with Buckminster Fuller. She also made "an immediate impression" on Elaine de Kooning (1918–1989), who taught there in the summer of 1948,[5] and on photography student Hazel-Frieda Larsen, whose portraits of Asawa were included in Edward Steichen's six women photographers exhibition at MOMA in 1949. She also met her future husband, architecture student Albert Lanier, at BMC. In 1948, Lanier left the college and moved to San Francisco, where Asawa would join him a year later in 1949.[6] These formative experiences, including the fundamental lessons of Albers, her personal study of indigenous craft practices in Mexico, and her attitude toward the integration of art and life all contributed to the innovative structure of Asawa's wire sculptures.

Before any of her sculpture appeared in an SFWA annual, Asawa and her work were represented in the society through a photograph by Imogen Cunningham. The older artist was a leading modernist since the 1910s and a member of SFWA at least since the 1930s. Her Ektachrome color photograph *Aiko with Mobile*, which refers to Asawa by her Japanese name, Aiko, instead of Ruth, with one of her wire sculptures, hung in the 1951 annual. It was awarded a prize by the photography jury, which included Bay Area modernists Minor White and Alma Lavenson (herself a perennial SFWA member and exhibitor).

The long-standing membership of Cunningham and others also provided SFWA with a sustained modernist credibility. A fixture in the Bay Area photography scene, Cunningham used her camera as an instrument to build community and to support other artists across generations, particularly women. Over the decades Cunningham made dignified portraits of many SFWA members, including Asawa, Ruth Cravath (1902–1986), Margaret Peterson (1902–1997), Leah Rinne Hamilton (1906–1960), Merry Renk (1921–2012), and the Bruton sisters Margaret, Helen, and Esther, frequently exhibiting these photographs in the annuals. These images often portrayed the artist in her studio or at work, which helped audiences to visualize women artists as individuals rather than stereotypes. Cunningham's concern for her subjects may relate to her early exposure to the philosophy of empathy, *Einfühlung*, or "in-feeling" (in contrast to alienation), which she learned when she was studying photography and chemistry in Germany in the early 1900s.

Separated in age by over forty years, Asawa and Cunningham formed a deep bond, abetted by the fact that they were neighbors in San Francisco's Corona Heights, overlooking the Castro district. The older woman, as a working artist and mother, encouraged Asawa's ambitions to blaze a new path as an artist, and simultaneously discouraged Asawa from having more children.[7] Cunningham knew from personal experience that it required ceaseless effort and creative solutions to be both an artist and mother, but she believed that the labor was worth it by conferring the full experience of life. Letters between Asawa and Cunningham document their bartering of Cunningham's photographs of Asawa's art in exchange for Lanier performing design and construction work in her house. Cunningham worried that she received more than her fair share from the deal and was also concerned whether her images would be convincing in Asawa's application for a Guggenheim Fellowship. "If you get it—I will be sure to think that that did it. If you don't get it, I will think that I am no good at all."[8] Alas, the application was not successful, but Cunningham's images over the years have become some of the iconic artist portraits of the midcentury. According to Asawa biographer Marilyn Chase, Cunningham also encouraged Asawa to sign her work with her original last name, not her husband's.[9]

It seemed possible that SFWA would present a salubrious opportunity for Asawa to show her work, and Cunningham invited her to join. As Asawa recalled, "The group wanted to get the membership up so they could sell more women's art. It would raise the level of women artists. They would become more equal to men [artists]. That was the effort, to be equal. Women artists were looked down upon."[10] As a member of SFWA, Asawa would be part of an organization that fostered the careers of artistic experimenters in a variety of media, including Plexiglas, mosaic, graphic design, and photography.

SFWA embraced a degree of diversity and change while maintaining meritocratic governing and art selection procedures typical of women artists associations. The organization has its roots in 1887, when a group of women artists, angry at the gender restriction of the Bohemian Club (the leading artists organization in the city), formed the Sketch Club. In 1925, Sketch Club members and other women's organizations merged to found the San Francisco Society of Women Artists. For the inaugural exhibition, they organized a large-scale decorative arts show with artists, designers, and architects. Within a few years the group embraced new strains of modern art, from Cubism to Social Realism. The sixth annual exhibition in 1931 at the Palace of the Legion of Honor, one of the city's fine arts museums (the San Francisco Museum of Art did not open until 1935), achieved extensive newspaper coverage. The presentation included an invited exhibition of works by about twenty women artists from outside the region, which included Frida Kahlo's first work in a U.S. exhibition, *Frieda and Diego Rivera* (1931). Mexican painter Kahlo became one of the most revered artists in the world, but at the time of the exhibition, a newspaper claimed the work's main interest was that it was by the wife of the famous Rivera, who had recently completed several commissioned murals in San Francisco.[11] Nevertheless, this and another newspaper deemed the painting meritorious of sizable illustrations and captions. Was it a coincidence that a women artists organization, and SFWA in particular, was the first in the United States to recognize the importance of a painter who candidly depicted her struggles as a woman and an artist?

SFWA fostered a community supportive of experimentation, reflecting the Bay Area's enthusiasm for the new. The group solidified this mission in partnership with the San Francisco Museum of Art (later renamed San Francisco Museum of Modern Art) from its inception in 1935. Founded by the San Francisco Art Association, the museum opened on the top floor of the Beaux-Arts-style civic center across the street from City Hall. The first curator and director of the museum, Dr. Grace McCann Morley (1900–1985), hailed from Berkeley and earned a doctorate from the Sorbonne in Paris. She joined SFWA and promptly made space for women in her progressive institution. One scholar calculated that the museum presented over forty solo shows by women artists before New York's Museum of Modern Art offered its first in 1942.[12] In 1935 SFWA began presenting its annuals at the museum, giving them equal footing with the San Francisco Art Association, which also presented its annuals there. Many women were members of both groups, and critics became accustomed to seeing their new work at least twice a year. SFWA members including Ruth Armer, Ruth Cravath, Imogen Cunningham, Claire Falkenstein, Alma Lavenson, Miné Okubo, and Jeanne Reynal (1903–1983) had solo exhibitions at the museum in the 1930s through the 1950s.[13] Morley invited SFWA to meet regularly at the museum, and SFWA members often presented lectures and participated in solo and group exhibitions. In 1946 Morley borrowed the exhibition "The Women" from the David Porter Gallery, rounding out the show with the addition of a few Bay Area artists, including SFWA members Falkenstein and Margaret Peterson.

Morley's internationalism and intellectual openness made her museum a dynamic institution in the United States at midcentury. She imported cutting-edge contemporary shows from the East Coast, supported new directions in the local scene, and staged surveys of the arts of Asia, Latin America, and Africa. An outspoken proponent of fairness and cooperation, she advocated to create a decentered, flexible, national network through which artists might be seen and appreciated. She understood perfectly well that women's advancement in the art world could be achieved through the expansion of access and equitable systems such as blind juries. Women artists organizations like SFWA relied on a two-stage jury system to ensure the quality of the works on view and to encourage its members to submit work to be vetted by recognized professionals and authorities, which lent prestige to the exhibition. One jury selected the works and a second awarded the prizes. The structure and ideals of the SFWA, coupled with its partnership with Morley and the San Francisco Museum of Art, created an environment hospitable to a cadre of women artists committed to both aesthetic innovation and community responsibility. Yet deep-seated biases persisted and the participating artists and jurors remained largely white.

The SFWA's progressive approach and openness to experimental media was embodied by the long-term involvement of sculptor Claire Falkenstein (1908–1997). She joined the organization in 1931, a year after graduating from the University of California, Berkeley. She consistently participated in the annuals, and her featured work reveals the evolution of her style from drawing and ceramics with tightly formed Cubist imagery to Constructivist sculptures in wood and metal. She served as SFWA president from 1942 to 1944, helping to make the annual exhibition a showplace for women artists' contributions to the war industry workshops of San Francisco and Berkeley through the display of blueprints and drafting plans. Through the late 1940s, SFWA annuals remained a suitable venue for Falkenstein's increasingly varied and rigorous innovation in diverse media. She contributed a design for a jazz album and a new enamel and metal sculpture to the 1947 annual, then presented a radical new Plexiglas sculpture, *Shalako III*, in 1949. The following year she moved to France, where she gained recognition from

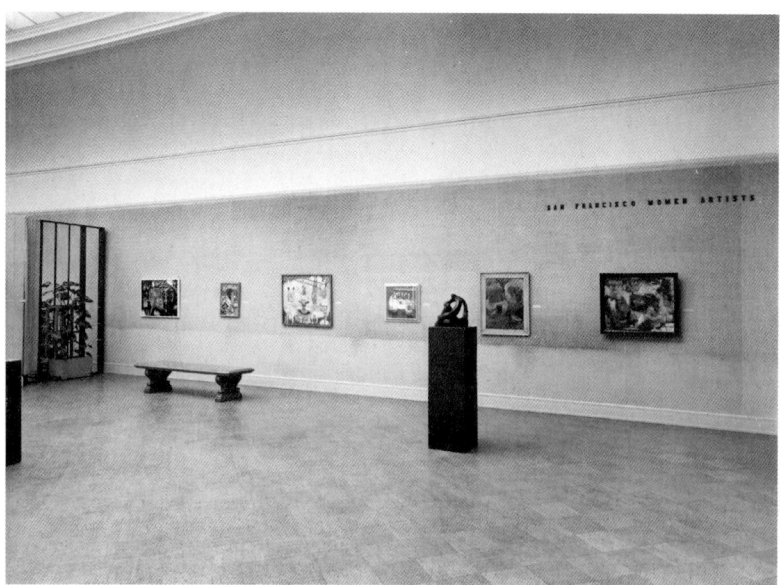

42 "San Francisco
Women Artists 27th
Annual Exhibition,"
installation view, 1952.

critic Michel Tapié as an American exponent of Art Informel, a mode
of process-based abstract art.[14]

The SFWA's 27th annual opened on November 14, 1952. Other
shows were also on view at the San Francisco Museum of Art at the
time: photographs by Minor White and Edward and Brett Weston, "30
U.S. Contemporary Artists," and "Six Canadian Painters." Based on
the four extant installation photographs of the annual, paintings generally occupied the walls of the large central skylight gallery, in which
one Asawa sculpture was displayed (illus. 42). One side gallery included
framed photographs, prints, and drawings (illus. 43). The exhibition
also included a large case inset in the wall with a lively display of metalwork, ceramics, and textiles (illus. 44). The interior spaces of the galleries appeared comfortable and inviting, well-lit with several benches and
a houseplant. The sculptures were generously distributed, with sufficient space between the pedestals and wall to permit aesthetic contemplation. The very existence of well-composed installation photographs
testifies to the seriousness with which the museum treated the exhibition. "They illustrate very well the variety of art work included in the
exhibition and the vitality of one group of artists in this area," a museum

43 "San Francisco
Women Artists 27th
Annual Exhibition,"
installation view, 1952.

44 "San Francisco
Women Artists 27th
Annual Exhibition,"
installation view, 1952.

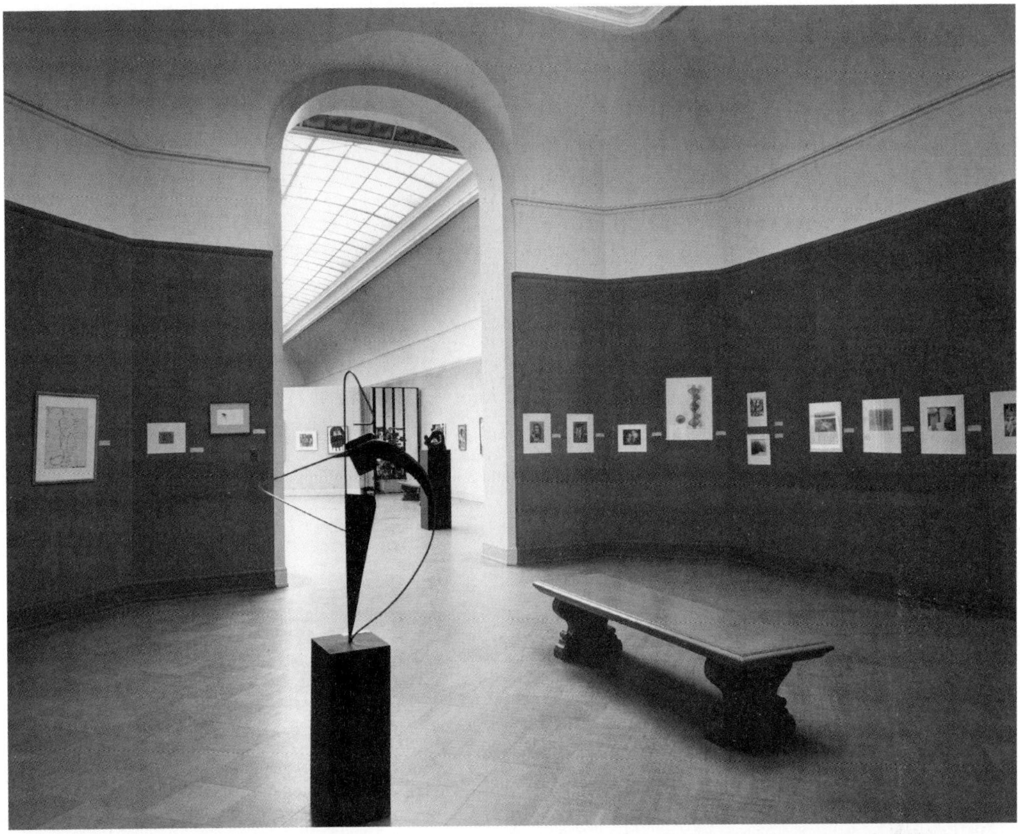

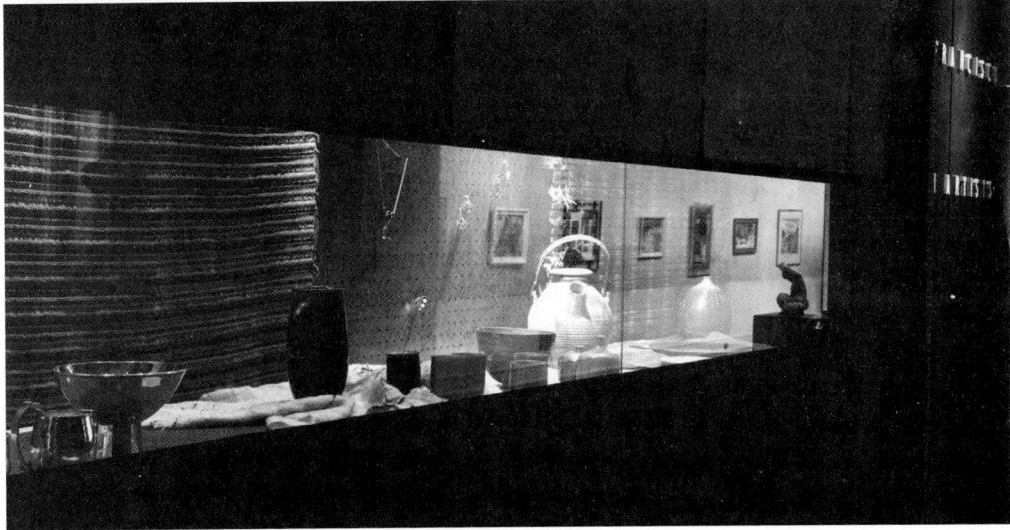

staff member wrote in a cover letter to *Look* magazine, which had requested prints to consider using in a future issue.[15]

Asawa's sculpture *Untitled* was installed at the far end of the long gallery. The work dominates the foreground of an installation photograph (see illus. 40), creating the appearance that it existed in its own sphere of influence. (Her second sculpture selected for the exhibition is not visible in any of the images.) Asawa's airy wire work contrasted with the earthy figural sculptures displayed on pedestals nearby. These works appear similar in both style and subject to sculpture by Gertrude Murphy and Miriam Hoffman, whose cast-stone pieces, entitled *Figure* and *Compositional Head*, respectively, each won a prize in this annual. The curvaceous sculpture of a sitting figure with long limbs may be Murphy's *Meditation*, and recalls the gracefully distended figures of Mary Callery, both influenced by the School of Paris.

The paintings in the gallery are difficult to identify in the installation photographs, though their titles and media are documented in the exhibition checklist. Some of these works are by artists who were widely known and respected in the Bay Area at midcentury but whose careers have been neglected subsequently, such as painter Ruth Armer (1896–1977), who showed two abstract works in her untitled number series. One work that can be definitively identified because of its graphic imagery is Margaret Peterson's *Abstraction 81* (illus. 43), depicting a bulbous creature-like form with four legs.[16] Flatly patterned and likely brightly hued, the tempera painting derived from her intensive studies of Indigenous art during extended travels in the Pacific Northwest and British Columbia. While Peterson was long esteemed in the region as a modern painter and educator—she taught at Berkeley from 1928—she is not as well known as her former students such as Jay DeFeo. The Red Scare and anti-communist fervor had arrived in liberal San Francisco in the early 1950s, and artists such as Peterson took a stand: she resigned from teaching in 1950 when refusing to participate in the so-called "loyalty oath" and declined the university's offer to rejoin the faculty in 1952. The *Oakland Tribune* cited the $100 prize awarded to Peterson's symbolistic *Canoe House Dance* (undated) as belated recognition of her underappreciated role in shaping the Bay Area art scene.[17] It is the single work illustrated in the review.

In a side gallery, several photographs by Cunningham are identifiable, as much of her corpus is catalogued. *Reeds* (1952) (illus. 45) depicts a stand of water plants as a screen of vertical lines, photographed by the artist on a visit to Tomales Bay, north of the city, with photographer Consuelo Kanaga. Two other Cunningham photographs depict Asawa sculptures. One, entitled *Mobile* (1951), closely crops an image of a folded Asawa wire sculpture, *Untitled* (s.535, Hanging Five-Lobed Continuous Form within a Form with Two Interior Spheres and One Teardrop Form) (1951), so it appears as an abstract biomorphic form. The second is a photocollage of two Asawa sculptures, *Untitled* (s.535) and *Untitled* (s.095), which appeared on the June 1952 cover of *Arts and Architecture*, a progressive journal based in Los Angeles that promoted modern design. Their abstracted, organic forms communicated the optimistic spirit that suffused California interior design, with clear lines, natural materials, and open spaces, in contrast to the angsty Expressionism then dominant in New York painting. Asawa's subtle innovation, springing from her sophisticated fusion of modernism and traditional craft, was not fully appreciated by all, and required defenders. The designer Charles Eames (1907–1978), according to Lanier, compared Asawa's sculpture to elementary pen-and-ink drawing studies at a gathering. Fortunately, Cunningham was there to remind Eames that Asawa's innovation was to fuse medium and method to invent new process-based open forms.[18]

The exhibition and brochure classified Asawa's work as sculpture, but it in fact shared more in common with modern textiles than cast-stone figures. Her looped-wire sculptures were formed into three-dimensional vessels through repeated manipulations of thin, pliable material to enclose space, utilizing basketmaking techniques she had learned in Mexico. Asawa's procedures, initially formulated at Black Mountain, complemented the "truth to materials" approach of other

Bauhaus-aligned sfwa members like Trude Guermonprez, a German-born weaver who presented an abstract textile curtain in the 1952 annual. They carefully explored the expressive capacity of materials and eschewed grandiose claims for the meaning of their art. As Anni Albers wrote in her book *On Weaving* (1965), the interrelation between the structure of the weave and the properties of the chosen materials constitutes the essence of weaving.[19]

The decorative and industrial arts section of the sfwa annual included fifteen artists working in textiles, twelve in metals and enamel, and six in ceramics. Florence Hickman's yellow upholstery weaving *Sunsand* (undated) won a textile prize. She discovered the craft when attending a lecture by San Francisco modern weaving pioneer Dorothy Liebes (1897–1972), and later moved to Dallas and became involved

45 Imogen Cunningham, *Reeds*, 1952, gelatin silver print.

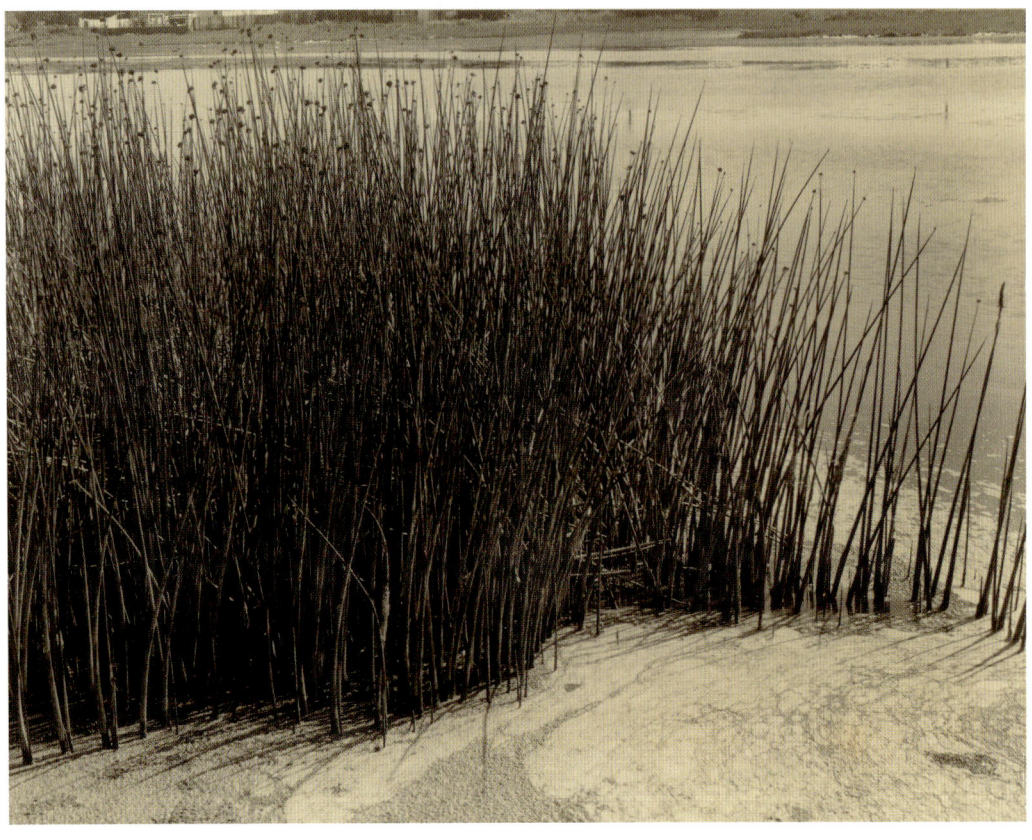

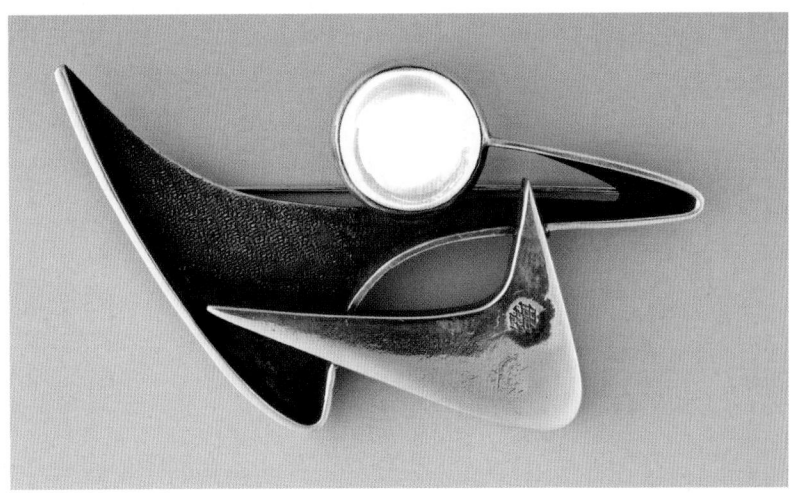

46 Margaret De Patta,
Pin no. 6, c. 1946–57,
silver, quartz.

with the Contemporary Handweavers of Texas. In the subcategory of architecture, Lois Davidson Gottlieb (1926–2018), a former student of Frank Lloyd Wright, displayed photographs of her first California house, the Val-Goeshen Residence in Marin County, north of San Francisco. The annual even featured a cattail fence constructed in redwood by Ginger Gester. The midcentury modern look, with its attention to natural materials, organic abstraction, and human scale, had already found a home with SFWA in the early 1950s.

Supporting contemporary craft and design was part of SFWA's mission from the beginning. Membership rolls from September 1948 indicate that artists working in the decorative arts comprised about half of the artist membership, 72 out of 151.[20] With modernist jewelry an emerging field, the SFWA served as a rare venue for contemporary metalsmiths to gather and show their work. The 1952 annual included jewelry by Merry Renk, as well as Irena Brynner (1917–2003), and Margaret De Patta (1903–1964) (illus. 46). These three artists, along with Vera Allison (1902–1993), were among the founders of the Metal Arts Guild in 1951, one of the first professional organizations for artistic jewelry and metalwork. Other leading Bay Area craft artists also showed with SFWA. Elena Montalvo Netherby (1891–1977), a building contractor and founder of the Mills College Ceramics Guild, won an award at the 1952 annual for her group of porcelain pots inspired by traditional Chinese ceramics and glazes.

As a progressive organization that sanctioned experimental work that blurred the boundaries of art, craft, and design, SFWA seems to have had some sensitivity to issues of race, ethnicity and class. Several Asian American artists joined SFWA and participated in its annuals before the Second World War. Miki Hayakawa (1899–1953) presented three paintings in the 1931 annual exhibition that also included work by Kahlo, Falkenstein, and Agnes Pelton. Born in Japan, Hayakawa immigrated with her family to the Bay Area, where she defied their wishes and attended art school on scholarship. As a young artist she attracted attention for her radiant paintings and portraits, which included nude studies, as discussed in a story in the *San Francisco Examiner* by writer Gobind Behari Lal.[21] Hayakawa appeared in the inaugural exhibition at the San Francisco Museum of Art in 1935. But with Japan emerging as an aggressor in the coming war, press coverage became racialized. One critic, complaining that Miné Okubo's (1912–2001) gouache *Fishing Boats*—displayed at the 1941 SFWA annual—appeared too Western in style, wrote, "we fear she has been eating corned beef and cabbage instead of tempura."[22]

After the bombing of Pearl Harbor on December 7, 1941, President Roosevelt issued an executive order on February 19, 1942 calling for the forced internment of legal residents and citizens of Japanese descent. The order ruptured the lives of thousands, including artists Hayakawa, Okubo, Asawa, Emiko Nakano, and Hisako Hibi. The experiences profoundly changed their lives, influencing their career paths and exposure to art and media. When Asawa was imprisoned at Santa Anita racetrack, living in former horse stables, she found refuge in drawing with Disney animators also interned there. Okubo also took to drawing to endure her internment in the Tanforan Assembly Center in San Bruno, California, and the Topaz concentration camp in Utah. After the war, she published *Citizen 13660* (1946), an illustrated account of her experiences and observations of systematic dehumanization. In

April 1946, Okubo presented some of her 2,000 eyewitness sketches in an art exhibition at Mills College in Oakland, coinciding with its Pan American Day. Asian American women artists in California, according to scholar Valerie Matsumoto, found their voices and built vibrant careers in midcentury America after the traumas of the Second World War.[23]

The SFWA and its annuals created a nexus of connections within the Bay Area art ecosystem of art associations, art schools, and university galleries, and as such they provided opportunities for exposure and critical response for a few young Asian American women artists. Printmaker and painter Emiko Nakano (1925–1990) joined SFWA for several years. Born in Sacramento, California, to immigrant parents from Japan, Nakano was interned with her family in several detention camps for three years. She returned to the Bay Area to study at the California School of Fine Arts and Mills College and gained attention for her gestural abstractions. Her work tuned in to the emerging methods of Abstract Expressionism, stemming from her studies with Clyfford Still and Richard Diebenkorn. Like Asawa she completed her education and established her career in the aftermath of the war, at a time when artists and critics found abstraction to be a universal language in which to express subjective experiences. Two of her prints appeared in the SFWA 1952 annual: a lithograph, *Abstraction in Texture No. 2* (undated), and an untitled etching. Photographic documentation is unavailable, but it is possible that they resembled her other landscape-derived abstract work of the period, such as the painting *Landscape in Green* (1954), an abstract assembly of varied marks faceting the surface into a chromatic prism (illus. 47). Nakano continued to show in other SFWA annuals and won several awards.

Asawa's participation in SFWA lasted for a single year, however. For the 1953 annual, she proposed two sculptures—wire pieces with legible subject-matter and the descriptive titles of *Motorcycle Rider* (undated) and *Imogen Cunningham* (c. 1953), a looped-wire caricature of her friend, replete with jaunty beret and bread pan base.[24] For unknown

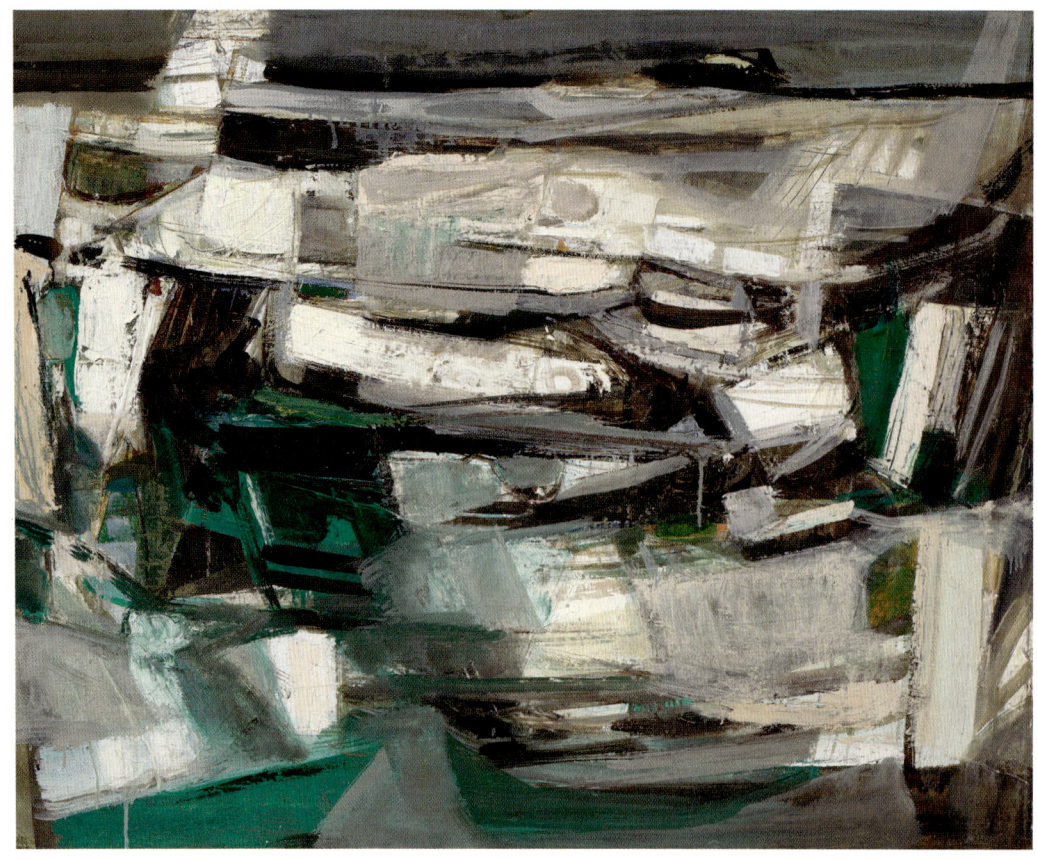

47 Emiko Nakano,
Landscape in Green,
1954, oil on canvas.

reasons, both were rejected by the sculpture selection committee of
Ruth Cravath, Sargent Johnson, and David Lemon. Whether the decision stung, or her own priorities shifted, Asawa never again showed
with the SFWA. As she later recalled, a regional membership group may
not have been worth the effort at such a formative stage in her career.
"I didn't join anything or belong to anything after that because I didn't
have time for it. I was busy being an artist and raising a family."[25] That
summer she had a two-person show with Jean Varda at the hip nightclub Tin Angel and a solo exhibition at the sophisticated Design
Research in Cambridge, Massachusetts.

Thanks to the curatorial program under Grace Morley, the San
Francisco Museum of Art continued to provide Asawa with exhibition

opportunities. In the 1954 exhibition "Four Artist-Craftsmen," a half-dozen of her wire sculptures were suspended adjacent to pottery by Marguerite Wildenhain, textiles by Ida Dean (Grae), and jewelry by Merry Renk. As with the case of MOMA's display of six women photographers, "Four Artist-Craftsmen" was an all-women show without a proclamation of gender-specificity; each of the two shows occurred in the context of a midcentury modern art museum that subordinated individual identity to common artistic values. Asawa's sculptures in "Four Artist-Craftsmen" gained the attention of Louis Pollack, director of the Peridot Gallery. At the end of 1954, she opened her first New York exhibition in his space, which five years earlier had mounted Louise Bourgeois's first sculptural installation. In 1955, Morley included Asawa's *Untitled* (S.250, Hanging Seven-Lobed Continuous Interlocking Form with Four Interior Spheres), a 10-foot-high (3 m) wire hanging sculpture, in the "Pacific Coast Art" section of the U.S. exhibition in the Third São Paulo Bienal.

Even without her direct participation in SFWA, Asawa's radical sculpture continued to be represented at the annuals through Cunningham's photographs. The 1957 annual featured an image of Asawa and four of her children sitting around a sculpture in her studio. Over the decade, Cunningham submitted images of her female friends, roughly one artist per annual, with Merry Renk represented in 1953 and Ruth Cravath in 1954. Another Cunningham portrait, of De Patta, poses her standing at home next to a work by Asawa in 1955. The camaraderie of photographers, sculptors, and jewelers exemplified SFWA's intended function to support women at any age and phase of their lives and careers.

In the 1950s, women artists associations continued to organize member exhibitions across the United States: from the venerable National Association of Women Artists (NAWA) in New York and Women Painters of the West in Los Angeles to newly formed regional groups like Arts Associated in Louisiana and Women Painters of Spokane (Washington). There were also professional organizations of women working in specific media, such as the National League of American Pen Women, for illustrators, founded in 1897. SFWA's inclusive and progressive stance, expressed through its encouragement of contemporary art media and openness to modernist Asian artists, can be better appreciated in comparison to the NAWA and its 1952 annual exhibition.

NAWA—the most prominent of the women artists groups in the United States—was founded as the Woman's Art Club of New York in 1889, and was later renamed in 1941. The organization was headquartered at 42 West 57th Street, a few doors down from Peggy Guggenheim's Art of This Century, and presented exhibitions in its in-house Argent Gallery. Prominent women painters of the late nineteenth and early twentieth centuries, including Mary Cassatt, Cecilia Beaux, and Elizabeth Sparhawk-Jones, joined or exhibited with the group.[26] It was not until 1934, however, that NAWA took a step toward racial integration and offered membership to Augusta Savage (1892–1962).[27] The sculptor showed in the annuals from 1935 to 1939, and had her first solo exhibition at NAWA's Argent Gallery in May 1939, in conjunction with her public commission for the New York World's Fair, *Lift Every Voice and Sing*, installed in the courtyard of the Contemporary Arts Building. However, Savage, a community organizer and entrepreneur, seems to have stepped away from NAWA soon after. She co-founded and became the first director of the Harlem Community Art Center in 1937, and two years later, and less than a month after her Argent show, opened the Salon of Contemporary Negro Art, the first gallery dedicated to the exhibition and sale of work by Black artists, on 125th Street in Harlem.[28] It closed after only three months, but proved the concept of a Black art movement independent of white-owned or -directed galleries and foundations.

NAWA installed its sprawling annual exhibitions at the National Academy of Design, a conservative artist membership organization with few women artists elected to join its ranks. The 1952 NAWA annual appeared in ten galleries spread over three floors, once described as "labyrinthine" by a less than sympathetic art critic.[29] None of the works in the 1952 NAWA annual were as daring as Asawa's wire sculptures or De Patta's metalwork. "The work is earnest and competent but seldom attains originality or a really superior level of craftsmanship—seldom communicates strong feeling, either," wrote James Fitzsimmons.[30] Adhering to established categories of painting, sculpture, watercolors, drawings, prints, and miniatures, NAWA maintained an old-fashioned image and did not present photographs, metalwork, textiles, or ceramics. Printmaking, however, was one area in which some innovation was evident: in the 1952 annual, Doris Seidler (1912–2010) presented abstract etchings made following her studies at the experimental workshop Atelier 17.

The sheer size of the NAWA, with eight hundred members, accommodated the participation of a few Asian and Latin American artists who moved to New York and sought avenues into the U.S. art world at midcentury. Painter Yu Jingzhi (b. 1890), then known as Ching Chih Yee, joined NAWA in 1952 and showed a watercolor, *Yang Kuei-Fei* (undated), depicting one of the legendary four beauties of ancient China, in that year's annual. She worked in a traditional Chinese painting style and prior to immigrating to the United States in 1937 taught at the Shanghai Art College and joined the Chinese Women's Society for Calligraphy and Painting. Activist and painter Mitsu Yashima (1908–1988), a Japanese anti-war protester who immigrated to the USA in 1939, joined NAWA in 1954, and showed a watercolor, *Dockyard* (undated), the following year. Bolivian sculptor Marina Núñez del Prado (1910–1995) received a fellowship from the American Association of University Women to travel to the United States in 1940. She joined NAWA and took part in "South America Day" at the 1947 annual exhibition.

Sculpture was one area in which NAWA harbored a group of progressive-minded artists. The bulk of the exhibited sculptures were figural representations of commonplace subject-matter like animals and family groups in traditional media like plaster, wood, bronze, and stone. Among these, however, a handful of works stood out:

semi-abstract sculptures by Helen Beling and Dora Menzes exhibited in the 1952 annual followed the formally reductive tendencies established by Barbara Hepworth and Herbert Ferber. In retrospect, the debut of new member Louise Nevelson, who showed a modest plaster sculpture, *Figures* (undated), was the most notable appearance at the 1952 NAWA annual. After abandoning her groundbreaking wood constructions of the mid-1940s, Nevelson, now in her early fifties, had entered a lull and needed to revitalize her career. She began sculpting blocky, figural plaster and terracotta sculptures and joined NAWA and several other artist groups in New York. Within NAWA, Nevelson mingled with a congenial group of sculptors, including Anna Walinska and Helen Wilson. The group offered one another mutual support, as sculpture had long played second fiddle to painting in New York. The following annual, Nevelson won a sculpture prize for her cast stone *The Ancient Figure* (undated). NAWA and its network incubated the resurgence of a formidable talent as Nevelson returned to creating wood constructions in the mid-1950s. Colette Roberts, the former director of NAWA's Argent Gallery, became the director of Grand Central Moderns gallery and presented Nevelson's breakthrough abstract sculptural environment in 1958.

NAWA as an institution did not prioritize innovation and maintained a defensive posture about its founding mission of gender-specificity in an era of supposed equality. "Strange as it may seem to us today, men did not welcome women to their exhibitions," president Nell Choate Jones wrote in an organizational history printed in the catalogue of the 1952 annual.[31] She measured their impact and diversity through national representation, not art media or identity, boasting that NAWA furthered a dual mission of supporting women artists and performing a charitable function and included members residing in 44 states. Despite their divergent cultural orientations and positions within their respective city's art worlds, both NAWA and SFWA endeavored to establish and maintain impartial and evenly applied standards for inclusion in exhibitions and awarding of prizes.

However, not all women, by reasons of aesthetics, temperament, or identity, chose to participate.

The traditional art-historical narrative suggests that modernism developed exclusively through the studio and social activities of heroic (male) avant-garde artists and the exceptional women in their circles. Research into the founding of women artists organizations, however, expands this narrative. In the nineteenth century, when many art societies barred women, women created their own parallel exhibition organizations to show and sell their work on the open market. As early as the 1850s, women artists in London began to imagine an artistic community of women that would foster creative equality. Pre-Raphaelite painter Anna Mary Howitt (1824–1884) advocated for "a beautiful sisterhood in Art," an idea that sprang from her experience studying with Jane Benham and Barbara Bodichon in Munich.[32] The notion of a women artists collective first cohered in England with the founding of the Society of Female Artists and its inaugural gallery exhibition on Oxford Street, London, in 1857. Since that time, professional groups of women artists in Europe and the United States have continued to promote their own work and resist capitulating to male dominance in contemporary art. They resisted the sexual politics of modernism, which encouraged women to conform to male-led institutions and deemed separate women-led institutions inherently second rate.

American women artists groups supported the artistic activities of thousands of women through their advocacy for women in art, stimulation of discourse on the topic, and creation of an alternate network of exhibition and criticism. Though they espoused the values of professionalism, egalitarianism, and social commitment, women artists groups in midcentury often catered to conservative tastes and failed to create a welcoming environment for all women. SFWA makes for an intriguing case study of the potential for one such group to genuinely cultivate an openness to ethnic and stylistic diversity. The organization contributed to the Bay Area contemporary art scene, and it enjoyed the respect and participation of influential curators, artists, and educators in the region. An artist's participation in the SFWA evidenced her awareness of her situation as a woman and artist, and her effort to create a positive identity for herself and other women-identified artists independent from the feminine characteristics ascribed by commercial galleries, critics, and art world gossip. As an Asian American woman artist working in non-traditional materials and craft techniques, Asawa's brief tenure in SFWA represents both the potential and the limitations for a community-minded women artists organization to truly support feminist and avant-garde art in the postwar United States.

6

Fiber Art: "Women in Art," Contemporary Arts Association of Houston, 1953

"I feel it is my duty as a teacher to look, read, listen, and be aware of the world in which I am living," Norma Henderson (1911–2000) wrote in a Texas teachers' association journal in 1957.[1] This high school art educator, artist, and curator embodied the unsung woman artist of the midcentury United States dedicated to enhancing her local art community. In the 1940s and '50s, Henderson made her living as a schoolteacher at Lamar High School, an elite public school in Houston. As a teacher, Henderson inspired some of her students to become artists and educators. As an artist, she contributed ceramic sculptures and oil paintings to regional exhibitions at the Dallas Museum of Fine Arts (renamed the Dallas Museum of Art in 1984). Henderson invested additional energy into social and artistic alliances to benefit the community as a volunteer and member of the exhibition committee of the Contemporary Arts Association of Houston (CAA). She made these contributions during the same period that the art patrons John and Dominique de Menil (1904–1973; 1908–1997) were living nearby, in the wealthy River Oaks neighborhood; the couple greatly influenced the association and underwrote headline-grabbing exhibitions. If the story of the de Menils is one of power and taste, the story of Henderson is one of the slow liberalization of the cultural institutions of Texas over the course of the twentieth century. Much like

Alouise Boker with the Camera Club of New York, Henderson used her platform on the exhibition committee of an artist membership organization to organize a groundbreaking exhibition of women artists. In so doing, she shined a light on women's artistic achievements and made a feminist intervention in the culture of the institution, even if short-lived.

Henderson's name is little known outside local histories of modern art in Houston. Yet her "Women in Art" was one of the most ambitious exhibitions of women in contemporary art and design at midcentury, and one of the few to be independently organized at a museum positioned on the cutting edge: it opened in May 1953 at the Contemporary Arts Museum, operated by the CAA (illus. 48). This survey of work by 57 artists in a dozen media aspired to demonstrate the emergence of women as forces in the new postwar fields of studio craft, interior design, and fiber art. "Women in Art" positioned women's creative responses to the atomic age as modern expressions within an ancient continuity, and was accompanied by a public relations campaign to bolster the profile of women in contemporary art by pointing to their accomplishments in art history. The need to "remember the ladies" took on new urgency in the rapid development of Texas, where postwar prosperity transformed the state into a hotbed of midcentury arts patronage in the United States.

New York Times writer Aline Louchheim credited women as mediating forces responsible for the development of museums and art centers in Texas. "All through the early days of the Southwest, 'culture' seems indeed to have been provided by the distaff side," she wrote in a 1954 article on the competition among the arts communities in

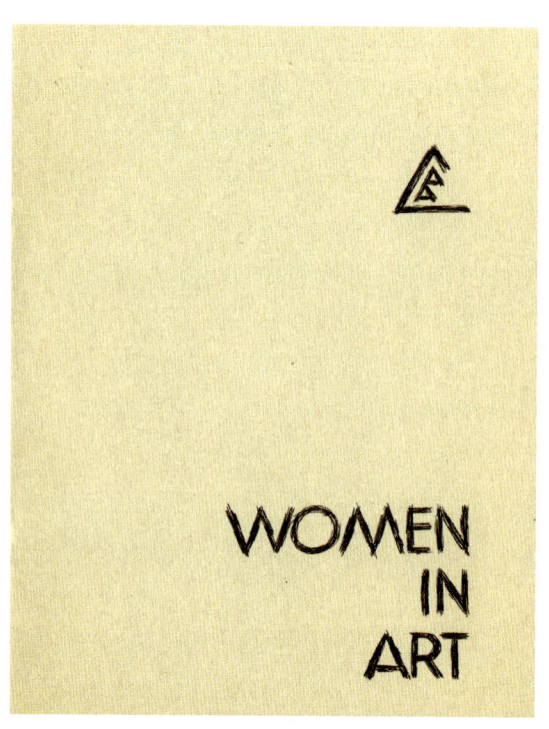

48 Contemporary Arts Association of Houston, *Women in Art,* exhibition catalogue, 1953.

Dallas, Fort Worth, Houston, and San Antonio.[2] Women initiated and funded many arts organizations and museums in Houston, and their names resided on museums and wings, but women artists remained overlooked. "Women in Art" stands as a signal midcentury exhibition that addressed the phenomenon, observed retrospectively by scholar Katie Robinson Edwards, of "how much Texas modern art owes to women."[3]

The Contemporary Arts Association was chartered in May 1948 by seven artists frustrated that the city's Museum of Fine Arts was not doing enough for contemporary art. Their goal was to present new art and explore its role in modern life through exhibitions, lectures, and other public programs. Texas painter Ola McNeill Davidson's (1884–1976) classes in abstract art had nurtured a generation of artists, including Robert Preusser (1919–1992) and Frank Dolejska (1921–1989), who were among the core group of volunteers to establish and run the CAA. Their fellow founding members were largely artists and creative types in architecture, design, and advertising, and the CAA maintained its original democratic ethos as a scrappy independent while being supported by a board populated by powerful arts philanthropists and oil executives. The CAA generally relied on a fleet of volunteers to curate shows, sit at the admissions desk, solicit publicity, and plan opening receptions. "Someone would take on an exhibition, organize it and bring it to us, and we'd display it," recalled Preusser.[4] The exhibition committee controlled the schedule of shows. All committee members had the opportunity to propose and, if approved by vote, organize an exhibition. The group clearly filled a need in the city: by the time of its inaugural exhibition, the CAA claimed more than two hundred members.

The premiere show, "This Is Contemporary Art," which opened at the Museum of Fine Arts on Halloween 1948, set an open-minded tenor. It included fine and decorative arts, with fabrics, jewelry, wallpaper, advertising, architecture, and industrial design exhibited along with painting, sculpture, and printmaking. Only a few women appeared in the show: sculptor Mary Callery, painter Irene Rice Pereira, jeweler Margaret De Patta, interior designer Helene Sprong, and artist and writer Mai-Mai Sze. From the time of its opening, the museum cultivated a Bauhaus-like attitude of using design and education to integrate art and life. Early exhibitions placed industrial design, craft, and art on an equal footing, and installation shots of "This Is Contemporary Art" show a didactic organization of materials based on function and social use. For its second exhibition, which opened seven weeks later, the CAA presented the traveling memorial to the recently deceased artist and Bauhaus professor László Moholy-Nagy, a move that emphasized the experimental artist-educator as a lodestar for the association.

In 1949 the CAA secured, for $1, the lease for a centrally located lot and by the end of the year had constructed and opened a modernist, industrial-looking A-frame exhibition space, designed by founding member and architect Karl Kamrath (1911–1988). The organization began to professionalize and hired two part-time workers, Ellen Sharp as administrator and Frank Dolejska as preparator, paying them similar salaries. Now with its own home, the Contemporary Arts Museum, the organization could maintain a full annual schedule of exhibitions. To do so they added powerhouse board members, some proponents of the International Style of geometric, unornamented architecture and patrons of Black artists. Nina Cullinan (1899–1983) commissioned Ludwig Mies van der Rohe (1886–1969) to design a new wing for the Museum of Fine Arts. Another, Susan McAshan (1905–2001), was instrumental in hiring painter John Biggers (1924–2001) to establish the art department at Texas Southern University (TSU), a historically Black college in the city. The de Menils, owners of an oil services corporation, moved to Houston in 1941 and tremendously impacted the city with patronage of new and existing institutions. The couple are commonly credited with putting the Contemporary Arts Museum on the map by organizing and underwriting popular exhibitions of Van Gogh in 1951 and Max Ernst in 1952. These powerful patrons brought with them a glow of wealth and power that cast in shadow less wealthy residents working at the grassroots to build Houston into a national center of modern and contemporary art.

By many reports, the spirit and operations of the CAA became a struggle between the DIY, all-volunteer committee—dubbed by its detractors the "burlap crowd" because of its homespun aesthetic—and the de Menils and allies who aspired to elevate the CAA into a Texas Museum of Modern Art.[5] In 1952 the couple attempted to hire a prominent full-time director, Douglas MacAgy, who turned them down, even though it was his wife Jermayne who had visited Houston on his behalf and submitted a detailed proposal for the position. Men usually took the lead in organizing the exhibitions in the early days of the CAA. An exception was Loraine Gonzalez, who sat on the exhibition committee. An amateur weaver, she curated a ceramics show in 1950 and design show in 1952 and was an early supporter of the American Craft Council. Women played an essential role in keeping the CAA afloat. A newspaper article detailed how the CAA's deeply committed female volunteers hired babysitters or enlisted their mothers to relieve them of their own domestic responsibilities in order to work during the museum's evening hours.[6] But these vital contributions did not translate into significant representation of women in exhibitions.

At the same time that women artists struggled for visibility, Texas art institutions remained racially segregated under Jim Crow laws. Black artists in Houston had access to few exhibition options other than at the Negro Arts Club and women's clubs with cultural missions, like the Ethel Ransom Art and Literary Club. The latter, like the Priscilla Art Club in Dallas, hosted an annual exhibition of members' needlework and craft. Sometimes works by contemporary Black artists crossed the color line. The CAA included a work by New York painter Jacob Lawrence in the premiere exhibition, and a color woodcut by sculptor and graphic artist Elizabeth Catlett (her nationality listed as Mexican, having relocated to Mexico City in 1946) in a 1950 exhibition drawn from local collections. The painter John Biggers played an instrumental role in the desegregation of the Museum of Fine Arts, which at the time restricted African Americans to visiting on Thursdays. These discriminatory rules prevented him from attending the Saturday opening of the 1950 annual contemporary art exhibition, in which his drawing *The Cradle* was awarded a purchase prize. The director asked Biggers to attend a special ceremony on Thursday night with the promise that the museum would integrate within a year.[7] Houston mayor Roy Hofheinz slowly began to desegregate other public cultural institutions and parks after his election in 1952.

In March 1953 the CAA opened "Painting, Sculpture and Ceramics from Texas Southern University," featuring the work of faculty and students from the historically Black university. Biggers and another teaching artist, Carroll H. Simms, contributed work, and the CAA's curators, Ava Jean and Herb Mears—she a secretary at CAA, he an artist recently arrived from New York—included 12 women among the 35 artists. Several of the participating artists went on to contribute to the further development of Black artists in the community. The CAA offered a summer art class to Black students in 1953, but according to board minutes it attracted no enrollees.[8]

The first CAA show with a sizable number of women artists was "Texas Contemporary Artists," co-curated in 1952 by Eleanor and Frank Freed in partnership with Knoedler Gallery of New York. Eleven of the 52 artists were women, including a contingent from the Fort Worth circle of painters and printmakers, which centered on a school and association founded by three women. The next year, the Freeds organized "Mexican Paintings and Drawings" with Diego Rivera, José Clemente Orozco (1883–1949), Rufino Tamayo (1899–1991), and others, in conjunction with the city's Mexican Art Week. Frida Kahlo was the lone woman in the show. In its first four years of operation, the CAA did not mount one solo exhibition by a woman artist. It is in this context that the exhibition committee of the CAA greenlighted its first exhibition to highlight women.

"Women in Art" must have been proposed in 1952, because Norma Henderson was already listed as the chair of the show in the minutes of an early 1953 meeting of the exhibition committee. In early March, she sent a letter inviting Louise Nevelson to participate, explaining, "the purpose of the exhibit is to show the best work which women are doing today in as many different types of art work as possible. We are trying to select two or three women in each field who, we feel, are doing particularly fine and unusual things."[9] Henderson deemphasized any activist dimension of the exhibition's purpose and painted an upbeat picture of women as prominent professionals in all areas of art and design in the United States. The short, unsigned statement in the eight-page brochure relied on gender stereotypes of women's essential differences to make these claims.

> As far back as man's knowledge goes, evidence has been found of the constant use to which woman has put her skillful hands and intuitive imagination—creating comfort and beauty in what-ever environment man has provided. Now, with the coming of new building materials, new concepts of space, a need has arisen for new line, new color, new shapes, and woman has found new work for her sensitive hands interpreting her environment with new materials, new ideas, and old skills—ingots and the blast of steel furnaces in needlepoint; the precision reach of skyscrapers in textiles; the simplicity of machines in watercolors; shapes from the laboratory and the burst of atomic color in ceramic.[10]

This text accepts the socially constructed binaries of the feminine and masculine, the soft and hard, the domestic and industrial, to define contemporary art by women in the exhibition as reactive to male-dominated social and economic structures.

A committee of dedicated teachers, artists, and crafts supporters formed around Henderson to assemble "Women in Art." Her former Lamar High School student Henry Gadbois designed the poster, and her Lamar colleague, Helen Greenwood, an English teacher, edited the brochure. Ellen Sharp, the CAA's executive secretary, also worked on the show. Kathryn Swenson, the typist and editor for the exhibition team, later opened the important New Arts Gallery. Another key member of the exhibition team was Loraine Gonzalez, a CAA board member (in the catalogue listed as "Mrs. Richard Gonzalez). A wide diversity of media, an inclusive spirit, and the integration of art and the domestic space were part of the CAA culture; it was Henderson's contribution to highlight women within this institutional framework.

Regrettably, there is no known checklist of exhibited works in the CAA's archives. Nor are there any installation photographs of the presentation in the A-frame. The list of artists in the brochure is the single record of the exhibition's participants. There is some guidance on the type of work exhibited by each artist, as artists are grouped by medium and technique. Other sources have furnished additional information about some artists' contributions. The CAA maintained a scrapbook, consisting mostly of newspaper clippings, some of which contain references to the imagery, style, or material used by several artists. Newspaper photographs record works like book bindings by Mariana Roach (1908–1976) and an unidentified animal figurine, possibly a ceramic piece by Leza McVey (1907–1984), being handled by Henderson and other volunteers and participants.[11] The images affirm that the highly engaged arts association membership took a hands-on approach to the works of craft and decorative arts selected for the exhibition; they send a message of accessibility and lack of preciousness.

The exhibition included representation of nationally known women in the fine arts. Many of them were already associated with the theme of "women in art," as they were frequently included in all-women gallery and museum shows. The presence of Mary Cassatt anchored the historical narrative of women's ongoing participation in modernism in the USA. To make these connections, the show included many of the widely exhibited women painters of the time, including Irene Rice Pereira, Loren MacIver, Hedda Sterne, and Dorothea Tanning. The sculpture selections favored craft media, with three artists working primarily in ceramics—Leza McVey, Nora Herz

(1906–1999), and Marianna von Allesch (1886–1972)—along with bronze work by the celebrated sculptor Mary Callery (1903–1977).

Callery lived in New York after a long residence in Paris, where she had interacted with Fernand Léger, Pablo Picasso, and others in the avant-garde. She invented a style of linear, open-form figural sculpture that was praised by curators and critics in the 1940s. "Mary Callery is one of the few sculptors present who is as interested in the areas which surround sculptured forms as she is in the sculptured object itself," a critic wrote.[12] She embodied the midcentury ideal of the versatile artist creating new work in dialogue with architecture, and received prominent private and public commissions. In 1948, after learning that the de Menils were in New York looking for a modernist architect to design their new house, she introduced them to Philip Johnson in her Manhattan studio. She developed a following in Houston, and her work appeared in the CAA's inaugural exhibition. It is not known which of her sculptures was included in "Women in Art," but it might have been one of her pieces that were already held in Houston collections, such as *Acrobats with Birds* (1952), which was in the collection of Mrs. E. J. Hudson, or *Tomorrow Is a Mystery* (1949), a 7-inch-tall (17.8 cm) bronze of a skeletal figure reclining by an elongated cruciform, which was in the Menil collection (illus. 49). The de Menils were listed as lenders in the exhibition brochure, but no records confirm whether *Tomorrow Is a Mystery* was the work in the show.

The presence of accomplished women artists was not the main story in Houston as it was at Smith College (see Chapter Three). Rather, the show's primary narrative was represented by a drawing of a pair of hands working knitting needles that appeared on the opening invitation: "Women in Art" sought to link the innovative contemporary artistic practices of women to the ancient association of women and needlework. About one-third of the artists in "Women in Art" worked in fiber. Many were trained in Europe and migrated to the United States during the rise of fascism in the 1930s, while others emerged as American-trained practitioners. The lessons of the Bauhaus, which focused on craft and the integration of art and design, effectively leveled the playing field and gave fiber and ceramic the same conceptual status as the traditionally male-dominated media of painting and sculpture.

Accordingly, the press focused on fiber as the newsworthy hook to the show. The more liberal of the two Houston dailies, the *Post*, thoroughly covered the exhibition, in part because several contributors to the newspaper also served on the CAA's publicity team. "Modern needlework is one of the least publicized and most intriguing of women's artistic endeavors," wrote a *Post* article on the exhibition that discussed the abstract material experiments and textile collages by

49 Mary Callery, *Tomorrow Is a Mystery*, 1949, bronze.

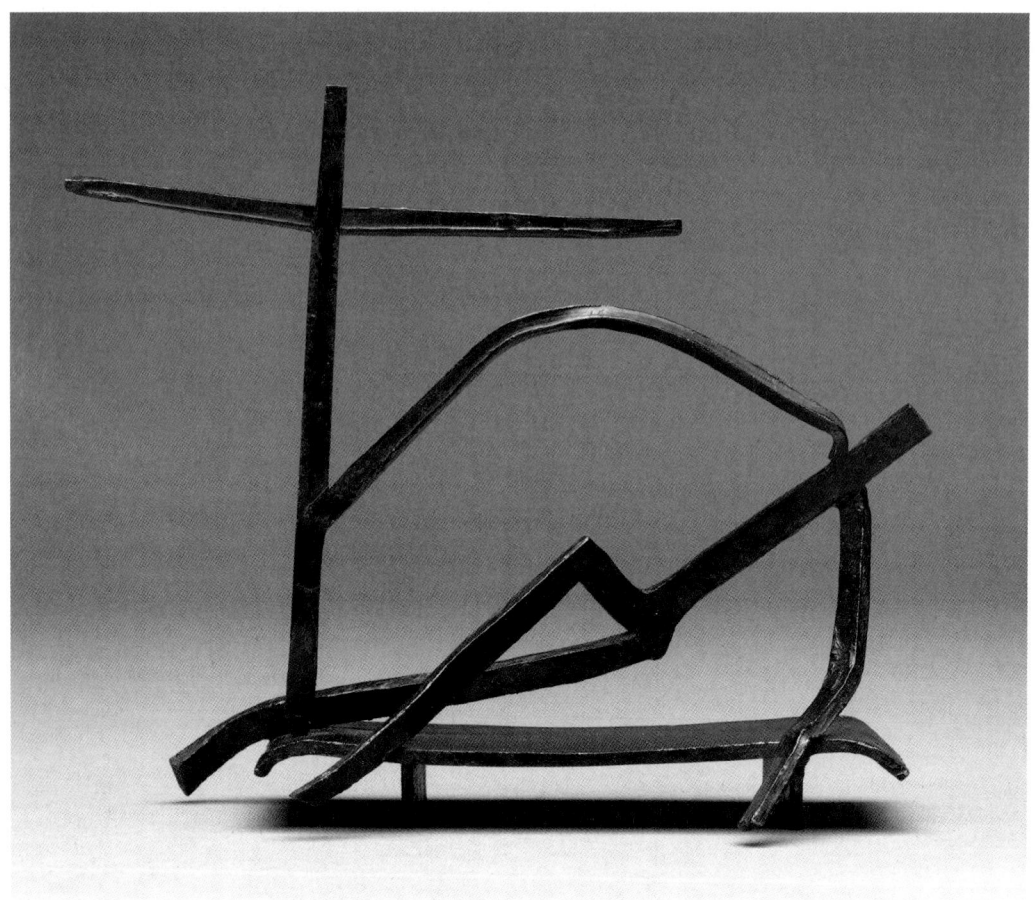

several participants.[13] The list of weavers and designers in the exhibition included many key figures in the modern textile movement in the United States. Dorothy Liebes and Florence Knoll were national artist-entrepreneurs in high-end textile design and fabrication, while Martha Taipale, Eszter Haraszty, Noémi Raymond, Isabell Scott, Marianne Strengell, Ruth Adler, Marion Dorn, Geraldine Funk, and Leslie Tillett innovated in design and handweaving. They ranged from individual artists, such as solo Texas weaver Doris Coulter, to craftspeople running workshops, like Maria Kipp, who opened a studio in California with sixteen looms operated by skilled artisans.

Architect and designer Florence Knoll's (1917–2019) marriage to company founder Hans Knoll (1914–1955) resulted in a powerful partnership: their name became synonymous with modern American interior design. In 1947 Florence launched the textile department and the Knoll Planning Unit, skillfully marketing the integrated interior design and sale of fabrics and furnishings to corporations and other clients. Like Callery, she had already made a mark in Texas by early 1953. Florence Knoll designed a demonstration room for the Dallas Museum of Fine Arts, which was photographed in the pages of *Life* in March, and was slated to design the interior of a new bank building in Austin.[14] There were other Knoll connections in the show. At the time of "Women in Art," Eszter Haraszty (1920–1994) was the head textile designer for the company, following in the footsteps of former department heads Marianne Strengell (1909–1998), who taught weaving at the Cranbrook Academy of Art in Michigan, and Noémi Raymond (1889–1980), who moved to Japan to open a design firm.

The organizers of "Women in Art" failed to include any Black women artists. This blind spot is particularly glaring because Henderson and the rest of the exhibition committee likely had seen work by a number of pertinent artists on view in the CAA exhibition of art from TSU two months earlier. Fannie Holman (1911–2005), a Houston native, later ran that university's weaving program. Athene

Watson (1915–1998) taught art education and aesthetics over four decades at TSU. And Ruth Mae McCrane (1929–2002) earned a master's degree in art education from TSU in 1955 and painted murals and religious paintings for decades while teaching in Houston public schools.[15] Theresa Pratt Allen (1913–2013), a Texas native with a master's degree in art from the University of Colorado, was not in the show, as she began teaching at TSU in 1955 after having taught for a number of years at Prairie View A&M University. At TSU she established a weaving workshop with extremely limited resources; as she recalled, "We used looms made from cardboard or picture frames with nails and cardboard shuttles. We even wove on soda straws!"[16] Allen built up the program and eventually acquired proper equipment, and her inventive adaptation of non-traditional techniques could have resonated with the avant-garde weavers selected for "Women in Art."

In addition to the weavers and textile designers, "Women in Art" included a selection of artists using fiber as an expressive art form outside the conventional functions of upholstery, curtains, or bedspreads. The brochure categorized some such works as "cloth pictures" that incorporated diverse materials such as burlap, sateen, percale, curtain mesh, braids, and sequins.[17] A review in the *Houston Post* praised the exhibition's devotion to modern textiles and singled out a number of artists, including Edith Lestz and her two-dimensional wall-hangings, *Birds in Flight* and *Cock Fight* (undated).[18] The *Post* reviewer also admired New York-based artist Eve Peri's (1897–1966) methods of employing fabric as a purely visual medium in the same way that a painter would use oil.[19] Peri's works were appreciated in their time as curious hybrids of abstraction and domestic arts, "sophisticated samplers" cross-breeding the masculine tradition of Picasso and the anonymous domestic crafts of Americana.[20] The work illustrated here, *Journey to the Moon* (c. 1945) (illus. 50), not known to have appeared in the show, embodies the visual and material characteristics described in the *Post* review: "an exciting and at the same time harmonious composition of textures, colors, and design."[21]

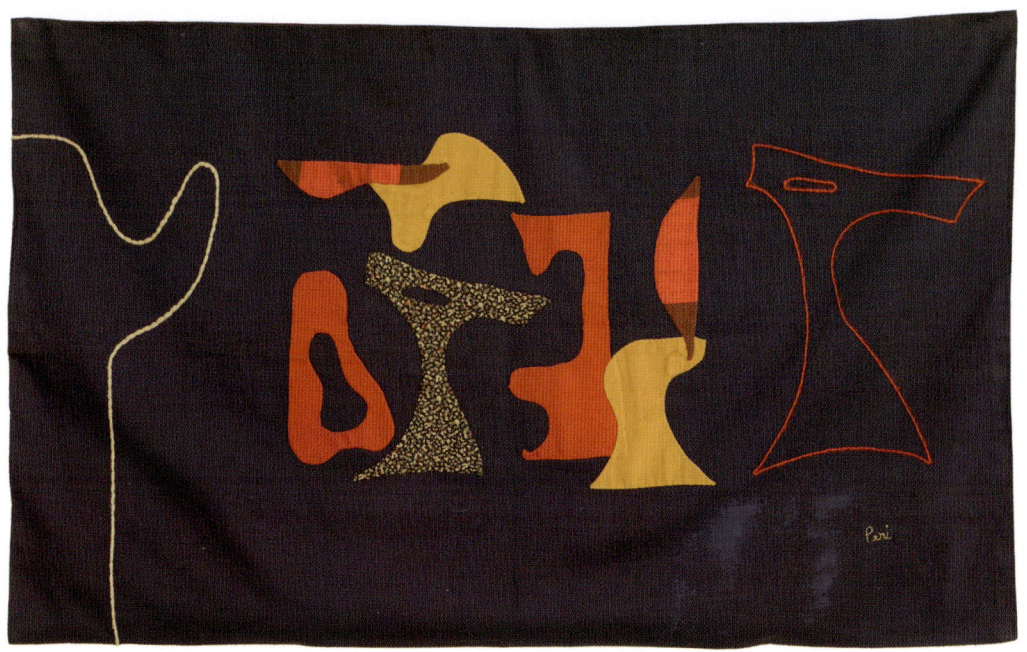

50 Eve Peri, *Journey to the Moon*, c. 1945, hand-appliqué and embroidery on fabric.

Another category, "needlework," included two-dimensional pictures with stitched imagery by three artists: needlepoint by Mildred T. Johnstone (1900–1988), abstractions in thread by Mariska Karasz (1898–1960), and embroidered tableaux by Nathalie Pervouchine Labrecque (1923–2002). Johnstone's work exemplified the exhibition's theme of modern design by women as a hybrid of industry and traditional craft. Her needlepoint wall-hanging *The Industrial Doll House* (1949) (illus. 51), depicting a cross-section of the interior operations of a steel furnace, was one of the few works in the show referenced in the exhibition's brochure text. The same work featured in a photograph in the *Houston Post*, which showed Henderson—sporting a distinctive pageboy haircut and cravat—handling the artwork in preparation for its installation.[22] Johnstone had developed the work using a multi-step process: she created a collage of newspaper and magazine clippings, then asked Chilean artist Pablo Burchard to draw them as cartoons, which she used to stitch the final piece. Her playful synthesis of industrial subject-matter and typically feminine media, though not

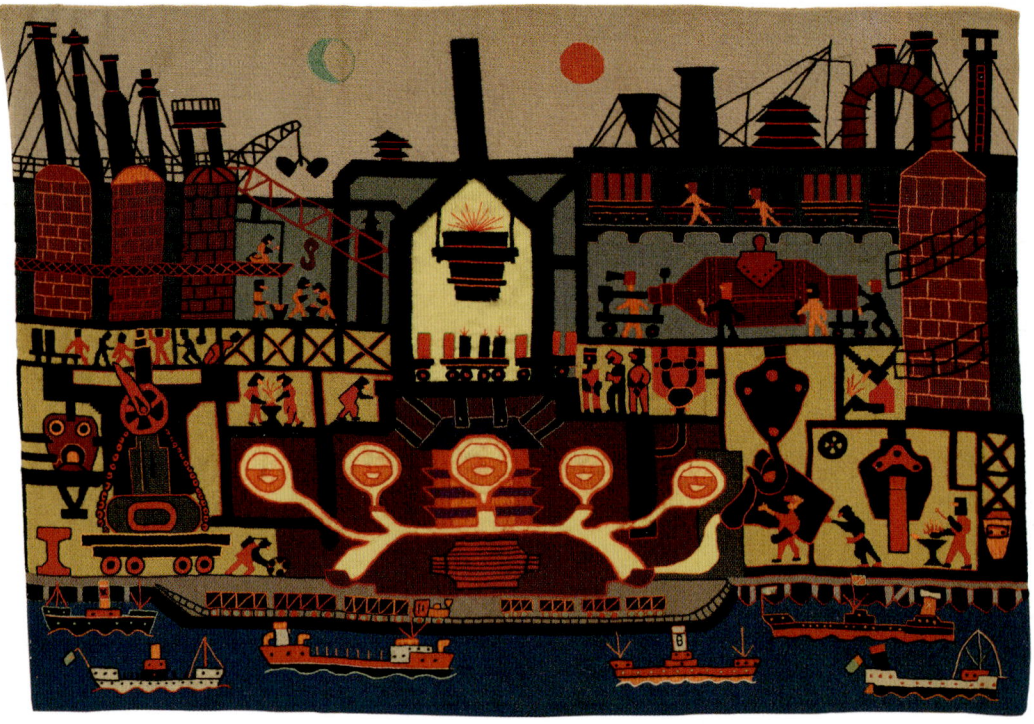

new in the craft world, continued to spark interest among journalists and critics. A few years later a newspaper mentioned the irony of the needlework hanging in the office of her steel executive husband.[23]

Also in the needlework category was Hungarian-born Karasz, a successful clothing designer who began artistic sewing after the Second World War. A fervent apostle of creative needlework, she published a book and served as guest editor at *House Beautiful* magazine to circulate her ideas to a national audience. She rejected the narrow association of sewing with grandmotherly handiwork and instead encouraged modern women to employ the needle as a supple tool for artistic creation, the same way that a painter might utilize a brush. "I feel that the needle is a chance for women to express herself in her world," she said.[24] Karasz also celebrated the beauty of the everyday by incorporating found objects and unusual elements in her work, such as copper telephone wire, rubber fly swatters, and natural materials like

51 Mildred T. Johnstone, *The Industrial Doll House*, 1949, linen plain weave with wool and angora diagonal tent stitch, stem stitch, straight stitch, French knots, and satin stitch embroidery, linen plain-weave lining.

moss and feathers. The *Post* article on modern textiles in "Women in Art" praises her usage of a variety of materials to make abstractions in thread that hung from rods or were framed, such as this representative example, *Skeins* (c. 1950) (illus. 52).[25]

The show also included a wide range of works by artists creating across the decorative arts. Among these were ceramics by Marguerite Wildenhain (1896–1985) and Eva Zeisel (1906–2011), silver by Margaret De Patta, plastic lamps by Zahara Schatz (1916–1999), glassware by Freda Diamond (1905–1998), book illustrations by Juliet Kepes (1919–1999), and more. These artists all had been included at least once in important contemporary design and craft exhibitions, such as MOMA's "Good Design" series. The national profile of many of the artists in the show spoke to the burgeoning system of exhibitions and publications in the U.S. postwar crafts field, which permitted the distribution of images and information.

The primacy of fiber art in the exhibition narrative likely influenced the selection of artists working in other media whose processes engaged with textiles either literally or metaphorically. Printmaking was one area of convergence of fine arts and textiles in the postwar U.S. art world. Led by Stanley William Hayter (1901–1988), the experimental printmaking workshop Atelier 17 in New York focused on etching and aquatint, and encouraged workshop participants to generate biomorphic patterns and textures with lace and other fabrics imprinted on the metal plate. Nevelson's etchings in "Women in Art" likely consisted of her images of diaphanous figures recently produced there. Atelier 17 was a hub for women artists working at the intersection of textiles and printmaking (see Chapter Eight).

Another printmaker in the show, June Wayne (1918–2011), favored a different technique for process-oriented experimental creativity. Working in Los Angeles, Wayne became a devotee of lithography, a popular medium for poster design, reinvigorated by Americans at midcentury because of its ability to record and reproduce brushstrokes with little distortion or loss of visual integrity. Many of her

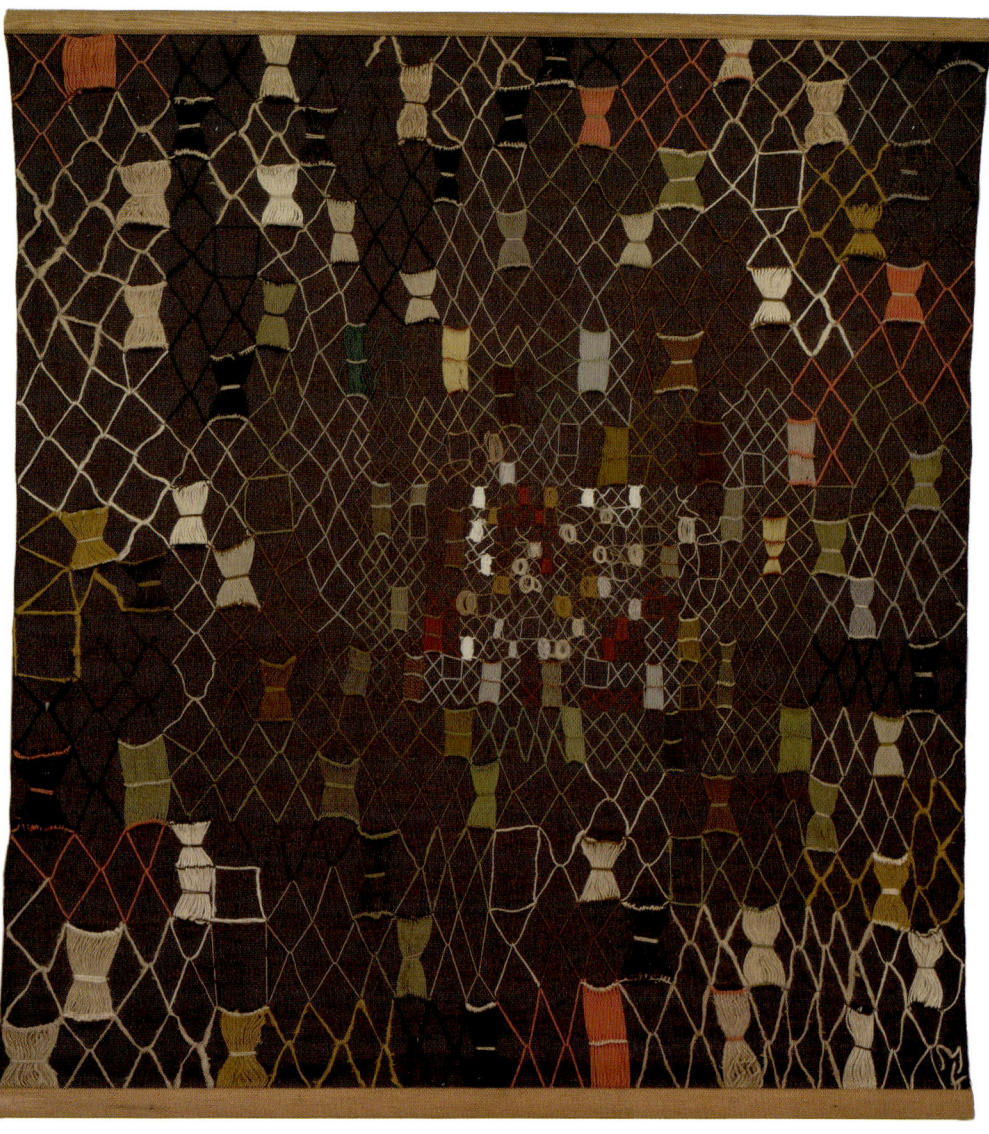

52 Mariska Karasz, *Skeins*, c. 1950, linen, cotton, and wool.

lithographs of the time possess textured surfaces that appear to be lattices or interlocking grids, suggesting the woven forms of textiles. The one Wayne print known to have been exhibited in the show, *The Witnesses* (1952) (illus. 53), was part of her *Justice* series, inspired by her personal experience attending a friend's court hearings and her readings of Kafka's *The Trial*.[26] Described in the *Post* as gentle and probing, the print's imagery of tapered columns with various patterns evokes an off-kilter and disorienting encounter.[27] A copy of the "Women in Art" brochure in Wayne's papers includes her annotations with corrected first names of participating artists, indicating her engagement with the exhibition.

The work by Sue Fuller (1914–2006) included in the exhibition, which blended aspects of sculpture, painting, and textiles, received its own category in the brochure: "String Composition." Building on the prewar Constructivism of Naum Gabo and Barbara Hepworth, Fuller adapted their use of thread and string to create spatial tensions between solid masses and extended the material into an image-making medium. Her prevailing formal interests in vectors and gravitational forces is

53 June Wayne, *The Witnesses*, 1952, lithograph in black with debossing on wove paper.

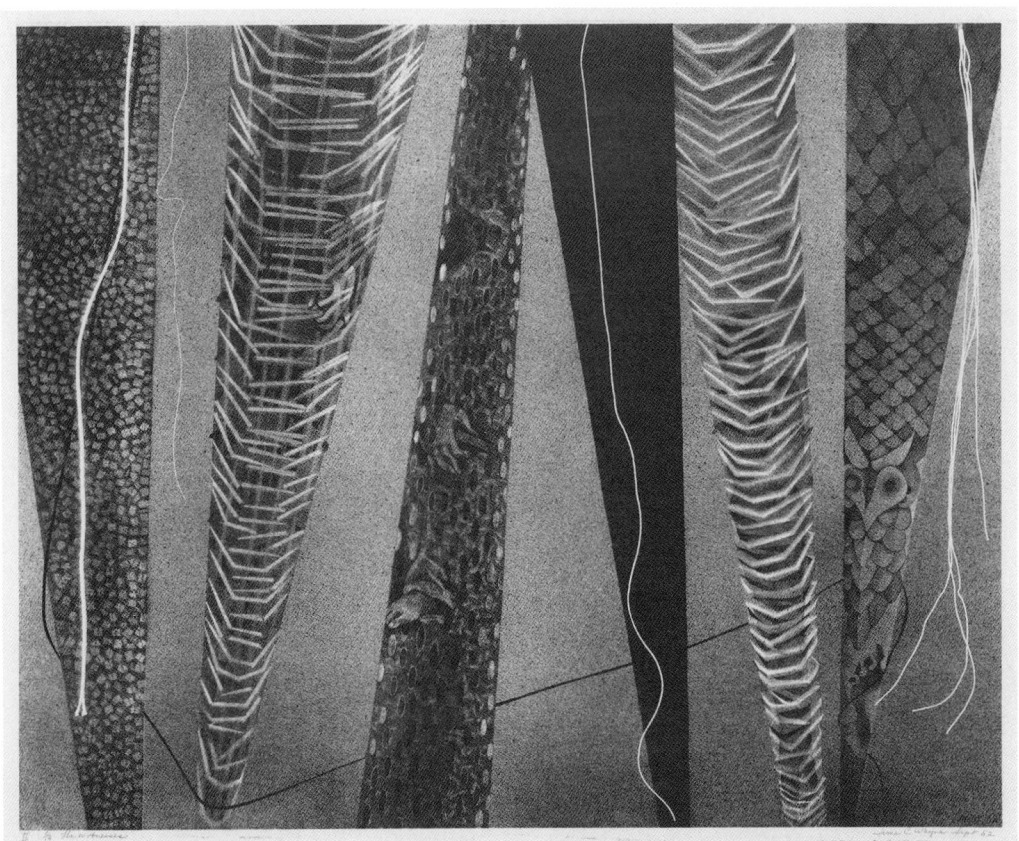

reflected in *String Composition #68* (1955) (illus. 54), a contemporaneous piece composed of plastic monofilament strung in taut, radiating lines within a thin steel frame. Fuller also employed string and textiles in her work at Atelier 17, producing soft-ground etchings.

The two photographers included in "Women in Art" also fit the exhibition's conceptual framework oriented around the flexible grid of fiber art: the selected prints highlighted photographic techniques to render abstract fields of lattices and waves. German-born New York resident Lotte Jacobi, well known since the 1920s for portraiture, embarked in the 1940s on her *Photogenics* series of abstract forms. She employed the photogram technique, shining a flashlight on pieces of glass or crinkled cellophane to cast abstract patterns that would be imprinted on photographic paper without the use of a camera. Three of these abstract photographs appeared in the show, described in the *Post* as "freeflowing forms."[28] Jacobi's photographic prints recorded light effects resembling fabrics or draperies, sometimes suggesting the topographies of the human body. These works, along with those by Nevelson, Fuller, and Wayne, expanded the conceptual and material potential of textiles and fiber to serve as vital wellsprings for modern art centering women's lives.

The other photographer in the exhibition, Carlotta Corpron (1901–1988), was among the cohort of Texas-based artists in "Women in Art." Born in Minnesota, she graduated from Teachers College of Columbia University and became a professor of art at the Texas State Women's College in Denton, north of Dallas, in 1935. In the 1940s Corpron began a body of abstract photographs depicting the interplay of light on the surfaces of solid objects within confined spaces. She pioneered the teaching of abstract photography in the United States, organizing a "light workshop" at the college by a visiting Moholy-Nagy in 1942. From time to time, one of her abstract images evoked the supple surfaces and geometries of textiles. Though her precise contribution to "Women in Art" is unknown, *Woven Light* (1944) (illus. 55) could have eloquently fit into the show. As suggested by the title, Corpron

54 Sue Fuller, *String Composition #68*, 1955, construction of plastic thread, nails, painted board and integral brass, steel and plexiglass frame.

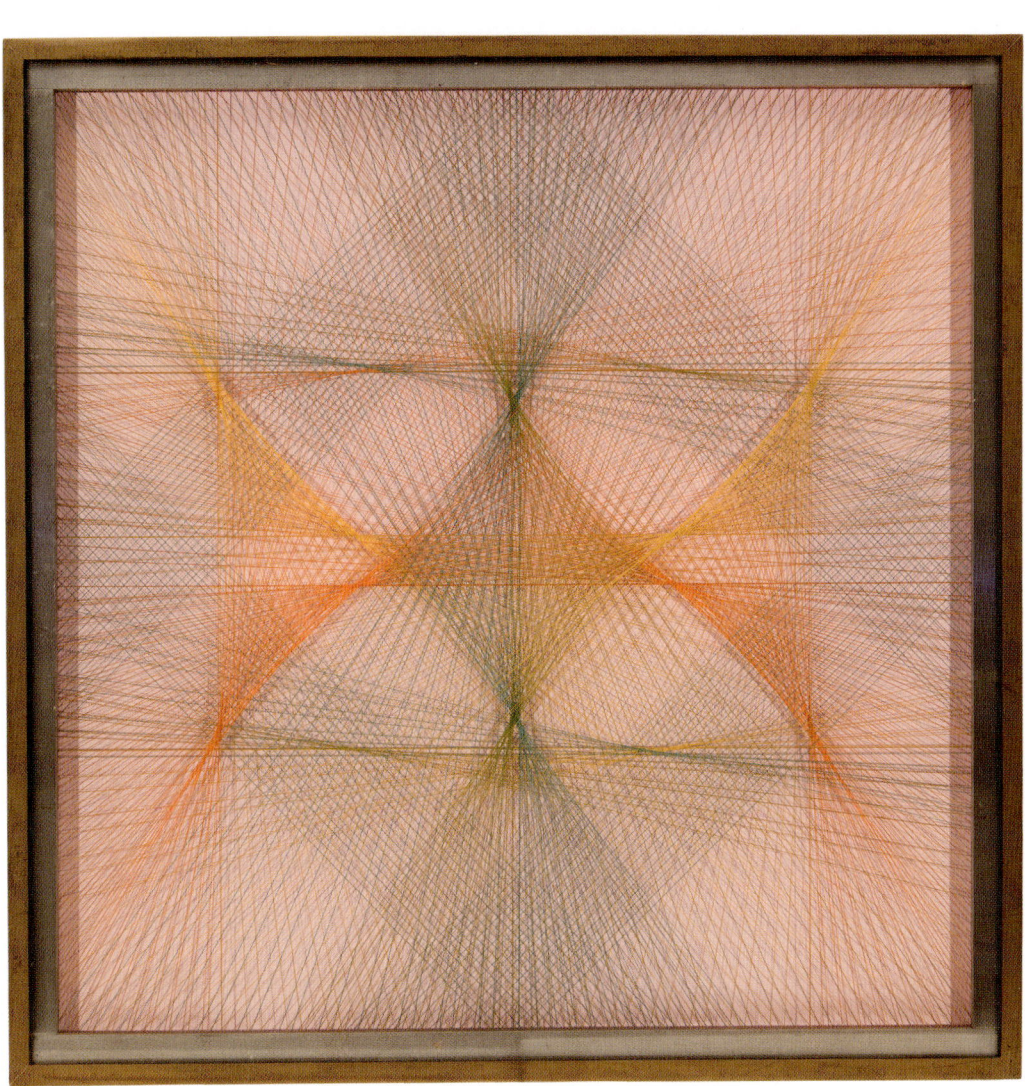

manipulated an artificial light source to create tightly controlled, repeated diamond-shaped patterns, not unlike those of a woven carpet. A leader of artistic photography in Texas, she was invited by the CAA to return to Houston to serve as a juror for its "Creative Photography" show in August, in advance of her solo exhibition at the Art Institute of Chicago.

Other artists in the exhibition filled out the story of the manifold contributions women made to art and design in midcentury Texas. Three artists in "Women in Art" had previously won prizes in the annual Texas Craft shows at the Dallas Museum of Fine Arts: book-binder Mariana Roach (Dallas), weaver Doris Coulter (Bryan, about 100 miles (160 km) from Houston), and potter Katherine Wilson (Austin). Roach's book bindings aligned with the larger category of needlework, as she utilized stitchery to join and adorn her fabric and leather covers. One of her works, entitled *Joseph's Coat*—visible in a black-and-white image in the *Post*—appears to possess vertical striped papers, reminiscent of the titular robe, as described in the Bible, applied to orange Oasis leather.[29] Other local artists included Kathleen Blackshear (1897–1988), who grew up in Texas and moved to Chicago, keeping a studio in Houston and often summering in her hometown Navasota, about 70 miles (113 km) away. Her crayon batik textile with owl-like bird in geometric patterns on orange ground was described as a favorite work by *Post* writer Catherine Louden.[30] Notably, Black-shear's longtime partner, Ethel Spears (1903–1974), contributed etchings to the exhibition as well.

At the opening, the CAA flipped its standard script of female volunteers providing smiling hospitality and assigned the roles of host committee and reception chair to male board members. The gender reversal sparked some amusement in the pages of the *Houston Post*, which relied on humor to deflect attention from the very real male anxiety about appearing even remotely feminine. *Post* columnist George Fuermann marveled at the "immense man's man" John Maher, head of the Oil Center Tool Co., also known as "Big Reb for his

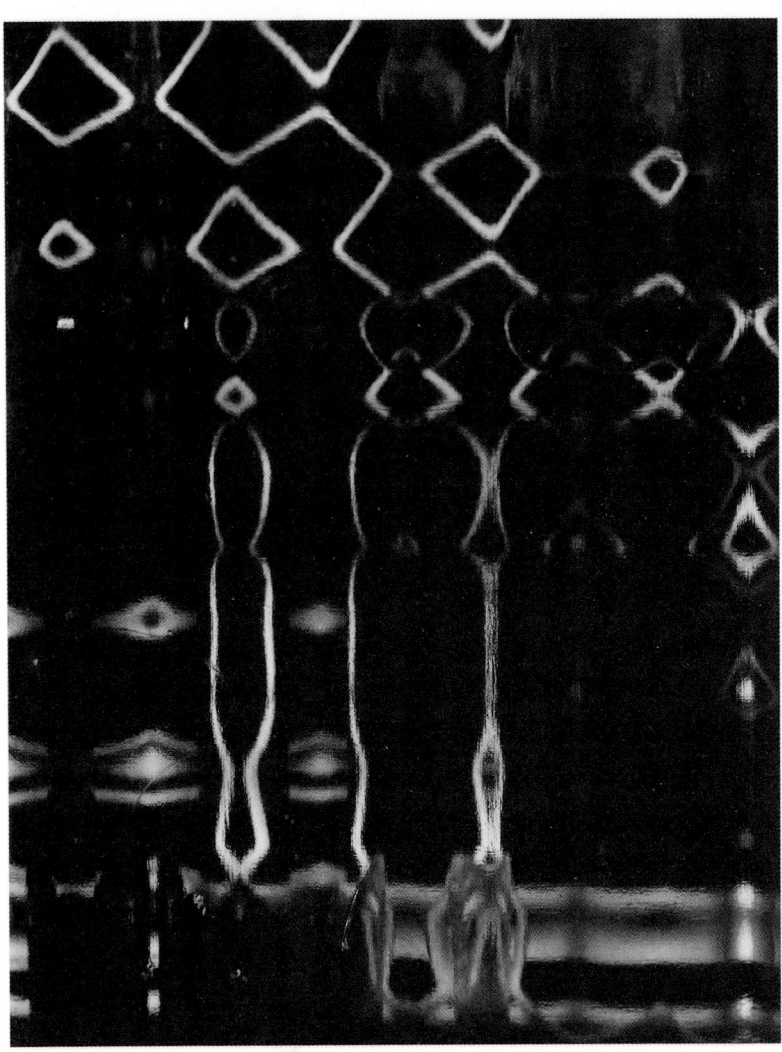

55 Carlotta Corpron,
Woven Light, 1944,
gelatin silver print.

remarkable knowledge of Confederate lore," serving as the host chair.[31]
To recuperate masculine pride, Fuermann insisted this was part of an
honorable tradition of men surrendering their superior positions,
opining, "men serving women is nothing new. Been going on for centuries."[32] Fuermann's snide attitude toward the idea of gender reversal
did not discourage the CAA from inviting him to moderate a public
panel discussion about women in the arts, presented in conjunction
with the show a week after the opening. The panel consisted of several

Texas women who impacted local and national art and culture. Writer Jewel Henson Gibson published two novels that narrated the underside of the Texas worship of God and money (exploring the territory before Edna Ferber's novel *Giant* popularized the Texas oil field drama in 1952). Also on the panel was Johnny Nelson George, the founder of Theatre Inc. and a pioneering theatrical presenter in the city. Painter Gertrude Levy, known locally for her progressive views on integration, was the sole female visual artist on the panel. Fuermann, in an advance item on the panel, billed it as a "battle of the sexes" in which he anticipated that he would have to defend the one male panelist, illustrator and CAA co-founder Edward "Buck" Schiwetz.[33]

The public opening and panel discussion of "Women in Art" staged predictable theatrics around gender roles—catnip to the press—that curated women's creative responses to the modern world and did not credit them with any role in building it. The contents of the exhibition itself, presented in the modernist museum, complicated these narratives and communicated an optimistic message of the inherent good in the fusion of new materials and techniques and old crafts in women's contemporary art. For all its contradictions, "Women in Art," by raising awareness of gender in art and indicating the growing role of women within the organization, contributed to CAA's institutional attempts to broaden its artists and outreach. The year 1953 witnessed the emergence of a socially aware ethos at CAA, with exhibitions dedicated to women in art, Texas Southern University, and Mexican painting and drawing. The CAA invited Niharranjan Ray, for example, a professor of fine arts at the University of Calcutta (1903–1981), to speak on Indian art and aesthetics. In November 1953 John Biggers contributed an essay to the catalogue of the optimistically titled exhibition "Integration: The Use of Painting and Sculpture with Architecture in Daily Life," organized by Frank Dolejska, on the need for experimental art and educational institutions to support free expression. By the end of the year, the CAA board formed the Women's Division to handle publicity and other public-facing aspects of the program, recognizing the disproportionate amount of free labor provided by women to make possible public access with only two paid staff.

This short period of inclusive community-building in the CAA occurred during a brief transitional period between the de Menils' hands-on patronage and the flamboyant exhibitions organized under the directorship of Jermayne MacAgy (1914–1964) starting in 1955. Their relationship began three years earlier when MacAgy traveled to Houston, met with the CAA board, and produced a detailed prospectus on the role of a director. The report sat for two years before the board began to take it seriously and assembled a committee to "pursue both the man and the money," as phrased by John Maher, according to board minutes.[34] CAA chair Marjorie Selden finally read MacAgy's report and realized that its author was the person they were looking for all along.[35] Her style of probing, thematic shows installed with theatrical flair, which she developed in her previous role as curator of the Palace of the Legion of Honor in San Francisco, consolidated the Contemporary Arts Museum's position as a leader in contemporary arts curating in the USA. The comingling of liberalizing culture, enthusiasm for experimental art exhibitions, and oil money found an uncommon and fluid equilibrium at CAA.

Many of the women involved with "Women in Art" continued to organize and participate in the Contemporary Arts Association's signature interdisciplinary shows during MacAgy's tenure. In 1956 Henderson, no longer on the exhibition committee, collaborated with two other artists on a silhouette projection screen included in the multimedia exhibition "Shadow and Substance: The Shadow Theater of Montmartre and Modern Art," organized by Ellen Sharp, and in 1958 Kathryn Swenson assembled "The Disquieting Muse: Surrealism," a reconsideration of the influential movement. But women remained underrepresented as artists in CAA exhibitions. It was not until 1960 that a woman, weaver Anni Albers, received a solo show there, which again reiterated the centrality of textiles in the thinking about women's contemporary art. Multiple forces—sometimes in competition, sometimes in harmony—coursed through the CAA, from a collective DIY volunteerism to authorial curation, from entrenched sexism to enthusiasm for women demonstrating the Bauhaus progressive ethos.

In a city newly attentive to embracing modern art, design, and architecture, Henderson organized an all-women art show as an apolitical vehicle to educate the public about women's achievements. But in affirming essentialist stereotypes and avoiding critical discourses, this prematurely celebratory narrative of the success of women artists in the United States neglected to address continuing institutional sex and race discrimination. "Women in Art" appears to have made little impact beyond Houston. It is unknown if any of the non-resident artists traveled to attend the exhibition. The exhibition did not receive any coverage in the pages of the New York and California art magazines, and just a few notices appeared in local newspapers outside Texas announcing participation of area residents. This bold survey of art and design by women in a leading U.S. contemporary arts museum unfortunately has been almost entirely overlooked in the art-historical and feminist literature.[36] Both ahead of and fully delimited by its time, "Women in Art" did not achieve broader institutional or critical support to fulfill its promise of a radical reclamation of the traditional women's arts as a foundation for feminist activism.

7

Greatness: "Great Women Artists: 16th to 20th Centuries," Delius Gallery, 1955

"It's puzzling that in major fields of art creation, women—though they show enormous talent—have never yet produced one toprank, ruling genius or leader," critic Alexander Fried wrote in response to the San Francisco Women Artists annual in 1952.[1] After decades of gains toward political and educational equality, women artists appeared to have attained greater recognition. But the problematic question of whether there are or have ever been "great women artists" continued to permeate the discourse around all-women exhibitions. "Even in this age of women's creativity there is no woman artist as dominant as Matisse, Picasso, Klee, or Henry Moore," the San Francisco critic deplored.[2] Such observations, without a critical feminist framing, defined artistic greatness by the image of the solitary male inventor of new forms and did not take into account the many institutional and psychological obstacles to women that remained firmly in place. American critics had by now repeatedly outlined the upward trajectory of female modern artists, starting with Mary Cassatt, but remained flummoxed by the fact that no woman had attained the status in art that Jane Austen and Charlotte Brontë achieved in English literature.

Few curators or institutions truly probed the whys and wherefores of the "greatness gap" directly. Women artists organizations shied away from making any claims of greatness, while individual women

EXHIBITION

"GREAT WOMEN ARTISTS"

(16th to 20th centuries)

Paintings — Drawings — Watercolors

It seems strange that in an age which keeps on expounding the characteristics, talents, and virtues of "The Second Sex," and which has even gone to the length of declaring "The Natural Superiority of Women," the power of women as creative artists has not yet been fully realized. Admittedly, there are no women painters of the stature of a Velazquez or a Picasso (though the most famous of all ancient pictures, "Alexander's Victory over Darius," has been attributed to a woman), nevertheless an astonishing number of them have made contributions which not only reveal the ability of their sex for outstanding and sustained craftsmanship, but have added a novel and altogether feminine element without which the great traditions of the Fine Arts would be so much the poorer. Any, even fragmentary exhibit will bring to the forth their distinctive flair as manifested in the re-occurring motherhood theme, and in the compassion, tenderness, grace, and intuition so typical for the Woman as an Artist.

SOFANISBA ANGUISIOLA
(Italian, 1527-ca. 1623)

LOUISE MOILLON
(French, 1610-1696)

RACHEL RUYSH
(Dutch, 1644-1750)

MARIE-LOUISE VIGÉE-LEBRUN
(French, 1755-1842)

ROSA BONHEUR
(French, 1822-1899)

BERTHE MORISOT
(French, 1841-1895)

MARY CASSATT
(American, 1845-1926)

PAULA MODERSOHN-BECKER
(German, 1876-1907)

SUZANNE VALADON
(French, 1869-1941)
(mother of Utrillo)

KAETHE KOLLWITZ
(German, 1867-1945)

Contemporaries:

BIALLA
SUZANNE CARVALLO
RUTH VAN CLEVE
SONJA DELAUNAY
LY JULIUS
MARIE LAURENCIN
GEORGIA O'KEEFFE
J. RICE-PEREIRA
RENÉE SINTENIS
VIEIRA DA SILVA

The Exhibit includes Christmas suggestions (drawings and prints).

•

The Delius Gallery wishes to thank the other Galleries and private collectors whose kindness and cooperation have made this Exhibit possible.

expressed their opinions on the matter in private correspondence and independent research. One exhibition tackled the issue head-on. With a provocative title, "Great Women Artists: 16th to 20th Centuries" opened at the Delius Gallery, New York, in late November 1955 (illus. 56). Presumably organized by gallery owner Frederick Delius Giese (1899–1957), the show presented works by twenty artists from

56 Delius Gallery, *Great Women Artists*, brochure, 1955.

Europe and America, divided equally between "old mistresses" (to borrow a term from Rozsika Parker and Griselda Pollock) like Sofonisba Anguissola (*c.* 1532–1625) and Rachel Ruysch (1664–1750) and contemporary modernists and abstractionists such as Marie Laurencin (1883–1956) and Irene Rice Pereira. The exhibition flatly insisted that women had achieved the status of greatness but hedged its bets on whether they had yet attained the highest levels of male genius. Whether the exhibition delivered on the promise of its title is explored in this chapter.

The evocation of female greatness might have been more of a marketing strategy than an art-historical intervention. "Great Women Artists" appeared in a small commercial gallery in midtown Manhattan specializing in drawings, with little track record of supporting women artists. Giese established a reputation for presenting high-quality old master artworks within a lively and interdisciplinary context. The gallery, whose name played on the fame of Giese's cousin, composer Frederick Delius, specialized in secondary market works by European and American artists from the Renaissance to modernism. Giese was known to be a connoisseur with an astute eye for quality, ferreting out treasures like a charcoal study by Frans Hals and detecting a group of Renoir forgeries by the infamous Elmyr de Hory. He was willing to take risks, too, staging exhibitions that introduced American audiences to overlooked media and artists, for example Picasso ceramics and a Mannerist group show. The gallery also presented new work by contemporary American and European artists practicing in representational styles.

One of many émigrés to set up shop in New York, Giese brought a distinctly Continental flavor to the gallery. Born in Germany in 1899, he studied art history and opened a gallery, which he moved to London in 1938. An early exhibition there spanned from old masters to Picasso, which initiated his specialty in thematic surveys across artistic schools and eras. After the Second World War, Giese moved to New York and reopened his gallery on 57th Street in 1948, with an opening show spanning several centuries, from Jusepe de Ribera to

Lyonel Feininger.[3] Delius Gallery exhibitions typically consisted of drawings and other works on paper and bore open-ended subtitles like "Through the Ages," "Cross-section," and "Old and New." Women appeared infrequently in these wide-ranging group shows, based on a review of the checklists of ten exhibitions. One of animal sculptures in 1952 included three women artists: Rosa Bonheur (1822–1899), and contemporary artists Renée Sintenis (based in Berlin) and Nora Herz (based in New York and later included in "Women in Art" in Houston). Cassatt and O'Keeffe, who had sterling reputations among American collectors, appeared in several Delius group shows. Surrealist-influenced painter Anne Saporetti (1914–1984) received a solo show at the gallery in 1952. "Great Women Artists" remained consistent with Giese's gallery program of clever surveys of various artists, media, and styles to generate sales opportunities and to compete in the heart of the city's gallery district.

Analysis of the exhibition's contents depends primarily on the brochure and a few contemporary documentary sources and reviews. There are no known archival records or installation views. Though the Delius Gallery's regular practice was to print a detailed checklist of works, the "Great Women Artists" brochure listed only the artists, not the works. This lack of specificity suggests that an exhibition dedicated to women remained unworthy of the standard practices of art-historical record-keeping and documentation. Giese probably selected conversation starters from what was pragmatically available. The title, list of artists, and critical responses in several local newspapers together form a critical jumping-off point for the analysis of an exhibition that constructed a new category of "great women artists" limited to artists of European descent.

The brochure listed the artists in two groups. The first ten, the titular "great women," appeared chronologically by year of birth: Sofonisba Anguissola, Louise Moillon, Rachel Ruysch, Élisabeth Louise Vigée Le Brun, Rosa Bonheur, Berthe Morisot, Mary Cassatt, Suzanne Valadon, Paula Modersohn-Becker, and Käthe Kollwitz. In one fudge, Delius listed Modersohn-Becker (1876–1907) before Valadon (1865–1938) and Kollwitz, though she was born after them, presumably because her premature death prevented her from working later in the twentieth century. All ten artists' significance was already well established in the United States. Works by Vigée Le Brun (1755–1842) and Bonheur achieved high prices at auction. *Vogue* dubbed Cassatt "America's Greatest Woman Painter."[4] Critic Elizabeth McCausland called Kollwitz (1867–1945) "the greatest woman artist of modern times."[5] The second group of ten artists fell under the category of "Contemporaries," listed alphabetically by surname. These living artists comprised a mixed bag, from the avant-garde pioneers Sonia Delaunay and Marie Laurencin to American artists largely disconnected from the main currents of advanced art: Susanne Carvallo, Ruth Van Cleve, and the now unknown artist Ly Julius.[6] The remaining contemporaries were American all-women exhibition veterans Janice Biala, O'Keeffe, and Pereira, and Europeans Maria Helena Vieira da Silva and Renée Sintenis. The gallery's two groups of artists seemed to distinguish the Great Women, as an established canon, and the "great" women, a loose determination applied to the truly venerated and scarcely known from today's perspective.

Notably, nine of the artists in the Delius show had appeared a decade earlier in a similar exhibition, "Famous Women Artists," a survey of thirteen artists that opened at New York's Feigl Gallery in October 1943.[7] Founded by Czech émigré Hugo Feigl, a specialist in French and German art, the gallery was located at 601 Madison Avenue, not far from Art of This Century, discussed in Chapter One. Less than a year after "31 Women" inspired artists and critics to reconsider contemporary women artists, the art world hardly noticed Feigl's historical survey. The *New York Times* review of the Feigl show did not address the all-women premise, and simply listed the artists and briefly described their works, offering sporadic linkages to male painters.[8] Cassatt was the lone American in the exhibition, which eschewed any emerging trends in contemporary American painting. Both Feigl and Delius, as Central

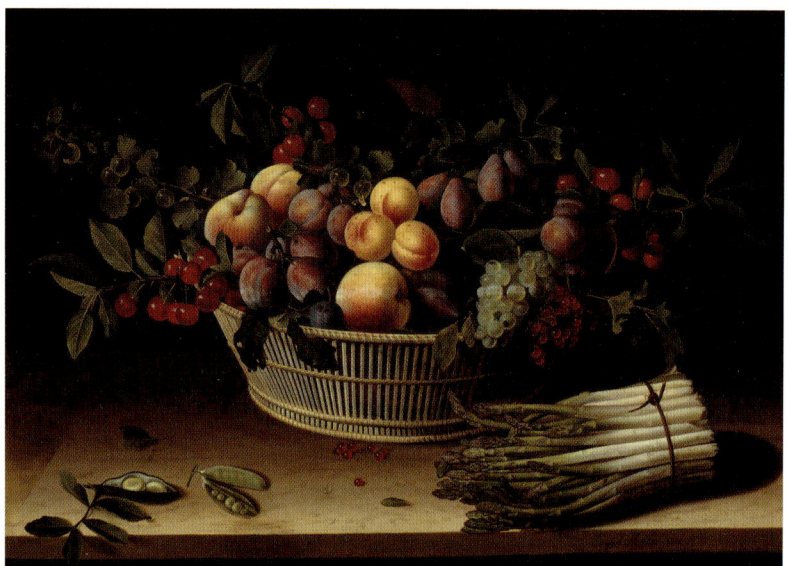

57 Louise Moillon, *Still-Life with a Basket of Fruit and a Bunch of Asparagus*, 1630, oil on panel.

European men, imposed their biases on the selection of women deemed to be "famous" or "great" and in doing so reinforced existing critical parameters.

A comparison between the two shows clarifies the particular contribution of the Delius exhibition. Giese's expansion of the category of "great" to include an equal number of contemporary artists acknowledged the culture was shifting, and more critics and artists engaged with the question of women's achievement. The Metropolitan Museum of Art, for example, published a book on women artists in 1956 with 24 tipped-in color plates as part of its series of books promoted as museums in miniature. Edith Appleton Standen, curator and author of the introduction, claimed that such a compendium was justified at a time when the museum's recent survey of contemporary art placed O'Keeffe on the cover of the catalogue and included Isabel Bishop, Loren MacIver, and Pereira:

> In New York at this moment in history there was nothing surprising about this choice for the cover or about the inclusion of these painters in the exhibition; whatever praise they received, it was not given

because, *though women*, they painted extremely well, and the critics did not look for their intrinsically feminine characteristics.[9]

Standen painted too rosy a picture of gender-neutral acceptance, yet she articulated the newly elevated status in terms of women's place in the history of art.

Although there are no known installation photographs of "Great Women Artists," general descriptions of the exhibited paintings, drawings, and watercolors are available from cursory reviews that appeared in secondary sources. Per the *Times*, French painter Moillon (1610–1696) and Dutch painter Ruysch (1664–1750) were represented by still-lifes, the genre for which they were known (illus. 57 and 58), and the show included "an attractive, serious portrait" by Italian artist Sofonisba Anguissola.[10] The *Herald Tribune* critic Carlyle Burrows confirmed other descriptions in the *Times* and provided additional information. He praised Sofonisba's painting as "a skillful Bronzino-like portrait of a woman."[11] It might have resembled the expertly composed *The Artist's Sister Minerva Anguissola* (*c.* 1564) (illus. 59).

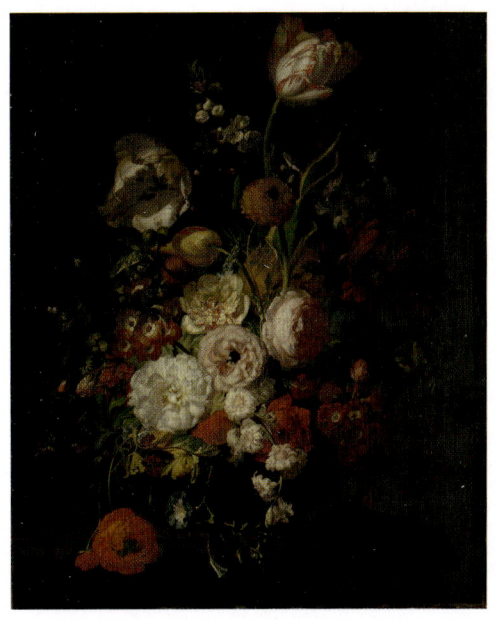

58 Rachel Ruysch, *Still-Life with Flowers in a Glass Vase*, c. 1690–1720, oil on canvas.

Burrows also described Élisabeth Louise Vigée Le Brun's pictures as "neo-classic portraits of the Empire period." A comparative work could have been the portrait *Mrs. Chinnery* (1803) (illus. 60), an Empire period painting when Roman art and architecture became fashionable in Paris. Burrows also noted works by Cassatt ("family group in crayon"), Bonheur ("a wonderfully sympathetic study of lions"), and Valadon (a "Cézanne-like study of a dog").[12] Extensive provenance research may in the future identify specific works. All but one of the illustrations in this chapter are representative examples based on secondary source descriptions.

Research for this chapter has yielded positive identification of one work in the show: Modersohn-Becker's small painting *The Artist's Sister Herma with Amber Necklace* (*c.* 1905) (illus. 61). In this stark frontal portrayal, the subject's head nearly fills the entire canvas. The figure has stylized facial features, with inscribed eyes and brows rhyming with the heavy beaded necklaces tied closely around her throat. Modersohn-Becker's younger sister Herma worked as an au pair in Paris at the time of this portrait, and her neat comportment suggests youthful

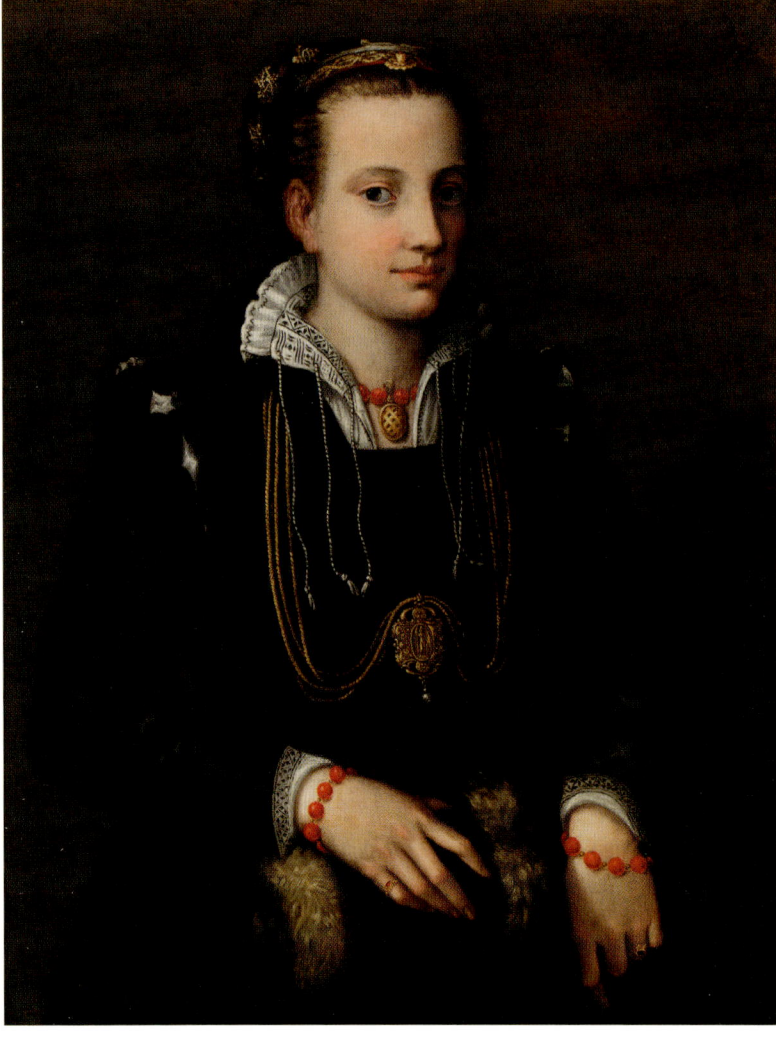

59 Sofonisba Anguissola, *The Artist's Sister Minerva Anguissola*, *c.* 1564, oil on canvas.

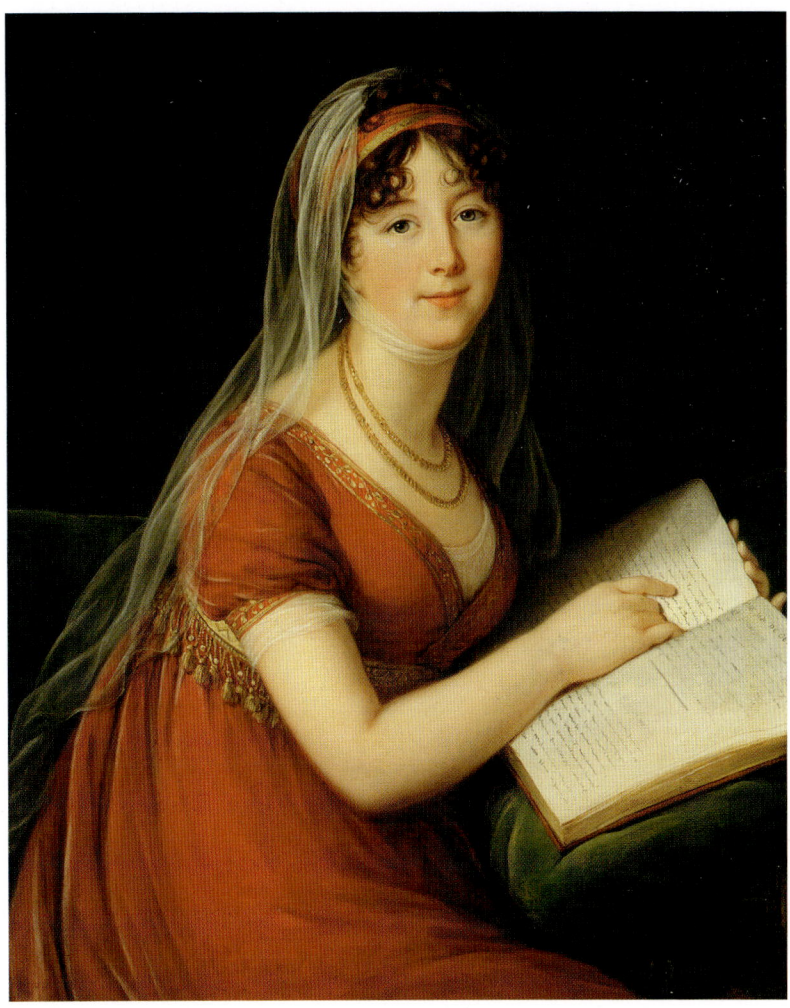

60 Élisabeth Louise Vigée
Le Brun, *Mrs. Chinnery*,
1803, oil on canvas.

responsibility. A black-and-white illustration of the painting appeared
in the graphic design magazine *Print*'s special issue dedicated to women
artists, in an eclectic portfolio of images selected by artist and art director Leo Lionni.[13] Critic James R. Mellow also admired the formal power
of the facial composition, calling Modersohn-Becker's two drawings
in the Delius show "monumentally structured" in a brief comment in
the magazine *Arts*.[14] It does not appear that the show included her
subversive nude self-portraits, depicting the curves of a pregnant body,
completed shortly before her death in 1907 at age 31. An artist's artist,

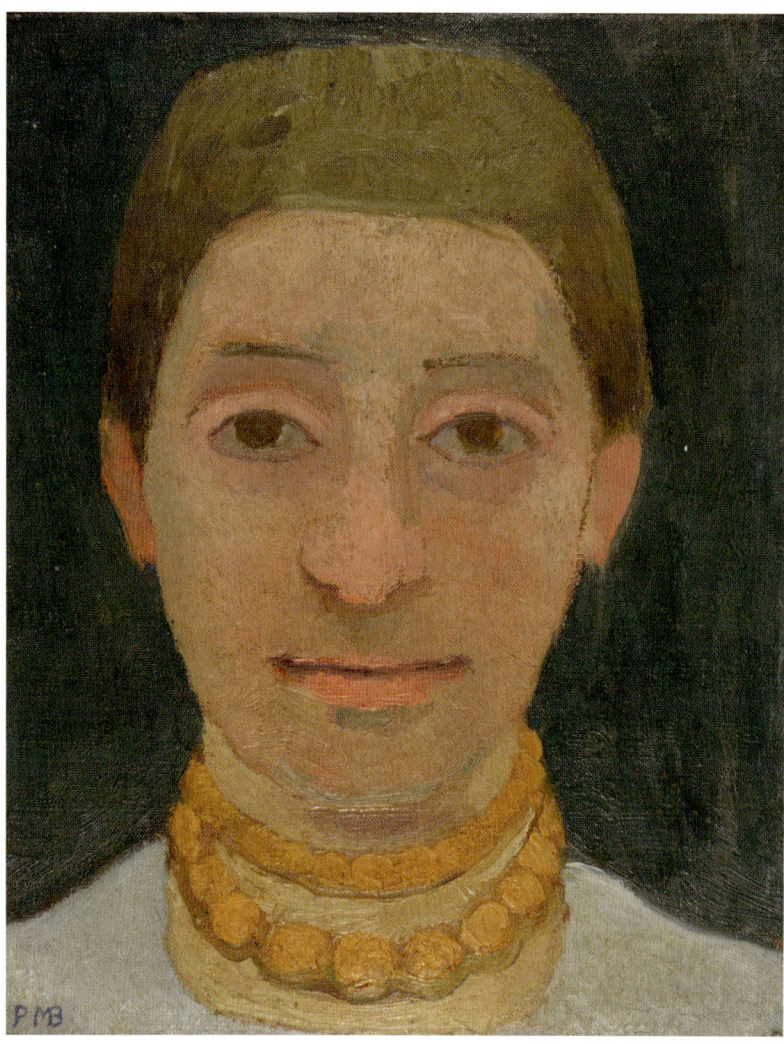

61 Paula Modersohn-Becker, *The Artist's Sister Herma with Amber Necklace*, c. 1905, oil on canvas.

she achieved a minor reputation in the United States, with modernist credentials bolstered by her posthumous appearance in Hitler's "degenerate art" show, and later gained in stature with the feminist art movement's celebration of female avant-garde pioneers.

Mellow's cursory exhibition notice highlighted the work of two artists in addition to Modersohn-Becker. He praised a "vibrant and firm line drawing of lions" by Bonheur.[15] Her mimetic paintings of animals made her one of the most famous women artists of the nineteenth century, and her dynamic canvas *The Horse Fair* became one of the most popular works in the collection of the Metropolitan Museum of Art upon its acquisition in 1887. Bonheur was known to have dressed in men's clothes in order to closely observe equine movement and anatomy in a distinctly macho environment. The unknown drawing of lions could be compared to other sheets of similar animal studies, such as an example now in the collection of the Morgan Library (illus. 62).

Mary Cassatt was represented in the Delius show, according to Mellow, by "a handsome pastel of a child," which presumably complemented the crayon drawing of a family group mentioned in another review in the *New York Herald Tribune*. Pastel was one of Cassatt's primary media, and her main subjects were women and children, so the work likely represented her achievement as an Impressionist portrayer of scenes of domestic nurture and care. Without knowing the age or gender of the child in question, any interpretation rests on the evaluation of the term "handsome." One of the few American artists, male or female, to achieve modernist standing in nineteenth-century Europe, Cassatt was the only woman and the only American in Delius's 1948

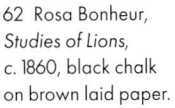

62 Rosa Bonheur, *Studies of Lions,* c. 1860, black chalk on brown laid paper.

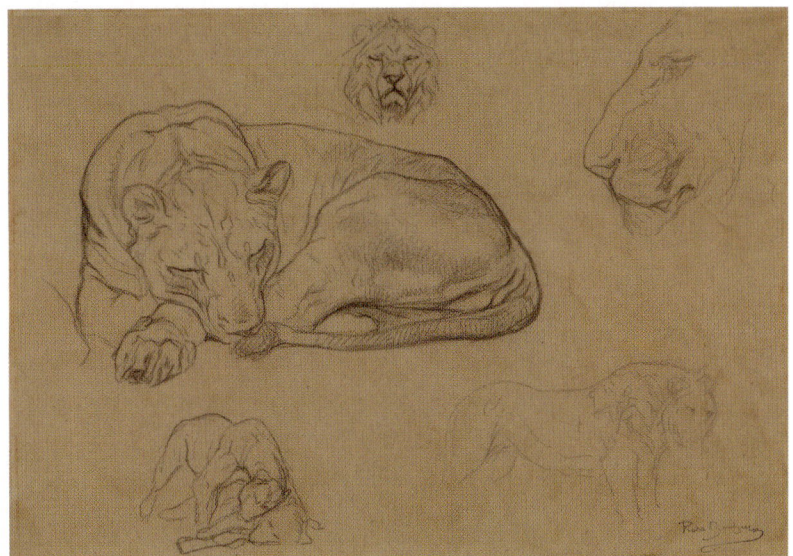

survey of French drawing, which featured her small pencil sketch of a young girl. The following year, her charcoal and pastel study for the print *Gathering Fruit* appeared in a Delius drawing survey. The image emerged from Cassatt's important body of work produced for the mural *Modern Woman* in the Woman's Building at the 1893 World's Columbian Exposition in Chicago: pastoral scenes of women decorating the tympanum of an edifice designed to celebrate women's social, artistic, and intellectual accomplishments. The colored sketch in the Delius drawing survey depicted a moment of intergenerational exchange, with an older woman on a ladder passing fruit to a toddler held in arms.

Few women artists escaped the interpretive lens of motherhood. Suzanne Valadon, whose forthright Expressionism broke societal taboos, had the distinction of being remembered as the mother of artist Maurice Utrillo, whose rather maudlin Parisian scenes conformed to American middle-class taste at midcentury. This genealogical fact is noted in the Delius brochure, a seemingly benign informational vehicle that reveals the art world's tendency to ascribe value to women artists through their associations with men. A later article in *Arts* on Valadon noted that she was represented in "Great Women Artists" with "two stunning oils": a small picture of a dog and a large flower piece, which could have resembled her painting *Bouquet de fleurs sur une petite table* (1932) (illus. 63).[16] These common subjects for women painters—animals and flowers—appealed to conventional expectation, and it is notable that Delius did not present Valadon's frank nudes that, like the work of Modersohn-Becker, depicted self-assured women and subverted the male gaze. Valadon's profile as Utrillo's mother, reiterated in the exhibition brochure, demonstrated the persistent belief among male cognoscenti that women's most significant creations emerged from their wombs, not their hands or minds. "It was still maintained, in some quarters, that the greatest contribution to the world of art that could be made by a woman was to be the mother of a genius," wrote art historian Albert Ten Eyck Gardner in a 1948 article on the history

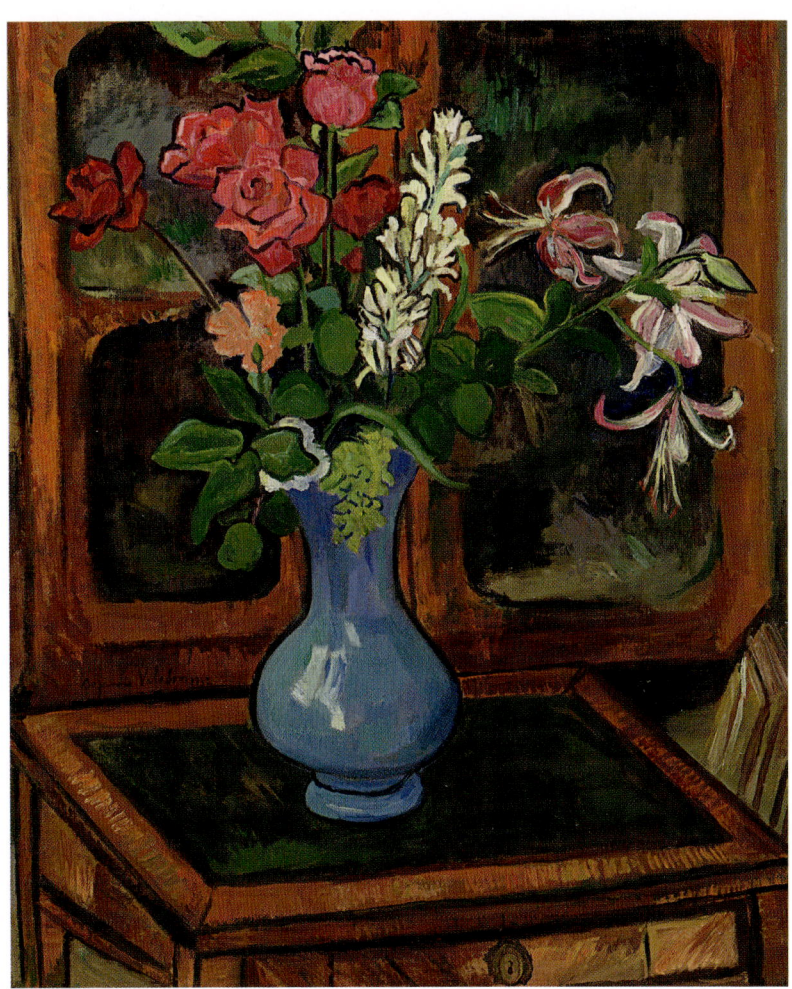

63 Suzanne Valadon, *Bouquet de fleurs sur une petite table*, 1932, oil on canvas.

of women artists on the centennial of the Seneca Falls Convention, considered the inaugural event of the women's rights movement in the United States.[17]

The Delius show responded to a period of rediscovery of the work of French avant-garde women in New York in the mid-1950s, with several receiving their first or significant solo exhibitions. Morisot (1841–1895), already widely exhibited in the United States, began to be considered a major figure in the Impressionist movement, as seen in *Young Woman Knitting* (*c*. 1883) (illus. 64). The traveling exhibition

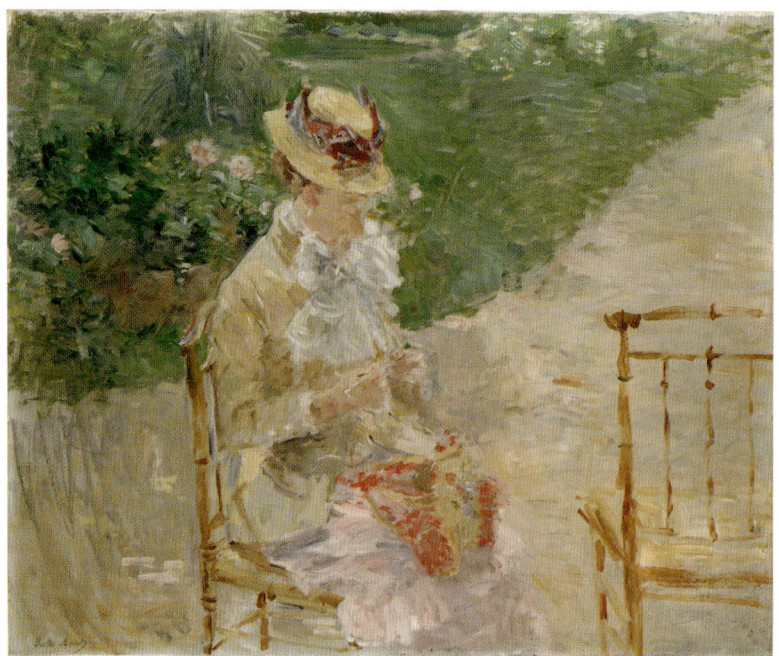

64 Berthe Morisot, *Young Woman Knitting*, c. 1883, oil on canvas.

"Berthe Morisot and Her Circle: Paintings from the Rouart Collection" (1952–4), which appeared at the Metropolitan Museum of Art, among other venues, secured this viewpoint for North American audiences. Sonia Delaunay had her first American solo show in 1955 at the Rose Fried Gallery. The first American exhibition of Valadon's drawings and prints occurred at the Peter H. Deitsch Gallery in 1956. Laurencin, also widely exposed in the States, died in 1956 and received a posthumous tribute show at the Rosenberg Gallery, her lifelong dealer. On Laurencin's passing, an editorial in the *Baltimore Sun* echoed the perplexity of Alexander Fried, Stuart Preston, and other critics. "Her death is a reminder, too, that for some inexplicable reason there has never been a woman painter of really first quality."[18] These pioneering European women served as role models and comparatives, and even, in the case of Valadon, cautionary tales, with her status as model and mother eclipsing that of artist for decades. U.S. critics, noting the surge of women in New York modernism, looked back to the Paris of the late nineteenth and early twentieth centuries as a precursor. Contemporary

American women artists in the New York School determined to avoid their fate of belated recognition.

Among her American contemporaries in the Delius show, Janice Biala (1903–2000) was the only artist aligned with this new generation. Born in Poland, Biala immigrated to America with her family at age ten. After studying art in New York and Provincetown, she established a growing reputation, but association with her artist brother Jack Tworkov restricted her independent artistic identity. In 1930 she dropped "Tworkov" and began signing her work as "Biala," the name of the town of her birth. This followed the tradition of Renaissance artists like Leonardo da Vinci and was a strategy of self-invention later adopted by feminist artists like Judy Chicago (b. 1939; formerly Judy Gerowitz). In 1950 Biala was one of three women (the other two were Hedda Sterne and Louise Bourgeois) among the 27 artists who participated in the Artists' Sessions at Studio 35, a landmark three-day round table conversation that crystallized ideas at the core of Abstract Expressionism. She regularly showed in the Stable Gallery's annual exhibition of vanguard New York artists, but still struggled to distinguish herself from the men in her life.

Biala's frustration boiled over in 1953 when the first sentence of an *ARTnews* review identified her as the sister of Tworkov. Three years earlier, the same journal had identified her as the wife of the cartoonist Alain. Incensed, she wrote a letter to the editor protesting how women are introduced to the art world through their male family relations:

> You seem to be a stern supporter of giving all the facts as to the family relationships of the painters reviewed. That seems to be particularly so in the case of the lady painters; they seldom appear in your pages detached from the conjugal yoke. I have never been given a review in your journal unaccompanied by one dear husband or another, and now the secret is out. I have a brother too![19]

This sarcastic missive appeared several months after the American publication of the English translation of Simone de Beauvoir's monumental feminist text *The Second Sex*. Biala's feminist protest in the pages of a U.S. art magazine in the 1950s corresponded to an eruption of feminist discourse inspired by Beauvoir's trenchant analysis.

Other contemporary artists in the Delius show lacked national recognition but enjoyed existing professional relationships with the gallery. Figural painter Susanne Carvallo, born in France, previously exhibited at Delius. She generally showed landscapes and still-lifes, and her portraits, especially of members of the German émigré community, are preserved in museum collections. Another of the contemporary contingent, Ruth Van Cleve (1898–1992), was born in Ohio and grew up in New Jersey. She studied at the Art Students League, where she later served as secretary. Known as much as a teacher and patron as an artist, she was a member of the National Association of Women Artists and her solo exhibition at the framemaker Newcomb-Macklin (a regular advertiser in the catalogue of the NAWA annual) in 1950 was listed in Robert Motherwell's publication *Modern Artists in America*. She may have shown an abstraction in the Delius show, but this cannot be confirmed.

Giese's uneven selection of living American women undermined the show's claim of consisting *of* "great women artists" and shifted the conversation to being *about* them. Burrows, in the *Herald Tribune,* found that the gallery overpromised. "The show at the Delius isn't all devoted to the great. Several are greatly gifted, others skilled and charming."[20] What was the discourse surrounding the exhibition, and the gallery's justifications to wade into the contested understanding of "great women artists"? As a commercial gallery, the primary goal would have been to create a presentation of saleable work by marketable artists. The rubric of "great women" attracted attention to and elevated artists in the gallery's orbit. The statement in the brochure is the one text available to discern the conceptual basis of the exhibition:

It seems strange that in an age which keeps on expounding the characteristics, talents, and virtues of "The Second Sex," and which has even gone to the length of declaring "The Natural Superiority of Women," the power of women as creative artists has not yet been fully realized. Admittedly, there are no women painters of the stature of a Velazquez or a Picasso (though the most famous of all ancient pictures, "Alexander's Victory over Darius," has been attributed to a woman), nevertheless an astonishing number of them have made contributions which not only reveal the ability of their sex for outstanding and sustained craftsmanship, but have added a novel and altogether feminine element without which the great traditions of the Fine Arts would be so much the poorer. Any, even fragmentary exhibit will bring to the forth their distinctive flair as manifested in the reoccurring motherhood theme, and in the compassion, tenderness, grace, and intuition so typical for the Woman as an Artist.[21]

The statement includes several key assumptions and literary citations that illuminate the contemporaneous understandings and debates around the greatness of women. The reference to women's painting beginning in ancient Greece, an argument made in the press release for "31 Women," established a European lineage for women artists. A canny promoter, Giese demonstrated casual fluency with the current literature in the study and politics of gender in referring to two recently published bestselling books.

The invocation of *The Second Sex* nods of course to Beauvoir, whose feminist landmark of that title appeared in English translation in 1953, after its two-volume French publication in 1949. The tome redefined the cultural basis of the secondary status of women in a sharply polemical prose designed to implicate the reader in her theory of sex and power. Gender myths collapse in her unmasking of the social construction of greatness. "Most female heroines are oddities," she wrote.[22] Comparing Joan of Arc to Lenin, she argues: "their greatness is primarily subjective: they are exemplary figures rather than historical agents. The great man springs from the masses and he is propelled onward by circumstances; the masses of women are on the margin of history, and circumstances are an obstacle for each individual, not a springboard."[23] In the final chapter of *The Second Sex*, Beauvoir examines how this dynamic plays out in the arts, specifically how the problems faced by female creators exemplify those of all independent women. Women turn to creative work to escape their situations, Beauvoir argued. But women's freedom is curtailed there as well. In her estimation, there were no great women artists because social conditions prevented them from achieving the fortitude and self-confidence to make the egocentric and grandiose choice to accept the burden of the world, the necessary act to strive for greatness. It requires women's entire effort just to discover themselves and achieve equal footing with men before they can begin the struggle to create a work of art, according to Beauvoir. Often limited to plying women's trades and minor genres, they are shut out from the transcendent realm of greatness. She flatly rejected the premise that there was any mystery surrounding women's failures to achieve greatness in Western society and culture: "in order to explain her limitations it is women's situation that must be invoked and not a mysterious essence."[24] The situation was obvious: social structures and ingrained psychology prevent women from achieving. "How could women ever have had genius when they were denied all possibility of accomplishing a work of genius—or just a work?"[25] The Delius brochure's appropriation of Beauvoir's title as an *au courant* synonym for women depleted the phrase of its critical content and turned it into an intellectual wink.

Another of the references is to *The Natural Superiority of Women*, the title of a popular book by anthropologist Ashley Montagu published in 1952. His theories fit into a broader midcentury trend of a "philo-feminine" discourse, largely promulgated by intellectual men, which examined the matriarchal roots of civilization and theorized the superiority of women based on their essential emotional and physical characteristics. Several other thinkers, ranging from André Breton to Jungian scholar Erich Neumann, published books in the 1940s and '50s arguing for the elevation of women to power: as everyday representatives of Mother Earth, it was posited that they would combat the runaway masculinity of Cold War politics and the military-industrial complex. Neumann concluded that the feminine archetype was necessary to balance "our one-sided patriarchal culture" because the feminine "symbolizes the essence of human relatedness, whose source lies in the primary relationship to the mother."[26] They challenged Darwin and Freud for claiming that male superiority is natural because of the male's greater physical strength, and disregarded the stereotypes of the active male and passive female. These arguments, necessary correctives, did not call for social change and still promoted the essential feminine qualities of women as gentle, emotional, and attuned to the life cycle.

The *New York Times* critic Stuart Preston's congenial but cursory exhibition review echoed some of these sentiments about the historical mismeasure of women. "Only a misogynist could deny the talent on view here," he wrote, but still pondered, "Just why there have been fewer eminent women artists than men is one of the mysteries of human nature."[27] The "mystery" had been addressed since the nineteenth century but gained greater urgency in the United States in the mid-twentieth century. He continued,

> For sensibility and imagination, the artist's two chief attributes, are by no means male monopolies. Social conventions and the relegation of women to domestic duties have undoubtedly had much to do with their minor artistic role in the past. But not all. Obstacles notwithstanding, certain women have come forward as painters during the past 500 years.[28]

Lacking a critical lens to situate the artists in a system of oppression, Preston's review exemplified the era's inability to think beyond the identification of women's shortcomings, decrying "misogynists" while wringing his hands in consternation about the "mystery" of critics withholding the label of greatness.

Two years later, another newspaper writer expressed similar mystification at women's absence from the artistic pantheon. "Why are there so few great women painters in all the long history of art?" asked Associated Press women's editor Dorothy Roe in 1957. "What ever happens to all those thousands of girls who major in art in college? What about that artistic temperament that women are always talking about? Is it confined to painting china and going over the living room?"[29] Her questions were prompted by her chagrin that just three women, O'Keeffe, MacIver, and Pereira, were among the fifty artists selected for the book *New Art in America: 50 Painters of the 20th Century*. She posed the questions directly to the editor, John I. H. Baur, a curator at the Whitney Museum of American Art, who reasoned that women are expected to perform domestic chores and do not have the courage to place art at the center of their lives.[30] These pressures resulted in women who studied art in college either getting married or becoming art teachers or interior decorators. His explanations were emblematic of the time in that he identified the social and psychological restrictions to women's success, but failed to envision an alternative, confirming Roe's palpable frustration with the under-recognition of women and the inaction of male gatekeepers.

These debates about greatness and the history of women artists were not merely academic. Since the mid-nineteenth century, when women emerged in significant numbers as professional fine artists in Europe and the United States, discussions of the natural abilities and historical accomplishments of women have been interwoven with the reception of contemporary women artists. Nearly a century before the Delius show, American historian and poet Elizabeth Fries Ellet published *Women Artists in All Ages and Countries* (1859), one of the first books of its kind, with the hope that it would bolster the spirits of contemporary women artists. "Should the perusal of my book inspire with courage and resolution any woman who aspires to overcome difficulties in the achievement of honorable independence, or should it lead to a higher general respect for the powers of women and their destined position in the realm of Art, my object will be accomplished," she wrote.[31] Women constantly battled the perception that greatness was unattainable to them in the present because no woman had achieved it in the past.

In midcentury America, a number of women artists delved into the history of women artists to correct the record and intervene in contemporary critical discourse. Painter Buffie Johnson investigated the history of women in art from the ancients to the present after *Time* magazine declined to review "31 Women" at Art of This Century. This research led her to discover scores of women artists and obtain insight into their social limitations, which she discussed in an article entitled "Embattled Women Artists."[32] Johnson circulated it to the art magazines but was unable to secure a publisher. "In 1943 I became a feminist. I understood what I was up against," Johnson recalled.[33] For women artists, even white women of privilege, the obstacles and challenges were crystal clear. The modern art community in which they aspired to take their places lacked a platform or sympathetic audience to hear them name their oppression. The question "why have there been no great women artists?" dogged women artists as a public embarrassment and private anxiety.

In another effort to understand the history of women artists, Elaine de Kooning researched the experiences of women artists for *Mademoiselle* magazine in 1949. The project was initially inspired by her experience in art school, where, like many female students, she turned to modeling for supplemental income. Her research into the history of women artists brought her far afield from canonical art history. "I began to get bogged down in all sorts of eccentric information and fascinating personalities," she recalled, from the outspoken feminist painter Marie Bashkirtseff to an unnamed Swiss woman born without arms who painted with her feet. "That was when I decided it was not a subject for a fashion magazine, and I gave up the whole project," de Kooning recalled.[34] *Mademoiselle* seemingly valued the arts as a profession for women, published substantive articles on women in society, and in the 1950s provided a platform for emerging talents such as poet Sylvia

Plath and artist Eva Hesse. De Kooning couldn't advance a narrative thread that reconciled the extensive presence of women in the history of art with their disappearance from contemporary consciousness beyond Virginia Woolf's formulation "anonymous was a woman." Her project addressed a mounting concern of the misalignment of women's ubiquitous presence in art and their exclusion from the norms and criteria of greatness.

Also in the late 1940s, artist Minna Citron (1896–1991) began an extensive research project, "Venus through the Ages: The Character of Woman as Portrayed in Art," a systematic examination of the images of women in the history of art, from ancient fertility goddess figurines to modern painting and sculpture, from a critical, feminist perspective. The concept emerged while giving a slide lecture she presented at the Art Students League, possibly the four-part series "The Grand Tradition and Modern Art," when she became curious about the social contexts accounting for the differences between the curvy Venus of Willendorf figurine and a lithe ancient Egyptian dancer painting.[35] Without directly addressing the question of greatness, her project, like the writing of de Kooning and Beauvoir, recognized the impediments women artists faced in overcoming their consideration as art objects rather than art creators.

In the 1950s, the community of artists and critics in New York began to harbor an expectation that the time was ripe for greatness to be legitimately pronounced in women artists. Grace Hartigan (1922–2008), one of the leading painters in the nascent Abstract Expressionist movement, attended a party in 1951 at painter Helen Frankenthaler's apartment with artists Jackson Pollock and Barnett Newman and critic Clement Greenberg. She reported in her journal,

Clem got on his stick of "women painters." Same thing—too easily satisfied, "finish" pictures, polish, "candy"; said Al [Leslie], Larry [Rivers] and [Robert] Goodnough all struggle. Makes me realize how alone I am. Am I to scream at him "I struggle too I do! I do!"

He said he wants to be the contemporary of the first great woman painter. What shit—he'd be the first to attack.[36]

Hartigan succinctly diagnosed the problem. The lack of acceptance of the struggle of women as artists rendered them invisible at a time when critics considered the act of painting an inherently masculine response to existential crisis. She dispelled the male critic's lament that there are no great women artists as the result of his refusal or inability to redefine the terms or respect what was before his eyes.

Around this time, Dorothy Brown (1899–1973) took another path to assert her position within a Western canon of women artists. An artist and professor at the University of California, Los Angeles, she assembled a rare private collection of artworks by women artists, many of whom appeared in the Delius show, like Cassatt, Laurencin, Morisot, Valadon, and Kollwitz, to address the gap in the public knowledge of their accomplishments. Brown began collecting in the late 1930s and by one report had acquired 35 pieces—primarily paintings, prints, watercolors, and drawings—by 1956.[37] She also acquired the art of Southern California women artists, including her mentor and fellow UCLA professor Annita Delano and her peers Lydia Takeshita, Helen Lundeberg, Vija Celmins, June Wayne, and Ynez Johnston. Frequent public exhibitions of the Brown collection, starting as early as 1948, often prompted local newspaper articles about women in art. One presentation, at Stanford University Art Gallery, was dubbed an exhibition of "famous women painters."[38] Brown often exhibited her own paintings, watercolors, and drawings with a selection of collection works, deftly creating a context for her work and elevating the public perception of its relative importance.

As it so happened, Judy Chicago, one of the founders of the feminist art movement in Southern California in the early 1970s, crossed paths with Brown when she began her art studies as an undergraduate at UCLA in 1958. According to biographer Gail Levin, Chicago was aware of Brown's collection, but dismissed it.[39] Ambitious students like Chicago found the concept laughable at the time, presumably to avoid the taint of association with supposed female mediocrity. Chicago aimed to be one of the boys, and later took pride in the fact that she was the only woman to train in an auto body school after she graduated with her MFA from UCLA in 1964. Ironically, a decade later Chicago lamented in her memoir that she had to discover the history of women artists on her own, in partnership with women of her generation.[40] That Brown's collection was easily available to her as an undergraduate suggests that Chicago as a student merely followed the period's conventional wisdom that women align with male gatekeepers and faculty members and avoid associations with overtly female contexts in order to become successful modern artists.

The growing presence of women in the upper echelons of U.S. art at midcentury broached the question of whether the canon should be expanded and the category of greatness redefined to make room for women. The Delius Gallery's "Great Women Artists" was one of the few exhibitions at the time to gauge the history of women in Western art, and provoked critics to consider the contradictions of aesthetic quality and historical amnesia. The exhibitions of "great women" by Giese, Feigl, and Brown remained largely confined to small, secondary-market commercial galleries and regional museums. Thus it was not entirely coincidental that it was a gallerist, Richard Feigen, who posed the question "why have there been no great women artists?" to art historian Linda Nochlin at a Vassar College commencement in 1970. Nochlin had heard this question for decades, dating back to her undergraduate years at Vassar in the late 1940s and early '50s. Her groundbreaking essay of the same name was her scholarly response. Nochlin demonstrated persuasively that "greatness" was denied to women because of social, psychological, and structural limitations, not inherent physical, mental, or spiritual deficiencies. Her essay was so effective in part because its title was so enduringly familiar. As she wrote, "The question tolls reproachfully in the background of discussions of the so-called woman problem, causing men to shake their heads regretfully and women to grind their teeth in frustration."[41]

8

Printmaking: "Women Printmakers," Philadelphia Museum of Art, 1956

Upon learning that two days remained before the exhibition "Women Printmakers" would close at the Philadelphia Museum of Art (PMA), bibliophile and archivist Miriam Y. Holden (1893–1977) packed her bag in her New York townhouse. "I shall be on the earliest train tomorrow morning for Phila. that I can take. To think that I came so close to missing one of the most exciting exhibits of women's achievements," Holden wrote to the curator, Kneeland McNulty (1922–1991).[1] The show was indeed the most substantial exploration of prints by women in a half-century, an overdue deep dive for audiences hungry for public demonstrations of women's history. Opening on March 16, 1956, "Women Printmakers" presented over 150 graphic works in a dense hang spanning roughly four hundred years and providing an extensive survey of contemporary stylistic and technical trends in the United States. A review in the *Philadelphia Inquirer* noted the significance that the museum "concentrated the resources of its scholarship and its collections on a still unexplored field."[2]

Indeed, large art museums with global collections almost never assigned their staff to conceptualize and curate women-focused exhibitions. The history of art at the time was generally categorized by national school, cultural geography, or style, not gender identity. Most all-women exhibitions that took place at museums were initiated and managed by women's organizations. A few art museums handled the responsibility of generating exhibitions dedicated to women artists

Claudia Stella

Diana Scultori

Knight   G L Ford   Converse   Hill
Whistler   Kimball   Metcalf   Dillon
Elyot L.   Ryerson   Keyston   Vahle
Ravent   Loggia   Pete Miller Cannon
Elsa Sel.   Cameron   Crawfors   Donaldson
                Huntin

WOMEN P

Carlott Justin   Duchamp Picasso

Anne Ryan   Sylvia...   Hirshhorn

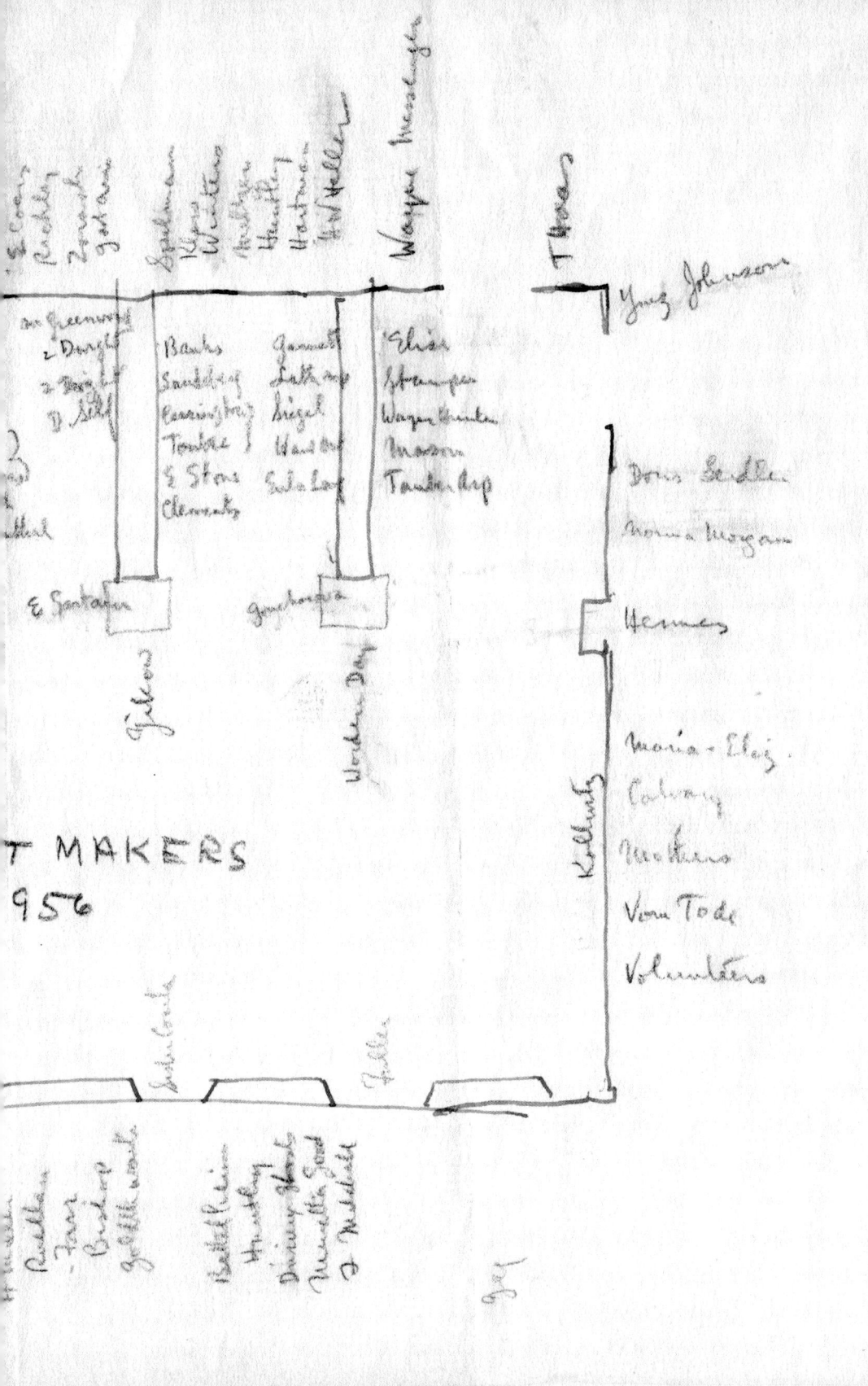

T MAKERS

956

when prompted by principled advocacy or material support. For example, after women protested the Detroit Institute of Arts's all-male 1942 annual exhibition, the museum devoted its 1943 annual to seventy paintings by fourteen women, as a curatorial apology in the fleeting wartime spirit of gender equality. Over a decade passed before another u.s. museum devoted staff time and collection resources to organizing an exhibition of women artists, outside hosting annual exhibitions of women artists groups. "Women Printmakers" is a landmark in the protracted emergence of women artists as a discrete field of art-historical study.

The PMA inhabited a relatively friendly climate for the education and appreciation of women artists. The exhibition, organized by the museum's print department, was drawn almost entirely from the PMA's own collection, which was strong in modern and contemporary prints by women from the nineteenth and twentieth centuries because of its ongoing partnership with the city's Print Club, which had been directed by women since its founding. To supplement these holdings, the museum borrowed about twenty prints, primarily etchings by esteemed Baroque-period European artists like Diana Scultori (1547–1612) and Elisabetta Sirani (1638–1665), from the collection of the nearby Pennsylvania Academy of the Fine Arts (PAFA). The academy, which began including women in its annual exhibitions in 1811, played an outsized role in the training of many prominent women artists of the late nineteenth and early twentieth centuries, including Mary Cassatt, Cecilia Beaux, Elizabeth Sparhawk-Jones, and Laura Wheeler Waring. The exhibition's existence in large part testified to women's significant participation in fine arts and print organizations in Pennsylvania, and the male curators who valued this history.

In many ways, historical surveys of women artists had to reinvent the wheel. One generation forgets the accomplishments of the prior generation, which, after surfacing briefly, sink back into the murk of memory as women artists remain underrepresented in collections and art-historical texts. The Philadelphia show opened 55 years after the previous foray into this "unexplored field" of women printmakers. In 1901 the New York antiquarian Grolier Club organized an exhibition of prints by women artists recently donated to the New York Public Library (NYPL) by Samuel Putnam Avery. He had purchased them in the 1884 Amsterdam auction of the estate of Henrietta Louise Koenen, who from 1841 to her death in 1881 had built a remarkable collection dedicated to prints and drawings by women artists.[3] NYPL print curator Frank Weitenkampf, in the Grolier Club catalogue essay, designated the exhibition as an intervention in the scant literature on women artists, focused mainly on painters and sculptors, and as an exercise in primary source work: "Many of the artists here represented are not mentioned in any of the reference-books; others are entered as men, or confused with other artists of the same name, or credited with work which they did not execute."[4] By his estimation, the assembly of work at the club would be "a novel experience to many."[5]

The emergence of women as independent printmakers in the mid-nineteenth century resulted in the first organizations and exhibitions of contemporary women etchers. Earlier, Mariana Griswold Van Rensselaer (1854–1934), one of the first American architecture critics, marveled at the discovery of such a vital area of new art in the 1888 catalogue of an exhibition of women printmakers at the Union League Club in New York. She noted the club's show, an expanded version of an exhibition held at the Museum of Fine Arts, Boston, in 1887, conjured "a peculiar degree of interest."[6] The exhibited works were drawn from both the museum's collection, assembled by its founding print curator Sylvester Rosa Koehler, and loans from numerous contemporary artists. Despite the gap of nearly seventy years between the Union League Club and PMA shows, their justifications remained consistent. "This exhibition aims to give a cross-section of women's achievements in the graphic arts through the ages," began the museum's exhibition statement.[7] Encyclopedic museums or libraries mounting exhibitions of women artists assumed little prior awareness by audiences, and relied on the specific passion and intellectual acumen of the few individual collectors and curators who prioritized work by women.

The PMA built its print collection under the auspices of curator Carl Zigrosser (1891–1975), one of the foremost proponents of modern printmaking in the United States. He became the director of the print-specialist Weyhe Gallery in New York in 1919 and the first print curator of the PMA in 1941. One of his early key decisions was to partner with the Print Club of Philadelphia. Founded in 1915, the club was one of the nation's leading organizations promoting the production and appreciation of prints. Women often won prizes in the club's exhibitions, and a significant number of women sat on the board. Its innovative director, Berthe von Moschzisker, supported new initiatives such as the creation of the Artist's Workshop and the facilitation of monthly visits by printmaker Stanley William Hayter. Zigrosser, a club board member and frequent juror and lecturer, stewarded the creation of a collection of prints funded by and named for the club and housed at the museum for study and exhibition. The Print Club became a pipeline for women artists to enter a major museum collection.

Zigrosser infrequently organized exhibitions devoted to women in the print department's dedicated galleries. The few instances were posthumous memorials to Anne Goldthwaite, Käthe Kollwitz, and Wanda Gág. The precise impetus for "Women Printmakers" is unknown, but was likely a constellation of institutional priorities, scheduling opportunities, and individual initiatives. The show was organized not by Zigrosser but by McNulty, who joined the print department as an assistant curator in 1952. McNulty considered the exhibition to be an opportunity to raise awareness of three centuries of women's accomplishments, relying heavily on the scholarship of Weitenkampf and the curatorial legacy of Zigrosser. Printmaking held a lower status in the art world than painting and sculpture because of its association with illustration, advertising, and commercial art. It thus afforded a more level playing field than the traditional high-status media, and several women artists, like Kollwitz and Gág, were recognized as working in the upper echelon of their fields. An alternate title proposed in the museum's press release, "Ladies of the Needle and Burin"—referring to the primary tools utilized in etching and engraving—associated the medium with a craft process, not a national school or style. There was no catalogue, and it received sparse coverage in the national art press and local newspapers. *ARTnews* included a brief mention in its print collector's column, reiterating the curatorial narrative that independent women printmakers were rarities until the last quarter of the nineteenth century.[8]

"Women Printmakers" ran for about two months in the museum's print gallery. The main narrative of the exhibition, articulated in a typed statement and press release, reiterated Weitenkampf's historical primer, newly informed by a half-century of innovations. The story outlined that the earliest women printmakers were born to families of artists and learned the craft of engraving and etching at home. Without independent studios, they made careers as links in the chain of artistic reproduction, working as copyists of other artists' compositions and techniques, often in collaboration with husbands or fathers and not venturing beyond the "family circle," according to McNulty.[9] "Rare women" like Anna Maria van Schurman (1607–1678) broke this precedent, "overcame all handicaps" and achieved the status of "a kind of universal genius."[10] This pattern in Europe held until the last quarter of the nineteenth century, when women, thanks to increased admissions to academies of art, established themselves as professionals and embarked on independent artistic experimentation. Artists like Morisot, Cassatt, and Valadon "approached their task as creative artists and not as copyists," McNulty wrote.[11] In the twentieth century women gained access to art training of all kinds, so the number of women artists grew, especially as new technologies and styles expanded the popularity of lithography and silkscreen.

A typewritten checklist in the museum exhibition files thoroughly documents the works in "Women Printmakers." This list, when cross-referenced with a hand-drawn annotated floor plan, provides a reasonably complete picture of the contents and arrangement of the exhibition, even without any extant installation photographs (illus. 65). The plan details the grouping of the artists within a large rectangular space with six alcoves, and the checklist provides the titles, media, and lenders. McNulty packed in more than 150 prints, hung in roughly chronological sequence, beginning with the earliest of the women printmakers and culminating in a selection of contemporary abstract art. Along the way the visitor encountered affinity groupings such as social commentary, animal prints, European contemporaries, and artists associated with the Whitney Studio Club. By hanging four or five works each by Angelica Kauffmann, Mary Cassatt, Mabel Dwight, Wanda Gág, and Käthe Kollwitz, McNulty defined a canon of key practitioners among the exhibited artists (of whom there were more than 120 in total). Singular color prints were hung in prominent locations along the gallery as punctuation marks and formed a show-within-a-show that enlivened the space. Overall, the layered exhibition design provided a rich experience for any visitor eager to discover both the history of Western printmaking since the seventeenth century, and the explosion of styles and techniques in contemporary American art from the 1920s to '50s in etching, woodcut, lithography, and silkscreen.

The entrance and first alcove presented about twenty engravings and etchings by European artists from the sixteenth to the eighteenth centuries, borrowed from the Pennsylvania Academy. Most of these prints reproduced a painting by a male artist in a new medium for wider circulation. The few original compositions were portraits of men, such as Schurman's engraving of poet Paul Fleming (1642) and Fanny Moreau Vernet's lithographs of the heads of her father, husband, and brother-in-law. This gallery established the narrative of women printmakers working in derivative and reproductive modes, setting the stage for the exhibition's emphasis on the creative work of the modern period.

The second alcove contained works by British and American artists from the first half of the twentieth century, many of them picturesque landscapes and genre scenes displaying varied stylistic influences, from Japanese *ukiyo-e* to French Cubism to American Scene painting.

McNulty also introduced an expanded range of media and techniques, including lithography, etching, linoleum cut, and woodblock. Some of the artists in this section maintained professional correspondences with Zigrosser for decades. The museum archive contains missives from Blanche Lazzell asserting her primacy in the invention of the white line print, one of the celebrated innovations of the Provincetown Art Colony, as seen in her *The Blue Jug* (1937). The print was published by the Federal Art Project of the WPA; it was one of several works in the second alcove that were realized through the federal government's financial support of American artists during the Depression. The WPA was the largest work program of the New Deal and many women artists gained employment or other support, but few became supervisors of any of the Graphic Arts Workshop divisions. Printmaker Mary Huntoon (1896–1970) served as director of her state Federal Art Project in Kansas. Her drypoint *Drug Store Lunch, Topeka, Kansas* (1935) appeared in this section of the exhibition.

Some women printmakers joined forces to counteract continued gender discrimination in the field. After the all-male Lone Star Printmakers Club denied membership to Bertha Landers (1911–1996), eight women artists living in the Dallas and Fort Worth area of Texas formed the Printmakers Guild in 1940. By 1945, their ranks had grown to sixteen and they organized a group show of thirty prints at the University of Texas Department of Art main building, dubbed in a newspaper as a show of "professional artists, housewives, public school teachers and a library worker."[12] Prints by three of its members, Blanche McVeigh, Janet Turner, and Emily Rutland, were included in the Philadelphia exhibition.

Dating back to his years at the Weyhe Gallery, Zigrosser supported printmaking as a medium for social commentary. Drawing on a collection shaped by his tastes, the Philadelphia exhibition included more works with social commentary than most all-women exhibitions of the time. Lucienne Bloch's (1909–1999) woodcut *Land of Plenty* (c. 1935) (illus. 66) depicts a family of presumably dispossessed farmers traveling across a landscape of American abundance, with fecund corn fields enclosed by a barbed-wire fence and surmounted by massive transmission towers. The ironic title critiques the disproportionate economic impacts of the Depression. This critical voice distinguishes the work from other prints in the show that cast a romantic look on the stoic rural woman, like Barbara Latham's engraving *The Highlander* (or *South Carolina Mountain Woman*, c. 1930). Bloch, a Swiss-born artist who traveled to Mexico to work with Diego Rivera on murals in the early 1930s and became one of Frida Kahlo's close friends, provided a

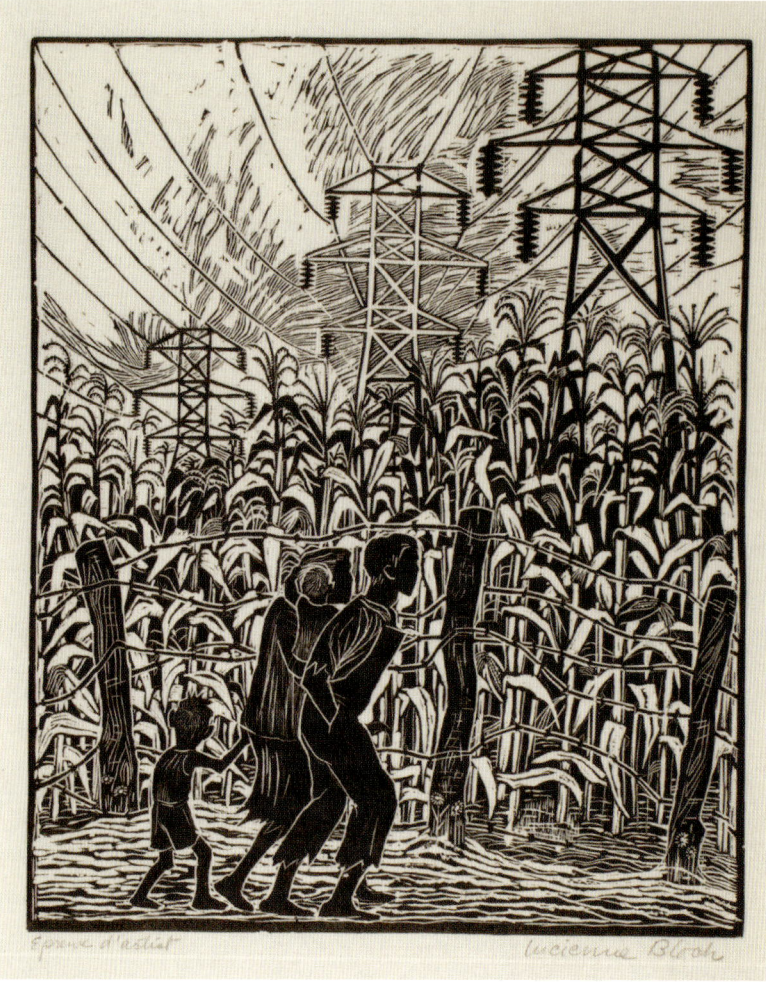

66 Lucienne Bloch, *Land of Plenty*, c. 1935, woodcut.

socially concerned outsider's point of view of American scenes of labor and agriculture.

Little critical imagery was found in the medley of prints in the third alcove, which focused on Philadelphia artists and color prints in lithography, woodcut, intaglio, and silkscreen, with subject-matter ranging from flower studies to landscapes to children's games. Some of these woodcut prints riffed on pop culture imagery, such as the beatnik-like character operating a turntable in Margo Hoff's *Favorite Song* (1953), and the congested retail space in Barbara Crawford's *Super Market* (1946). According to the press release, the 74 Americans in the exhibition included 16 artists from the Philadelphia area, a number of whom held leadership roles in the local chapter of the National Color Print Society. One local artist, Razel Kapustin (1908–1968), was the aunt and role model for a young Louise Fishman, who became a prominent feminist artist in the 1970s.

The fourth alcove included a strong selection of work by Peggy Bacon, one of the quintessential satirical printmakers at midcentury. Trained as a painter, she learned to make drypoints with a few friends using an old press at the Art Students League in 1918. Bacon became a central figure in the modern American art scene of Greenwich Village, which began to coalesce around the Whitney Studio Club after its establishment by Gertrude Vanderbilt Whitney in 1918. Her drypoint *Frenzied Effort (The Whitney Studio Club)* (1925) (illus. 67), included in the exhibition, archly portrays a room crowded with a disheveled lot of intergenerational students straining for good sightlines of a nude female model. The expressionistic style of jagged lines and foreshortened perspective accentuates the chaotic mood. As a member of this community, Bacon permits the audience to laugh alongside her at the unruly democratization of fine art. The print records the paradox of both gender parity, with nearly as many women in dresses as men in suits, and the persistence of the male gaze and the objectification of women in art.

Also in the alcove was Mabel Dwight (1875–1955), a late bloomer nearly twenty years older than Bacon who became one of the more

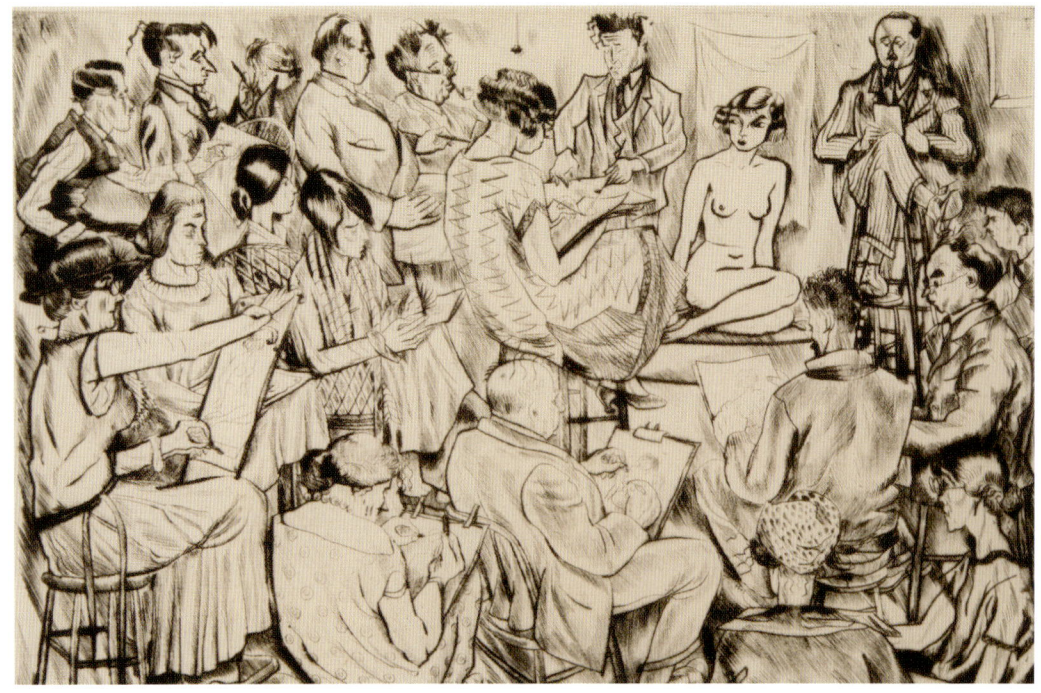

67 Peggy Bacon, *Frenzied Effort (The Whitney Studio Club)*, 1925, drypoint.

circulated midcentury printmakers in the United States. Her lushly detailed lithographs, with intense chiaroscuro, lend her figures a massive, sculptural presence; they nearly pop from the surface. Her lithograph *Life Class* (1931) revisits the subject of Bacon's print, but reverses the angle. The female nude is seen from behind, revealing to the viewer her vantage on the scowling, ogling visages of the mostly male sketchers. This inversion of perspective and clever attention to social hierarchies is palpable in *Queer Fish* (1936) (illus. 68), which was also illustrated in Zigrosser's survey *The Book of Fine Prints*.[13] Set in the recently opened New York Aquarium, a rotund grouper is the protagonist in a stare-down with an equally round man in front of the glass. To the left, the backside of a woman leaning forward completes the triangle of ample flesh and the obliviousness of the well-fed American middle class.

The fifth alcove assembled a notable selection of prints with Surrealist imagery or psychological themes: unsettling interiors or single figures gazing inwardly. The work of Los Angeles artist Grace Clements (1905–1969) was represented in the lithograph *Reconsideration of Time and Space* (1937), which illustrates her attempts to depict psychological states with controlled use of psychoanalytic methods. These effects also relate to the telescoping of time and space in the lithograph *Planets* (1937) by Helen Lundeberg (1908–1999), with its miniaturization and domestication of the cosmos on a cafe table. Leonora Carrington was represented by an etching of cartoonish creatures, *Untitled* (or *The Dogs of the Sleeper*, 1942), published in a portfolio by the American Surrealist journal *VVV*. The animal subject of this work linked it to an agglomeration of more prosaic animal prints. For all the innovative works included in the show, many banal prints served as didactic examples of technique and variety of subject-matter.

Within the architectural limitations of the gallery, McNulty devised the exhibition to highlight Käthe Kollwitz and Wanda Gág by giving them pride of place in the main space of the room, separate from the row of alcoves. The five prints by Kollwitz, recognized by reviewers as the

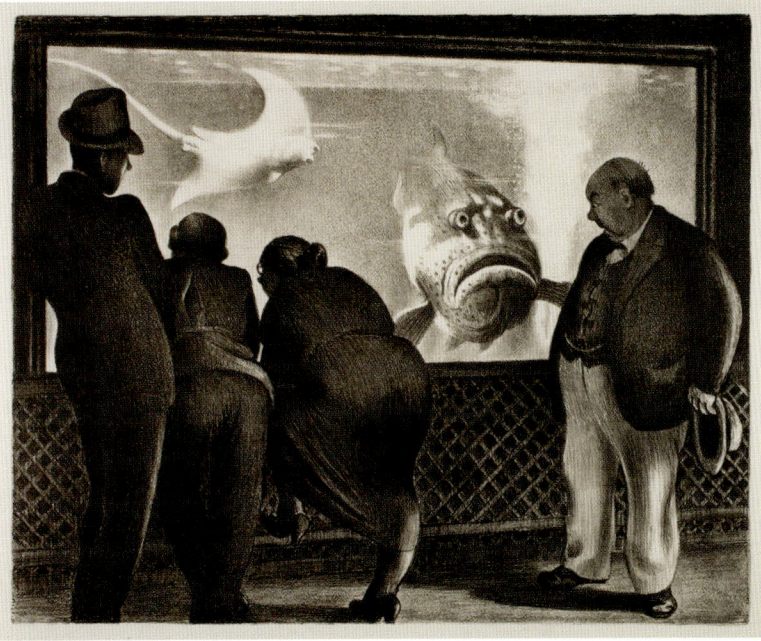

68 Mabel Dwight, *Queer Fish*, 1936, lithograph.

foremost printmaker in the show, were hung in a prominent location directly across from the entrance. A master of lithography, Kollwitz worked in the searing anti-war tradition of Goya, and her heavy lines and somber faces lent a gravity and humanity to her imagery (illus. 69). Gág received her own space on the adjacent wall. Nationally known for children's books like *Millions of Cats* (1928), illustrated with her woodcut prints, Gág's five lithographs depicted benign situations with a sense of mystery. *Lamplight* (1929) (illus. 70) won a prize from the Philadelphia Print Club and was illustrated in Zigrosser's book.[14] The dark shadows warp perception, curving straight lines and distorting a square room. A feminist who contributed illustrations to the socialist journal *New Masses*, Gág once published an autobiographical statement describing her choice to dedicate herself to art instead of

69 Käthe Kollwitz, *The Mothers*, 1919, lithograph.

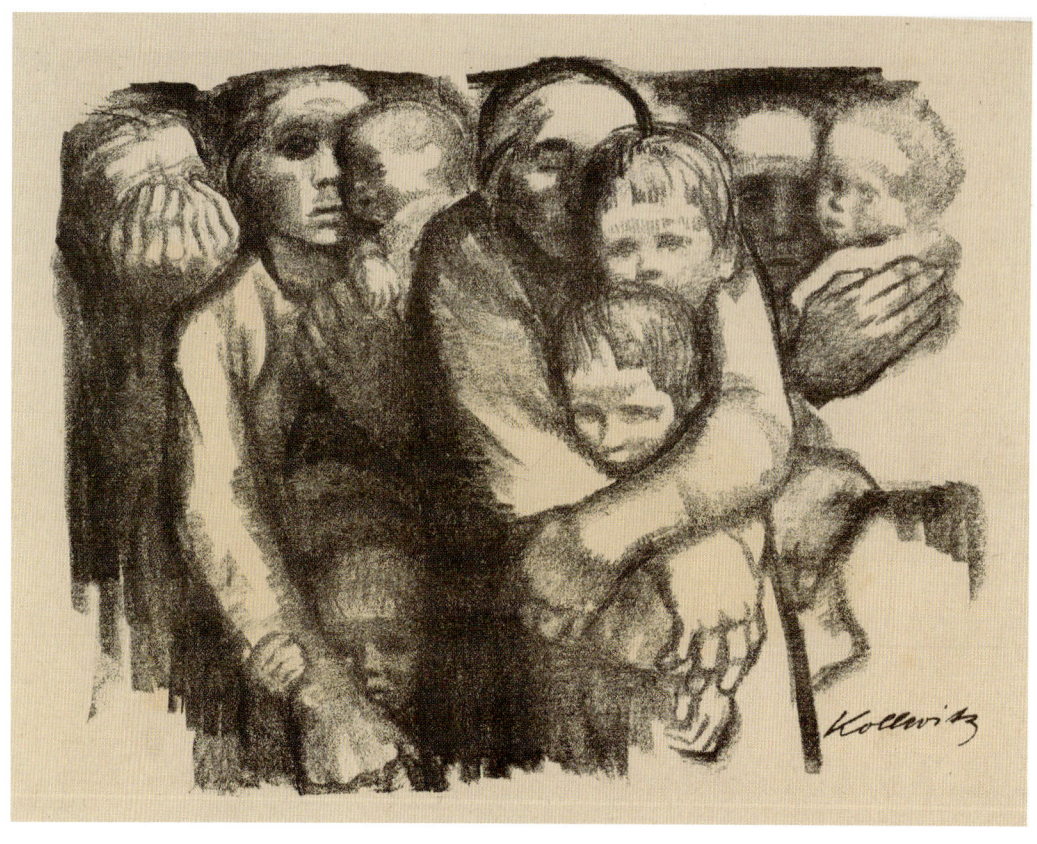

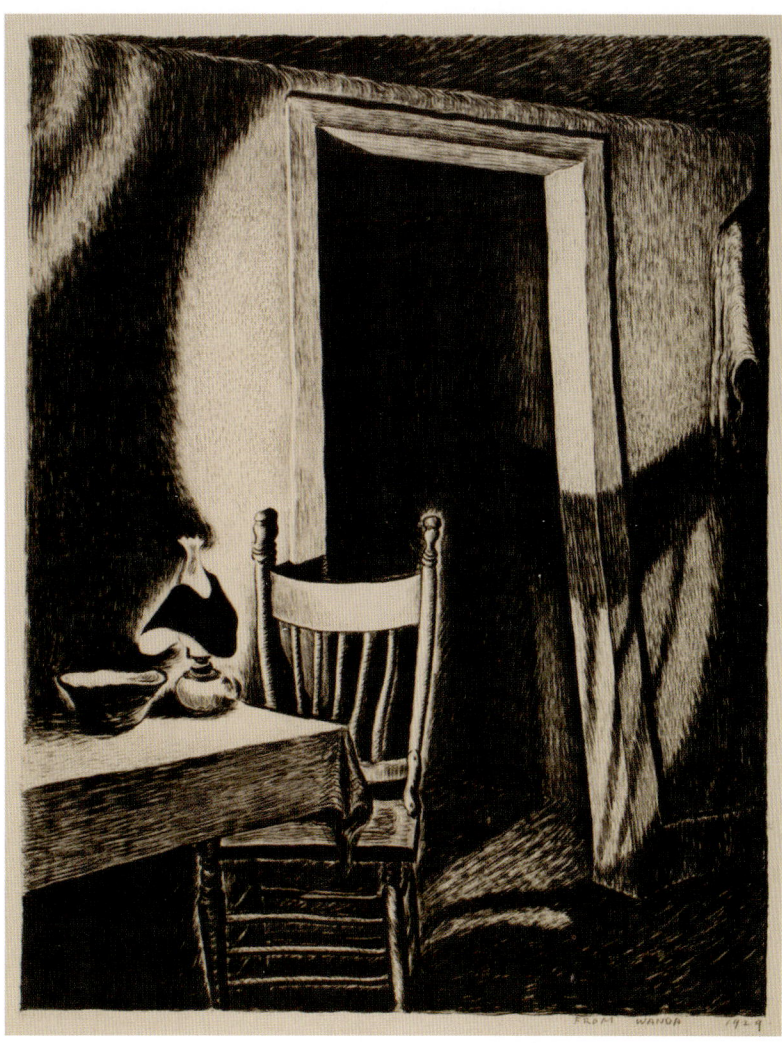

70 Wanda Gág,
Lamplight, 1929,
lithograph.

motherhood in *The Nation* magazine's essay series "These Modern Women" in 1927.[15] Her images cast a skeptical eye on domestic space and rural environments as fraught sites complicated by a nostalgia for childhood *Gemütlichkeit*, or warmth and sense of belonging.

By the time the exhibition appeared in the mid-1950s, abstraction had taken hold as the predominant style in American art. The culminating group of works in this vein, in the sixth and final alcove, appropriately reflected the present and future of printmaking. Continuing his American focus, McNulty selected just one European pioneer of abstraction, Sophie Taeuber-Arp. Her rather minimalist etching *Untitled* (or *Formes*, 1935), from *23 Gravures* published by Anatole Jakovski, primarily consists of wavy lines suggesting landscapes in outline. Among the Americans, Maybelle Stamper's (1907–1995) lithograph *Abstraction: Energy* (c. 1941), a work of cosmic imagery, was earlier reproduced in Zigrosser's anthology of fine art prints.[16] Stamper had established the print department at the Cincinnati Art Academy before relocating full-time to Captiva Island, Florida, where she was free to pursue her artistic visions. The exhibition's abstract section also included three artists working in and around Los Angeles: Elise Armitage, Ynez Johnston, and June Wayne.

The largest grouping in the abstract section included etchings and woodcuts by artists who had worked at Atelier 17, the innovative workshop established by British etcher Stanley William Hayter. Among them were Worden Day, Sue Fuller, Terry Haass, Alice Trumbull Mason, Norma Morgan, Anne Ryan, and Doris Seidler. Hung elsewhere in the show were etchings of a flower still-life and landscape by two others who had studied at Atelier 17, Jean Francksen and Frances Mitchell, respectively. As art historian Christina Weyl has extensively researched, the scores of women who worked in Atelier 17 during its fifteen-year run in New York from 1940 to 1955 both developed their artistic skills, leading to technical breakthroughs, and expanded their social and professional networks.[17] The intimate and inspiring workshop, with classes open to about ten artists at a time, served as a crucial meeting ground, fostering dialogue among artists interested in technical and material experimentation in a tactile medium.

The workshop's focus on the hard-edge printmaking techniques of engraving, etching, and woodcut required an intense physical relationship to the medium through carving and scratching lines on a copper plate or wood panel; as such, the atelier attracted artists interested in achieving an expressive precision and structure. Anne Ryan's (1889–1954) color woodcut *Mobile* (1947) (illus. 71) is a case in point.

71 Anne Ryan, *Mobile*, 1947, color woodcut.

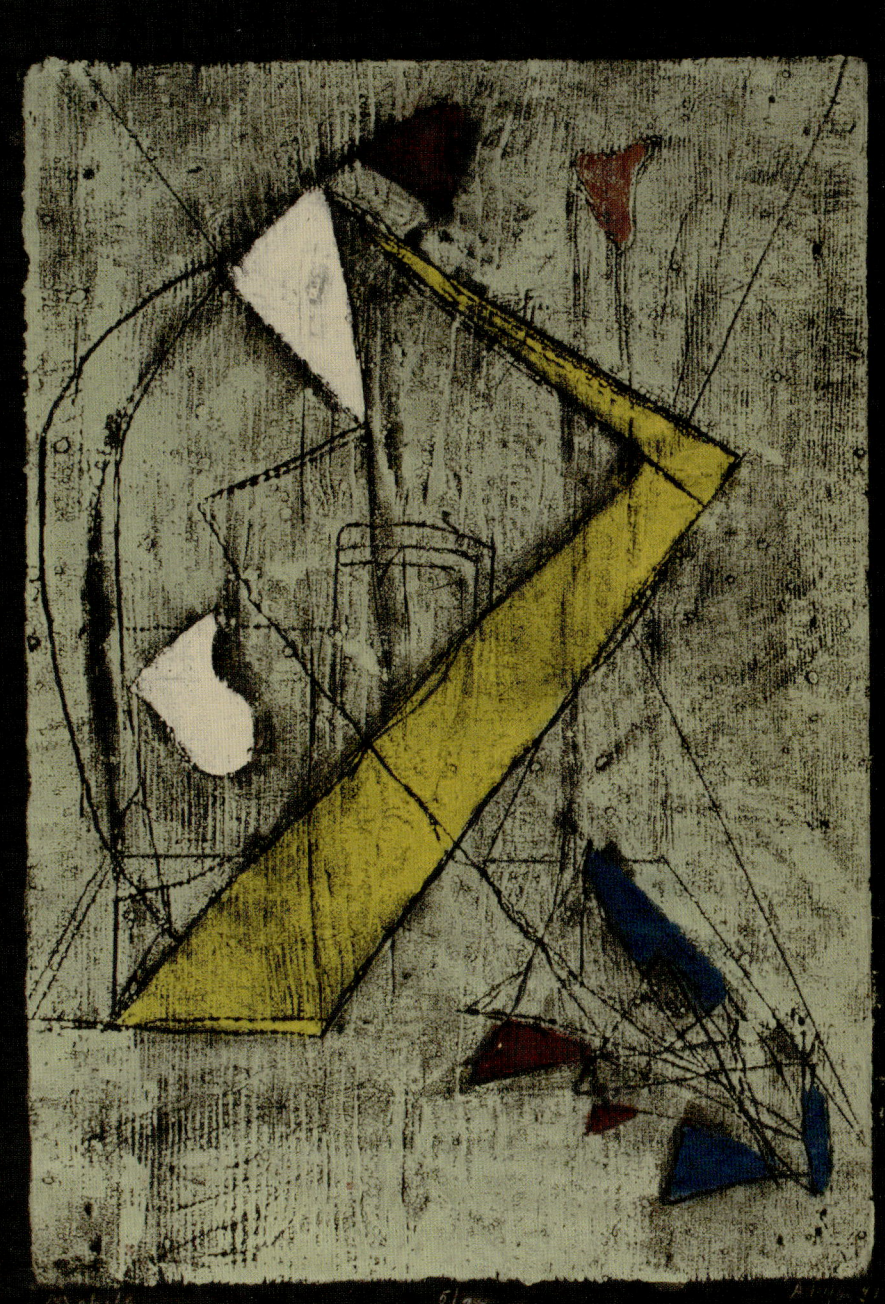

Mobile   5/30   AH 31

152-31-60   #36

The composition deftly balances different abstract weights and masses. The linear imagery, reminiscent of open mesh or soft lattice, relates to the work of other Atelier 17 artists who used textiles or string. In this process, a copper plate is covered with a soft ground of wax, then an impression is made with lace, muslin, or another textile, thus exposing some of the copper surface to create the positive image of the print. An etching by Sue Fuller, *Little Girl Jumping Rope* (1948), appears to have been made with strings arranged in loops and pressed into the wax surface. The strings themselves eventually became Fuller's central concern as a constructive material as well as a technical tool, as seen in her abstract *String Compositions*. Atelier 17's embrace of textiles and fibers to create organic patterns in soft-ground etching popularized an efficient means of achieving an abstract all-over print.

Fuller's deep engagement with this printing process inspired her to make an intervention in art history. As an experimental printmaker, Fuller admired Mary Cassatt both as a role model and as an artist who had not fully received her due. With guidance from scholar and Baltimore Museum of Art director Adelyn D. Breeskin, Fuller studied Cassatt's "revolutionary" collage technique via the direct application of textured material in soft-ground etching.[18] Fuller attempted to recreate these effects in her own studio, which formed the basis of a published article; she credited Cassatt as an early developer of the techniques that Fuller and her peers rediscovered three-quarters of a century later at Atelier 17. A native of Pittsburgh, Cassatt had studied at the Pennsylvania Academy of the Fine Arts, and the PMA already possessed a substantial collection of her prints by the 1950s. Among Cassatt's five works in the show, one soft-ground etching, *The Umbrella* (1879) (illus. 72), may display some of the effects that Fuller described in her article, created by Cassatt pressing paper and other material directly into the wax to render textures in the muted background and chair upholstery. Without explicating issues of gender, Fuller addressed Cassatt's constrained social situation. "It required wisdom, courage and independence to perform the kind of work she did in the age in

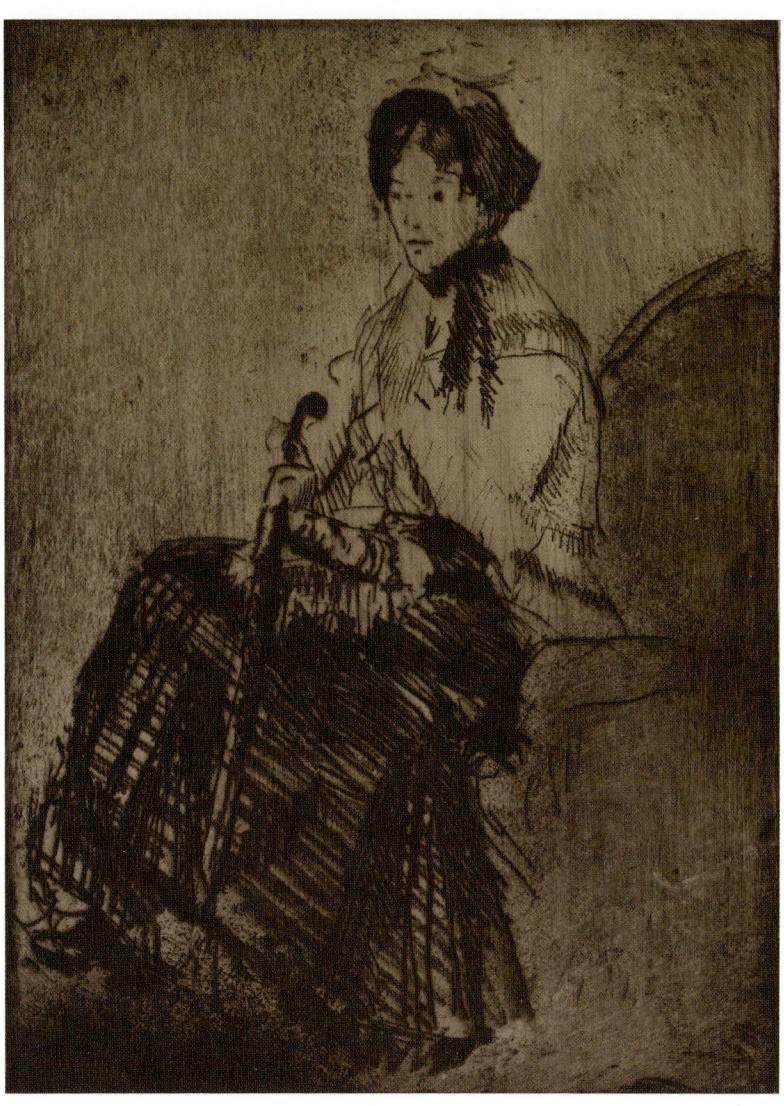

72 Mary Cassatt,
The Umbrella, 1879,
soft-ground etching.

which she lived," Fuller wrote.[19] She reasoned that Cassatt was not merely a Degas follower notable for her gender and nationality, as she was often defined, but an inspirational experimentalist who presaged abstract printmaking of the twentieth century.

One print in the sixth alcove stands out as both an impressive print and unusual story. Norma Morgan's (1928–2017) engraving *Granite Tor* (1954) (illus. 73), depicting a rock outcropping, appeared in the abstract section. The print's technical skill and massing of abstract monoliths formally resonated with nearby prints by Terry Haass and Doris Seidler. Notably, Morgan appears to have been the only Black woman to have been included in this exhibition. Born in New Haven, Connecticut, she moved to New York and studied printmaking at the Art Students League and painting at Hans Hofmann's school. She joined Atelier 17 around 1950, and there further developed skills in engraving, producing the abstract composition *Turning Forms* (1950), with dynamic arcs, assertive cross-hatching, and red and yellow shapes to complement a network of black lines. Morgan participated in several Atelier 17 exhibitions, and her figural etching *Youth* (1951) was acquired by MOMA and exhibited in a survey of recent prints. Fascinated by English literature, Morgan received a fellowship from the John Hay Whitney Foundation to study the British countryside from the southeast to the Scottish Highlands, retracing the steps of Thomas Hardy and the Brontë sisters. *Granite Tor* was part of this body of work.

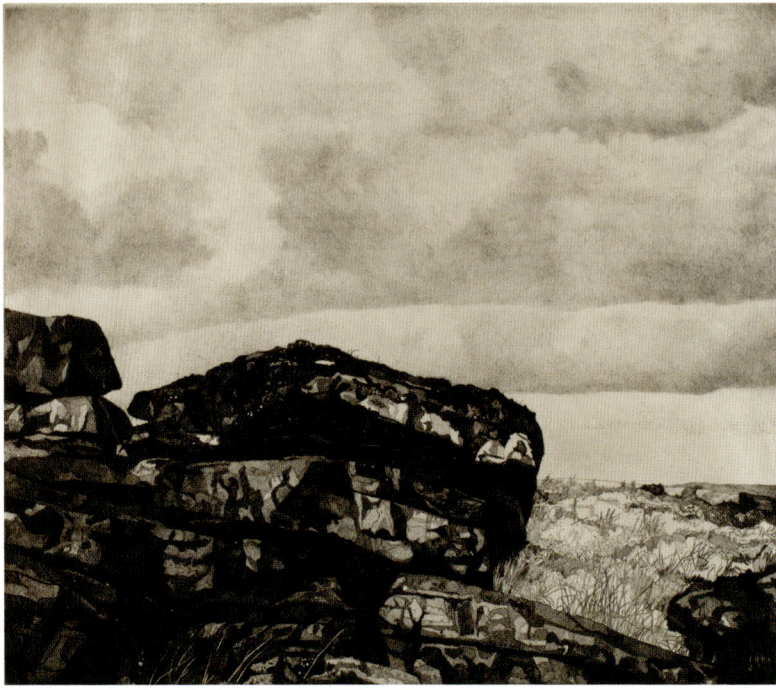

73 Norma Morgan, *Granite Tor*, 1954, engraving.

Spare to the point of abstraction, the work depicts one of the famous exposed masses of granite in Cornwall and Devon. It won the purchase prize at the Print Club's annual print show and became part of the collection of the PMA in 1955. Elton Fax (1909–1993), a prominent printmaker and early mentor of Morgan, later wrote, "one is tempted to believe that her deliberate choice of decaying, eroding subject-matter—her harsh, desolate English countryside and her strong handling of it—are symbolic. Who is to say that the restrictions imposed upon her as a woman who is also black have not evoked this kind of stark creative response?"[20] It could be said that Morgan reversed the gaze on the literary imagination of white Protestant England. Morgan may also have used this opportunity to riff on Hayter's name, which coincidentally was shared by one of the famous Dartmoor outcroppings, Haytor, making this print a witty homage. Morgan probably crossed into McNulty's line of sight because of her involvement in Atelier 17 and the Print Club. Zigrosser later wrote a recommendation for her Fulbright application to return to England in 1959.[21] Had McNulty directed his research towards other institutions, he might have discovered a wealth of additional accomplished Black women printmakers with careers adjacent to white artists but rarely invited to join their ranks in all-women shows.

Elizabeth Catlett (1915–2012) produced an important body of prints over the course of her long career. Born in Washington, DC, and educated at Howard University, her 1947 solo exhibition "Paintings, Sculptures, and Prints of the Negro Woman" at her hometown's integrated Barnett Aden Gallery conveyed the story of Black women in America through multiple perspectives and diverse media. One component of this show was Catlett's series of fifteen linoleum-cut prints depicting Black women, ranging from portraits of famed activists like Harriet Tubman to scenes of anonymous farm laborers. The series articulated a poetic first-person narrative of oppression and resilience, which concluded with a print with a hopeful title: "My right is a future of equality with other Americans."[22] By that time Catlett had relocated to Mexico City to escape McCarthyism and to work at the socially progressive Taller de Gráfica Popular. The print collective, a vestige of the Mexican muralism movement and popular front, attracted fellow traveling Americans.

A friend of Catlett's, the Chicago artist Margaret Burroughs (1917–2010) worked at the Taller de Gráfica Popular from 1952 to 1953, producing a powerful lithograph of the abolitionist Sojourner Truth that was part of the collective print series *Against Discrimination in the u.s.*, coordinated by Catlett. Burroughs was raised in Chicago and became instrumental in founding the South Side Community Arts Center, which opened its building in 1940. She studied printmaking at the School of the Art Institute of Chicago (SAIC) with Max Kahn, the husband of Eleanor Coen (1916–2010), a friend of Burroughs who also worked at the Taller, traveling there on a SAIC fellowship in 1941. Coen's color lithograph depicting her children, *Katie and Noah* (1952), was in the PMA exhibition and collection. Burroughs's and Catlett's work was not. The museum heralded technical variety and diverse subjects by white artists and overlooked distinctive socially conscious work by Black artists.

Another printmaking artist to come up through Howard University was Louise Jefferson (1908–2002). Born in Washington, DC, into an artistic family, she moved to New York in the 1930s, studying printmaking at Hunter College and Columbia University. She taught at the Harlem Community Art Center and roomed with future Black feminist scholar, activist, and lawyer Pauli Murray. Jefferson's lithographs of Harlem nightlife in the late 1930s provided a viewpoint on a subject area increasingly popular among voyeuristic white artists. Jefferson's lithograph *Nightclub Singer* (c. 1938) was not included in "Women Printmakers," but a similar image by a white artist, Mildred Rackley's color screenprint *Boogie-Woogie* (1941), which depicted four Black revelers, was acquired by the museum and later included in the exhibition. Jefferson continued to attain notable professional achievements and in 1942 became an art director and production assistant for a New York publisher. She worked for nearly two decades at Friendship Press, the publishing arm of the National Council of Churches, designing book jackets, annotated maps, and other illustrations, while continuing to produce and exhibit wood engravings and lithographs.

As was typical of the representational art exhibited in museums at the time, Black women were more frequently portrayed as the subjects of art in all-women spaces than invited as artists themselves. "Women Printmakers" included several works by white artists that depicted Black figures in genre scenes of picturesque activity and labor, such as Anne Goldthwaite's etching Saturday (1920), South Carolina artist Anna Heyward Taylor's Harvesting Rice (1937), and Sylvia Wald's color screenprint of a housekeeper in Spring Cleaning (1941). Zigrosser especially admired a print by Blanche McVeigh (1895–1970), one of the Fort Worth printmakers, whose dramatic Insurance Man (1940) depicts a man in a business suit soliciting a harried woman with multiple children in her charge. He holds a sheet of paper, presumably some sort of contract, and she reacts with a look of disbelief. In a similar vein, a number of prints contained subject-matter collected on white artists' travels and sojourns to Asia, Mexico, and the Southwestern United States, in search of authentic indigenous traditions, architecture, and costume—yet apparently no Asian, Native American, or Latina artists were included in the show. McNulty sought a diversity of representations in subject-matter but failed to include a diversity of artists, resulting in a clear imbalance of representation.

Discussions of printmaking invariably involve an examination of the particularities of media and process. "Women Printmakers," through an inclusive approach to media, presented works by artists who paved the way for women to take on greater roles as leaders in the resurgence of lithography. The exhibition included a color lithograph by Margaret Lowengrund (1902–1957), *Milkweed* (1952), previously exhibited in a National Association of Women Artists (NAWA) annual. She founded The Contemporaries in New York, a gallery and printmaking workshop, as an independent space for artists to access lithography, etching, and silkscreen equipment.

McNulty also included in the exhibition *This Beginning of Miracles* (1952) (illus. 74), a screenprint by Corita Kent (1918–1986), then a nun in the Order of the Immaculate Heart of Mary, Los Angeles. This inclusion demonstrates the rapid national ascendance of an artist who had started using an abandoned screen-printing machine in the basement of Immaculate Heart College a few years earlier after receiving instruction from the skilled printmaker María de Sodi Ramos Martínez. Corita achieved popular acclaim in the 1960s when her printmaking classes became public happenings and sites of interchange between progressive Catholics and Pop artists. *This Beginning of Miracles*—a semi-abstract rendition of the Wedding at Cana, the site of Jesus's first miracle of turning water into wine—could be interpreted as an allegory for the onset of her own series of spiritual transformations.

The exhibition was right up the alley of at least one prominent critic. Dorothy Grafly, an arts reporter based in Philadelphia, had a long interest in prints and had authored a history of the Print Club in 1929. She also promoted women artists, frequently reviewing NAWA annuals, and wrote a brochure text for an exhibition of women sculptors. "The American woman has not only invaded but conquered what was once virtually masculine territory," she boldly claimed in 1950.[23] Grafly's review of the print show for the *Christian Science Monitor*, a nationally distributed Boston-based newspaper, tacked a moderate course and largely rehashed the press release's succinct history of the evolution of women printmakers and the contemporary American renaissance. Grafly agreed with the press release's premise, writing, "the findings are provocative."[24]

It was Grafly's article that caught the eagle eye of Miriam Holden, the New York-based collector who amassed a large private library dedicated to women's history and culture. She wrote to McNulty immediately, requesting materials from the exhibition to add to her collection.[25]

The exhibition's public surfacing of women's history rekindled her memories of frustrating attempts to access the Avery collection of women printmakers at the New York Public Library, which was locked in a rare book room. She hoped that the Philadelphia show would spur the library to exhibit its own collection, which it had not done since 1901. Holden encouraged McNulty to send materials to William Dix, librarian at Princeton University, with whom she was working to increase the presence of women. Indeed, the library later acquired Holden's 6,000 books and extensive archive after her death. She also shared the article with her comrade in women's history, bibliophile Madeleine B. Stern, who was researching a book on women's "career firsts" in nineteenth-century America.[26] Stern wrote to McNulty and sought his advice on identifying the first American woman printmaker.

74 Corita Kent, *This Beginning of Miracles*, 1952, color screenprint.

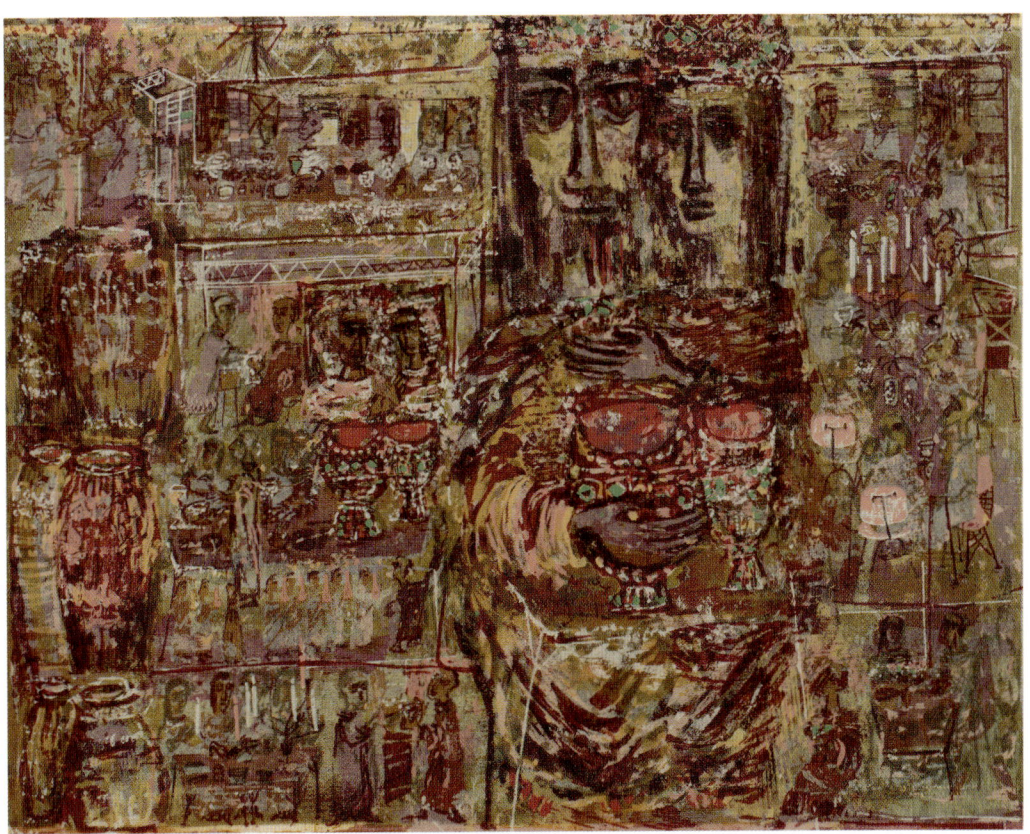

In the wake of "Women Printmakers" and its inducement for further scholarship, no other museum in the United States took up the mantle of devoting its curators and collections to studying, preserving, and presenting the history of women artists until nearly a decade later. In 1964, curator William H. Gerdts assembled "Women Artists of America, 1707–1964" at the Newark Museum in New Jersey. With 135 works by 129 artists, partly drawn from the museum's permanent collection, it surveyed 250 years of painting and sculpture (but not printmaking) from the colonial period to the present. Both the Philadelphia and Newark shows responded to the creative and innovative output of American women artists in the 1950s and relied on the depth of their museum's collections to create a historical context and teleological narrative.

Coinciding with "Women Printmakers," the year 1956 represented a transitional moment with the new energy in printmaking shifting from etching to lithography and screenprinting. Atelier 17 closed its doors for good in 1955 after several years of financial struggle and relocations. Following the Philadelphia show, two women established important experimental print workshops and publishers. In 1957 Tatyana Grosman (1904–1982) opened Universal Limited Art Editions on Long Island, a location she chose for its proximity to New York School artists in Manhattan and the East End. She frequently paired painters and poets to collaborate on portfolios. In Los Angeles, June Wayne opened the Tamarind Lithography Workshop in 1960. A leading voice in lithography, Wayne's print in the Philadelphia show, *The Hunter* (1952), won a prize and had been acquired by the Print Club of Philadelphia. It had been printed by Lynton Kistler, whose retirement was one of the factors that inspired Wayne to establish Tamarind to train a new generation of lithograph printers.

It was not until the women's movement of the 1970s that a new round of exhibitions and catalogues on women printmakers appeared. The NYPL finally got around to displaying prints from the Avery collection in 1973. That same year, Mount Holyoke College Art Museum opened the exhibition "14 American Women Printmakers of the 30's and 40's," which traveled to the Weyhe Gallery, New York. "Women Printmakers" arrived not as a triumphal pronouncement of the new equality of women but as a survey of their steady accomplishment.

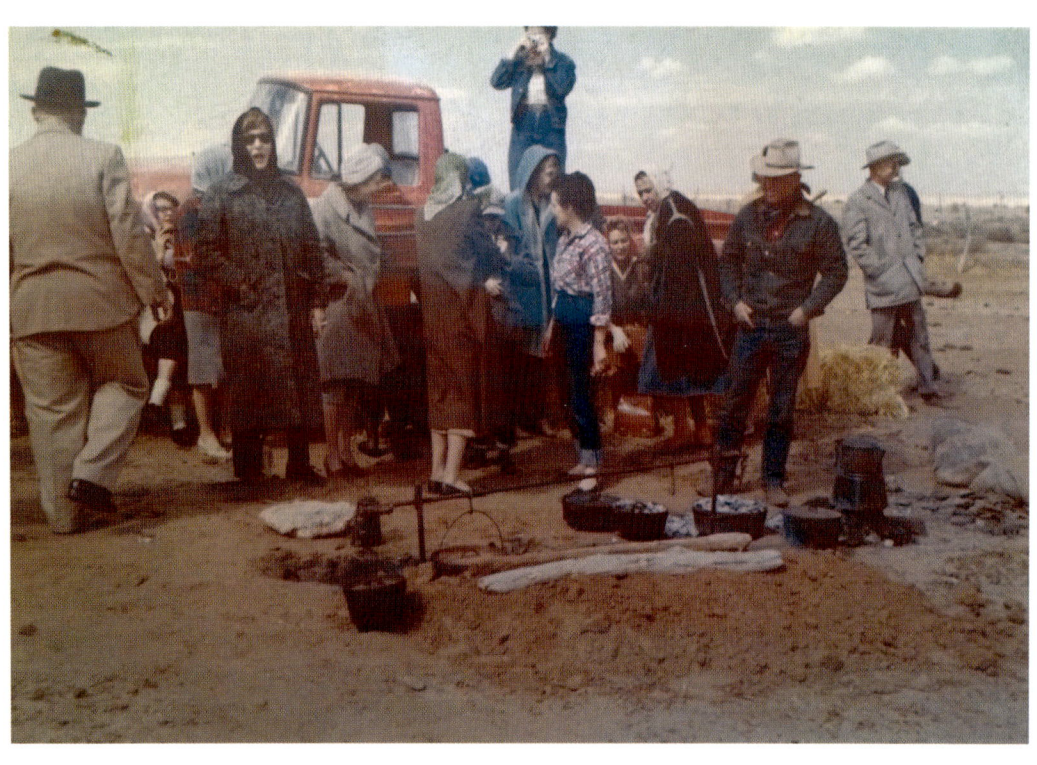

9

Abstract Expressionism: "17 of the Women Tops in Art," Dord Fitz Gallery, 1960

On a windy day in mid-March 1960, the New York artists Elaine de Kooning, Jeanne Reynal, Yvonne Thomas, Linda Lindeberg, and Louise Nevelson, along with dealer Martha Jackson, found themselves driving out to the central pasture of the massive 80-square-mile (210 sq. km) Durr Cattle Ranch near Dumas, Texas. They were heading there for an open-fire cooked lunch, served from a mule-drawn chuck wagon, in honor of the opening of their group exhibition (illus. 75). Three plainsman cooks surprised their guests with a feast comprising "calf fries," better known as prairie oysters, along with sourdough biscuits, gravy, pickles, banana bread, and coffee. The scene echoed a similar moment in Edna Ferber's novel *Giant* (1952) when the newly arrived bride Leslie Benedict, an educated and outspoken Virginian, faints at the spectacle of Texas heiresses and matrons devouring cow brains and eyeballs during a ranchero feast of traditional barbacoa.[1] According to Carolyn Fitz, the New York artists enjoyed the Western hospitality and history, but the comparison remains useful in drawing attention to the way Texans engaged food rituals to challenge Eastern gender norms. The chuck wagon lunch was part of a series of echt Texas celebrations of the landmark exhibition "17 of the Women Tops in Art," often abbreviated as "The Women," at the Dord Fitz Gallery in Amarillo, at the time known more for meat-packing than contemporary art (illus. 76). The artists also enjoyed a barbecue dinner, rodeo entertainment, visits to the historic XIT Ranch, and afternoon tea with the local women's club.

75 Women from New York at the Durr Cattle Ranch, near Dumas, Texas, March 1960. Third from left: Elaine de Kooning; third from right: Louise Nevelson; seated to the left of Nevelson: Martha Jackson.

The gallery's press release played up the larger-than-life stereotypes of the Lone Star State, emphasizing size above all: "The pictures will be large, as becomes Texas, and the sculptures will be a surprise, especially when we stop to realize that this show is exclusively by women!"[2]

George "Dord" Fitz (1914–1989) presented a comprehensive exhibition of women Abstract Expressionists in the implausible location of the Texas Panhandle, a region closer to Oklahoma and New Mexico than Dallas and Houston. The indefatigable educator parlayed his connections to New York's downtown scene and collaborated with artists Jeanne Reynal and Elaine de Kooning to exhibit three canvases each by prominent Abstract Expressionist painters, including Nell Blaine, Perle Fine, Helen Frankenthaler, Jane Freilicher, Pat Passlof, Miriam Schapiro, Ethel Schwabacher, Hedda Sterne, Yvonne Thomas, Jane Wilson, and others, including de Kooning herself. Grace Hartigan and Joan Mitchell would have participated had their new work been available. In addition to the impressive assembly of painting, "The Women" also included important sculptures by Louise Nevelson and Claire

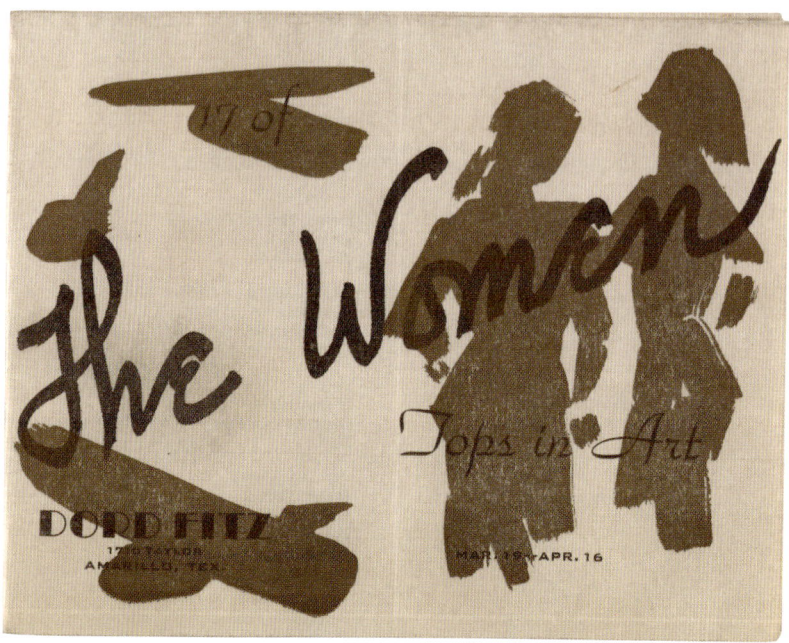

76 Dord Fitz Gallery, *17 of the Women Tops in Art*, brochure, 1960.

Falkenstein and mosaics by Reynal, bringing the total works in the exhibition to 51.

The dominant force in American art from the late 1940s to the early 1960s, Abstract Expressionism was clouded with rhetoric espousing the individuality of the artists in the coded vocabulary of virility, strength, and force. This discourse gendered the style, tailored to the personas of the male proponents of the movement like Jackson Pollock, Willem de Kooning, and Barnett Newman. By the late 1950s, artists and critics of the younger generation resented the narrow framing of a new aesthetic that in fact inspired artists of diverse identities to express individual subjectivity on the canvas. Creative women were increasingly expected to be outspoken and independent, as depicted in novels such as Rona Jaffe's *The Best of Everything* (1958). Fitz caught wind of the growing frustration of women artists who had been integral players in the New York School from its inception but found themselves eclipsed by their male peers. The novelty of Fitz's exhibition sprung from its unique situation: two women artists, de Kooning and Reynal, curated an exhibition in a freethinking gallery far from the standard institutional parameters and social hierarchies.

Born in Oregon in 1914, Dord Fitz grew up in Oklahoma. After studying music, he decided to make a career as an art educator, earning a bachelor's degree at Eastern Kentucky State Teachers College in 1935 and studying for two semesters at the School of the Art Institute of Chicago in 1937. He earned a master's from the University of Iowa in 1943, with Philip Guston serving as thesis advisor and Grant Wood inspiring his love of regionalism. A closeted gay man married with three children, Fitz was fired from teaching at the University of Kentucky because of a sexual encounter with another man.[3] This experience may have contributed to his drive to create an independent art center with a positive message of regional pride and social inclusivity.

Fitz purchased a ranch in northwest Oklahoma and soon after began teaching art classes in a church basement. He first established the Westerner Art Center in 1952 with adult students who playfully called themselves the Sand Hill Daubers. He began offering satellite classes in small cities and towns across the Panhandle area, and in 1953 relocated to Amarillo, where he opened the Dord Fitz School of Art and gallery. An inspirational leader, he built a following of several hundred amateur artists, doctors, business leaders, and housewives. Some were philanthropic and funded his growing ambitions to bring the values of modern art to his high-plains corner of the United States. The area also had a few wealthy collectors like Houston and Dallas, and Fitz built a patron class by teaching the fundamentals, insisting on the importance of direct study of works of art and espousing personal integrity and self-expression, stemming from a philosophy of selflessness discerned from his readings of Lao Tzu and other Eastern thinkers.[4] In 1954 Fitz launched the Creative Arts Association, a group of students and collectors committed to supporting the visual arts in Amarillo.

Part of Fitz's pedagogy included exposing his students to advanced contemporary art and artists across the country. He opened the Dord Fitz Gallery to create commercial opportunities for regional artists and to import quality exhibitions to the region. And in 1956 he arranged the first in a series of annual exhibitions of student work at the Burr Galleries in New York. The gallery, on 55th Street in midtown Manhattan, was directed by artist Patricia Allen (Burr) Bott (1911–1994). In a brochure from one such student show, Fitz enthusiastically claimed that his network of schools had "sparked an art movement that may well become the nucleus of an American Art Renaissance, independent of European trends, native to and typical of our own great country."[5] The tabula rasa of the Panhandle as an emerging art nexus appealed to Fitz more than the sophisticated coastal art districts of Greenwich Village and Hollywood. As an artist himself, Fitz looked to other artists, not necessarily critics and curators, for ideas and inspiration.

New York artists Reynal and de Kooning played vital roles in Fitz's ambition to become a national player, and in return he introduced their work to a passionate local community. Reynal and de Kooning were born seventeen years apart and spanned two generations, with

Reynal directly involved with the Surrealists and de Kooning intimately connected with the younger generation of painters, critics, and poets. Both showed their work at Eleanor Ward's Stable Gallery in the mid-1950s. Well known and respected as artists, they also promoted other artists, Reynal as a collector and de Kooning as a critic. Both women acted as agents for Fitz in New York, suggesting names of artists to consider. These relationships would prove decisive in the development of "The Women."

Reynal met Fitz at the premiere exhibition at the Burr Galleries and immediately expanded his horizons. The artist, collector, and salon host was born in New York in 1903, and returned to the city in 1946 after extended stays in Paris in the 1930s and San Francisco in the early 1940s. She was an important early advocate for Arshile Gorky and had exhibited in the legendary "Bloodflames" at the Hugo Gallery—dubbed the last Surrealist show in the United States—in 1947. As an artist, Reynal devoted her practice to the modern mosaic, revitalizing an ancient tradition while cultivating the ambitions of her generation to create abstract art with the potential to transform consciousness. Works such as *Amarillo* (1960) (illus. 77), with hand-cut glass and shell tesserae set in pigmented cement, similar to her pieces later shown at Dord Fitz, blended art, craft, design, and architecture.

Reynal encouraged Fitz to drop in on Abstract Expressionist painter (and fellow Gorky follower) Milton Resnick (1917–2004), who lived with the artist Pat Passlof (1928–2011) in a cold-water loft in the downtown art hub on East 10th Street. Fitz did so, and then accompanied Resnick to a party, which brought him in contact with other artists, including de Kooning, Franz Kline, and Nevelson. The rush of sudden access to a group of artists bursting with confidence inspired Fitz to transport the energy of the emerging downtown scene to Texas. On a return trip to New York during his spring 1957 exhibition at the Burr Galleries, Fitz convened with the artists at the Cedar Street Tavern to finalize arrangements for his initial foray into exhibiting New York art, titled "7 Contemporary Painters." The show opened in Amarillo

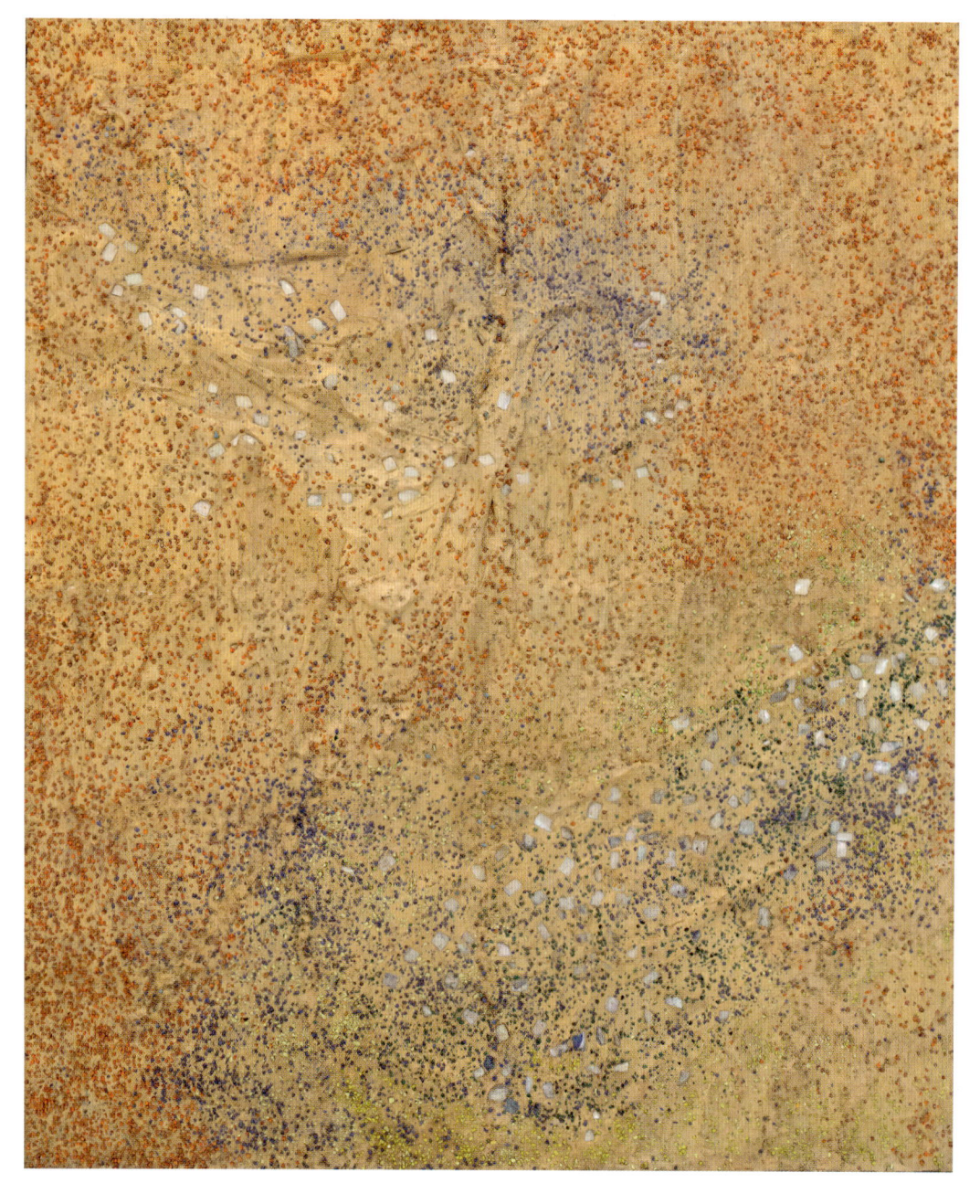

in September 1957 with several dozen paintings by de Kooning, Resnick, Passlof, and Kline, along with Joe Stefanelli, John Grillo, and Miles Forst. To save costs, Fitz removed the canvases from their stretchers, rolled them, and drove them to Texas in a station wagon.[6]

Fitz relied especially on de Kooning to help organize the show and asked her to solicit photos and biographies from the other artists.[7] She attended the opening, which could be seen as a sign of her considerable investment of time and personal capital into the endeavor. De Kooning's journey introduced her to the Southwest, an area that became increasingly important to her as a source of aesthetic inspiration, subject-matter, and patronage. The vast landscape spoke to the lifelong New Yorker, born in Brooklyn in 1918. She became interested in art as a teenager and soon found her way to the studio of Willem de Kooning (1904–1997), who took her on as a pupil. They married in 1943. Vivacious and witty, she established a reputation as a discerning art critic in *ARTnews*, frequently contributing to its popular monthly series of in-depth articles on artistic process. De Kooning's feature article in *ARTnews* in 1953, "Reynal Makes a Mosaic"—praising the artist's achievement of dematerializing stone into pictorial energy—was the only one of her "paints a picture" articles dedicated to a woman artist (out of fourteen in total).[8] De Kooning exhibited a survey of her gestural paintings and drawings—both abstractions and recalibrated figural images of portraits and basketball players—at her first solo at the Stable Gallery in 1954, through which she asserted her place in the crowded field of action painters. She continued to revisit themes of nature in abstraction, such as the painting *March Sky* (1959), which she later showed in "The Women" (illus. 78). In November 1959, de Kooning joined another New York contemporary painting show at the Fitz gallery, with an expanded roster of thirteen artists, including two other women, Jane Wilson (1924–2015) and Jane Freilicher (1924–2014).

Fitz may have conceived the idea of an all-women exhibition around the time that he opened his gallery, but the actual working concept for the show cohered after he began to travel to New York for

77 Jeanne Reynal, *Amarillo*, 1960, smalti and dyed Japanese shell on pigmented cement.

exhibitions at the Burr Galleries.[9] Director Patricia Bott happened to be a longtime exhibiting member of NAWA, an affiliation speaking to her concern for the historical marginalization of women. And Fitz, himself impacted by the patriarchal and homophobic sexual mores of the era, must have commiserated with the challenges faced by women to overcome restrictive gender stereotypes. Fitz also may have been attuned to the new wave of interest in the collective identity of the young women painters emerging as forces in the new abstraction in the United States. In 1957 *Life* magazine proclaimed five artists under the age of 35—Grace Hartigan, Helen Frankenthaler, Nell Blaine, Joan Mitchell, and Jane Wilson—as a "group" of young American women who, for the first time, equaled their male peers in terms of sales, exhibitions, and critical reputations.[10]

Bristling at the gap between the glossy images of glamorous art stars, as photographed by Gordon Parks in *Life*, and the sense of isolation experienced by most women artists, a group of women assembled in the studio of artist Ilse Getz (1917–1992) to discuss their need for greater cooperation. Mitchell, Nevelson, Worden Day, and Minna Citron answered an open call to plan a "comprehensive exhibition of both well-known and less known women artists, intending to awaken the museums, galleries and critics to the high aesthetic level of their work," Day recalled.[11] Unsure of how to proceed, they polled a few other artists, who discouraged them. The group disbanded, agreeing not to meet again or organize an all-women show lest they "rock the boat."[12] Yet the need persisted, and the next year, 1958, another collective of young New York artists formed a women's cooperative gallery. Gallery 15 remained open for about a year, but drew little attention, and was promptly forgotten, but its transitory existence testifies to the increased activity by women clamoring to create opportunities outside the gallery system.

The practical plans for the exhibition "The Women" were set into motion during a studio visit with Reynal in October 1959. According to one of Fitz's students, who accompanied him on the study trip to

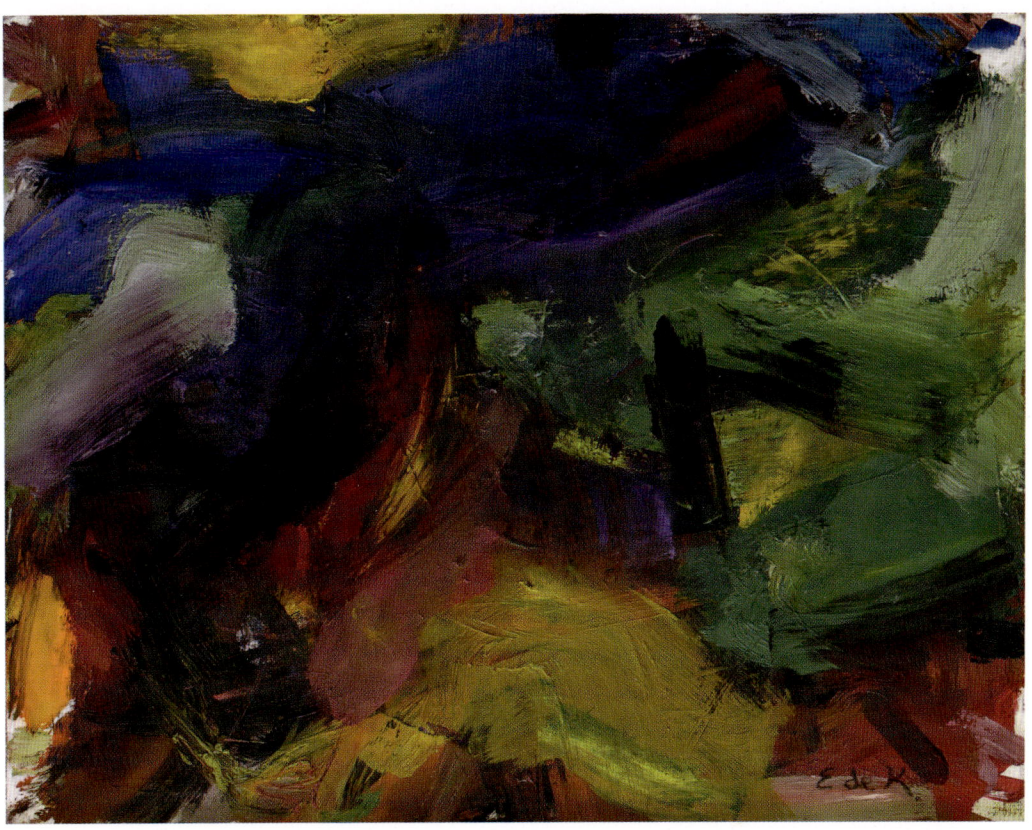

78 Elaine de Kooning, *March Sky*, 1959, oil on canvas.

New York, the conversation with Reynal led to "lamenting that the men artists had recognition, but the women artists were seldom mentioned."[13] Reynal had long been concerned about the junior position that women held in modern art. She was a member of San Francisco Women Artists when Claire Falkenstein was president of the group, and presented mosaics in the 1942 and 1943 annual exhibitions. In a series of letters to Agnes Gorky, Reynal described how she debated with the French painter and Surrealist artist Jacqueline Lamba about the problem of women being unable to achieve independent reputations beyond becoming "a sort of toy or ornament" in art by men.[14] At that point in the 1940s, Reynal observed the cultural and psychological patterns but did not publicly articulate a structural critique of gender discrimination. Over a decade later, Fitz heard her message and humbly

239

admitted that he, too, was guilty of assembling all-male exhibitions. He vowed to correct the injustice and organize an all-women show.[15] Abetted by rising interest in women artists and their increased exposure in the art market, Reynal's private feminist critique reached the right ears at the right time.

Fitz initially set a wide scope and considered inviting artists from across the country, but eventually encountered the typical surprise of anyone first delving into the history of women in art. The vague sense of their absence is quickly overwhelmed by a deluge of names. The problem was not a lack of women in art, but the fact that the endless churn of male-dominated canon-formation suppressed their existences. As soon as curators foreground women, their omnipresence is easily perceived. As a practicality, Fitz limited the exhibition concept to New York City artists. By October 20, 1959, the working title became "12 Top Women Artists."[16] Fitz relied on the on-the-spot expertise of Reynal and de Kooning, who applied a few key criteria in the curation of the show: the artists must identify as women, live in New York, have achieved recognition, and work in a contemporary style. Another essential criterion was working on a large scale. As Reynal wrote to Fitz: "Both Elaine and I have added people who would enhance the overall look and we are emphasizing major works."[17] The epic proportions of New York School painting, inspired by the Mexican muralists, distinguished the ambitions of the American upstarts, who pushed the limits of physical display within the confines of uptown galleries.

Reynal and de Kooning finalized their artist list by January 1960. After they made initial contacts and secured handshake agreements, Fitz mailed formal letters to dealers and artists to secure the loans and organize shipping, listing Reynal as the local New York contact who could be telephoned to provide additional information about the project. The ready cooperation of prominent galleries complicates the assumption that participating in an all-women exhibition was considered a career liability. The New Yorkers seemed just as intrigued by the novelty of showing in Amarillo as Fitz was excited to import their gravitas to his community. The recently organized Area Arts Foundation, composed primarily of his students, underwrote additional costs incurred by the exhibition.

As an artist-curated endeavor, "The Women" reflected the stylistic diversity of the New York School. It had more in common with the community spirit of the legendary artist-run "9th St. Exhibition of Paintings and Sculpture" of 1951—which announced the emergence of a new movement with 74 artists, 11 of them women—than subsequent canon-forming museum survey exhibitions and art-historical studies that largely eliminated women from the Abstract Expressionist discourse. All but three of the eighteen artists in "The Women" had shown in at least one of the annual downtown independent exhibitions of contemporary art, which began with the "9th St. Show" and were taken over by the Stable Gallery until the sixth and final iteration in 1957. The three artists in "The Women" who did not show in any of the Stable Annuals were not part of the downtown community: Falkenstein, an old acquaintance of Reynal's, lived in Los Angeles after a decade in Paris, and New York residents Mickey Wagstaff and Bott were not Abstract Expressionists and were likely added to the show by Fitz.

With no known installation photographs, the exhibition largely lives on in the form of the brochure, loan letters from galleries and artists, and an incomplete typewritten installation plan, all found in the Dord Fitz papers at the University of Oklahoma. Incongruously, the title of the show on the cover of the brochure bears the words "17 of the Women Tops in Art," despite the addition of Bott (listed in the catalogue as Patricia Allen) to make eighteen artists in the show. The cover was adorned with an olive-green sketch of two standing female figures, one leaning slightly toward the other and one posing for the viewer. No statement explaining the gender-specific curation appeared in the brochure. Instead, Fitz included a poem, reproduced here in its entirety, with original formatting, that articulates his metaphysical call for aesthetic independence to achieve sensory, mental, and spiritual unification.

> Let us not dangle from strings
>   That hang loose from the leashed
>   Free mind to see
>   When space and time are one
>   Mind opens from sightlessness
>   To infinite vision.[18]

The poem's imagery nods to the suspended open-wire constructions of Falkenstein, and to the free gestures of the abstract paintings, in a shift of values away from restrictive hierarchies of taste and quality toward egalitarian respect and acceptance.

For Fitz, the show fulfilled both educational and commercial purposes, with all but one work for sale. The evening of the opening included a panel discussion on contemporary art with several artists at the local community college. The Federation of Women's Clubs hosted a reception tea during the opening weekend. Several weeks later, 125 people in Fitz's Advanced Criticism class attended the show. He knew that few of his students would become professional artists but hoped that through art training based on enduring principles and wisdom, they would become open-minded members of the community and enlightened patrons of the arts. "These people know that love and respect for human kind is synonymous with the creative mind," Fitz wrote, describing his pedagogy to artist Linda Lindeberg (1915–1973).[19] Notable is his inclusive phrasing that refuses the faux universalist default "mankind."

The Dord Fitz Gallery was located in a late nineteenth-century wood-frame house that Fitz had purchased in 1958 to upgrade his previous gallery, which had been located in a second-floor loft over a lumber store. The property also included a brick garage that he converted to a studio-workshop. An incomplete checklist in the archives documents the exhibition installation in at least six of the ten rooms, plus the hall. Works by each artist were distributed around the various rooms, reinforcing the curatorial intent to focus on formal qualities, not individual style. "Dord has it all beautifully arranged so the colors don't fight and all the rooms are as harmonious as possible," reported one of his students.[20] The domestic milieu must have posed a challenge for the exhibition team's desire for large-scale work. The two North Rooms accommodated substantial pieces, with Perle Fine's layered oil and collage *The Wave Roaring, Breaking* (1959) and Pat Passlof's brushy painting *Promenade for a Bachelor* (1958) (illus. 79) on the upper floor, and Louise Nevelson's imposing 8.5 by 8 foot (2.6 × 2.4 m) wall sculpture *Moon Garden* (1959) on the lower (illus. 80). Other, smaller rooms allowed for intimate pairings, such as Jane Freilicher's *The Green Stripe* (1958) and Ethel Schwabacher's *Evening* (1958) in the Red Room. The installation, particularly the juxtaposition of certain works within distinct rooms, explored connections among the artists and revealed a

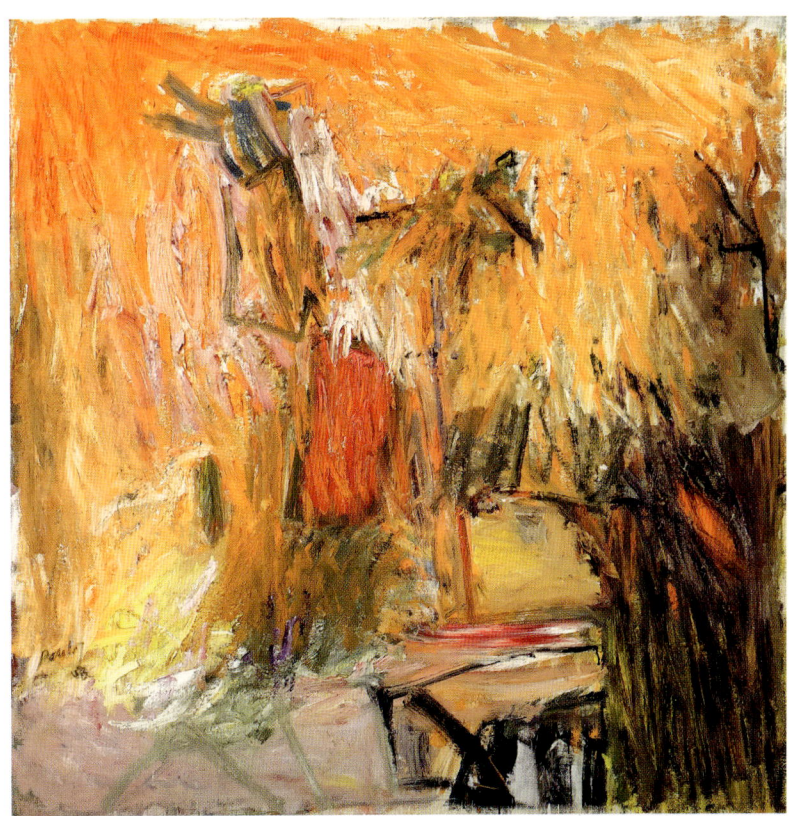

79 Pat Passlof, *Promenade for a Bachelor*, 1958, oil on linen.

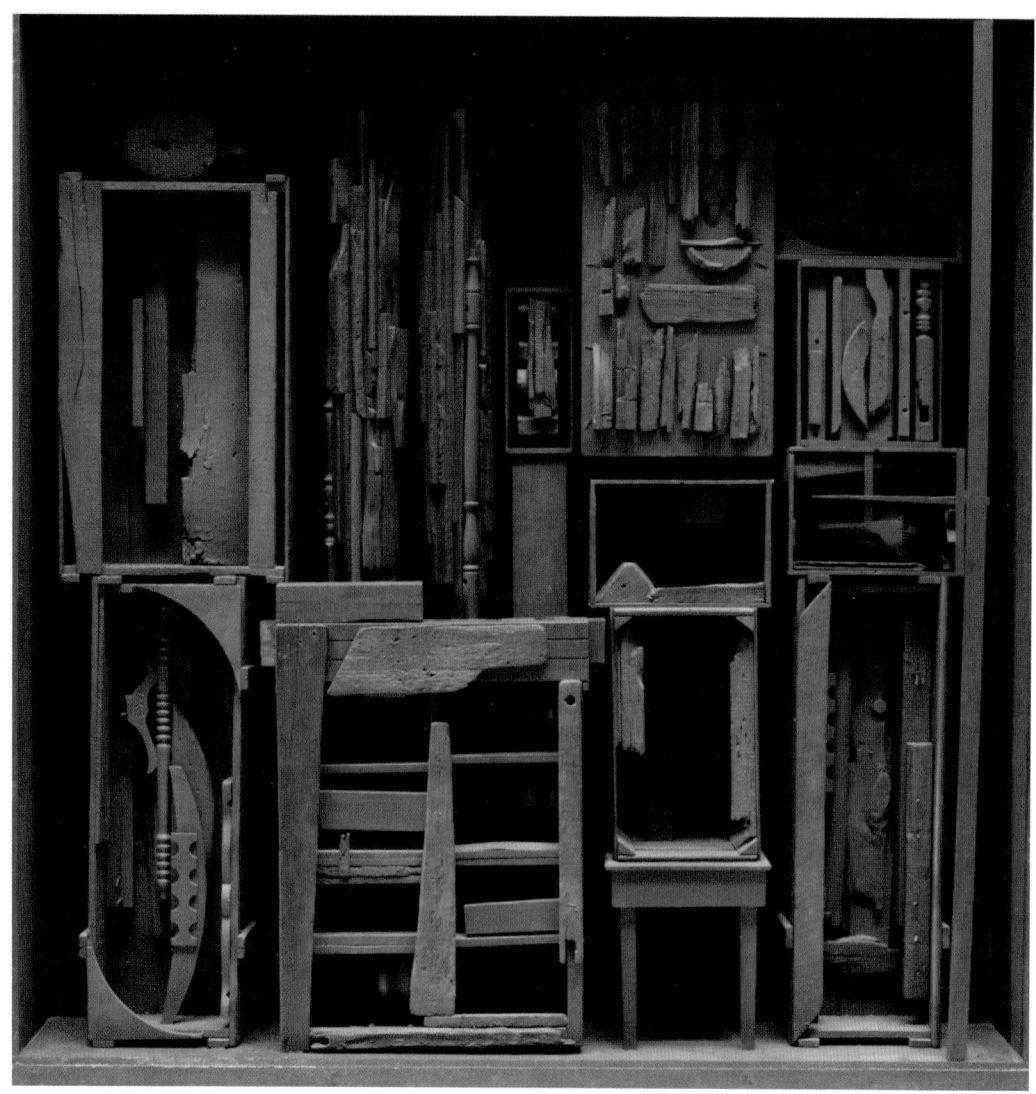

larger truth about the situation of women in Abstract Expressionism on the cusp of its imminent eclipse by the new styles of Pop and Minimalism.

80 Louise Nevelson, *Moon Garden*, 1959, painted wood.

The Living Rooms contained a diverse group of artists and media, and can be considered representative of the curatorial intentions for the show. All three sculptures by Falkenstein hung here, each demonstrating a different outcome from her disciplined assembly of basic metal units into complex abstract structures. The steel wire *Envelope* (1958), a cocoon-like piece shrouding inner mysteries, closes in on itself, in contrast to another work on view, *Sun no. 16* (1958–9), a construction of welded and brazed copper wire and tubing that extends outward in tangled tendrils. *ARTnews* called her "a sculptor of force" in a review of her solo show at Mayer Gallery in New York later that year.[21] Reynal, who like Falkenstein spent nearly a decade in Paris, adorned the room with two mosaics: the gray-and-white *Legends of the Rain* (c. 1960) and the *Graying Rain* (1959). Both Falkenstein and Reynal manipulated small units of an obstinate material to create a macrocosmic imagery.

The Living Rooms also included an impressive abstract painting by the youngest artist in the show, Helen Frankenthaler. Red, blue, and green circular splatters of paint radiate around centralized voids in the 13½-foot-wide (4 m) *Madridscape* (1959) (illus. 81), suggesting figures, caves, or the depths of time and space. The painting, with its active surface, is one of a series of works inspired by the art and landscape of Spain,

81 Helen Frankenthaler, *Madridscape*, 1959, oil on canvas.

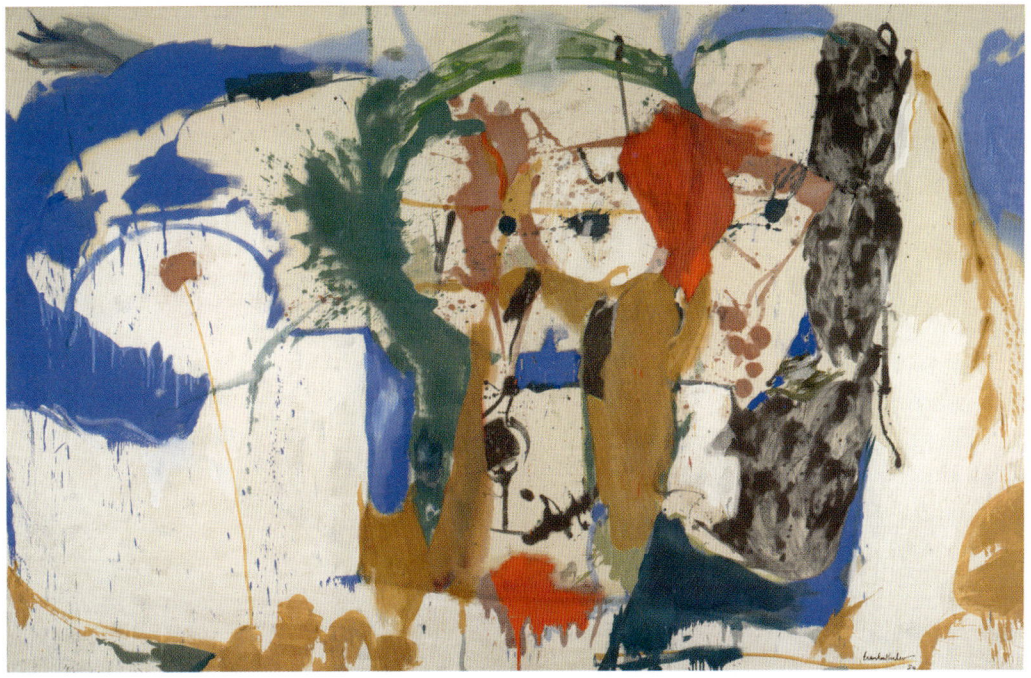

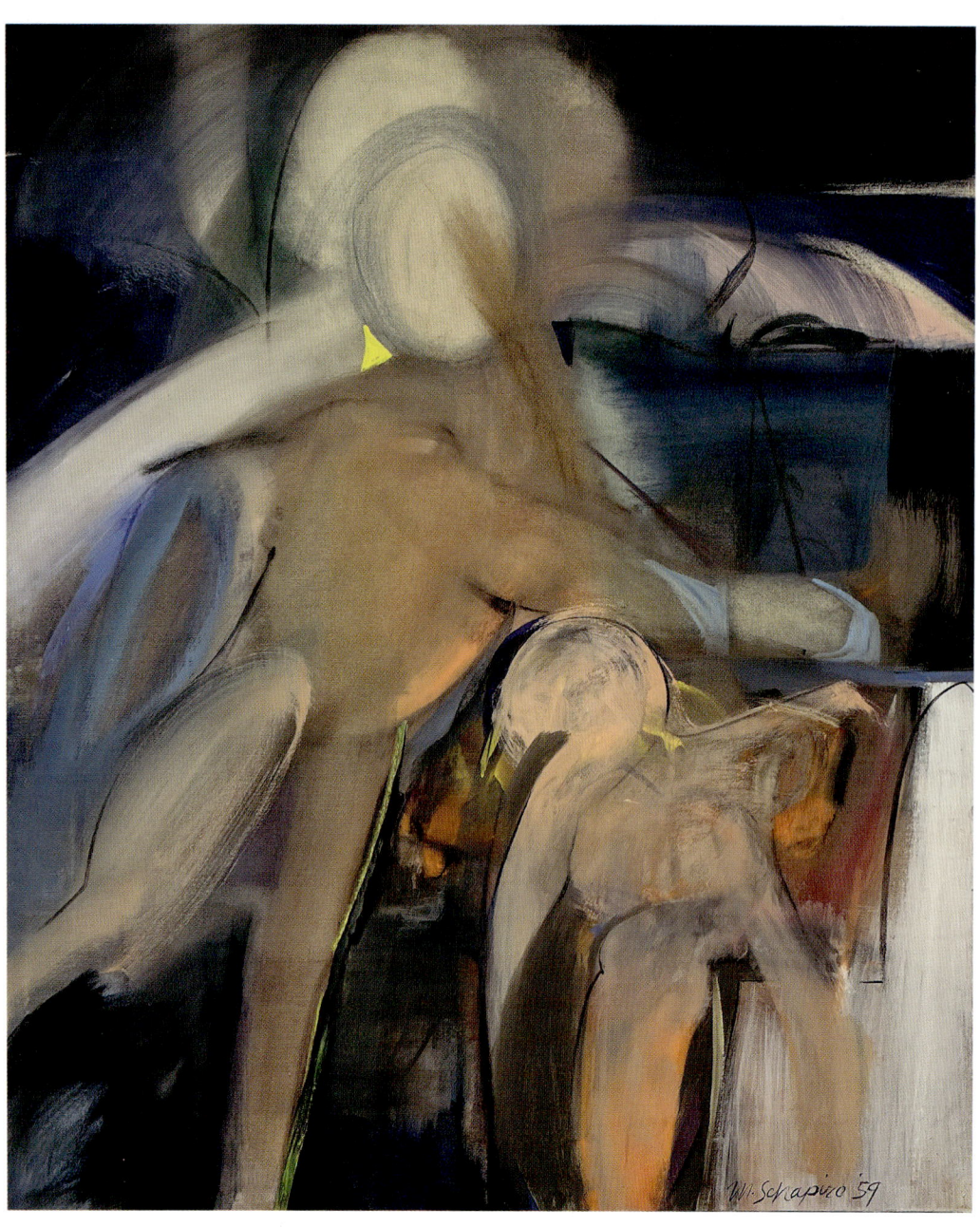

where Frankenthaler had traveled the year before. At the time of "The Women," Frankenthaler, at age 31, had recently closed her first solo museum show, at the Jewish Museum in New York, curated by critic and poet Frank O'Hara. It provoked a malicious *ARTnews* review imputing sexualized imagery in her art-historical references and personal symbolism.[22] Abstraction alone did not eliminate the risk that women's work would be interpreted through the lens of femininity.

Painter Miriam Schapiro (1923–2015), like Frankenthaler, showed at the prestigious André Emmerich Gallery. Her painting in the Living Rooms, *Pandora* (1959) (illus. 82)—an abstraction based on a photographic self-portrait—represents her conflicted place in the art scene of the day. At the time Schapiro was an admired member of the second generation of the New York School, but she later perceived these public successes through her private resentment of the sexism she encountered and the refusal of women artists to band together to combat it. In retrospect, after she became a leader in the feminist art movement, Schapiro lamented that women in the 1950s were both emotionally entwined with and professionally isolated from one another. "We talked about our love lives, and shared each other's romance. But I can assure you we never came together over painting," she recalled.[23] This sentiment, consistent with the narrative of the feminist movement at the time, seemingly overlooks the existence of projects like "The Women," which emerged from the efforts of two women artists specifically to bring attention to their peers.

The Abstract Expressionist movement, despite its name, in fact encompassed a diversity of imagery and subject-matter, from pure abstraction to symbolic forms to gestural representation. Over the course of the 1950s, the style expanded to accommodate artists like Schapiro, who employed its techniques to paint figural and narrative images. "The Women" embraced several of these gestural stylists, including Jane Wilson, Jane Freilicher, and Nell Blaine. One landscape by each hung in the Living Rooms, with Wilson's 8-foot-wide (2.4 m) panoramic landscape *River Port* (c. 1958) (illus. 83) complementing Freilicher's

82 Miriam Schapiro, *Pandora*, 1959, oil on canvas.

6½ by 6½-foot (2 × 2 m) view of a cluster of purple flowering plants in *The Mallow Gatherers* (1958) (illus. 84). Wilson's painting *Reclining Nude* (1955), a frontal image of a nude woman relaxing in a chair looking casually aside, hung in the Fitz Studio and more explicitly addressed the status of women in the art world. Like Valadon, de Kooning, and Hartigan, Wilson once posed as a model before painting as an artist and reclaiming images of feminine beauty. *Reclining Nude* appeared in her solo show at Hansa Gallery in New York in 1955, illustrated in the *ARTnews* review, with critic Parker Tyler writing that her "personality and design" appeared distinctly in this painting.[24] Two years later the painting appeared in the background of the photograph of Wilson in the *Life* article, "Women Artists in Ascendance." The mein of the figure in the painting mirrored Wilson's intention to upend the Western academic tradition of the odalisque, which objectified the female body for the pleasure of the male gaze.

The other artists with works displayed in the Living Rooms were Yvonne Thomas, Linda Lindeberg, Janice Biala, and Pat Passlof. De Kooning's modestly sized *March Sky* (1959) rounded out the grouping. The largest of her three works was the 5-foot-tall (1.5 m) *Climber* (1956), a vigorous and rhythmic gestural abstraction. This painting hung in the gallery labeled Dord's Room, and it is tempting to assign special status to the three works there. Adjacent to *Climber* were Frankenthaler's *The Red Sea* (1959) and Schapiro's *By the Sea* (1958), a swirling, gestural abstraction derived from a photograph of Frankenthaler.[25] In sum, the exhibition told the story of a confident, assertive group of women artists who found their voices in the visual language of gestural painting and abstract sculpture, though the term "Abstract Expressionism" did not appear in the press release.

Reynal and de Kooning's curatorial focus on one generation of gestural painters and allied sculptors resulted in a number of significant exclusions. For the first time in a decade, a curated survey of midcentury American women artists did *not* include Loren MacIver or Irene Rice Pereira, the two iconic "women artists" of their generation. Their

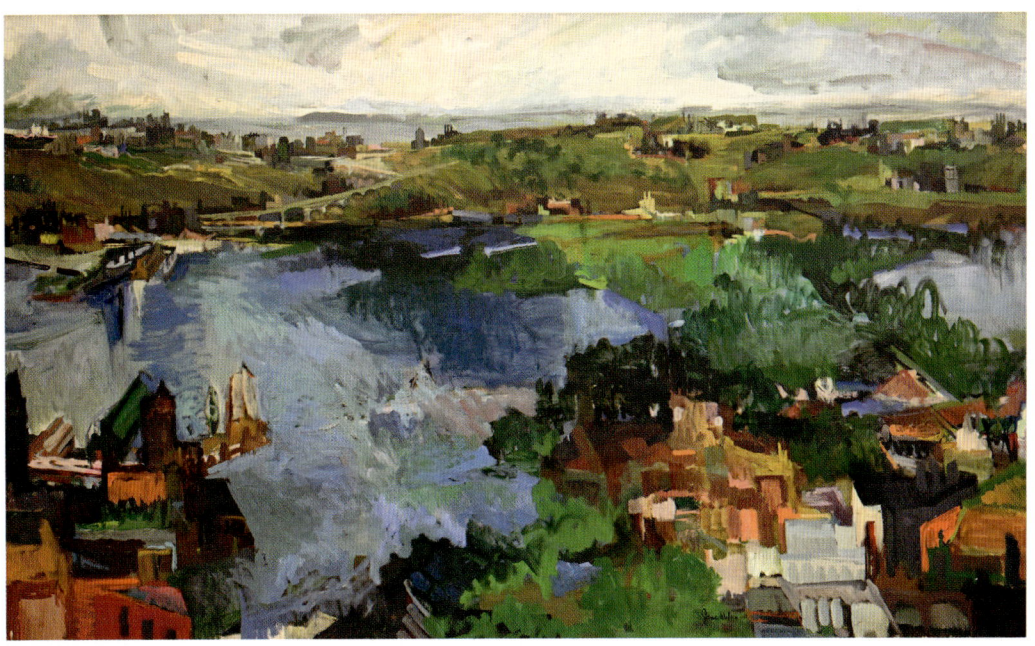

83 Jane Wilson,
River Port, c. 1958,
oil on canvas.

well-crafted, modestly sized paintings in lyrical representation and non-objective abstraction had fallen out of favor among critics and curators enthralled by the pugnacious energy of Abstract Expressionism and its rhetoric of American assertiveness and rejection of European finish and composition. Further, the New York focus eliminated artists working in other urban centers of the style, such as the San Francisco Bay Area, home to Joan Brown, Emiko Nakano, and Jay DeFeo.

Because Fitz, Reynal, and de Kooning sought to exhibit recent work, they foreclosed the participation of several key artists. The press release listed Joan Mitchell and Grace Hartigan as among participating artists, but in the end neither sent any works. A handwritten letter from Hartigan, dated a few weeks before the opening, reiterated her position that she had hoped to contribute at least one painting, but all of her new work was on consignment, with the exception of a very thickly painted canvas drying in the studio. There is no direct correspondence from Mitchell, who was in France at the time, so it is unclear if she

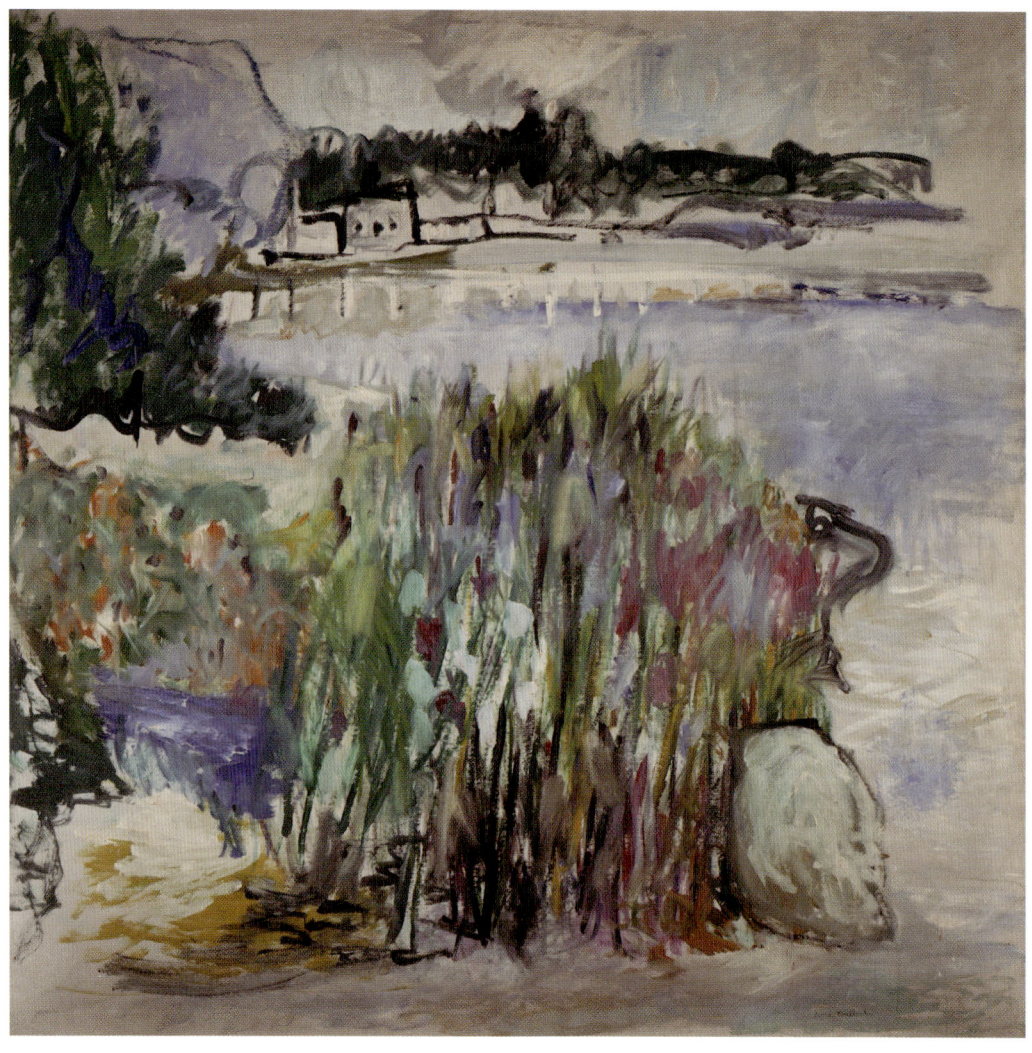

84 Jane Freilicher, *The Mallow Gatherers*, 1958, oil on linen.

personally assented to the show. Eleanor Ward from the Stable Gallery, which represented Mitchell, wrote on her behalf, expressing regret that there was no new work in inventory to lend.

"The Women" provided a panoramic view of female painters and sculptors in the vibrant New York art scene circa 1960, but neglected to recognize racial diversity in Abstract Expressionism. Reynal and de Kooning's focus on new work, culled through studio visits and phone calls, overlooked artists like Rose Piper (1917–2005), who had contributed to the formation of the New York School in the 1940s but had left the city and evolved her practice toward textile design and commercial art. The nearly exclusive curation from a coterie of downtown New York artists precluded the participation of Black women abstractionists working outside the city, like artist and educator Alma Thomas, who had initiated a new direction in gestural abstraction in the late 1950s in Washington, DC. Thomas revitalized her career in her late sixties, when she shifted from representational painting to synesthetic explorations of color and light, such as *Blue Abstraction* (1958), which was exhibited in the 26th Biennial Exhibition of Contemporary American Painting at the Corcoran in 1959. Thomas gained national attention later in the 1960s when she adopted a hard-edge style and became associated with the Washington Color School.

The Dord Fitz exhibition also did not feature abstract painting by any Asian American women artists, several of whom became visible in the late 1950s with the dovetailing of aesthetic interest in the Western gestural techniques of abstraction and Eastern calligraphic ink painting. A number of works by Asian and Asian American artists circulated nationally and could have been noticed by Fitz, de Kooning, or Reynal. California painter Noriko Yamamoto (1925–2022) worked in the Abstract Expressionist idiom and exhibited in a group show at the Institute of Contemporary Art, Boston, in 1958 and a two-person show with Falkenstein in San Francisco in 1959. In New York, Yayoi Kusama (b. 1929) had her first show of all-over *Infinity Net* paintings at the downtown cooperative Brata Gallery in 1959, and Ruth Asawa had multiple solo shows and participated in the Stable Annual in 1955. Chinese-born abstract landscape painter Tseng Yuho (1924–2017), a resident of Hawaii, began circulating her paintings on the mainland with a solo exhibition at the Walker Art Center in Minneapolis in 1959. Notably, she was the one artist of color in the all-women exhibition "37 Contemporary Americans" at the IBM Gallery, New York, in April 1960. The collaboration between Reynal, de Kooning, and Fitz created a congenial context that allowed the women to pursue a separatist exhibition, far outside the orbit of New York critics and collectors yet still marked by the city's tastes and biases.

Proud of the exhibition, Fitz strove to extend its reach beyond the Panhandle. He attempted to partner with the American Federation of the Arts to tour it to Dallas and wrote to Martha Jackson that "some of the girls want a show at a museum there [in New York]."[26] Aiming for national media attention, he sent press releases and letters to the regional offices of *Time, Life, Horizon,* and other publications with substantive arts coverage, as well as *ARTnews,* de Kooning's former employer. "This show is evidence of the spreading interest in contemporary art and underlines the importance of women's role in art today," Fitz wrote to executive editor Tom Hess.[27] His pitch touted the novelty and newsworthiness of the exhibition, claiming that "The Women" was the largest show of its kind outside New York and ever in the Southwest. (He made these claims notwithstanding a similar show in Houston seven years earlier, "Women in Art," which also included Nevelson and Sterne.) Neither the tour nor the national coverage panned out. *ARTnews* ran an advance notice for the show, inaccurately listing Mitchell and Hartigan among the participants. Local newspapers in many of the small cities and towns served by Fitz's schools printed articles derived from the press release and offered little fresh reporting or critical response.[28] Publicity photographs of Sterne, Reynal, and Wilson appeared in local newspapers. One news photo showed two of Fitz's volunteers with a painting by Wilson and a work on paper by de Kooning. Curiously, the titles in the caption do not match those of works on the checklist.

Although it had little influence on the national discourse around women artists, "The Women" did impact the lives and careers of its participating artists. De Kooning especially benefited from her ongoing interactions with Fitz's gallery and the Southwest region in general. She became enamored with the high-plains landscape and frequently traveled to Amarillo and New Mexico, where she served as a visiting artist at the state university in Albuquerque. "The Southwest is developing an art style all its own, one with a feeling of quiet and remoteness. It is entirely different from the turbulent art of the east and west coasts," she said in a Texas newspaper.[29] The simplified lifestyle and desolate landscape had already attracted painters like Georgia O'Keeffe and Agnes Martin. Through Fitz, de Kooning connected to the community and its ethos, and its influence on her work was significant. Reynal and Nevelson also continued to travel to Amarillo for workshops and exhibitions.

Few famous male artists from New York ventured to Amarillo, so women held "center stage," according to Amy Von Lintel and Bonnie Roos, scholars of modern and contemporary art in the Panhandle.[30] Fitz successfully placed works in the show with local collectors. Thrilled with the presence of Nevelson's sculpture, the Area Arts Foundation purchased *Moonscape Chapel* (now titled *Moon Garden*) (1959), an impressive example of her pioneering installation art. The foundation pooled the $1,500 down payment through sales of $1 raffle tickets for the acquisition, toward the final sale price of $5,822.50, after a 15 percent discount.[31] The following year, Nevelson returned to Texas to install the work in a dedicated room in Fitz's new gallery, around the corner from the Victorian house, which was slated to be demolished to make way for a new freeway ramp. His personal commitment to artists in "The Women" meant that he continued to show and sell works by de Kooning, Nevelson, Reynal, Thomas, and Wilson. From a marketing standpoint, it made sense to claim "The Women" as the first and most important show of its kind, positioning Fitz as the local guru who discovered the American women painters taking the lead in the contemporary art market. Indeed, he rode the wave of a larger trend. In May 1960, *Time*, the country's premier news magazine, with a circulation in the millions, declared the reign of outspoken women in American art, with Frankenthaler, Hartigan, and Mitchell its primary exponents.[32] "The Women" marked the narrative shift from emphasizing individual women's competition for coveted positions among men to women as a group with shared concerns, challenges, and accomplishments.

An exhibition with a similarly triumphant message of women's commercial and critical success, "Women of American Art," opened in the fall of 1960 in New York, at the World House Galleries, located in the upscale Carlyle Hotel. "Probably never before in history have so many women been able to emerge as artists of the first rank," the press release quoted *Look* writer Charlotte Willard.[33] Her article, which appeared in conjunction with the show and included photographs of the seven artists with statements, marveled at the market potential for women in the wake of a Cassatt selling at auction for an impressive $39,000.[34] "Women of American Art" featured one work each by seven artists, three of whom were also in the Dord Fitz show: Nevelson, Falkenstein, and Frankenthaler, along with O'Keeffe, Hartigan, and two emerging talents, sculptor Lee Bontecou (1931–2022) and painter Joan Brown (1938–1990) (both in their twenties). Treading similar aesthetic territory, both shows included Falkenstein's sculpture *Sun no. 16*, Nevelson's wood construction elements from immersive installations, and Frankenthaler's symbolic abstractions painted from her memories of Europe (*Hotel Cro-Magnon* (1958) at World House and *Madridscape* at Dord Fitz). Even Fitz's open-sky theme of the American West was represented at World House in the form of O'Keeffe's *From the Plains II* (1954), a vibrant painting of a glowing orange sky streaked with a yellow serrated arc. The reduced formal elements of the work responded to the light and vistas of the Texas high-plains landscape, which first enraptured O'Keeffe as a young artist teaching in Amarillo in 1912. *From the Plains II*, if not quite a work of Abstract Expressionism, approached the style's vibrant spatial opticality, perhaps anticipating its evolution into Color Field painting. Contrasting with the Fitz gallery's location in a converted residence in Amarillo, the ultramodern World House gallery was conceived by Frederick Kiesler (designer of Art of This Century) and Armand Bartos as a bespoke showplace to integrate architecture, lighting, and art objects.

The culmination of the unique partnership of de Kooning, Reynal, and Fitz, "The Women" forthrightly proclaimed that a cohesive group of women had come to the fore in the leading art movement of the day. The Texas Panhandle, a region built on a frontier mythos located over a thousand miles from both the East and West coasts, offered an advantageous setting to assert women's presence within Abstract Expressionism, which itself was associated with the cowboy image of blue jean-clad Jackson Pollock, a son of Wyoming. The Texas rhetoric of size, freedom, and rugged individuality befit a certain kind of (white) woman artist. The Western openness to women artists as artistic pioneers, as articulated by Fitz, continued nearly a half-century later when the Denver Art Museum in Colorado organized the largest historical survey of women in Abstract Expressionism to date.

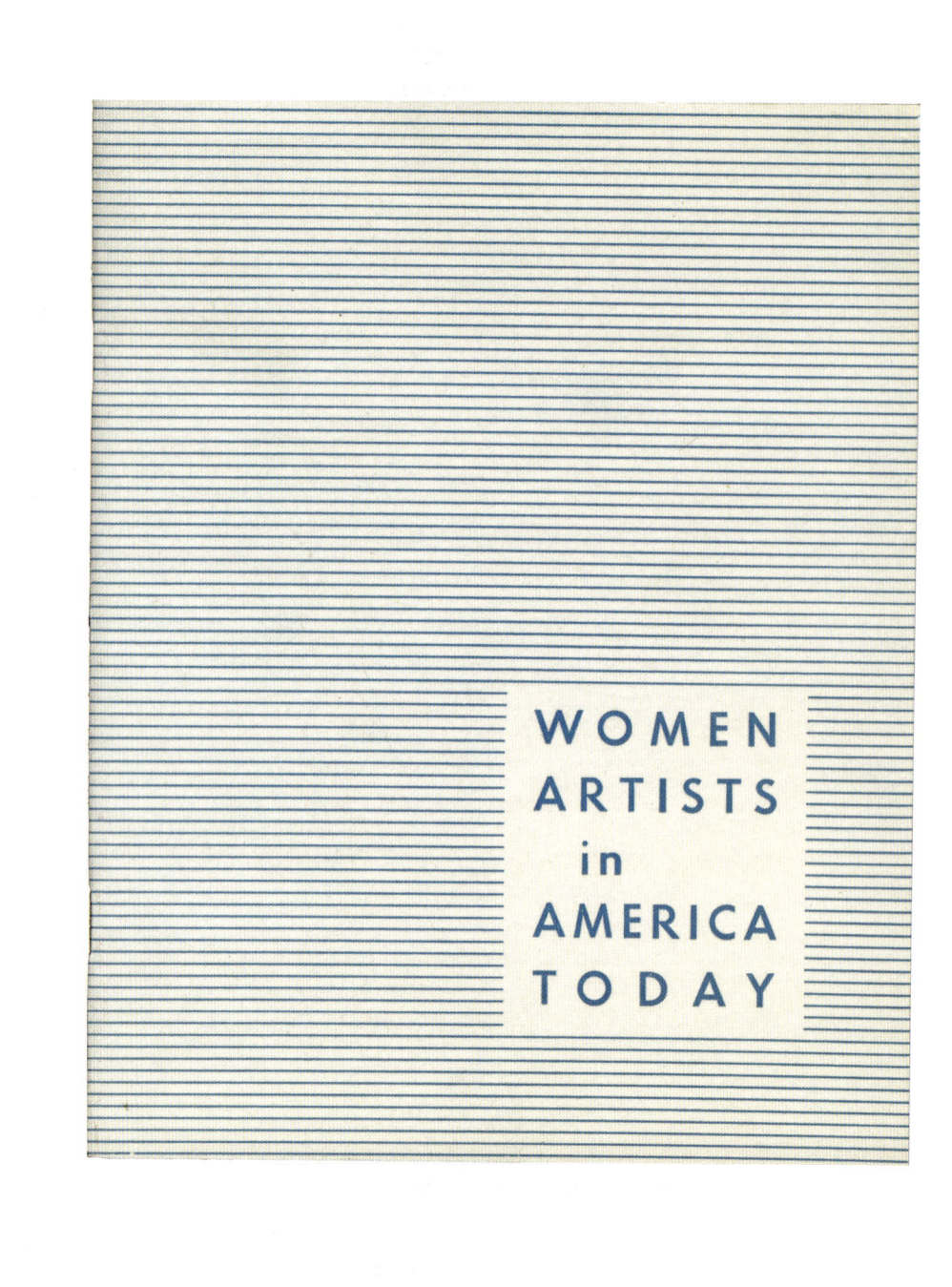

WOMEN
ARTISTS
in
AMERICA
TODAY

10

Democracy: "Women Artists in America Today," Mount Holyoke College Art Museum, 1962

"Women Artists in America Today: A Loan Exhibition" gathered the best and brightest to survey a heady swath of contemporary art in celebration of the founding of Mount Holyoke College, a women's liberal arts school in western Massachusetts (illus. 85). A photograph from the opening night reception shows a tuxedoed Arthur M. Schlesinger, Jr. (1917–2007), special assistant to President John F. Kennedy, facing the intricate welded metal tubing of Claire Falkenstein's large floor piece *Sun no. 20* (1960). He is flanked by college trustee Janet Brewster Murrow and art critics Dorothy Adlow and Emily Genauer (illus. 86).[1] Their eyes study something up and out of the frame, perhaps Falkenstein's sculpture *Envelope* (1958), which would have been suspended from the ceiling. Looming in the background like the opening of a cave was Lee Bontecou's cavernous 5½-square-foot (165 × 165 cm) *Flit* (1959), a mound made of canvas tied with wire to a metal armature. Black velveteen fabric lined the interior space within the large aperture at the center to absorb light and simulate the sense of a dark void. The contrast between the genteel celebrants of an all-women's exhibition and its presentation of disquieting abstract sculpture illustrates an era on the cusp of feminist transformation.

The show opened on April 10, 1962, fifteen months into the Kennedy administration, the confluence of an adventuresome contemporary art show at the nation's oldest women's college and the political agenda of the youngest president in U.S. history. The opening

85 Mount Holyoke College Art Museum, *Women Artists in America Today*, exhibition catalogue, 1962.

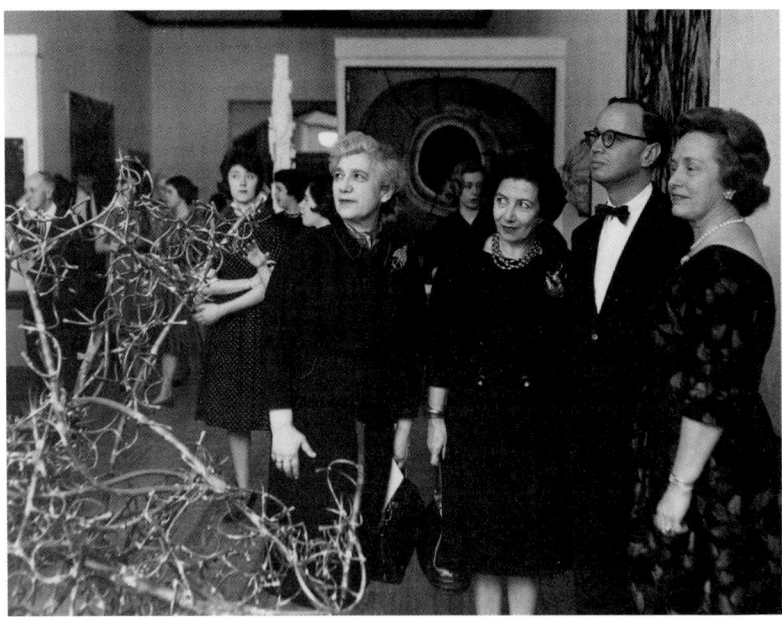

86 "Women Artists in America Today" opening: (L–R) Dorothy Adlow, Emily Genauer, Arthur M. Schlesinger, Jr., Janet Brewster Murrow, with Claire Falkenstein's *Sun no. 20* at left, Lee Bontecou's *Flit* at rear.

weekend of the exhibition included a lecture by Schlesinger on the subject of government and the arts. Kennedy's embrace of modernity in science, culture, and politics as essential components of a robust democracy ushered in a constellation of new initiatives, including the push for a federal arts policy as well as amplified focus on the role of women in U.S. society and politics. At the end of 1961, Kennedy issued an executive order creating the President's Commission on the Status of Women, the first federal panel to address discrimination against women and to identify proposals to remove barriers to success. These twin initiatives of the Kennedy administration—to support artistic freedom and women's advancement—can be seen as animating principles shared by the exhibition.

"Women Artists in America Today" and related public programs occurred under the rubric "Art and the Artist in Today's Society" on the occasion of Mount Holyoke College's year-long celebration of its 125th anniversary. The scope of the exhibition reflected the growing excitement around innovative women in contemporary American art. Included were over 50 works by 26 artists, a number greatly exceeding

Smith College's ten-work 75th anniversary exhibition thirteen years earlier. If, as stated in the Mount Holyoke press release, the exhibition celebrated the "coming of age" of women artists in the United States, the narrative remained stubbornly limited to predetermined institutional markers of success.[2] None of the artists were women of color, conforming to a pattern of centering white middle-class women as the archetypes of "woman" that would remain in place for decades. Nevertheless, due to its scale and stylistic inclusivity, "Women Artists in America Today" can be considered the most complete survey of women artists in the major movements of contemporary art before the emergence of Pop, Minimalism, and political activism. The show's importance stems not from its direct impact—like many of the all-women exhibitions in this period outside New York, it received little critical response—but from its signaling of the convergence of new political and cultural crosscurrents.

Mount Holyoke art history professor Jean C. Harris (1927–1988), a Smith College graduate with a doctorate from Radcliffe, skillfully curated the Mount Holyoke exhibition. It was installed in the galleries of the Dwight Memorial Art Building, which housed the department of fine art and its collections and galleries. Harris specialized in nineteenth-century French modernism, and the curation was abetted by an exhibition committee comprising professors Dorothy Cogswell (1909–2008), a painter and the first woman to receive a Master of Fine Arts degree from Yale, and Marian Hayes (b. 1906), an art historian who helped build the college's art collection. The Mount Holyoke Friends of Art, which included patrons like financier and modern art collector Roy Neuberger, sponsored the show. With loans from museums in New York and elsewhere, the budget equaled those of all of the museum's other exhibitions that year combined, a worthy expense for such an ambitious endeavor, Harris concluded in her report to the Friends of Art.[3] Two paintings in the show were from the museum's collection at the time: Doris Lee's *The Tree* (1947), acquired in 1952, and *Woman Reclining* (c. 1904), then attributed to Mary Cassatt, but now of undetermined authorship.[4] All but two artists appeared in at least one of the all-women exhibitions discussed in this book. As for the exceptions, Lee Krasner had been selected for Peggy Guggenheim's "The Women" but never delivered a work, and Stephanie Scuris (1931–2023) was an emerging artist in her early thirties. The recurrence of certain artists and even a few specific works in midcentury all-women shows reiterates the persistence of an established pool of "women artists."

The curatorial criteria were broad and nonspecific, emphasizing artistic quality and artist reputation. As with Smith College's anniversary exhibition (see Chapter Four), the curatorial team focused on biography and self-identification when selecting the "noted women artists."[5] Harris's letter of inquiry to Joan Mitchell, sent care of Stable Gallery, plainly stated, "Since we hope that each piece will be an important and representative example, we are asking each artist for suggestions as to the works which she would like to see included."[6] This deference to the artists' preferences, and the dependency on the availability of work, opened the door to a random assortment, which Harris had to integrate into a cohesive exhibition. As she explained in a short statement in the exhibition catalogue:

> Although some attempt was made in arranging this exhibition to present a survey of the styles and media in which women artists are working today, our main concern was to select objects which would present a vivid picture of the impressive contributions being made to the American scene by women artists. Certainly such contributions deserve more recognition than they have hitherto received. It is hoped that this exhibition will play a small part in attaining this goal.[7]

A local newspaper reporter agreed, writing, "The 1950s will probably go down in the annals of American art as the period when women achieved their full emancipation as artists."[8]

In laying out this narrative that women artists were "coming of age" to take their place among the men in the United States in the early 1960s, Harris began the artistic story in the usual place: Mary Cassatt. In the catalogue introduction, she quotes critic Forbes Watson from 1932 that "[Cassatt] was never a 'lady' painter, always a 'woman' painter," an assessment Harris found applicable to the other artists in the show.[9] While shedding the aura of dilettantism and elitism of the "lady," Harris's framework still fell short of making a strong claim for women as innovators, instead considering them the humanizing force of male avant-garde disruption. "Like Mary Cassatt, the women artists in America today transform the often disturbing and iconoclastic expressive devices initiated by their male colleagues in very personal ways," Harris wrote. Without offering a definition of radical formal invention in the work of women artists, Harris resorted to the persistent stereotypes that modernist women merely "tidy up" the radical styles of their husbands and peers.[10]

The collective tastes and insights of the exhibition committee capaciously formulated several selections of artists that highlighted many of the key trends in painting and sculpture of the previous two decades. The show prioritized both the celebrated figures of advanced art and interesting lesser-known artists. "Women Artists" was the only all-women exhibition at midcentury to bring together works by Abstract Expressionist painters Lee Krasner, Joan Mitchell, Grace Hartigan, Elaine de Kooning, and Helen Frankenthaler. The show also, unusually, devoted significant space to sculptors, from the multimedia abstractions of Falkenstein and Bontecou to figural bronzes by Minna Harkavy (1886–1987) and Luise Kaish (1925–2013). The exhibition rounded out a canon of American women artists through the inclusion of all the regulars in midcentury "woman artist" shows—Isabel Bishop, Perle Fine, Doris Lee, Loren MacIver, Georgia O'Keeffe, and Irene Rice Pereira—who embodied the era's standards of quality and also all appeared in Smith College's 1949 show. And the Mount Holyoke show recognized artists like Surrealist Kay Sage and geometric abstractionist

Charmion von Wiegand, representing the predominant styles of Peggy Guggenheim's two all-women projects.

"Women Artists in America Today" distinguished itself among other painting-centric midcentury all-women exhibitions for including a larger group of sculptors. The photograph of the opening showed several large works by Falkenstein, Bontecou, and Nevelson in close proximity, evidencing the exhibition's expansive focus on abstract sculpture by women. Falkenstein's *Envelope* had been previously installed at Dord Fitz's "The Women," and Nevelson's white assemblage *Hanging Column (from Dawn's Wedding Feast)* (1959), a 6-foot-tall (1.8 m) element of a room-sized, white-painted wood installation, hung nearby. Bontecou was represented with *Flit* and the smaller *Untitled*, a canvas-and-wire piece borrowed from the collection of nearby Smith College. Bontecou's technique of building a superstructure from an assemblage of smaller components related to the methods of Falkenstein and Nevelson, which offered contemporary artists a set of procedures to scale up intimate gestures and everyday materials into monumental forms.

Bontecou studied in Florence and rapidly emerged after joining Leo Castelli's New York gallery in 1959. The solemnity of her work contrasted the cool irreverence of Castelli's stable of newly minted neo-Dada stars like Jasper Johns. In this regard, Bontecou correlated to Lee Krasner, whose adjacent painting *Entrance* (1960), a tensely composed canvas more than 7 feet (2 m) high, exuded an air of portentous occasion. In the early 1960s, Bontecou assembled, welded, stitched, and twisted army surplus and industrial detritus into mysterious presences. Widely exhibited in their day, these mixed-media reliefs demanded new modes of criticism, grounded in phenomenology, to account for their command of the surrounding space and their ability to evoke the body without directly representing it. This nearly complete transfiguration of found objects distinguished her work from other contemporaneous assemblage artists, with whom she was frequently grouped, and in turn inspired younger women like Eva Hesse. After dinner one night with

Bontecou, Hesse wrote, "I am amazed at what that woman can do . . . The complexity of her structures, what is involved, absolutely floored me."[11]

The inclusion of Louise Bourgeois made a statement on women's advanced work in sculpture achieving the status of painting and breaking free from the lingering post-Cubism of David Smith and others. Born in France, Bourgeois immigrated to the United States in 1938. Like Krasner and Hedda Sterne, she participated in the formation of Abstract Expressionism in the late 1940s and was one of four women to sign the infamous open letter denouncing the conservative jury selecting the Metropolitan Museum of Art's upcoming show *American Painting Today* in 1950. The ensuing controversy resulted in Nina Leen's photograph of a group of the signatories, dubbed "the Irascibles," in *Life* magazine in 1951, which became the definitive image of the Abstract Expressionist painters. The famous photograph omitted all the sculptors, however, and notoriously included just one woman, Sterne.

As a sculptor, Bourgeois pioneered environmental installation. Her two solo exhibitions at the Peridot Gallery in New York in 1949 and 1950 presented carved and assembled wooden totemic figures, known as the *Personages*, distributed throughout the space. These works addressed in part the complexities of women's roles as daughters, wives, and mothers, grounded in the artist's psychological and philosophical responses to her own experiences. The Mount Holyoke show included a bronze casting of one of these pieces, *Sleeping Figure* (1950; cast 1959). A second work, *One and Others* (1955) (illus. 87), consists of a cluster of vertical forms, each uniquely painted, standing on a panel, distilling the room-sized configurations of *Personages* into a tabletop piece. Bourgeois, like Krasner, had previously been sidelined, but by the early 1960s both reappeared to acclaim in New York. Bourgeois's new body of work comprising plaster biomorphic forms with sexual overtones, not present in the Mount Holyoke show, appealed to a younger generation of proto-feminist critics like Lucy Lippard, who had graduated from Smith College in 1958 and later included Bourgeois in the groundbreaking group show "Eccentric Abstraction" at the Fischbach Gallery in 1966.

The two artists to have attended the Mount Holyoke opening happened to be sculptors. One was Nevelson, who participated in the panel discussion. Her international renown, flamboyant persona, and exhortations on the creative license of artistic expression embodied the archetype of the woman artist as grande dame. One of two women selected to represent the United States at the Venice Biennale later that summer (the other was MacIver), Nevelson took on an outsize presence as a colorful avatar of women's professional accomplishment. The other artist who traveled to South Hadley, Massachusetts, was Minna Harkavy, a figural sculptor who had achieved some recognition in the 1930s and '40s but had not adapted to the changing times. One of Harkavy's two works at Mount Holyoke, the blocky, representational bronze *American Miner's Family* (1931), was borrowed from the

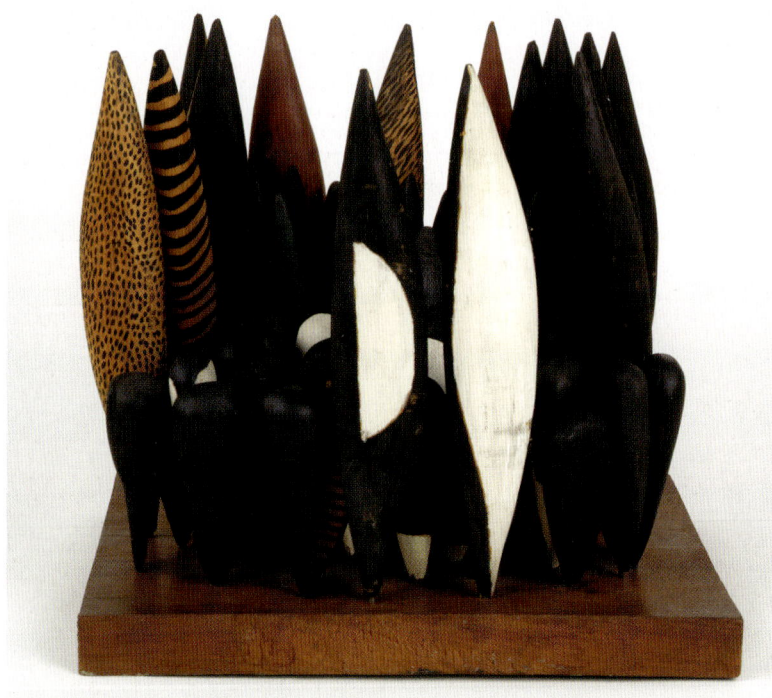

87 Louise Bourgeois,
One and Others, 1955,
painted and stained wood.

88 Jean Harris and Minna Harkavy at the opening of "Women Artists in America Today" with Harkavy's *Woman in Thought*, undated, bronze.

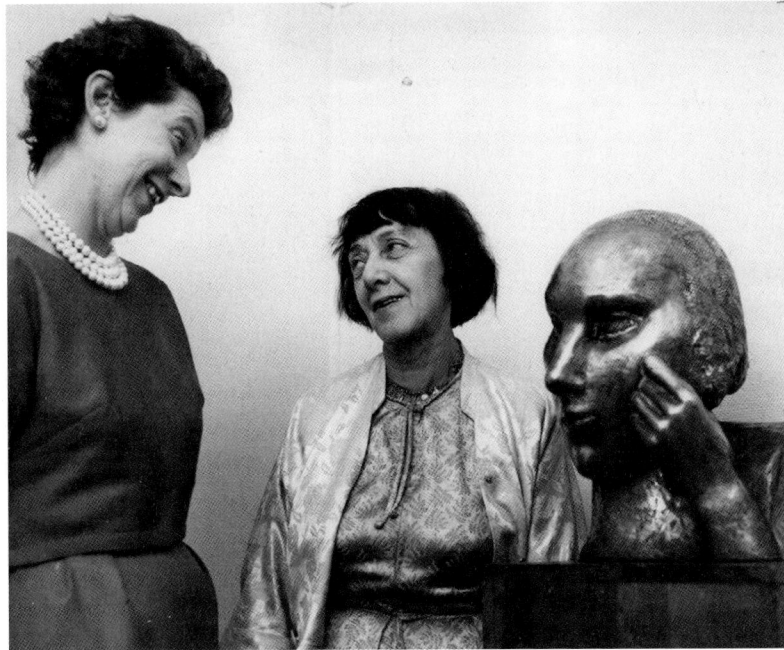

Museum of Modern Art, but the work was subsequently deaccessioned as socially conscious figural art had fallen out of favor in the face of both the Cold War and the new taste for abstraction. A photograph of curator Jean Harris towering over Harkavy at the opening documents the sculptor's other work in the show, the stylized bronze *Woman in Thought* (undated) (illus. 88). Born in Estonia, Harkavy immigrated to the United States around 1900 and lived mainly in New York. She was active in numerous artist groups, including NAWA, and helped organize an all-women exhibition titled "Six Sculptors" that opened at the association's Argent Gallery in May 1948. The show was slated to travel to Paris as part of the "Women's International Exposition," which was also to include Nancy Newhall's photography exhibition. But the exposition canceled all fine arts exhibits because of lack of funds for insurance and transportation expenses. Harkavy, with the support of NAWA, arranged for the exhibition to travel to Paris two years later, under the new title "New York Six," at the Petit Palais. An earlier brochure for the show included a philo-feminine statement by

Le Corbusier praising American women for focusing on creation and "the special part of life," in contrast to men who singularly chased the dollar.[12]

Several other sculptors in the Mount Holyoke show had long-standing involvement with NAWA. Rhys Caparn (1909–1997) also participated in "New York Six," and at Mount Holyoke presented two bronzes of monolithic abstracted shapes from the late 1950s that up-dated her Cubist figural style. Mary Callery loaned two recent bronzes of swirling linear forms, further abstracting the "drawing in space" imagery she had developed over a decade earlier. By 1960 a self-conscious group of sculptors in NAWA believed that they set the standard for high-quality, advanced work within a women artists organization. Helen Wilson, the chair of the NAWA sculpture committee, wrote to sculptor Jane Teller in 1960, "We already have most of the best women sculptors including Nevelson, Callery, Harkavy, Caparn, [Dorothy] Dehner, [Helen] Phillips, [Lu] Duble, [Lily] Ente, etc. If sculpture is to be shown as 'women's work,' or in fact is shown at all, I want it to be good!"[13] Despite their commitment to excellence, these sculptors have been largely omitted from histories of postwar American art. Only Nevelson made the transition from being one of the "Guild ladies" (members of both NAWA and the Sculptors Guild) to a celebrated innovator in modern sculpture.

Representing a younger generation, Luise Kaish, born in Atlanta, took traditional bronze sculpture in a new direction. She joined NAWA around the time she exhibited in the landmark "Women Welders" with seven other artists at the Sculpture Center in 1953. Kaish's two works in the Mount Holyoke show were cast bronzes, not welded assemblages, displaying her personal and aesthetic engagement with places of wor-ship and religious imagery. *Abraham, Abraham* (1958) (illus. 89) depicts the climactic moment in the book of Genesis when God's messenger summons the biblical patriarch to sacrifice a ram in place of his son Isaac. By the early 1960s, Kaish had become a leading sculptor of eccle-siastical art in a wave of modernist synagogue construction in the

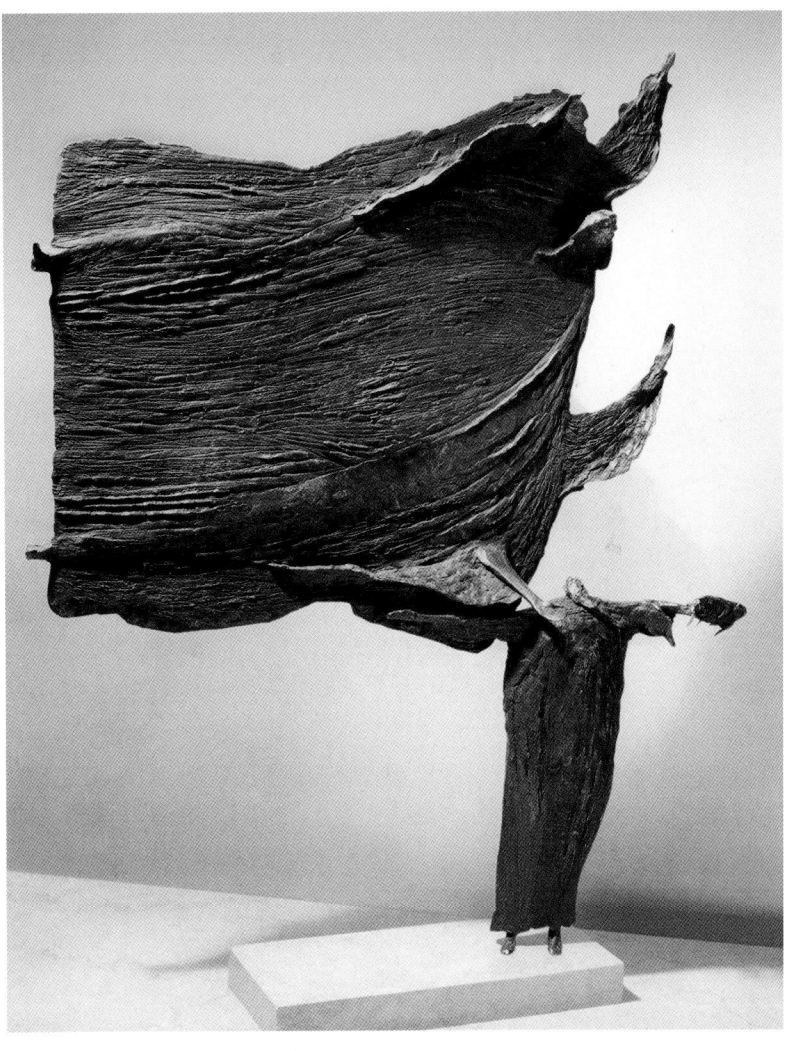

89 Luise Kaish, *Abraham, Abraham*, 1958, bronze.

suburbs that signaled the assimilation of the Jewish community into the American mainstream. A few days before the opening of the Mount Holyoke show, Kaish received a letter from the chairman of Temple B'rith Kodesh in Rochester, New York, approving her proposal for the ambitious bronze *Ark of Revelation* for a new building designed by architect Pietro Belluschi. Kaish's sculpture revisiting cultural myths and religious narratives must have appealed to Harris's expansive thinking about representational art.

Kaish's theme of life hanging in the balance was addressed by another figural sculptor in the exhibition, Marianna Pineda (1925–1996). Born Marianna Packard in Illinois, the artist changed her name in homage to Mariana Pineda, the protagonist of Federico García Lorca's eponymous play about a resistance activist in nineteenth-century Spain. Her life-size bronze *Prelude* (1957) (illus. 90) portrays a woman in labor, her limbs and torso torqued in tension. Women artists commonly represented mothers and children in painting and sculpture, but infrequently explored the subjective experience of pregnancy and childbirth as did Pineda. The same year that *Prelude* appeared in Mount Holyoke, Pineda become a fellow of the Radcliffe Institute for Independent Study in Cambridge, Massachusetts. Founded by Radcliffe College president Mary Bunting to provide critical support to mid-career female academics and creative artists who were also mothers and wives, the institute played an important role in recognizing the challenges faced by women to advance their careers without sacrificing their determination to have a family. The fellowship accommodated reality, rather than tried to change the system, and fostered new networks among women artists. In the first class of fellows,

90 Marianna Pineda, *Prelude*, 1957, bronze.

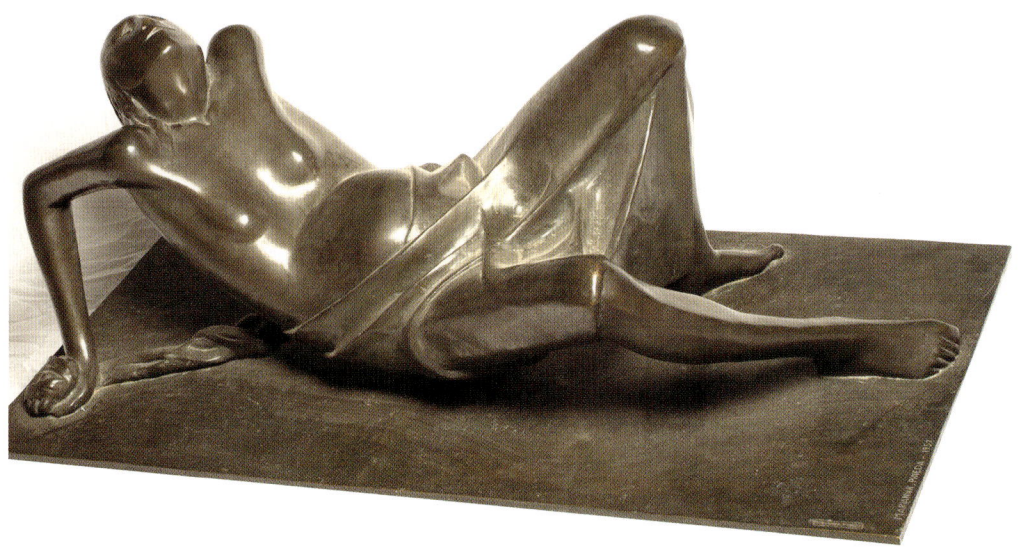

writers Anne Sexton, Maxine Kumin, and Tillie Olsen encouraged one another's efforts to develop proto-feminist critiques of the social and psychological constraints placed upon women. They, along with kindred spirit Sylvia Plath, discovered in the early 1960s that there was suddenly a market for literature that unflinchingly exposed their struggles as women and artists. Works by Pineda in the Mount Holyoke exhibition were visual analogues to contemporary confessional poetry. With its sagacious and wide-ranging exploration of contemporary sculpture, the Mount Holyoke exhibition welcomed both cutting-edge abstract art and traditional bronze sculpture exploring women's autobiography.

A third photograph of the opening provides an entry point to a discussion of another significant theme in the show: institutional recognition of women in Abstract Expressionism. A jovial Janet Brewster Murrow (1910–1998), college trustee and journalist, stands next to a woman holding a copy of the exhibition catalogue and points toward something out of frame. Two dynamic paintings by Joan Mitchell, *Harbor December* (1956) and *Summer Slide* (1960–61), hanging on the wall behind (illus. 91), captured the physicality of Mitchell's brushstrokes, often attributed to her athletic muscle memory from experiences as a competitive figure skater. She painted the 80 by 80-inch (2 × 2 m) *Harbor December* when she was emerging as a new talent, and the explosive brushwork breaks from artistic influences legible in earlier paintings. "Power is written all over Joan Mitchell's new canvases," critic Dore Ashton (1928–2017) wrote in 1958.[14] Boldness was Mitchell's calling card, and she distinguished herself from other American women artists of her generation by moving to France and forswearing bourgeois life, writing to a lover that she never wanted to be Marjorie Morningstar.[15]

A number of all-women shows had reckoned with the rise and efflorescence of Abstract Expressionism, from "The Women" at Art of This Century in 1945, to "Nine Women Painters" at Bennington College in 1953, to "The Women" at Dord Fitz Gallery in 1960. Together, these

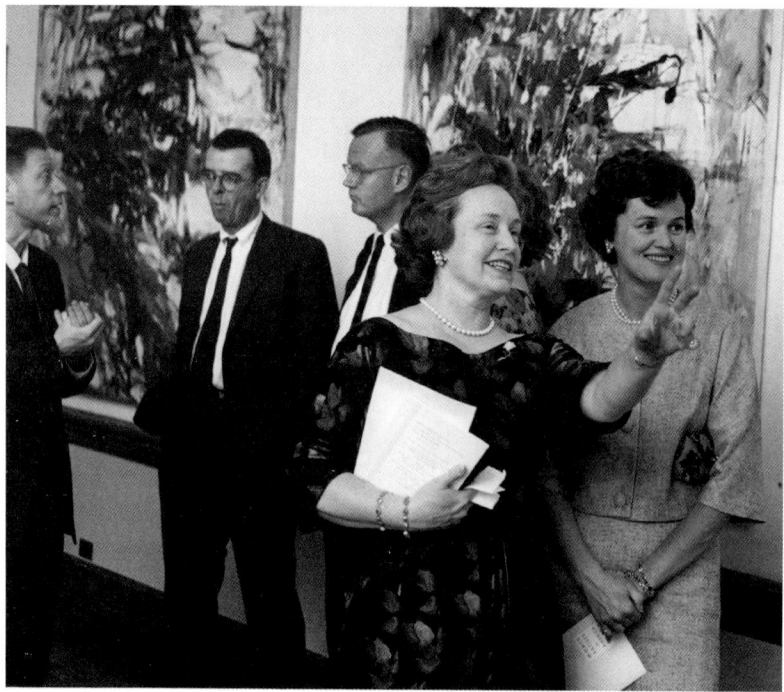

91 The opening of "Women Artists in America Today": (L–R) Peter Viereck, Mr. Tighlman, John L. Cooper, Janet Brewster Murrow, Mrs. Cooper, with Joan Mitchell's *Harbor December*, 1956, and *Summer Slide*, 1960–61.

shows included most major female Abstract Expressionist painters in New York with one notable exception: Lee Krasner. She agreed to, but did not deliver, a painting to "The Women" in 1945 and thereafter remained distant from other all-women exhibitions. Like many women artists of her generation, Krasner masked her gender: she did so by changing her name from Lenore to the unisex Lee, and sometimes signed her canvases with the initials LK. At Mount Holyoke, Krasner took her place among Abstract Expressionist women at least a decade younger: Frankenthaler, Hartigan, Mitchell, and de Kooning. Krasner was an originator of the movement, but struggled to gain attention for her intimate abstractions in the late 1940s and collages of cut-up pieces of older work in the early 1950s. Only after her husband Jackson Pollock's death in the summer of 1956 did she reassert her public identity. She took over Pollock's barn studio and stretched large canvases on the wall—fresh territory, as Pollock had previously worked on the floor— and erupted in multiple series of energetic gestural abstractions suffused

with symbolism relating to narratives of rebirth, nature, and the cycle
of life. Two paintings from this important body of work, *Entrance*
(1960) and *Night Watch* (1960) (illus. 92), appeared at Mount Holyoke.
With a new group of younger supporters, like poet Richard Howard
and dealer Howard Wise, Krasner earned new acclaim and recognition.
The younger Frankenthaler, Hartigan, and Mitchell had achieved
greater renown and curatorial and institutional recognition in the 1950s,
yet it was the belated emergence of Krasner that indicated American
art's new openness to the hidden, even traumatic personal narratives of
women as artists. Krasner later remained skeptical of feminist politics
in art while accepting the critical interventions of younger curators like
Marcia Tucker, who organized Krasner's first American museum show
at the Whitney Museum of American Art in 1973.

In the late 1950s, Hartigan also began to participate in all-women
exhibitions after becoming one of the few exceptional women at the
center of the Abstract Expressionist movement. She was known as both
a physically statuesque person who modeled at the Art Students League
in her early days, and as a denizen of the gritty Lower East Side who
adopted men's attire. Hartigan flouted fixed gender lines, positing
gender as masquerade in paintings like *The Persian Jacket* (1952) and
Grand Street Brides (1954). In her first three solo exhibitions at the
Tibor de Nagy Gallery, New York, she showed under the name "George
Hartigan," both a camp sobriquet inspired by her playful interactions
with a coterie of gay male poets such as Frank O'Hara and an earnest
homage to George Sand and George Eliot, two influential female
novelists of the previous century with male pen names (Sand experi-
mented in painting as well). For her 1954 show at Vassar College, she
appeared as "Grace George Hartigan." By the time Dorothy Miller
selected her as the sole woman in MOMA's "Twelve Americans" in 1956,
Hartigan dropped the male pseudonym. After her exceptional position
was further secured when she became the only woman in MOMA's landmark traveling exhibition "The New American Painting" (1958–9),
Hartigan participated in a number of all-women shows, such as

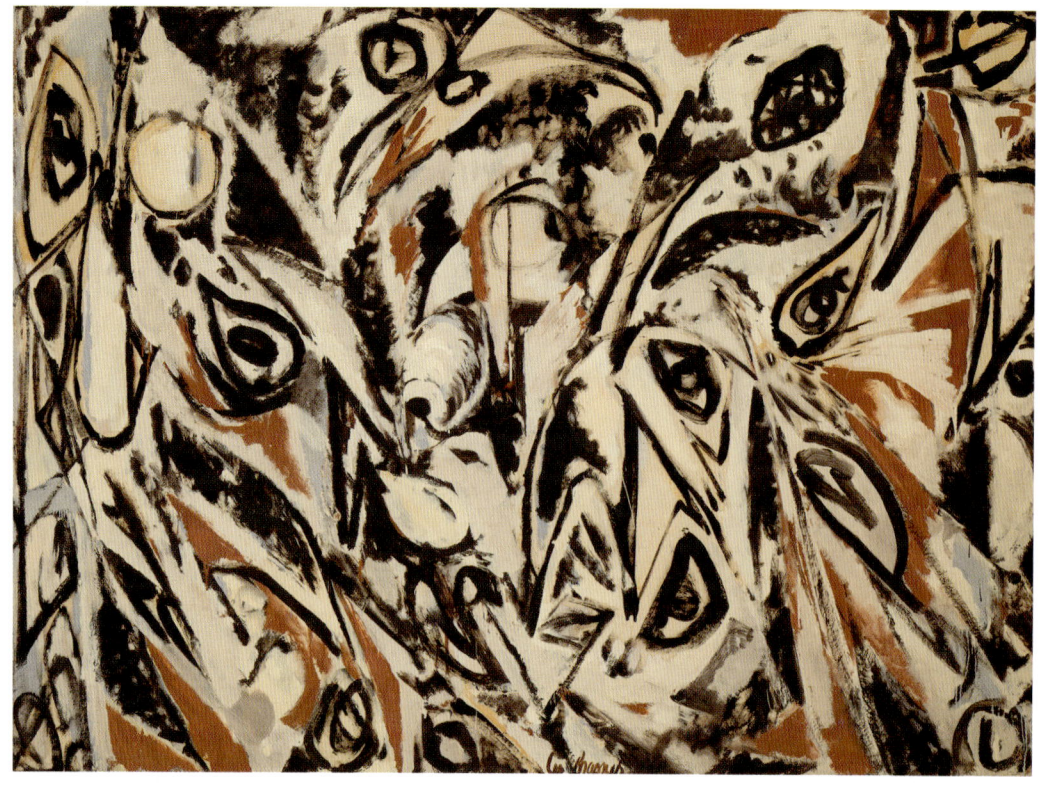

92 Lee Krasner,
Night Watch, 1960,
oil on canvas.

"Paintings by Some Contemporary American Women: 48th Annual Exhibition" at Randolph-Macon Woman's College in Virginia in 1959 and "37 Contemporary Americans," sponsored by the National Council of Women of the United States, at the IBM Gallery in midtown Manhattan in 1960.

In 1960, she married for a fourth time, moved to Baltimore, and began painting in a lyrical manner. For the Mount Holyoke show, she contributed a recent painting that, like Krasner's, recorded her intensification of self-confidence. *New York Rhapsody* (1960) (illus. 93), a bold arrangement of color nestled in an interlocking armature of black brushstrokes, nods nostalgically to her residence in that city. Nearly 8 feet (2.4 m) wide, it was among the larger canvases in the show, evidencing the physical scale of postwar women's ambitions in Abstract Expressionism—a theme that was central to Dord Fitz's "The

Women"—and distinct from the smaller abstractions by Pereira and O'Keeffe. The toned-down painting muted some of the jarring chromatic juxtapositions of Hartigan's mid-1950s abstract style. *City Life II* (1956), which appeared in the IBM Gallery show, was described in *Time* magazine as exemplifying this phase, where "her colors are pounded into every available space, her strokes seem committed out of rage; the effect is one of extraordinary power."[16]

The Smolin Gallery on the Upper East Side also addressed women artists' status a few months before the Mount Holyoke show. The press release for "The Women of '62," an exhibition of seven painters, pronounced that women had realized the promise that "'artist' has no gender."[17] The seven painters included four—Pennerton West, Charmion von Wiegand, Nell Blaine, and Marjorie McKee—who had continued to evolve their work since appearing in one of Peggy Guggenheim's all-women shows. Elaine de Kooning participated as well, and Alice Neel might have been in the show, but documentary sources conflict. Von Wiegand appeared in both the Mount Holyoke and Smolin exhibitions after a decade-long break from New York gallery shows, as her spiritually-informed geometric abstractions reemerged from under the secular shadow of Abstract Expressionism. In Mount Holyoke, her primary-colored *Night Intersection* (1957–9) (illus. 94) explores Mondrian's legacy, engaging with hard-edge geometry's potential to visualize her spiritual study and practice of Hinduism and Buddhism. In a short review, critic Natalie Edgar observed, "this is an 'idea' show but about artists and not art," indicating that the emerging conceptual frameworks for the exhibition and interpretation of art included gender.[18]

That powerful figures in art, media, finance, and government gathered at Mount Holyoke to fete women's artwork suggests that an invigorated category of "women artists" was part and parcel of the validation of the arts in the United States as a central component of a modern liberal democracy. "Women Artists in America Today" served as one of many platforms for promoting the country's democratic

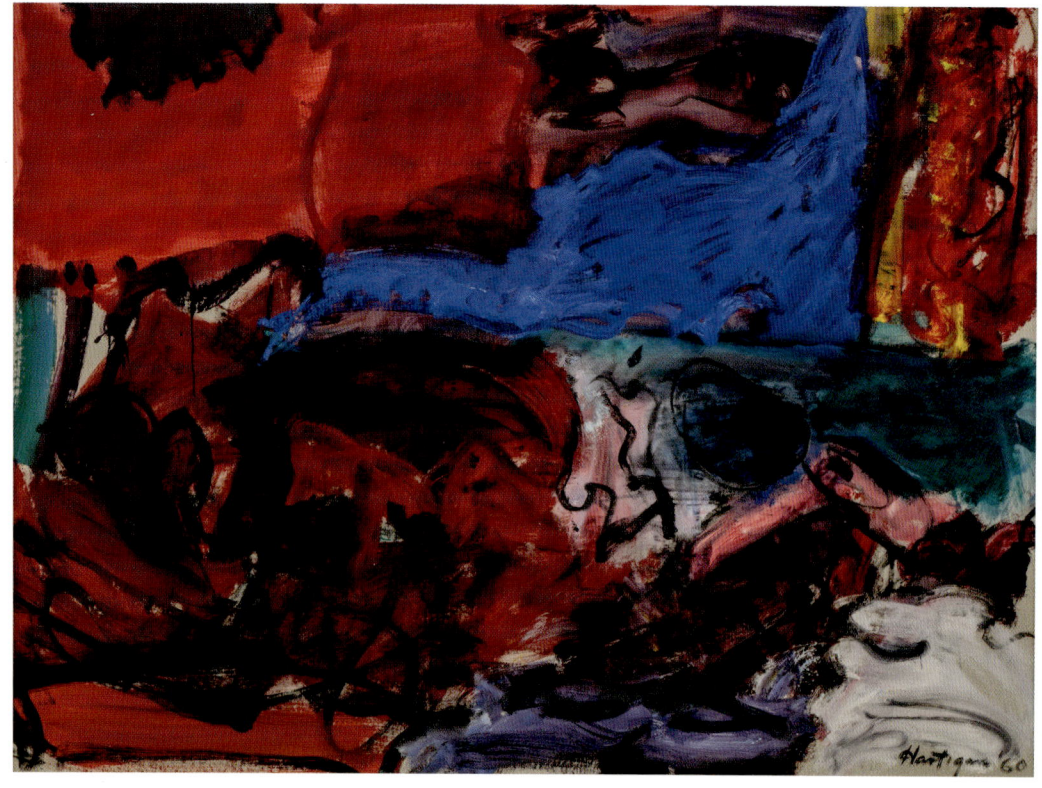

93 Grace Hartigan,
New York Rhapsody,
1960, oil on canvas.

values and facilitating social progress. And what more appropriate location than Mount Holyoke, the alma mater of Frances Perkins (class of 1902). Perkins (1882–1965) became the first female presidential cabinet member when Roosevelt appointed her Secretary of Labor. She used her position to support women's work as essential to the national economy by instituting Social Security and other public welfare programs.

A generation later, President Kennedy claimed Roosevelt's mantle of liberal democratic leadership and championed the incremental expansion of rights. He did so in part through the continuation of the work of Perkins and other labor leaders like Esther Peterson. Kennedy's 1961 executive order to create the Commission on the Status of Women acknowledged that "prejudices and outmoded customs act as barriers to the full realization of women's basic rights which should be respected and fostered as part of our Nation's commitment to human dignity, freedom, and democracy."[19] The president called for the commission to deliver by October 1963 a report with recommendations to overcome discrimination and to support women's roles as wives and mothers. This initiative both circumvented any immediate action on the long-proposed Equal Rights Amendment and assembled a powerful group of leaders who helped fuel the resurgence of the women's rights movement in the later part of the decade. The commission of eleven women and fifteen men was chaired by Eleanor Roosevelt and first convened in May 1962, later forming committees and working groups of activists, writers, and academics, among them lawyer Pauli Murray. The commission's legacy lay in creating a federal-level, pragmatic, scholarly conversation about women that acknowledged structural sexism and institutional obstacles to setting political priorities.

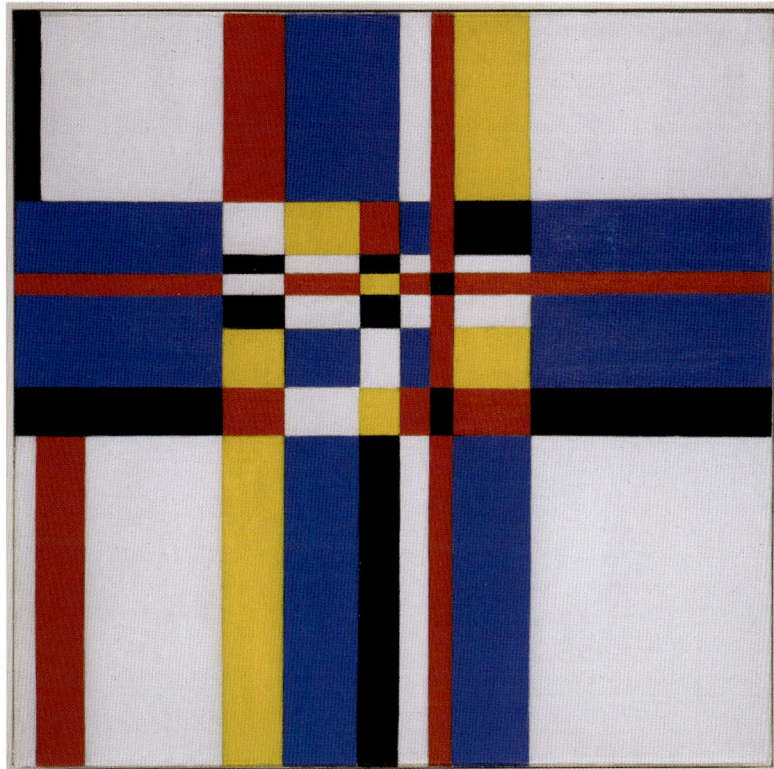

94 Charmion von Wiegand, *Night Intersection*, 1957–9, oil on canvas.

No visual artists sat on the commission, but the arts did hold an important place in the Kennedy administration. In March 1962, August Heckscher II was sworn in as Kennedy's special consultant on the arts—the first White House cultural advisor—with the goal to create a policy framework for government support of the arts. A month later at Mount Holyoke, Schlesinger's well-attended lecture, "Government and the Artist," directly brought "Women Artists in America Today" into the orbit of the formation of Kennedy's arts policy. Indeed, the lecture was part of his administration's strategy of laying the groundwork to establish an agency and advisory councils for the federal support of the arts, a controversial idea at the time. Republican critics associated government support for culture with New Deal overreach and state-sanctioned (read: communist) propaganda.

A copy of Schlesinger's speech is not available, but based on contemporary newspaper accounts, it seems that he charted a cautious path toward federal funding, weighing the pros and cons of government support of the arts in recent history. The Associated Press coverage of his talk focused on his call for grants for artists in all creative disciplines as both a social good for average Americans and a tactic in global Cold War competition.[20] He reassured listeners that the administration did not want to create a department of arts, and distinguished his vision for a blue-ribbon advisory committee from sweeping Roosevelt-era artist employment programs. Schlesinger proposed that creativity resides in the individual, and that the government can strengthen democracy by supporting artists. The tantalizing prospect of funding from the government attracted a good deal of local and national attention. Many regional directors and administrators of college art programs attended the Schlesinger talk, hoping for insight or entry into government support. An editorial in the student newspaper the *Mount Holyoke News* supported Schlesinger's positions and urged the government to create a truly independent council empowered to support experimental arts, such as electronic music, to gird against the nation's growing leisure time appetite for "mindless entertainment" in the form of movies, television, and paperback novels.[21] Newspaper reports suggest that he did not directly address gender in his remarks.

The Mount Holyoke newspaper ran at least four news articles and one editorial about the exhibition and its panel and lecture, printed in the same issues as ads for diets, slimming clothing lines, and cigarettes blatantly objectifying women, such as Winston cigarettes' "Girl Watchers Guide." One issue contained a piece by a student, "Women Agree to Status Quo with Required 'Reticence,'" about how most women eschew feminism and accept their second-class status in exchange for a secure position on the pedestal of femininity.[22] Such contradictory messages about democratic ideals and sexist stereotypes remained the lingua franca for college-educated middle-class women from the 1940s to the 1960s. The elevated status of women poets and painters in theory did not ensure their liberation. Another article in the newspaper suggested that the students desired more insights from the exhibition than curator Harris offered in her brief catalogue introduction. An interview prodded Harris to frame the exhibition as a survey of women artists' growing roles in social commentary as much as a celebration of women's accomplishments.[23] These ideas echo the period's conventional wisdom that a strong modern democracy accommodated social protest and critique in art.

The panel discussion the day after Schlesinger's talk was moderated by *Christian Science Monitor* critic Dorothy Adlow. It included Nevelson, who played the role of the enthusiastic, if eccentric, artist, counterpunching the cynicism of newspaper critic Emily Genauer and cultural commentator Marya Mannes, who warned against the decay of standards and quality in contemporary art. "No problems were solved but there was an energetic exchange," Adlow reported.[24] One scheduled speaker, former Baltimore Museum of Art director Adelyn D. Breeskin (1896–1986), canceled her engagement due to illness. She would have been a strong representative of the celebration and exhibition's ideals. A woman with power in the midcentury U.S. art world, she was one the period's few female museum directors, along with Grace McCann

Morley and Jermayne MacAgy. Among her accomplishments were securing the bequest of Etta Cone's extraordinary Matisse collection, commissioning the U.S. Pavilion at the Venice Biennale in 1960, and becoming the preeminent authority on Cassatt, publishing several catalogues of the artist. Breeskin also spoke frequently on women artists and the situation of women working in the arts at women's groups and colleges. A graduate of the elite women's Bryn Mawr College in Pennsylvania, she readily acknowledged her reliance on the work of others to provide household help so that she could parent her children and work as a museum director.[25]

The issue of marriage was not directly addressed by the exhibition or the works. Yet women's lives and choices were scrutinized in the media and by their peers, especially college women's changing ambitions, with marriage eclipsing professional accomplishment as a life goal. Mount Holyoke's survey of different generations of alumnae revealed that 96 percent of the class of 1957 married by age 25, compared to 14 percent of the class of 1912, reported an article in the *New York Times* about a 125th anniversary benefit event.[26] Betty Friedan (1921–2006) had made a similar discovery in 1957 when she surveyed her Smith College 1942 classmates for their fifteenth reunion. Shocked by her peers' diminished expectations of professional accomplishment, Friedan began her investigation into unmasking the midcentury iteration of age-old sex discrimination. She dubbed the paradox of white middle-class women's ennui—at a time when they had never had so much freedom, opportunity, and leisure—"the problem that has no name."[27] "Women Artists in America Today" marked one of the last uncritically celebratory exhibitions of contemporary women artists as bourgeois success stories.

For a short period of time in the Kennedy years, the concept of the emancipated "woman artist" became a symbol of the superiority of American democracy, idealistic yet still delimited by race and class. From this perspective, it was no mere coincidence that an artist in the Mount Holyoke show, Elaine de Kooning, painted the only life portrait of Kennedy during his presidency. At the end of 1962, the Truman Library in Missouri commissioned de Kooning and sent her to West Palm Beach, Florida, to draw the president from life. She was somewhat of a specialist in portraiture of cocksure men in action, as seen in the bullfighting scene *Juarez* (1960) in the Mount Holyoke show, and skillfully recorded the edgy assuredness of the New Frontier in the image of the president. One of her portraits, now in the National Portrait Gallery in Washington, DC, depicts a casual Kennedy, in shirt sleeves, rendered in slashing brushstrokes and an acid-green palette. Her depiction symbolized his strategic deployment of American cultural power, self-confident enough to accept ambiguity, dissonance, and even critique. Kennedy's inspirational Space Age technocratic optimism modulated an undercurrent of nascent social foment—from the sexual revolution ushered in by the birth control pill and the New Left youth movement for civil rights, represented by the Congress of Racial Equality and Students for a Democratic Society. Women artists like de Kooning and others in the Mount Holyoke show were both the subjects of change and among its agents and visualizers.

"Women Artists in America Today" represents the apotheosis of the midcentury all-woman show, with multiple blind spots and a check-list stocked with names of artists who in subsequent decades achieved major solo exhibitions in international museums and million-dollar auction prices. The exhibition's success in defining a canon of mid-century white American women painters and sculptors can be clearly seen in the checklist of an exhibition mounted three years later at the Newark Museum, "Women Artists of America, 1707–1964." All but four of the artists in Mount Holyoke appeared at Newark. Yet the exhi-bition certainly had its ambiguities and limitations. The curators and advisory team, too focused on crafting what was perhaps the one exhi-bition of women artists allied with the agenda of Kennedy's New Frontier, omitted artists of color and avant-garde artists soon to reshape the American art world. A younger generation of artists weaned on postwar mass-market culture and the contradictions of imperialism began innovating in the realms of Pop, performance, assemblage, and intermedia art. In New York, the scene centered on a number of lively small galleries and the Judson Church in Greenwich Village. A year after the exhibition came the publication of Friedan's landmark book *The Feminine Mystique*, and soon the resurgence of new feminist consciousness and critique dissolved the artificial integrity of the category of "women artists." For all the blue-ribbon panels and optimistic exhibitions, women determined that activism, not accolades, would bring about true social change.

Afterword

In tracing the arc of all-women exhibitions from Peggy Guggenheim's two freewheeling shows of the 1940s to Mount Holyoke College's celebration of women and democracy in 1962, we can observe how all-women art shows primarily served as passion projects to educate the public about women's achievements. For all their accomplishments in centering the work of hundreds of artists, these upbeat narratives of the abilities of women in the United States invariably affirmed essentialist stereotypes, marginalized women of color, and avoided challenging institutional sex and race discrimination. The study of all-women exhibitions in the United States at midcentury illustrates common themes surrounding the emancipation of women—themes that have threaded through modern art since the nineteenth century—and allows a better appreciation of the disruptive rise of the feminist art movement in the late 1960s.

A shift in the language of all-women shows can be seen in 1963 in "Women in Contemporary Art," at the Woman's College Gallery of Duke University. The exhibition expanded the scope of "American" to include women artists from the Americas, rather than solely the United States. The show included three Latin American painters—Argentinians Raquel Forner and Sarah Grilo and Cuban Amelia Peláez—among fifteen "major twentieth century artists" like Nevelson and O'Keeffe. In justifying the show, catalogue essayist Leslie Judd Ahlander, who had worked on the visual arts programs at the Pan American Union, identified sexual and racial discrimination as social evils: "Any form of segregation is an abomination—and in this respect women have suffered more than most."[1] Ahlander expands the definition of "woman artist" to encompass women's common social situation rather than innate feminine characteristics.

The naming of women artists as a class united by discrimination harbingered a new, more assertive demand that repositioned the all-women exhibition as an activist tool. By 1970, after nearly a decade of political agitation, artists began to set new expectations for all-women art exhibitions, investing them with the power not merely to add women to the established art-historical narrative but to rewrite the narrative entirely. The tone of these new exhibitions rejected the midcentury's circumspect proclamations of quality, professionalism, and distinction to explore a wider spectrum of emotions, from anger to joy, among women artists and their audiences.

Possibly the first second-wave feminist all-women show was organized by artists Carolyn Mazzello and Vernita Nemec in February 1970, "X[12]: 12 Artists, 12 Women," at Museum: A Project of Living Artists, New York. Emerging from nascent radical feminist organizations such as Women Artists in Revolution (WAR), the show confronted both the present-day neglect of women artists and the perennial obliteration of women's history. Reflecting on the fact that she belatedly became aware of exhibitions such as the Woman's Building in Chicago and "Women Artists in America Today" at Mount Holyoke, Nemec recalled, "Little did I or my art history professors know that women had been having exhibitions excluding men since 1893."[2] The inclusion and acknowledgment of intersectional identities expanded the conversation about women and art, with Black women artists creating self-defined spaces for artist-organized all-women exhibitions, such as "Sapphire Show" at Gallery 32 in Los Angeles in July 1970, and "Where We At" at Acts of Art Gallery in New York in June 1971. Women artists staged targeted protests at New York museums, such as picketing the Whitney Museum of American Art, New York, in December 1970 for the low percentage of women selected for its prestigious annual sculpture exhibition. These actions forced mainstream institutions to revalue the women artists already in their collections as a first step to increase the representation of women across exhibitions and programs. An early such example was "Permanent Collection: Women Artists," a group show of 52 artists at the Whitney curated by Elke Solomon in direct response to protests by WAR.

New feminist groups like the all-women cooperative A.I.R. Gallery, founded in New York in 1972, reclaimed all-women exhibitions as effective organizational and public relations mechanisms to create community and redress marginalization in the art world. After a half-century, the all-women art exhibition has been normalized by most mainstream American art museums as a critical tool of art history, with major exhibitions occurring regularly across the country and around the world. Continued study and interpretation of all-women's exhibitions centers women's history and releases the conception of midcentury art from its narrow New York-centric perspective.

REFERENCES

Introduction

1 Martica Sawin, "Women Welders," *Arts Digest*, 28 (November 1, 1953), p. 22.

2 Sahl Swarz, *Women Welders*, exh. cat., Sculpture Center, New York (1953), n.p.

3 Catherine Dossin and Hanna Alkema, "Women Artists Shows·Salons·Societies: Towards a Global History of All-Women Exhibitions," *Artl@s Bulletin*, VIII/I (2019), article 19.

4 Judy Chicago, *Through the Flower: My Struggle as a Woman Artist* (New York, 1975), p. 150.

1 Avant-Garde: "Exhibition by 31 Women," Art of This Century, 1943

1 Jasper Sharp, "Serving the Future: The Exhibitions at Art of This Century, 1942–1947," in *Peggy Guggenheim and Frederick Kiesler: The Story of Art of This Century*, ed. Susan Davidson and Philip Rylands (New York, 2004), p. 292.

2 "Spring Days in the Art Galleries," *New York Times* (April 25, 1926), p. X12.

3 Virginia Dortch, *Peggy Guggenheim and Her Friends* (Milan, 1994), p. 110.

4 Peggy Guggenheim, *Out of This Century: Confessions of an Art Addict* (New York, 1979), p. 229.

5 Art of This Century, advertisement, *View*, 3 (October 1942).

6 Sharp, "Serving the Future," p. 288.

7 Guggenheim, *Out of This Century*, p. 233.

8 Jimmy Ernst, *A Not-So-Still Life: A Memoir* (New York, 1984), p. 236.

9 The American Woman's Association Clubhouse in New York—the same venue as Dreier's "13 Women Painters" in 1934—sponsored a solo show of O'Keeffe's work in 1937, "Exhibition of Paintings (1924–1937) by Georgia O'Keeffe."

10 "Georgia O'Keeffe," *ARTnews*, XXIV/19 (February 13, 1926), p. 7.

11 Edward Alden Jewell, "No Priority on the Spice of Life," *New York Times* (January 10, 1943), p. X9.

12 Geoffrey T. Hellman and Harold Ross, "Ribbon Around Bomb," *New Yorker* (November 12, 1938).

13 Sharp, "Serving the Future," p. 292. Barr also proposed Gertrude Greene and Eleanor de Laittre.

14 Karen Anne Bearor, *Irene Rice Pereira: Her Paintings and Philosophy* (Austin, TX, 1993), p. 162.

15 Ibid.

16 Robert M. Coates, "The Art Galleries," *New Yorker* (January 16, 1943), p. 56.

17 A. Z. Kruse, "At the Art Galleries," *Brooklyn Eagle* (January 17, 1943), p. 36.

18 Henry McBride, "Women Surrealists: They, Too, Know How to Make Your Hair Stand on End," *New York Sun* (January 9, 1943), p. 28.

19 Ben Bindol, "Art Events," *Aufbau*, IX/3 (January 15, 1943). Louise Nevelson papers, Archives of American Art, Smithsonian Institution, Box 5, Folder 32, scrapbook, loose items and pages, 1918, 1935–1955.

20 Alexandra de Lallier, "Buffie Johnson: Icons and Altarpieces to the Goddess," *Woman's Art Journal*, III/1 (Spring–Summer 1982), p. 31.

21 R. F. (Rosamund Frost), "Thirty-Odd Women," *ARTnews*, XLI/17 (January 1–14, 1943), p. 20.

22 Ibid.

23 Robert Beverly Hale, "The Vernal Return of Women's Work," *ARTnews*, XLII/5 (April 15–30, 1943), p. 12.

24 Frost, "Thirty-Odd Women," p. 20.

25 Coates, "The Art Galleries," p. 56.

26 Jewell, "No Priority," p. X9.

27 "Jackson Pollock," *ARTnews*, XLII/13 (November 15–30, 1943), p. 23.

28 Jacqueline Bograd Weld, *Peggy: The Wayward Guggenheim* (New York, 1986), p. 334.

29 Sharp, "Serving the Future," p. 325.

30 Edward Alden Jewell, "Chiefly Modern in Idiom: Painting and Sculpture in New Shows," *New York Times* (June 13, 1945), p. X2.

31 Weld, *Peggy*, p. 254.

32 Jewell, "Chiefly Modern in Idiom," p. X2.

33 "The Passing Shows," *ARTnews*, XLIV/9 (July 1945), p. 29.

34 "Art: Mexican Autobiography," *Time*, LXI/17 (April 27, 1953), p. 92.

2 Race: "Portraits of Leading American Negro Citizens," Smithsonian Institution, 1944

1 Laura Wheeler Waring to William E. Harmon, letter, January 15, 1928, Harmon Foundation Records, Box 43, Library of Congress, Manuscript Division.

2 Tuliza K. Fleming, *Breaking Racial Barriers: African Americans in the Harmon Foundation Collection*, exh. cat., National Portrait Gallery, Washington, DC (San Francisco, CA, 1997), p. 16. See also *Against the Odds: African-American Artists and the Harmon Foundation*, exh. cat., Newark Museum (1989).

3 Waring to Harmon, January 15, 1928.

4 "Paris Art Notes," *New York Herald* (Paris) (July 21, 1929), p. 4.

5 Lisa E. Farrington, *Creating Their Own Image: The History of African-American Women Artists* (New York, 2005), p. 82.

6 Jacqueline Francis, *Making Race: Modernism and "Racial Art" in America* (Seattle, WA, 2012), p. 106.

7 Alain Locke, "The American Negro as Artist," *American Magazine of Art*, XXIII/3 (September 1931), pp. 210–20.

8 "Betsy G. Reyneau Exhibits," *New York Times* (December 5, 1922), p. 19.

9 H. L. Dungan, "$350,000 in Tapestries to Be Shown," *Oakland Tribune* (February 8, 1948), p. 69.

10 Romare Bearden, "The Negro Artist and Modern Art," *Opportunity*, 12 (December 1934), pp. 371–2.

11 David C. Driskell, "Mary Beattie Brady: Remembering the Legacy," in Fleming, *Breaking Racial Barriers*, pp. 6–7.

12 Mary Beattie Brady to Margaret Just Butcher, letter, March 30, 1953, Harmon Foundation Papers, MS02.00, Box 4, Folder 12, David C. Driskell Center Archives, University of Maryland.

13 Fleming, *Breaking Racial Barriers*, pp. 12–13.

14 George Washington Carter to Betsy Graves Reyneau, letter, undated, Record Unit 311: National Collection of Fine Arts, Office of the Director Records, Box 40, Folder 10, Smithsonian Institution Archives.

15 Mary Beattie Brady to Alain Locke, letter, January 14, 1943, Harmon Foundation Papers, MS02.00, Box 6, Folder 3.

16 Brady to Butcher, March 30, 1953.

17 "Negro Artists Give Exhibition," *Philadelphia Inquirer* (November 14, 1945), p. 11.

18 "Smithsonian Gets Carver Portrait," *New York Times* (May 3, 1944), p. 16.

19 Laura Wheeler Waring, "Paintings of Negro Americans," *Pulse* (June 1944), pp. 3, 34. Record Unit 311, Box 40, Folder 10, Smithsonian Institution Archives.

20 Eleanor Roosevelt, "My Day," *St. Louis Post Dispatch* (May 4, 1944), p. 28.

21 Eleanor Roosevelt, "My Day," *St. Louis Post Dispatch* (February 3, 1944), p. 28.

22 Cornelia Otis Skinner, "Marian Anderson," Record Unit 311, Box 40, Folder 10, Smithsonian Institution Archives.

23 Channing Tobias, "Mary McLoed Bethune," Record Unit 311, Smithsonian Institution Archives, Box 40, Folder 10.

24 Pauli Murray, *Song in a Weary Throat: An American Pilgrimage* (New York, 1987), p. 215.

25 Ibid., p. 217.

26 Fiorello LaGuardia, "Jane Bolin," April 25, 1944. Record Unit 311, Smithsonian Institution Archives, Box 40, Folder 10.

27 Mary Beattie Brady to Alain Locke, letter, June 26, 1944, Harmon Foundation Papers, MS02.00, Box 6, Folder 3.

28 Mary Beattie Brady to Alain Locke, letter, October 1, 1943, cited in Fleming, *Breaking Racial Barriers*, p. 19.

29 Mary Beattie Brady to Alain Locke, letter, March 6, 1944. Harmon Foundation Papers, MS02.00, Box 6, Folder 3.

30 Ibid.

31 Ibid.

32 Alain Locke to Mary Beattie Brady, letter, November 25, 1944; n.d. (1944); and November 22, 1944, Harmon Foundation Papers, MS02.00, Box 6, Folder 3.

33 *Report of the General Managers of the Exhibit of the State of New York at the World's Columbian Exposition* (Albany, NY, 1894), pp. 208ff.

34 Ida B. Wells, *The Reason Why the Colored American Is Not in the World's Columbian Exposition* (Chicago, IL, 1893), p. 69.

35 Mary Cole, "Minnesotan Touring Nation with Art Series on Negroes," *Winona Republic* (October 6, 1947).

36 "Anacostia Musuem Exhibits Rats as Part of Neighborhood Effort to Teach, Learn," *Pittsburgh Courier* (September 26, 1970).

37 Amy Mooney, "The Terra Lectures in American Art: Regarding the Portrait: The Pragmatists," June 15, 2020; Steven Nelson, "Combating Racism: Betsy Graves Reyneau, Laura Wheeler Waring and Representation of Black Achievement," November 17, 2020, www.youtube.com.

38 Brady to Butcher, March 30, 1953, Harmon Foundation Papers, 1929–1994, MS02.00, Box 4, Folder 12.

3 Photography: "First Women's Invitation Exhibition," The Camera Club, 1947

1 Vicki Goldberg, *Margaret Bourke-White: A Biography* (New York, 1986), p. 252.

2 C. B. Neblette, "Careers in Photography," *Popular Photography*, XIX/2 (August 1946), p. 171.

3 Board of Trustees Meeting minutes, February 6, 1948, Camera Club of New York records, Box 2, Folder 12, New York Public Library, Manuscripts and Archives Division.

4 Ibid.

5 *First Women's Invitation Exhibition*, exh. cat., Camera Club of New York (1947).

6 *Camera Club Notes* (November 1947), p. 6. Camera Club of New York records, Box 8, Folder 4.

7 Photography album 1940–49, Camera Club of New York records, Box 15.

8 Jacob Deschin, "Women's Exhibit: Show Is Interesting, but Faults Weaken It," *New York Times* (November 9, 1947), p. X13.

9 Margaretta K. Mitchell, *Ruth Bernhard: Between Art and Life* (San Francisco, CA, 2000), p. 78.

10 Naomi Rosenblum, *History of Women Photographers* (New York, 1994), p. 156.

11 "Former Illustrator Is First Lady of Photographic Salons," *Des Moines Register* (October 20, 1940).

12 Camera Club Board of Trustees Meeting minutes, May 1, 1947, Camera Club of New York records, Box 2, Folder 11.

13 Catherine Weed Barnes, "Why Ladies Should Be Admitted to Membership in Photographic Societies," *American Amateur Photographer,* 1/6 (December 1889), pp. 223–4.

14 "Photographs All Made by Women," *Hartford Courant* (April 7, 1906), p. 14.

15 Les Sipes, "More Anent Meaning of 'Pictorialism,'" *Oakland Tribune* (October 21, 1951), p. 76.

16 "Camera Notes," *New York Times* (April 6, 1947), p. X21.

17 "Photographs by Mildred Hatry," May 2, 1946 through June 2, 1946, press release, www.brooklyn-museum.org; "Photographs by Eleanor Parke Custis," November 22, 1946 through December 22, 1946, press release, www.brooklynmuseum.org.

18 "Homemaker Honored: Detroit Woman's Print Heads for Smithsonian," *Detroit Free Press* (August 26, 1948), p. 17.

19 Kathryn Sullivan, "Constance Bannister: Camera Girl," *Popular Photography*, XII/3 (September 1943), p. 77.

20 "St. Louis Monkeys," *Life* (September 1, 1947), pp. 71–3.

21 Mary Henderson, *Stars on Stage: Eileen Darby and Broadway's Golden Age: Photographs, 1940–1964* (New York, 2005), p. 24.

22 "She Leads a Hectic Life and Loves It!" *Parade* insert in *Detroit Free Press* (April 8, 1945), p. 50.

23 "Selections from the First Women's Invitational Photo Exhibit," *u.s. Camera*, XI/2 (February 1948), p. 32.

24 Goldberg, *Margaret Bourke-White*, p. 310.

25 Imogen Cunningham, "Photography as a Profession for Women," *The Arrow*, XXIX/2 (January 1913), p. 203.

26 Jeanne Moutoussamy-Ashe, *Viewfinders: Black Women Photographers* (New York, 1985), p. 125.

27 *Camera Club Notes* (April 1948), p. 5. Camera Club of New York records, Box 8, Folder 5.

28 Camera Club Board of Trustees Meeting minutes, June 10, 1948. Camera Club of New York records, Box 2, Folder 12.

29 Nancy Newhall to Margaret Bourke-White, letter, March 18, 1948. Beaumont and Nancy Newhall papers, Box 10, Folder 10, Getty Research Institute.

30 Nancy Newhall to Margaret Bourke-White, letter, April 8, 1948. Beaumont and Nancy Newhall papers, Box 10, Folder 10.

31 Mildred Stagg, "Women in Photography," *u.s. Camera*, XI/9 (September 1948), p. 61.

32 Jacob Deschin, "Women's Show: Exhibitors from Thirteen States Display Prints," *New York Times* (October 31, 1948), p. X15.

33 *Camera Club Notes* (October–November 1948), p. 11. Camera Club of New York records, Box 8, Folder 6.

34 Alouise Boker to Laura Gilpin, letter, September 24, 1948, Laura Gilpin Papers, Amon Carter Museum of American Art Archives.

35 *Camera Club Notes* (December 1948), p. 9. Camera Club of New York records, Box 8, Folder 6.

36 Jacob Deschin, "High School Yearbooks," *New York Times* (October 16, 1949), p. X13.

4 Education: "Ten Women Who Paint," Smith College Museum of Art, 1949

1 "Ten Women Who Paint," *Art Digest*, XXIV (November 1, 1949), p. 12.

2 Edgar C. Schenck to Georgia O'Keeffe, letter, April 2, 1949, Smith College Museum of Art, exhibition files.

3 Honoré Sharrer to Edward Schenck, letter, March 26, 1949, Smith College Museum of Art, exhibition files.

4 Linda Eisenmann, *Higher Education for Women in Postwar America, 1945–1965* (Baltimore, MD, 2007), p. 45.

5 John H. Fenton, "Smith Installs Wright as President; He Asserts Changes Are Inevitable," *New York Times* (October 20, 1949), p. 31.

6 Frances Burns, "Mrs. Roosevelt Presents Four-Point Peace Plan," *Boston Globe* (October 20, 1949), p. 2. Note, the phrase from Article 1 of the UDHR was misquoted. The original text reads: "All human beings are born free and equal in dignity and rights."

7 Talbot Faulkner Hamlin, "The Tryon Art Gallery—An Appreciation," *Bulletin of Smith College Museum of Art* (June 15, 1926), p. 1.

8 Henry-Russell Hitchcock and Edgar C. Schenck, "Foreword," in *Ten Women Who Paint*, exh. cat., Smith College Museum of Art, Northampton, MA (1949), n.p.

9 Margaret L. Johnson, "Foreword," in *75 Books by 75 American Women, 1875–1949*, exh. cat., Tryon Gallery, Smith College Museum of Art, Northampton, MA (1949), n.p.

10 Eisenmann, *Higher Education for Women*, pp. 80–81.

11 "White Birth Rate (Adjusted for Under Registration) and Proportion of Teaching Faculty Who Were Women, 1910–1960," in Jessie Bernard, *Academic Women* (University Park, PA, 1964), p. 74.

12 Schenck to O'Keeffe, letter, April 2, 1949, Smith College Museum of Art, exhibition files.

13 "What the Artists Are Doing," *ARTnews*, XLII/9 (August–September 1943), p. 37.

14 "She Paints on Her Pulse," *American Artist*, VIII (September 1944), p. 10.

15 Elizabeth Sparhawk-Jones to Edgar C. Schenck, letter, March 12, 1949, Smith College Museum of Art, exhibition files.

16 "Elizabeth Sparhawk-Jones," *ARTnews*, XLVI/1 (March 1947), p. 25.

17 Cora Schley, "Contemporary American Art Goes on Exhibit at Center," *The Town Talk* (Alexandria, LA) (December 11, 1950).

18 Doris Bry to Smith College Museum of Art, letter, October 24, 1949, Smith College Museum of Art, exhibition files.

19 Grace Pickett, "Twelve Women Painters of Distinction," *Independent Woman*, 25 (November 1946), pp. 336–8, 348.

20 James Thrall Soby, "To the Ladies," *Saturday Review*, XXIX/27 (July 6, 1946), pp. 14–15.

21 James Thrall Soby, "The Younger American Artists," *Harper's Bazaar* (September 1947), p. 196.

22 Irene Rice Pereira, "How I Work," *ARTnews*, XLVI/7 (September 1947), p. 27.

23 *Fourteen Americans*, exh. cat., Museum of Modern Art, New York (1946), p. 28.

24 James Thrall Soby, "Again, to the Ladies!" *Saturday Review*, XXXVI (February 7, 1953), p. 50.

25 "Tribute to the Working Man," *Life*, XXXI/25 (December 17, 1951), pp. 12–13; Dorothy Seckler, "Sharrer Paints a Picture," *ARTnews*, L/2 (April 1951), pp. 40–67.

26 Howard Devree, "Vital and Diverse: New Current Group Exhibitions Stress Work by Contemporary Americans," *New York Times* (June 5, 1949), p. x6.

27 *75 Books by 75 American Women, 1875–1949*, exh. cat., Tryon Gallery, Smith College Museum of Art, Northampton, MA (1949).

28 Elizabeth McCausland, "Why Can't America
  Afford Art?" *Magazine of Art*, XXXIX (January
  1946), pp. 18–21.

29 Cynthia Lowry, "Isabel Bishop Says: American
  Painter Can't Make Decent Living from
  His Art," *Washington Post* (August 24, 1947),
  p. L5.

30 Helen Markel Herrmann, "The Saga of Sophia
  Smith," *New York Times Sunday Magazine*
  (October 16, 1949), pp. 14, 54–5.

31 Mabel Newcomer, *A Century of Higher Education
  for American Women* (New York, 1959), p. 206.

32 Ibid., p. 207.

33 "Women and Dimensions in Art," Irene Rice
  Pereira papers, Roll 2395, Frames 233–261, Archives
  of American Art, Smithsonian Institution.

34 Linda Nochlin, conversations with the author,
  May 2008.

35 E. C. Goossen, *Nine Women Painters*, exh. cat.,
  Bennington College Gallery, Bennington, VT
  (1953), n.p.

5 Women Artists Groups: "San Francisco Women
  Artists 27th Annual Exhibition," San Francisco
  Museum of Art, 1952

  1 *Jane Todd* show, "San Francisco Women Artists
  Twenty-seventh Annual Exhibit," radio transcript,
  Box 8, San Francisco Women Artists (SFWA)
  records, Archives of American Art, Smithsonian
  Institution.

  2 Walter Snelgrove, "Women Artists Show Ranges
  from Oils to a Picket Fence," *Oakland Tribune*
  (November 30, 1952), p. 75.

  3 R. H. Hagan, "Big Art Exhibits on for Holiday
  Season," *San Francisco Chronicle* (November 30,
  1952), p. 29.

  4 Alexander Fried, "Museum Holds Annual
  Women's Art Display," *San Francisco Examiner*
  (November 30, 1952), p. 183.

5 Elaine de Kooning, "de Kooning Memories,"
  Vogue, CLXXII/12 (December 1983), p. 353.

6 Addie Lanier and Henry Weverka kindly clarified
  this and other biographical details of Asawa's
  early life.

7 Ibid.

8 Imogen Cunningham to Ruth Asawa, letter,
  February 19, 1953, Ruth Asawa papers (M1585), Box
  6, Folder 1, Department of Special Collections and
  University Archives, Stanford University Libraries.

9 Marilyn Chase, *Everything She Touched: The Life of
  Ruth Asawa* (San Francisco, CA, 2020), p. 75.

10 Ruth Asawa to author, email, August 4, 2006.

11 H. L. Dungan, "Three Exhibitions to Open at
  Legion of Honor in S.F.," *Oakland Tribune*
  (November 8, 1931), p. 22.

12 Berit Potter, "Gathered Another Way: Early
  Surrealist Exhibitions at the San Francisco
  Museum of Modern Art," *The Space Between:
  Literature and Culture, 1914–1945*, XIV (2018).

13 Information gathered from SFWA exhibition
  brochures and archival materials, cross-referenced
  with SFWA exhibition history.

14 Noreen Larinde, "Claire Falkenstein," *Woman's
  Art Journal*, I/1 (Spring–Summer 1980), p. 52.

15 Clifford R. Peterson to Natalie Leighton, letter,
  December 12, 1952, San Francisco Museum of
  Modern Art Library, exhibition files.

16 The painting, titled *Abstraction 81* in the SFWA
  checklist, is labeled *Blue on Blue* in an installation
  photo of Peterson's 1953 exhibition at the Art
  Gallery of Greater Victoria, 1953. Robert Amos,
  An Archival Mosaic: The Margaret Peterson Fonds
  (Victoria, BC, 2019), p. 14.

17 Snelgrove, "Women Artists Show Ranges from Oils
  to a Picket Fence," p. 75.

18 Albert Lanier to John Entenza, letter, May 5, 1952,
  Ruth Asawa papers, Box 100, Folder 8.

19 Anni Albers, *On Weaving* (Middletown, CT, 1965),
  p. 38.

20 SFWA records, Archives of American Art, Smithsonian Institution, Box 8.

21 Gobind Behari Lal, "Japanese Girl's Paintings Challenge Attention: Work of Four Years Proves Her Genius," *San Francisco Examiner* (June 2, 1929), p. 59.

22 H. L. Dungan, "Women Artists Are Radical Enough, Good Show in S.F.," *Oakland Tribune* (November 16, 1941), p. 55.

23 Valerie J. Matsumoto, "Pioneers, Renegades, and Visionaries: Asian American Women Artists in California, 1890s–1960s," in *Asian American Art: A History, 1850–1970*, ed. Gordon H. Chang, Mark Dean Johnson, Paul J. Karlstrom, and Sharon Spain (Stanford, CA, 2008), p. 169.

24 *San Francisco Women Artists 28th Annual*, exh. cat., San Francisco Museum of Modern Art Library, exhibition files.

25 Asawa to author, email, August 4, 2006.

26 Clark S. Marlor, "Centennial Roster: National Association of Women Artists," in *One Hundred Years: A Centennial Celebration of the National Association of Women Artists*, exh. cat., Nassau County Museum of Fine Art, Roslyn Harbor, NY (1988), pp. 87–95.

27 Frederick Koppel to Augusta Savage, letter, November 5, 1934. Augusta Savage Papers, Schomburg Center for Research in Black Culture, New York Public Library.

28 "Distinguished Audience at Opening of Augusta Savage's Harlem Studio," *New York Age* (June 17, 1939), p. 7.

29 Belle Krasne, "Women Artists Annual— Is Sex Necessary?" *Arts Digest* (July 1, 1950), p. 13.

30 James Fitzsimmons, "All-Woman Annual," *Arts Digest*, XXVI (May 15, 1952), p. 15.

31 Nell Choate Jones, "Foreword," in *60th Annual Exhibition*, exh. cat., National Association of Women Artists, New York (1952), p. 3.

32 Anna Mary Howitt, "An Art Student in Munich," in *Canvassing: Recollections by Six Victorian Women Artists*, ed. Pamela Gerrish Nunn (London, 1986), p. 36.

6 Fiber Art: "Women in Art," Contemporary Arts Association of Houston, 1953

1 Norma Henderson, "Inspiration for Painting," *Texas Trends in Art Education, Journal of the Texas Art Education Association* (March 1957), p. 29.

2 Aline B. Louchheim, "Diverse Museums: Institutions of Our Southwest Present a Wide Variety of Aims and Outlook," *New York Times* (December 27, 1953), p. X12.

3 Katie Robinson Edwards, "Bookshelf," *aether: A Visual Arts Dialogue* (Fall–Winter 2014), p. 49. See also Edwards, *Midcentury Modern Art in Texas* (Austin, TX, 2014).

4 Oral history interview with Robert O. Preusser, January–October 1991, Archives of American Art, Smithsonian Institution.

5 Sarah C. Reynolds, *Houston Reflections: Art in the City, 1950s, 60s, and 70s* (Houston, TX, 2008), p. 10. Another essential source is *In Our Time: Houston's Contemporary Arts Museum, 1948–1982*, exh. cat., Contemporary Arts Museum, Houston (1982).

6 Nedra Jenkins, "Contemporary Art Has New Home at Houston," *Fort Worth Star-Telegram* (March 21, 1954), p. 57.

7 Olive Jensen Theisen, *Walls that Speak: The Murals of John Thomas Biggers* (Denton, TX, 2010), p. 29.

8 Minutes of the Meeting of the Board of Directors, December 8, 1953, Contemporary Arts Museum, Houston records, MS 690, Box 1, Folder 33, Woodson Research Center, Fondren Library, Rice University.

9 Norma Henderson to Louise Nevelson, letter, March 3, 1953, Louise Nevelson papers, Box 1,

Folder 28, Archives of American Art, Smithsonian Institution.

10 "Foreword to Catalogue," in *Women in Art*, exh. cat., Contemporary Arts Association of Houston (1953), n.p.

11 Margaret Young, "Marginalia," *Houston Post* (May 3, 1953); "CAA Panel Members," *Houston Post* (May 12, 1953). Clippings in scrapbook in Contemporary Arts Museum, Houston records, MS 690, Box 207, Folder 36.

12 Judith Kaye Reed, "Distaff Sculpture," *Arts Digest*, XXIV (March 1, 1950), p. 13.

13 "Modern Needlework Asks More than Thread, Cloth," *Houston Post* (May 3, 1953). Clipping in scrapbook in Contemporary Arts Museum, Houston, records, MS690, Box 207, Folder 36.

14 "Drum Beaters for Modern: Knolls Use Dramatic Displays," *Life* (March 2, 1953), pp. 72ff.

15 Some biographical information is available in Ruthe Winegarten, Janet G. Humphrey, and Frieda Werden, *Black Texas Women: 150 Years of Trial and Triumph* (Austin, TX, 1995).

16 Lazette Marie Jackson, "Weaving: The Threads of Our Past," *ashe*, 1/2 (Summer–Fall 1990), n.p.

17 "Artists Represented in Exhibition," in *Women in Art*, exh. cat., Contemporary Arts Association of Houston (1953), n.p.

18 "Modern Needlework Asks More than Thread, Cloth," *Houston Post*.

19 Ibid.

20 Lucy Key Miller, "Front Views and Profiles," *Chicago Tribune* (April 27, 1953), p. 50.

21 "Modern Needlework Asks More than Thread, Cloth," *Houston Post*.

22 Ibid.

23 Polly Henry, "Executive's Wife Tells Story of Steel in Needlepoint," *Bradenton Herald* (Bradenton, FL) (January 6, 1957), p. 17.

24 Mary P. Packwood, "Needle Gives Woman Chance to Express Creative Talents,"

Press and Sun-Bulletin (Binghamton, NY) (January 27, 1953), p. 11.

25 "Modern Needlework Asks More than Thread, Cloth," *Houston Post*.

26 June Wayne to Carroll Hogan, letter, September 3, 1953, June Wayne Papers, Box 29, Folder 6, University of California, Los Angeles, Library Special Collections. The catalogue is in Box 177, Folder 5.

27 Catherine Louden, "Ladies Day in Art at CAA Museum," *Houston Post* (May 10, 1953). Clipping in scrapbook in Contemporary Arts Museum, Houston records, MS 690, Box 207, Folder 36.

28 Ibid.

29 Young, "Marginalia." Clipping in scrapbook in Contemporary Arts Museum, Houston records, MS 690, Box 207, Folder 36.

30 Louden, "Ladies Day in Art at CAA Museum."

31 George Fuermann, "Post Card," *Houston Post* (May 1, 1953). Clipping in scrapbook in Contemporary Arts Museum, Houston records, MS 690, Box 207, Folder 36.

32 Ibid.

33 Fuermann, "Post Card." Clipping in scrapbook in Contemporary Arts Museum, Houston records, MS 690, Box 207, Folder 36.

34 CAA, Minutes of the Meeting of the Board of Directors, May 4, 1954. Contemporary Arts Museum, Houston records, MS 690, Box 1, Folder 33.

35 William Middleton, *Double Vision: The Unerring Eye of Art World Avatars Dominique and John de Menil: Paris, New York, Houston* (New York, 2018), p. 387.

36 Jenni Sorkin included it as one of the few midcentury all-women exhibitions in her timeline in "The Feminist Nomad," in *WACK! Art and the Feminist Revolution*, exh. cat., Museum of Contemporary Art, Los Angeles (2007), p. 474.

7 Greatness: "Great Women Artists: 16th to 20th Centuries," Delius Gallery, 1955

1 Alexander Fried, "Museum Holds Annual Women's Art Display," *San Francisco Examiner* (November 30, 1952), p. 183.

2 Ibid.

3 Frederick Giese, "Editor's Letters," *ARTnews*, XLVIII/9 (January 1950), p. 6. See also "Frederick D. Giese, Art Gallery Head," *New York Times* (November 24, 1957).

4 Frederick A. Sweet, "America's Greatest Woman Painter: Mary Cassatt," *Vogue*, CXXIII/3 (February 1954), pp. 102–3.

5 Jean Owens Schaefer, "Kollwitz in America: A Study of Reception, 1900–1960," *Woman's Art Journal*, XV/1 (Spring–Summer 1994), p. 29.

6 Ly Julius is not in the Union List of Artist Names.

7 Ruysch, Vigée Le Brun, Bonheur, Cassatt, Modersohn-Becker, Valadon, Kollwitz, Laurencin, and Sintenis. The four artists exhibited in Feigl and not Delius were Angelica Kauffmann, Jeanne-Philiberte Ledoux, Margaret Sarah Carpenter, and Anna Roskot.

8 Howard Devree, "A Reviewer's Notes: Paintings by European Women Artists," *New York Times* (October 31, 1943), p. X7.

9 Edith Appleton Standen, *Women Artists* (New York, 1956), n.p. Emphasis in original.

10 S. P. (Stuart Preston), "About Art and Artists: 500 Years of Work by Women Painters Covered in Delius Gallery Display," *New York Times* (December 3, 1955), p. 37.

11 Carlyle Burrows, "'Open Air' Art Show Features Hassam," *New York Herald Tribune* (December 18, 1955), p. E9.

12 Ibid.

13 Leo Lionni, "The Lion's Tail: Leo Lionni's Pages of Visual Miscellanea, Mostly Graphic, All Feminine," *Print* (September–October 1956), pp. 60–67.

14 J.R.M. (James R. Mellow), *Arts*, XXX/3 (December 1955), p. 59.

15 Ibid.

16 Alfred Werner, "The Unknown Valadon," *Arts*, XXX/8 (May 1956), p. 20.

17 Albert Ten Eyck Gardner, "A Century of Women," *Metropolitan Museum of Art Bulletin*, VII/4 (December 1948), p. 118.

18 Editorial, "Woman as Artist," *Evening Sun* (Baltimore) (June 16, 1956), p. 4.

19 Janice Biala, "Editor's Letters," *ARTnews*, LII/4 (Summer 1953), p. 6.

20 Burrows, "'Open Air' Art Show," p. E9.

21 *Great Women Artists*, exh. cat., Delius Gallery, New York (1955). Delius Gallery file, Brooklyn Museum Library.

22 Simone de Beauvoir, *The Second Sex*, trans. H. M. Parshley (New York, 1989), p. 131. I am quoting from the first English translation, which though incomplete and in some places misrepresentative, was the text available to American readers at midcentury.

23 Ibid.

24 Beauvoir, *The Second Sex*, p. 714.

25 Ibid.

26 Erich Neumann, *The Archetypal World of Henry Moore*, trans. R.F.C. Hull (New York, 1959), p. 129.

27 S. P., "About Art and Artists," p. 37.

28 Ibid.

29 Dorothy Roe, "Why Are So Few Women Renowned as Artists?" *Boston Globe* (September 3, 1957), p. 11.

30 Ibid.

31 Elizabeth Fries Ellet, *Women Artists in All Ages and Countries* (New York, 1859), p. v.

32 Buffie Johnson, "Women in Art (The Embattled Woman Artist)," in *Art of This Century: The Women*, exh. cat., Pollock-Krasner House and Study Center, East Hampton, NY (1997), pp. 33–7.

33 Alexandra de Lallier, "Buffie Johnson: Icons and Altarpieces to the Goddess," *Woman's Art Journal* III/1 (Spring–Summer 1982), p. 31.

34 Elaine de Kooning with Rosalyn Drexler, "Dialogue," in *Art and Sexual Politics: Why Have There Been No Great Women Artists?*, ed. Thomas B. Hess and Elizabeth C. Baker (New York, 1973), pp. 57–8.

35 Minna Citron and Jan Gelb, "Prefatory Statement," in *Venus Through the Ages*, c. 1959, Jan Gelb and Boris Margo Papers, Roll 998, Frame 443, Archives of American Art, Smithsonian Institution.

36 William T. La Moy and Joseph P. McCaffrey, eds, *The Journals of Grace Hartigan, 1951–1955* (Syracuse, NY, 2009), p. 18.

37 Norma H. Goodhue, "Woman Artist Collects, Too," *Los Angeles Times* (October 21, 1956), p. 80.

38 "Women Painters' Work to Be Put On Exhibit," *Los Angeles Times* (April 26, 1953), p. 98.

39 Gail Levin, *Becoming Judy Chicago: A Biography of the Artist* (New York, 2007), p. 71.

40 Judy Chicago, *Through the Flower: My Struggle as a Woman Artist* (Garden City, NY, 1977), p. 146.

41 Linda Nochlin, "Why Are There No Great Women Artists?," in *Women in Sexist Society: Studies in Power and Powerlessness*, ed. Vivian Gornick and Barbara K. Moran (New York, 1971), p. 244. A shortened version of the quote appears in Nochlin's better-known version, "Why Have There Been No Great Women Artists?," *ARTnews*, LXIX/9 (January 1971), p. 24. The Feigen story is told in "Forget to Be Afraid," a video by Julia Trotta.

8 Printmaking: "Women Printmakers," Philadelphia Museum of Art, 1956

1 Miriam Holden to Kneeland McNulty, letter, May 18, 1956, Prints, Photographs, and Drawings Exhibitions Records, Box 12, Philadelphia Museum of Art, Library and Archives.

2 Gertrude Benson, "Vast Photo Exhibit Opens," *Philadelphia Inquirer* (March 25, 1956), pp. S1, 10.

3 *Les Femmes artistes: Catalogue d'une collection unique de dessins, gravures et eaux-fortes composés ou exécutés par des femmes* (Amsterdam, 1884).

4 Frank Weitenkampf, "Introduction," in *Catalogue of a Collection of Engravings, Etchings and Lithographs by Women*, exh. cat., The Grolier Club, New York (1901), p. v.

5 Ibid., p. viii.

6 M. G. Van Rensselaer, "Introduction," in *Exhibition Catalogue of the Work of the Women Etchers of America*, exh. cat., Union League Club, New York (1888), n.p.

7 *Women Printmakers*, exhibition statement, 1956, Prints, Photographs, and Drawings Exhibitions Records, Box 12, Philadelphia Museum of Art, Library and Archives.

8 Irvin Haas, "The Print Collector," *ARTnews*, LV/3 (May 1956), p. 63.

9 *Women Printmakers*, exhibition statement, 1956.

10 Ibid.

11 Ibid.

12 Donald Goodall, "Texas Women Artists Showing Prints Now at Main Building," *Austin American* (May 13, 1945), p. 7.

13 Carl Zigrosser, *The Book of Fine Prints: An Anthology of Printed Pictures and Introduction to the Study of Graphic Art* (New York, 1948), pl. 422.

14 Ibid., pl. 423.

15 Anonymous (Wanda Gág), "A Hotbed of Feminists," *The Nation* (June 22, 1927), p. 691.

16 Zigrosser, *The Book of Fine Prints*, pl. 500.

17 Christina Weyl, *The Women of Atelier 17: Modernist Printmaking in Midcentury New York* (New Haven, CT, 2019). See also her invaluable online biographical supplement, https://atelier17.christinaweyl.com.

18 Sue Fuller, "Mary Cassatt's Use of Soft-Ground Etching," *Magazine of Art*, XLIII/2 (February 1950), p. 54.

19 Ibid.

20 Elton C. Fax, *Seventeen Black Artists* (New York, 1971), p. 254.

21 Carl Zigrosser to Norma Morgan, letter, September 15, 1959, Carl Zigrosser Correspondence, Box 11, Folder 2, Philadelphia Museum of Art, Library and Archives.

22 Elizabeth Catlett, *Paintings, Sculptures, and Prints of the Negro Woman*, exh. cat., Barnett Aden Gallery, Washington, DC (1947), n.p.

23 Dorothy Grafly, *Women Sculptors*, exh. cat., Philadelphia Art Alliance, Philadelphia (1950).

24 Dorothy Grafly, "Women Printmakers," *Christian Science Monitor* (May 12, 1956), p. 6.

25 Miriam Holden to Kneeland McNulty, letter, May 14, 1956, Prints, Photographs, and Drawings Exhibitions Records, Box 12, Philadelphia Museum of Art, Library and Archives.

26 Madeleine B. Stern, *We the Women: Career Firsts of Nineteenth-Century America* (New York, 1963).

9 Abstract Expressionism: "17 of the Women Tops in Art," Dord Fitz Gallery, 1960

1 Edna Ferber, *Giant: A Novel* (Garden City, NY, 1952), p. 178.

2 "Show Devoted Entirely to Women Artists Is Making History in the World of Art," n.d., press release, George (Dord) Edward Fitz Papers, Box 4, Folder 2, Western History Collections, University of Oklahoma Libraries.

3 Carol Mason, *Oklahomo: Lessons in Unqueering America* (Albany, NY, 2016), p. 125.

4 Wallace Truesdell, "Artist Commutes to Instruct Beginners," *Pampa Daily News (Texas)* (March 30, 1958).

5 *Dord Fitz Art Center: Art from Amarillo, Texas*, exh. cat., Burr Galleries, New York (1960).

6 Graziella Marchicelli, *The Broadcast Is Always On: The Area Arts Foundation and Dord Fitz*, exh. cat., Amarillo Museum of Art, Amarillo, TX (2008). See also sources in note 30.

7 Dord Fitz to Elaine de Kooning, letter, June 24, 1957, Dord Fitz papers, Box 1, Folder 10.

8 Elaine de Kooning, "Reynal Makes a Mosaic," *ARTnews*, LII/8 (December 1953), pp. 34–7, 51–3.

9 "Federation to Participate in All-Woman Art Showing," newspaper unknown, February 10, 1960, Dord Fitz papers, Box 4, Folder 2.

10 Dorothy Seiberling, "Women Artists in Ascendance: Young Group Reflects Lively Virtues of U.S. Painting," *Life*, XLII/19 (May 13, 1957), pp. 74–7.

11 Worden Day to Rosalyn Drexler, letter, January 29, 1973, Worden Day papers, Archives of American Art, Smithsonian Institution.

12 Ibid.

13 Press release, draft, n.d., Dord Fitz papers, Box 4, Folder 2.

14 Jeanne Reynal to Agnes Gorky, letter, September 1, 1946, Jeanne Reynal papers, Roll N69–66, Frame 762, Archives of American Art, Smithsonian Institution.

15 Press release, draft, n.d., Dord Fitz papers, Box 4, Folder 2.

16 Mickey Wagstaff to Dord Fitz, letter, October 30, 1959, Dord Fitz papers, Box 2, Folder 13.

17 Jeanne Reynal to Dord Fitz, January 14, 1960, Dord Fitz papers, Box 4, Folder 2.

18 Dord Fitz, in *17 of the Women Tops in Art*, exh. cat., Dord Fitz Art Gallery, Amarillo, TX (1960), n.p.

19 Dord Fitz to Linda Lindeberg, letter, February 22, 1960, letter, Dord Fitz papers, Box 4, Folder 2.

20 Dorothy Hastings to Helene (Huff), letter, n.d., Dord Fitz papers, Box 4, Folder 2.

21 J.H.B., "Claire Falkenstein," *ARTnews*, LIX/7 (November 1960), p. 15.

22 A. S. (Anne Seelye), "Helen Frankenthaler," *ARTnews*, LIX/1 (March 1960), pp. 39, 57. See also letters to the editor in April and May issues.

23 Miriam Schapiro, "Notes from a Conversation on Art, Feminism, and Work," in *Working It Out: 23 Women Writers, Artists, Scientists, and Scholars Talk about Their Lives and Work*, ed. Sara Ruddick and Pamela Daniels (New York, 1977), p. 287.

24 P. T. (Parker Tyler), "Jane Wilson," *ARTnews*, LIV/7 (November 1955), p. 49.

25 Thalia Gouma-Peterson, *Miriam Schapiro: Shaping the Fragments of Art and Life* (New York, 1999), p. 45.

26 Dord Fitz to Martha Jackson, letter, April 24, 1960, Dord Fitz papers, Box 1, Folder 26.

27 Dord Fitz to Tom Hess, letter, January 29, 1960, Dord Fitz papers, Box 4, Folder 2.

28 See various clippings in Dord Fitz papers, Box 4, Folder 2.

29 Sally Bivins, "Visiting Artist Sees Southwest as Area of Distinctive Expression," *Amarillo Globe-Times* (October 25, 1962), p. 12.

30 Amy Von Lintel and Bonnie Roos, "Expanding Abstract Expressionism: Elaine de Kooning, Action Painting, and the American West," *American Art*, XXXII/2 (Summer 2018), pp. 52–79. See also Von Lintel and Roos, *Three Women Artists: Expanding Abstract Expressionism in the American West* (College Station, TX, 2022).

31 Martha Jackson Gallery, statement, December 1, 1960, Dord Fitz papers, Box 1, Folder 26.

32 "The Vocal Girls," *Time*, LXXV/18 (May 2, 1960), pp. 74–6.

33 World House Galleries, "Women in American Art," press release, September 19, 1960, Louise Nevelson Papers, Reel D296B, Frame 619, Archives of American Art, Smithsonian Institution.

34 Charlotte Willard, "Women of American Art," *Look*, XXIV/20 (September 27, 1960), pp. 70–75.

10 Democracy: "Women Artists in America Today," Mount Holyoke College Art Museum, 1962

1 "Presidential Aide Schlesinger Speaks on Art and Government at Mt. Holyoke," *Holyoke Transcript-Telegram* (April 12, 1962).

2 "Women Artists in America Today," press release, c. March 1962, Mount Holyoke College Archives and Special Collections.

3 Annual Report of the Mount Holyoke Friends of Art, c. June 1962, Mount Holyoke College Archives and Special Collections.

4 *A Woman Reclining*, at https://museums.fivecolleges.edu, accessed March 26, 2023.

5 Jean C. Harris to Joan Mitchell, letter, October 17, 1961, Stable Gallery records, Box 2, Folder 13, Archives of American Art, Smithsonian Institution.

6 Ibid.

7 Jean C. Harris, "Introduction," *Women Artists in America Today: A Loan Exhibition*, exh. cat., Mount Holyoke College Art Museum, South Hadley, MA (1962), n.p.

8 Wayne C. Smith, "Mount Holyoke Activities High Points in Busy Week," *The Republican* (April 15, 1962). Mount Holyoke College Archives and Special Collections.

9 Harris, "Introduction," n.p.

10 G.T.M. (Gretchen T. Munson), "Man and Wife," *ARTnews*, XLVIII/6 (October 1949), p. 49.

11 Elizabeth A. T. Smith, "All Freedom in Every Sense," in *Lee Bontecou: A Retrospective*, exh. cat., Museum of Contemporary Art, Chicago (2003), p. 176.

12 Le Corbusier, "Femmes-Sculpteurs," Rhys Caparn Papers, Reel 680, Frame 10, Archives of American Art, Smithsonian Institution.

13 Helen Wilson to Jane Teller, letter, April 9, 1960, Jane Teller papers, Archives of American Art, Smithsonian Institution.

14 Dore Ashton, "Art," *Arts and Architecture*, LXXV/5 (May 1958), p. 29.

15 Joan Mitchell to Michael Goldberg, letter, June 10, 1954, Michael Goldberg papers, Archives of American Art, Smithsonian Institution.

16 "The Vocal Girls," *Time* (May 2, 1960).

17 "Women—1962: Smolin Gallery a No-Man's Land for Four Weeks," press release, 1962, "Women Printmakers" exhibition file, Philadelphia Museum of Art, Library and Archives.

18 N. E. (Natalie Edgar), "Seven Women," *ARTnews*, LX/9 (January 1962), p. 15. Alice Neel is listed as a participant in the review, but not in the press release, which lists Anne Tabachnick as the seventh artist.

19 John F. Kennedy, Executive Order 10980— Establishing the President's Commission on the Status of Women, www.presidency.ucsb.edu, accessed March 27, 2023.

20 "U.S. Arts Grants Urged," *Fort Worth Star-Telegram* (April 11, 1962), p. 2.

21 "Political Art?" *Mount Holyoke News*, XLVII/30 (April 13, 1962), p. 2.

22 Martha George, "Women Agree to Status Quo with Required 'Reticence,'" *Mount Holyoke News*, XLVII/29 (March 23, 1962), p. 6.

23 "Women Artists Excel in Social Commentary," *Mount Holyoke News*, XLVII/29 (March 23, 1962), p. 1.

24 Dorothy Adlow, "Women Artists at Mt. Holyoke: Display, Discussion Mark Anniversary," *Christian Science Monitor* (April 19, 1962). Mount Holyoke College Archives and Special Collections.

25 "New Museum Trends," talk given at a Bryn Mawr Alumnae Meeting, *c.* 1947. Adelyn Dohme Breeskin papers, Archives of American Art, Smithsonian Institution.

26 Grace and Fred M. Hechinger, "125 Years of Holyoke Girls," *New York Times Magazine* (February 11, 1962), pp. 34–5.

27 Betty Friedan, *The Feminine Mystique* (New York, 1964), p. 11.

Afterword

1 Leslie Judd Ahlander, *Women in Contemporary Art*, exh. cat., Women's College Gallery of Duke University, Durham, NC (1963), n.p.

2 Vernita Nemec, "X12: Feminist Artists First Show Together," *womanart* (Summer 1976), p. 4.

BIBLIOGRAPHY

This general reading list does not include archival materials or biographies and monographs of individual artists.

Beauvoir, Simone de, *America Day by Day*, trans. Carol Crosman (Berkeley, CA, 2000)
—, *The Second Sex*, trans. H. M. Parshley (New York, 1989)
Birnbaum, Paula, *Women Artists in Interwar France: Framing Femininities* (Farnham, 2011)
Blackman, Lynne, ed., *Central to Their Lives: Southern Women Artists in the Johnson Collection* (Charleston, SC, 2018)
Blair, Karen J., *The Torchbearers: Women and Their Amateur Arts Associations in America, 1890–1930* (Bloomington, IN, 1994)
Butler, Cornelia, and Lisa Gabrielle Mark, eds, *WACK! Art and the Feminist Revolution*, exh. cat., Museum of Contemporary Art, Los Angeles (Los Angeles, CA, 2007)
Butler, Cornelia, and Alexandra Schwartz, eds, *Modern Women: Women Artists at the Museum of Modern Art* (New York, 2010)
Chadwick, Whitney, *Women Artists and the Surrealist Movement* (New York, 2002)
Conaty, Siobhán M., *Art of This Century: The Women*, exh. cat., Pollock-Krasner House and Study Center, East Hampton, NY (New York, 1997)
Cummins, Victoria H., "Black Clubwomen and the Promotion of the Visual Arts in Early Twentieth-Century Texas," *Southwestern Historical Quarterly*, CXIX/1 (July 2015), pp. 1–22
Davidson, Susan, and Philip Rylands, eds, *Peggy Guggenheim and Frederick Kiesler: The Story of Art of This Century* (New York, 2004)
De Zegher, Catherine M., ed., *Inside the Visible: An Elliptical Traverse of 20th Century Art: In, of, and from the Feminine* (Cambridge, MA, 1996)
Doherty, Maggie, *The Equivalents: A Story of Art, Female Friendship, and Liberation in the 1960s* (New York, 2020)
Dossin, Catherine, and Hanna Alkema, "Women Artists Shows·Salons·Societies: Towards a Global History of All-Women Exhibitions," *Artl@s Bulletin*, VIII/1 (2019), article 19, https://docs.lib.purdue.edu/artlas/vol8/iss1
Eisenmann, Linda, *Higher Education for Women in Postwar America, 1945–1965* (Baltimore, MD, 2007)
Fajardo-Hill, Cecilia, Andrea Giunta, and Rodrigo Alonso, eds, *Radical Women: Latin American Art, 1960–1985*, exh. cat., Hammer Museum, University of California, Los Angeles (Los Angeles, CA, 2017)
Farrington, Lisa E., *Creating Their Own Image: The History of African-American Women Artists* (New York, 2005)

Fisher, Andrea, *Let Us Now Praise Famous Women: Women Photographers for the U.S. Government, 1935 to 1944* (London, 1987)

Fleming, Tuliza K., *Breaking Racial Barriers: African Americans in the Harmon Foundation Collection*, exh. cat., National Portrait Gallery, Washington, DC (San Francisco, CA, 1997)

Friedan, Betty, *The Feminine Mystique* (New York, 1963)

Gabriel, Mary, *Ninth Street Women: Lee Krasner, Elaine de Kooning, Grace Hartigan, Joan Mitchell, and Helen Frankenthaler: Five Painters and the Movement that Changed Modern Art* (New York, 2018)

Garb, Tamar, *Sisters of the Brush: Women's Artistic Culture in Late Nineteenth-Century Paris* (New Haven, CT, 1994)

Gibson, Ann Eden, *Abstract Expressionism: Other Politics* (New Haven, CT, 1997)

Grasso, Linda M., *Equal Under the Sky: Georgia O'Keeffe and Twentieth-Century Feminism* (Albuquerque, NM, 2019)

Hall, Lee, *Betty Parsons: Artist Dealer Collector* (New York, 1991)

Herskovic, Marika, *New York School Abstract Expressionists: Artists Choice by Artists: A Complete Documentation of the New York Painting and Sculpture Annuals, 1951–1957* (New York, 2000)

Hess, Thomas B., and Elizabeth C. Baker, eds, *Art and Sexual Politics: Why Have There Been No Great Women Artists?* (New York, 1973)

Hirshler, Erica E., *A Studio of Her Own: Women Artists in Boston, 1870–1940*, exh. cat., Museum of Fine Arts, Boston (Boston, MA, 2001)

Jakubowska, Agata, and Katy Deepwell, *All-Women Art Spaces in Europe in the Long 1970s* (Liverpool, 2021)

Langa, Helen, and Paula Wisotzki, eds, *American Women Artists, 1935–1970: Gender, Culture and Politics* (New York, 2018)

Lewis, Emma, *Photography, a Feminist History: Gender Rights and Gender Roles on Both Sides of the Camera* (San Francisco, CA, 2021)

Macel, Christine, ed., *Women in Abstraction*, exh. cat., Musée national d'art moderne, Paris (Paris, 2021)

Madeline, Laurence, et al., *Women Artists in Paris, 1850–1900*, exh. cat., American Federation of Arts, New York (New York and New Haven, CT, 2017)

Marter, Joan, *Women and Abstract Expressionism: Painting and Sculpture, 1945–1959*, exh. cat., Sidney Mishkin Gallery, Baruch College, New York (1997)

—, ed., *Women of Abstract Expressionism*, exh. cat., Denver Art Museum (Denver, CO, 2016)

Massey, Anne, *Women in Design* (London, 2022)

Matsumoto, Valerie J., "Pioneers, Renegades, and Visionaries: Asian American Women Artists in California, 1890s–1960s," in *Asian American Art: A History, 1850–1970*, ed. Gordon H. Chang, Mark Dean Johnson, Paul J. Karlstrom, and Sharon Spain (Stanford, CA, 2008)

Meskimmon, Marsha, *We Weren't Modern Enough: Women Artists and the Limits of German Modernism* (Berkeley, CA, 1999)

Morris, Catherine, and Rujeko Hockley, eds, *We Wanted a Revolution: Black Radical Women, 1965–85: A Sourcebook* (New York, 2017)

Moutoussamy-Ashe, Jeanne, *Viewfinders: Black Women Photographers* (New York, 1985)

Munro, Eleanor C., *Originals: American Women Artists* (New York, 1982)

Nelson, Maggie, *Women, the New York School, and Other True Abstractions* (Iowa City, IA, 2007)

Nemser, Cindy, *Art Talk: Conversations with 12 Women Artists* (New York, 1975)

Nochlin, Linda, *Women, Art, and Power and Other Essays* (New York, 1988)

Parker, Rozsika, and Griselda Pollock, *Old Mistresses: Women, Art, and Ideology* (New York, 1981)

Pisano, Ronald G., *One Hundred Years: A Centennial*

Celebration of the National Association of Women Artists, exh. cat., Nassau County Museum of Fine Art, Roslyn, NY (Roslyn Harbor, NY, 1988)

Pollock, Griselda, *Killing Men and Dying Women: Imagining Difference in 1950s New York Painting* (Manchester, 2022)

Prieto, Laura R., *At Home in the Studio: The Professionalization of Women Artists in America* (Cambridge, MA, 2001)

Reckitt, Helena, ed., *The Art of Feminism: Images that Shaped the Fight for Equality, 1857–2017* (San Francisco, CA, 2018)

Rosenblum, Naomi, *History of Women Photographers* (New York, 1994)

Sachs, Sid, and Kalliopi Minioudaki, *Seductive Subversion: Women Pop Artists, 1958–1968*, exh. cat., University of the Arts, Philadelphia (Philadelphia, PA, and New York, 2010)

Schimmel, Paul, ed., *Revolution in the Making: Abstract Sculpture by Women, 1947–2016*, exh. cat., Hauser Wirth & Schimmel, Los Angeles (New York, 2016)

Seaton, Elizabeth Gaede, and Marianna Kistler, *Paths to the Press: Printmaking and American Women Artists 1910–1960*, exh. cat., Marianna Kistler Beach Museum of Art, Kansas State University (2006)

Siegel, Katy, ed., *The Heroine Paint: After and Around Helen Frankenthaler* (New York, 2015)

Silver, Kenneth E., Cynthia A. Drayton, and Nancy Hall-Duncan, eds., *JFK and Art*, exh. cat., Bruce Museum, Greenwich, CT (2003)

Smith, Laura, ed., *Action, Gesture, Paint: Women Artists and Global Abstraction 1940–70*, exh. cat., Whitechapel Gallery, London (2023)

Swinth, Kirsten, *Painting Professionals: Women Artists and the Development of Modern American Art, 1870–1930* (Chapel Hill, NC, 2001)

Von Lintel, Amy, and Bonnie Roos, *Three Women Artists: Expanding Abstract Expressionism in the American West* (College Station, TX, 2022)

Wagner, Anne, *Three Artists (Three Women): Modernism and the Art of Hesse, Krasner, and O'Keeffe* (Berkeley, CA, 1996)

Weyl, Christina, *The Women of Atelier 17: Modernist Printmaking in Midcentury New York* (New Haven, CT, 2019)

Wije, Michele, ed., *Sparkling Amazons: Abstract Expressionist Women of the 9th St. Show*, exh. cat., Katonah Museum of Art, New York (2019)

Wolf, Amy J., *New York Society of Women Artists, 1925*, exh. cat., ACA Galleries, New York (New York, 1987)

ACKNOWLEDGMENTS

This book has been nearly twenty years in the making. The first iteration was my Institute of Fine Arts dissertation, defended in 2008. In the interim I've curated exhibitions and published articles on women artists in midcentury America. In 2020 Katy Siegel encouraged me to seek a wider audience for my research, and connected me to Vivian Constantinopoulos and Reaktion Books, for which I am beyond grateful. The Reaktion editorial team has been a pleasure to work with and vastly improved the rigor and quality of the original manuscript. Thank you Vivian, Amy Salter, Aimee Selby, and the design team. Costs for color reproductions were underwritten by the Malka Fund and the late Mildred Weissman, thanks to Joan Rosenbaum. Special thank yous as well to Carolyn Fitz, Risa Kaufman, Addie Lanier, Karen Leader, Kalliopi Minioudaki, Amy Von Lintel, Henry Weverka, Christina Weyl, and Michele Wije who astutely commented on draft versions. I would also like to acknowledge Siobhán M. Conaty, Tuliza Fleming, and Amy Von Lintel, whose scholarship significantly informed Chapters One, Two, and Nine, respectively. I've attempted to synthesize an enormous amount of material and any inadvertent errors of fact or interpretation are entirely my own.

The development of some of the concepts and histories animating this book occurred in essays published in a variety of catalogues, exhibitions, and journals. I am grateful to the support and editorial comments of Julie Cortella, Julia Drost, Fabrice Flahutez, Hélène Gheysens, Mark Godfrey, Anne Helmreich, Christine Macel, Kalliopi Minioudaki, Lise Motherwell, Maura Reilly, Martin Schieder, Martha R. Severens, Katy Siegel, Elizabeth Smith, Jonathan Stuhlman, and Michele Wije. I've had the good fortune of participating in two Archives of Women Artists, Research and Exhibitions (AWARE) conferences, which gave international perspectives to my American subject. Many artists have shared personal stories and offered valuable insights. I treasure my interviews with Ruth Asawa, Louise Bourgeois, Louise Fishman, Grace Hartigan, Martha Rosler, Carolee Schneemann, Joan Snyder, Mierle Laderman Ukeles, June Wayne, and Zuka.

Dialogue with experts and friends over the years has sharpened my research and writing, especially with Glenn Adamson, Patricia Albers, Jo Applin, Elizabeth Baker, Yaron Ben-Zvi, Maya Benton, Christa Blatchford, Ulrich Boser, Phong Bui, Barbara Castelli, Cathleen Chaffee, Christiane Citron, Carol Cole, Jack Cowart, Thomas Crow, Cathy Curtis, Catherine Dossin, Douglas Dreishpoon, Charles Duncan, Matt Erlich, Tuliza Fleming, Sue Frank, Howard Greenberg, Helen Hsu, Sarah Huag, Christina Hunter, Andrew Ingall, Matthew Israel, Melissa Kaish, Morton Kaish, Nathan Kernan, Norman Kleeblatt, Shaina Laravee, Karen Levitov, Sarah

Lewis, Courtney Martin, Laura Morris, Nicole Myers, Nell Painter, Sara Pasti, Hart Perry, Judith Piniero, Dick Polich, Helaine Posner, Brooke Kamin Rapaport, Katy Rogers, Maureen St. Onge, Irving Sandler, Corinna Schaming, Dan Schifrin, Ryan Senser, Natasha Staller, Ilan Stavans, Catharine Stimpson, Robert Storr, Anne Swarz, Murtaza Vali, Laurie Wilson, Reva Wolf, Tom Wolf, and Maggie Wright.

The decision to frame my ongoing study of women artists with all-women exhibitions required new research into institutional histories. Countless archivists and librarians have digitized and provided access to essential archival and visual materials. This book would not have been possible without the generosity and resources of the following institutions: Amon Carter Museum of American Art, Archives of American Art, Art Students League, AWARE, Brooklyn Museum Library, California African American Museum, Center for Creative Photography, Chicago History Museum Abakanowicz Research Center, Contemporary Arts Museum Houston, Detroit Institute of Arts Archive, Frick Art Reference Library, Georgia O'Keeffe Museum, Getty Research Institute, Hammer Museum Grunwald Center for the Graphic Arts, Houston Public Library System Special Collections Division, Illinois State Museum, J. Paul Getty Museum, Library of Congress Manuscript Division, Menil Collection, Mount Holyoke College Archives & Special Collections, Museum of Modern Art Library, National Archives & Records Administration, National Museum of Women in the Arts, New York Public Library (Rare Books and Manuscripts, Schomburg Center, and Billy Rose Theatre Division), New York State Library and Archive, Philadelphia Museum of Art Library and Archives, Phillips Collection, Princeton University Art Museum, Princeton University Library Special Collections, Rice University Woodson Research Center, San Francisco Museum of Art Library, San Francisco Women Artists Gallery, Schlesinger Library of Harvard Radcliffe Institute, Smith College Museum of Art, Smith College Special Collections, Smithsonian American Art and Portrait Gallery Library, Smithsonian Institution Archives and Libraries, Solomon R. Guggenheim Museum, Stanford University Libraries Department of Special Collections, Syracuse University Libraries Special Collections Research Center, University of California–Los Angeles Library Special Collections, University of Louisville Archives and Special Collections, University of Maryland–College Park David C. Driskell Center, University of Maryland Library Special Collections, University of New Hampshire Lotte Jacobi Archive, University of Oklahoma Libraries Western History Collections, University of Pennsylvania Carey Law School, and Whitney Museum of American Art.

I'm grateful to the following individuals for contributing to image research and permissions: MB Abram, Lucienne Allen, Lynda Bannister, George Barker, Toby Bielawski, Tracy Boyd, Jean Bubley, Katherine Bussard, Chris Chapman, Emma Crumbley, hallie harrisberg, Sarah Kay, Emily Lenz, Meg Partridge, Erik Preminger, Lisa Tatsuko Prince, Madeline Murphy Rabb, Jennifer Samet, Jenna Segal, Rex Stevens, Susan Teller, and Bruce Weber. Joyce Faust at Art Resource and JR Pepper at ARS NY shepherded through multiple image requests.

A special shout out to Mara Held and the board and staff of the Al Held Foundation, my happy home the past seven years. The field of artist-endowed foundations and estates is refreshingly collaborative. I am fortunate to have so many wonderful colleagues in the legacy business. A tip of the hat to my friends at the Association of Art Museum Curators and at RiverArts; I am a proud board member of both.

My parents, the late Steven Belasco and Fran Belasco, and Claire Eisenstadt and Sandy Bogin instilled a love of art and architecture, and feminist values. Other family members lift me up: Judith Belasco, Sara Belasco, Mark Berkowitz, Karen and Michael Rosner, Hattie and Allan Kaufman, and Barbara and Bob Dreyfuss. My teens, Frieda and Reuben, keep me on my toes with their curiosity and freely shared opinions on aesthetics and life. I can state with confidence that I have definitely learned far more from them than they have from me. And to Risa, my bashert and partner in life, I could not have completed this book without your time, energy, support, and encouragement, not to mention willingness to gently issue astute feedback on multiple drafts over the years. I love you all.

Finally, a note on the book's dedication to the memory of two beloved teachers. In high school Judy Cook lit a fire when she introduced me to using a gender lens to interpret culture and society. One critical read of *Tess of the d'Urbervilles* and I've never looked back. And Linda Nochlin took me under her wing at the Institute of Fine Arts and generously shared her guidance, memories, critical insight, and vast art-historical knowledge. I am grateful to Linda for being my friend and teacher, and always reminding me that I was *her* student.

PHOTO ACKNOWLEDGMENTS

The author and publishers wish to thank the organizations and individuals listed below for authorizing reproduction of their work:

The 31 Women Collection, © Sonja Sekula Estate: 7; Allentown Art Museum, PA (gift of Mildred T. Johnstone): 51; Amarillo Museum of Art, TX (gift of the Area Arts Foundation in honor of Dord Fitz), © 2023 Estate of Louise Nevelson/Artists Rights Society (ARS), New York: 80; Amon Carter Museum of American Art, Fort Worth, TX (gift of the Dorothea Leonhardt Fund of the Communities Foundation of Texas, Inc.), © 1988 Amon Carter Museum of American Art: 55; Archives of American Art, Smithsonian Institution, Washington, DC (Claire Falkenstein papers): 76; Art Institute of Chicago (Wirt D. Walker Fund): 57; The Baltimore Museum of Art, MD (anonymous gift), photo Mitro Hood, © 2023 Helen Frankenthaler Foundation, Inc./Artists Rights Society (ARS), New York: 81; Bivins Foundation, Amarillo, TX, photo Amy Von Lintel, © Estate of Jane Wilson, courtesy DC Moore Gallery, New York: 83; Brooklyn Museum, NY (bequest of Edith and Milton Lowenthal), © 2023 Georgia O'Keeffe Museum/Artists Rights Society (ARS), New York: 34; Brooklyn Museum Libraries and Archives, NY: 56; Esther Bubley Archive: 27; Buffalo AKG Art Museum, NY (Room of Contemporary Art Fund, 1943), photo Brenda Bieger, © Estate of Doris Lee, courtesy

D. Wigmore Fine Art, Inc., New York: 31; © 2024 Estate of Leonora Carrington/Artists Rights Society (ARS), New York: 4; Constance Bannister Archive: 26; © 2024 Contemporary Arts Museum Houston, TX: 48; Danforth Art Museum, Framingham State University, MA (gift of Pyracantha Hannah Shapero, daughter of the artist): 38; Detroit Institute of Arts, Research Library and Archives, MI (The Clyde H. Burroughs Exhibition Records), © Estate of Laura Wheeler Waring: 13; © Elaine de Kooning Trust: 78; Eskenazi Museum of Art, Indiana University, Bloomington, photo Kevin Montague: 60; courtesy Carolyn Fitz: 75; Elizabeth Hazan and Stephen Hicks, NY, courtesy Kasmin Gallery, New York: 84; collection of the Hedda Sterne Foundation, © 2023 The Hedda Sterne Foundation, Inc./Artists Rights Society (ARS), New York: 6; Hirshhorn Museum and Sculpture Garden, Washington, DC (The Joseph H. Hirshhorn Bequest, 1981): 94; The J. Paul Getty Museum, Los Angeles: 25 (gift of Daniel Greenberg and Susan Steinhauser, © Ruth Bernhard Archive, Princeton University Art Museum, NJ), 45 (© Imogen Cunningham Trust); courtesy Kallir Research Institute, New York: 61; © Estate of Lisa Larsen: 29; Los Angeles County Museum of Art (Decorative Arts and Design Acquisition Funds), photo © 2023 Museum Associates/LACMA, licensed by Art Resource, NY, © Estate of Margaret De Patta: 46; Memorial Art Gallery, Rochester, NY (gift of the Jewish Community of

Rochester), courtesy the Luise and Morton Kaish Foundation: 89; The Menil Collection, Houston, TX, photo Adam Neese: 49; The Metropolitan Museum of Art, New York (bequest of Miss Adelaide Milton de Groot, 1967): 64; courtesy Michael Rosenfeld Gallery LLC, New York: 50, 54 (© Estate of Sue Fuller, courtesy Susan Teller Gallery, New York); Mildred Lane Kemper Art Museum, Washington University in St. Louis, MO (University purchase, Bixby Fund, 1960), © Estate of Grace Hartigan: 93; © 2023 Milton Resnick Pat Passlof Foundation, courtesy Eric Firestone Gallery, New York: 79; Milwaukee Art Museum, WI (Layton Art Collection Inc., gift of the family of Mrs. Frederick Vogel Jr., L1952.1), photo John R. Glembin: 59; The Morgan Library & Museum, New York (gift of the Christian Humann Foundation): 62; Mount Holyoke College, Archives and Special Collections, South Hadley, MA: 85, 86 (photo Neil Doherty), 88 (photo Neil Doherty), 91 (photo Neil Doherty, artwork © Estate of Joan Mitchell); Munson/Art Resource, NY, © Estate of Irene Rice Pereira, courtesy D. Wigmore Fine Art, Inc., New York: 35; photo © Museum of Modern Art Library, New York, licensed by SCALA/Art Resource, NY: 21; Museum of Fine Arts, Boston (Hayden Collection – Charles Henry Hayden Fund), photo © 2024 Museum of Fine Arts, Boston: 32; © Estate of Emiko Nakano, courtesy Berry Campbell, New York: 47; National Archives at College Park, MD: 18 (H-HNE-22-15), 19 (H-HNE-22-30), 20 (H-HNE-22-49); National Gallery of Art, Washington, DC (gift of June Wayne), © Estate of June Wayne, courtesy MB Abram: 53; National Portrait Gallery, Smithsonian Institution, Washington, DC (gift of the Harmon Foundation): 12 and 16 (© Estate of Laura Wheeler Waring), 14 and 15 (© Peter Edward Fayard); New Britain Museum of American Art, CT (gift of the artist's family): 90; Newark Museum of Art, NJ (bequest of Kay Sage Tanguy, 1964), photo Art Resource, NY, © 2023 Estate of Kay Sage/Artists Rights Society (ARS), New York: 10; The New York Public Library (Camera Club of New York records, Manuscripts and Archives Division): 22, 23, 24; The New York Public Library for the Performing Arts (Gypsy Rose Lee Papers, Billy Rose Theatre Division): 9; Philadelphia Museum of Art, PA: 5 (125th Anniversary Acquisition, purchased with funds contributed by C. K. Williams, II, © 2023 Artists Rights Society (ARS), New York/ADAGP, Paris), 66 (purchased with the Lola Downin Peck Fund from the Carl and Laura Zigrosser Collection, © Lucienne Bloch, courtesy Old Stage Studios), 67 (gift of Carl Zigrosser, © The Estate of Peggy Bacon), 68 (purchased with the Lola Downin Peck Fund from the Carl and Laura Zigrosser Collection), 69 (gift of Carl Zigrosser), 70 (gift of the estate of Wanda Gág), 71 (purchased with the Thomas Skelton Harrison Fund, © the Estate of Anne Ryan, courtesy Susan Teller Gallery, New York), 72 (gift of R. Sturgis Ingersoll, Frederic Ballard, Alexander Cassatt, Staunton B. Peck and Mrs. William Potter Wear), 73 (gift of the Print Club of Philadelphia, 1955, © Estate of Norma Morgan), 74 (Print Club of Philadelphia Permanent Collection, 1953, © 2023 Corita Art Center/Immaculate Heart Community/Artists Rights Society (ARS), New York); Philadelphia Museum of Art, PA, Library and Archives: 30, 33, 37 (© Estate of Honoré Sharrer, courtesy Hirschl and Adler Modern, New York), 65; The Phillips Collection, Washington, DC (acquired in 1944), © Loïs Mailou Jones Pierre-Noël Trust: 2; private collection, photo Maurice Berezov, © A. E. Artworks, LLC: 39; © 2023 Estate of Jeanne Reynal/Artists Rights Society (ARS), New York: 77; Richard Green Gallery, London: 63; Rijksmuseum, Amsterdam (purchase 1814): 58; San Francisco Museum of Modern Art Archives: 40 (artwork © 2023 Ruth Asawa Lanier, Inc./Artists Rights Society (ARS), New York, courtesy David Zwirner), 41, 42, 43, 44; © 2023 Estate of Miriam Schapiro/Artists Rights Society (ARS), New York: 82; Schlesinger Library, Radcliffe Institute for Advanced Study, Harvard University, Cambridge, MA (Marjory Collins Papers), © President and Fellows of Harvard College: 28; SculptureCenter, New York, courtesy the Luise and Morton Kaish Foundation: 1; Seattle Art Museum, WA (gift of the Friday Foundation in honor of Richard E. Lang and Jane Lang

INDEX

Illustration numbers are indicated by *italics*